Occasional Glory

ALSO BY DAVID M. JORDAN

Happiness Is Not My Companion:
The Life of General G.K. Warren
(Indiana University Press, 2001)

The Athletics of Philadelphia:
Connie Mack's White Elephants
(McFarland, 1999)

A Tiger in His Time: Hal Newhouser
and the Burden of Wartime Ball
(Diamond Communications, 1990)

Winfield Scott Hancock: A Soldier's Life
(Indiana University Press, 1988)

Roscoe Conkling of New York:
Voice in the Senate
(Cornell University Press, 1971)

Occasional Glory

The History of the Philadelphia Phillies

David M. Jordan

McFarland & Company, Inc., Publishers
Jefferson, North Carolina, and London

Except where otherwise noted, all photographs are from the National Base-ball Hall of Fame Library.

Library of Congress Cataloguing-in-Publication Data

Jordan, David M., 1935–
    Occasional glory : the history of the Philadelphia Phillies /
David M. Jordan.
      p.   cm.
    Includes bibliographical references and index.

    ISBN-13: 978-0-7864-1260-0
    (softcover : 50# alkaline paper) ∞

    1. Philadelphia Phillies (Baseball team)— History. I. Title:
History of the Philadelphia Phillies. II. Title.
GV875.P45J67 2002
796.357'64'0974811— dc21   2001008056

British Library cataloguing data are available

Manufactured in the United States of America

Cover photograph: Pitchers from the 1915 Phillies, *from left,* Stan Baum-gartner, Pete Alexander, Ben Tincup, Erskine Mayer, Al Demaree, Joe Oeschger, and George McQuillan.

McFarland & Company, Inc., Publishers
  Box 611, Jefferson, North Carolina 28640
    www.mcfarlandpub.com

To the memory of a great researcher, writer, fan, and friend. Jerry Malloy.

Table of Contents

Introduction   1

CHAPTER 1: The Coming of the Phillies   5
CHAPTER 2: The Phillies in the 1890s   14
CHAPTER 3: The American League Invasion   24
CHAPTER 4: Dooin Takes the Reins   36
CHAPTER 5: A Pennant for Pat Moran   47
CHAPTER 6: For Pickles Dillhoefer???   54
CHAPTER 7: Hitting Isn't Everything   67
CHAPTER 8: Doormats of the National League   77
CHAPTER 9: The Wartime Phillies   86
CHAPTER 10: Postwar Vistas   96
CHAPTER 11: Jubilee   108
CHAPTER 12: Middle-Class Baseball   118
CHAPTER 13: The Coming of Gene Mauch   128
CHAPTER 14: Tote'm Home Pennant   138
CHAPTER 15: Last Years of an Old Ballpark   150
CHAPTER 16: The Vet   160
CHAPTER 17: The Ozark Years   165
CHAPTER 18: The Team That Wouldn't Die   180
CHAPTER 19: Another Flag   195
CHAPTER 20: Michael Jack and the Dude   208

CHAPTER 21: Winning — and Losing — Wild 224
CHAPTER 22: More Losing Seasons 241
CHAPTER 23: Glory Nevertheless 250

Notes 255
Bibliography 271
Index 275

Introduction

In the spring of 1943, when I was eight years old, I spent a good bit of time with my father's Uncle George Barnes, a longtime die-hard Phillies fan. I had only recently discovered the game of baseball, and I found it fascinating to sit in his living room on North Franklin Street above Erie Avenue, listening to Byrum Saam describe games on the radio and Uncle George talk about the Phillies. He spoke of some of the oldtimers like Chuck Klein and Pinky Whitney and Ethan Allen as well as the great current Phillies outfielder Danny Litwhiler. To my young ears the feats of the great Litwhiler, an extraordinary fielder and a fine hitter, were wondrous indeed.

At the end of that May my father and Uncle George took me to Shibe Park for the first time, although much to the latter's disgust we saw the Athletics and not the Phillies. (Uncle George was the same age as Connie Mack and for some reason had no time for the venerable A's manager.)* I loved what I saw and was hooked for life. Uncle George made my father promise to take us again a few days later when the Phillies were back in town, so we could see Danny Litwhiler play. And so he did, when the world champion St. Louis Cardinals came in. At last I was going to see the great Litwhiler! On the way to the ballpark, Uncle George told me sadly that, indeed, we would see the great Litwhiler, but there was one problem. The Phillies had just traded him to the Cardinals, and we would see Danny Litwhiler in gray road flannels, with an "StL" on his cap. This was my introduction to life with the Phillies.

Over the years since I have been privileged to witness a lot of Phillies history, much of it in person at Shibe Park or Veterans Stadium. I've also had the chance to see the Phils play at Ebbets Field, Wrigley Field, Shea

---

George Barnes was also the Democratic committeeman in his division, but it was many years before I heard the theory about the connections between the local political parties and the baseball teams, that Phillies fans were Democrats and A's fans Republicans.

1

Danny Litwhiler, left with teammate Babe Dahlgren, before his 1943 trade to St. Louis.

Stadium, Busch Stadium, Fulton County Stadium, and Camden Yards. I was there the night Bubba Church was nailed by Ted Kluszewski's liner and the night Von Hayes hit two first-inning homers in a 26–7 rout of the Mets. I was at Connie Mack Stadium for three games of the infamous final homestand in 1964, and my wife Barbara and I took our little girl Diana down to the airport to welcome Gene Mauch's crew back from Cincinnati at the end of that doomed season. I saw Koufax no-hit the Phillies, saw the Phils pull off a pitcher-to-short-to-first-to-home triple play against the Pirates in 1950, and watched Greg Luzinski hit a ball off the Liberty Bell at the Vet. I saw the game Jimmie Foxx started for the Phillies as a pitcher in September 1945 against the Reds. I've seen a bunch of World Series games and the first three All-Star games played in Philadelphia. I've had season ticket plans, a few freebies, and a chance to get to know a number of Phillie ballplayers. And in the years since 1943 I've seen countless numbers of Phillies games of no particular historical moment, except they're all in the record books of the greatest game on earth.

During the summer of 2000, I was privileged to accompany Don Hasenmayer to Veterans Stadium on the night that the Phillies honored the 1950 Whiz Kids. Don Hasenmayer is a warm and kindly man who had the traditional "cup of coffee" with the Phillies in 1945 and 1946, appearing in eleven games altogether. His is not a name that turns on baseball fans, but that evening I learned a bit more of what is important in the game. Don played in the minor leagues and in spring training with many of the Whiz Kids being honored, and he was their contemporary and teammate. The "pecking order" among players is something much different from what fans understand. For Robin Roberts, Curt Simmons, and the others, Don Hasenmayer was one of them, a man who had persevered through the bad infields, the bus rides, and the flickering lights of the bush leagues. With them, he is a baseball man.

I've always been a great believer in reading the newspapers to find out when or how something happened. This is not to say that newspaper reports should not be taken with a grain of salt, especially the oldtime reporters' quotes from ballplayers, but they offer a good way to check out tales of storytellers like Fred Lieb and Bill Veeck and old ballplayers. The Newspaper Division of the Free Library of Philadelphia and Urban Archives at the Temple University Library have accordingly served as great resources for me, as has the National Baseball Library at the Hall of Fame in Cooperstown. In addition, I want to offer my thanks to my friends in the Philadelphia SABR regional chapter, among them Kit Crissey, Joe McGillin, Frank Phelps, and Joe Dittmar, to Larry Gerlach, as well as to my friends in the Philadelphia Athletics Historical Society like Ernie Montella, Max

Silberman, Bob Warrington, Steve Harlem, Clara McGonigal, Tony Risi and others. And my wife Barbara has put up cheerfully with more baseball throughout our marriage than she surely ever thought possible.

Finally, I want to thank the young lady who knows more about the Phillies than almost anyone I know, who attended with me the closing game at Connie Mack Stadium, the 1976 All-Star game, the horrendous 15–14 Game Four loss in the '93 World Series, and so many other games along the way, who applied her critical editorial eye to parts of this manuscript and suggested numerous improvements, and who pitched in again on the index, my daughter Diana. This one is for her, despite her weakness for Terry Francona.

And one other thing. I still think Gene Mauch is the best manager the Phillies ever had.

David M. Jordan
Jenkintown, Pa.

Chapter 1

The Coming of the Phillies

In 1876, the first season of play for the National League, the newly-created baseball organization featured a team from Philadelphia called the Athletics, which had long antecedents in the city. The Athletics had been an independent club as well as the original Philadelphia representative in the first professional baseball league, the National Association. Indeed, the Athletics won the first National Association pennant in 1871. The team had less success in the first year of the National League. Losing a fistful of money, the club's president, G.W. Thompson, decided to cut his losses by skipping its final western trip of the season. As a result, the Athletics were booted out of the league (the same fate also befell the New York entry), and there was no Philadelphia team in the National League from 1877 to 1883.

Another major league, the American Association of Base Ball Clubs, was organized in 1882. The new league was called unofficially "the Beer-and-Whisky League" from the source of much of its financial backing. The Athletics, homeless since 1876, were invited to join the Association, and in 1883 they brought another pennant to Philadelphia. The Athletics' stars, like Harry Stovey and Bobby Mathews, were highly-regarded heroes in the Quaker City, but they no longer had Philadelphia to themselves in 1883. In that year the National League returned to town, for the first time since the expulsion of the 1876 Athletics. President A.G. Mills of the National League knew that his circuit should be represented in New York and Philadelphia, and the appearance of the American Association in those towns made such representation imperative.

Mills had watched the American Association thrive in its first season, and when the upstart league added two more franchises for 1883, in New York City and Columbus, Ohio, Mills decided his organization had better make peace. A National Agreement was concluded, providing a frame-work for the two major leagues to function together.[1]

Mills knew that Philadelphia, the greatest industrial center in the nation, could support two baseball teams. The city had recently celebrated its great triumph with the Centennial Exposition of 1876, hosting more than ten million visitors, and it basked in such tributes as that of a reporter from Chicago who wrote that Philadelphia was "as cosmopolitan as Paris and as lively as Chicago."[2]

The city's population in 1880 reached 847,000, and it was growing steadily. Of this number only about 200,000 were foreign-born, small in comparison to other large American cities. In 1882, the mighty Pennsylvania Railroad opened its Broad Street Station, just west of City Hall, symbolic of the industrial giants that dominated Philadelphia's economy. These giants, like the Cramp shipyards and Baldwin locomotive works, together with a myriad of smaller enterprises, particularly textile manufacturers, provided steady employment to thousands of workers, many of whom were or became devoted baseball fanatics.

The settled portion of the city now stretched for some seven miles up and down the Delaware and three or four miles to the west, across the Schuylkill River. Unlike physically-constricted cities like New York and Boston, Philadelphia had room for growth; it was known for its single-family and owner-occupied homes. An extensive system of street railways tied the various neighborhoods together. No organization claiming to be national in scope and first-rate in quality could ignore the Quaker City.

For the 1883 season, League president Mills moved the Troy, New York, National League club to New York City, and he started working on shifting the Worcester, Massachusetts, franchise to Philadelphia. Before the Civil War, Mills, playing for the Washington Nationals, had become friendly with Al Reach, the star of the rival Brooklyn Eckfords and one of the great performers of early baseball. Mills asked Reach, now a sporting goods entrepreneur in Philadelphia, to take on the new National League franchise in his adopted city.

Reach had prospered in his sporting goods business. In partnership with a leather expert named Ben Shibe, Reach had a retail store on Market Street downtown and a factory in Kensington, manufacturing such items as baseballs and gloves. With his wealth and his love of baseball, Reach was quite open to Mills's proposition and soon agreed to head up the new Philadelphia National League franchise.

The man Reach procured to work with him in running the new ballclub was a well-connected lawyer-politico named Colonel John I. Rogers. At first Rogers, who could be arrogant and overbearing at times, was content to be the silent member of the partnership; the well-known baseball name of Reach represented the Phillies, as the new team soon came to be known.

Reach leased a tract of ground, bounded by 24th and 25th Streets, Columbia Avenue, and Ridge Avenue, for his ballpark. The field was leveled, wooden grandstands and bleachers were erected, and by May 1, 1883, Recreation Park was ready for the return of the National League to Philadelphia.

The Worcesters had had their moments: on June 12, 1880, Brown University grad John Lee Richmond pitched the first perfect game in major league history, and they finished fifth that year (Richmond won and lost 32 games). The following two seasons, though, the Brown Stockings finished a dismal last. In September 1882, they committed 21 errors in a single game, and on September 29 only eighteen spectators showed up to watch their final defeat, 10–7 to Troy.[3]

The team which appeared in Philadelphia the next year was no better; indeed, its abysmal record of 17–81 was considerably worse, called by the *Spalding Guide* "almost the poorest record known in league history." The team *was* different. None of the Brown Stockings made the trip south to Philadelphia, with two notable exceptions: slugger Harry Stovey and pitcher Fred Corey came to town but with the Athletics and not the Phillies. Many of the Worcester players were picked up by somebody, but Reach and Rogers had to scratch around for players for their new team.[4]

Pitcher Jack Coleman of the new Phillies won 12 games but lost 48. Coleman's staffmate, Arthur "Cut" Hagan, won one and lost 14 before being shipped off to Buffalo, where he lost two more. When Hagan made his debut for the Phillies, a reporter said he was "very nervous, but may do well when this wears off." Sadly, it never did, and his big-league career was short.[5]

Player-manager Bob Ferguson, who bore the superb nickname "Death to Flying Things," held down second base and hit .258; the financially-acute Ferguson, who had been the president of the National Association from 1872 to 1875, also handled the club's business matters. Third baseman-outfielder Blondie Purcell, who took over the field management from Ferguson after seventeen games (of which the Phillies won only four), hit .268. The rest of the team was worse.

Ferguson was relieved of his field authority because the players resented his tyrannical manner, but he continued to handle the club's finances so well that the dismal organization actually made money. One reason was a special dispensation from the league allowing the Phillies to lower ticket prices from 50 cents to 25 cents in order to compete against the Athletics.

It was hard to overlook that 17–81 record, though. The new National League entry was not much of an attraction against the champion Athletics, even though in postseason exhibitions the Phillies were able to win five out of nine games with the tired Athletics.[6]

The next season there was a *third* league fighting for the fans' dollars, an organization called the Union Association, founded and bankrolled by a wealthy railroad millionaire named Henry V. Lucas of St. Louis. The Unions scorned the reserve clause, the backbone of the relationship between the players and the two older leagues, and it attempted to raid the established clubs for players, but with only moderate success.[7] A total of twelve franchises started the season in the ill-starred league, but only five were around at the end.

The Union Association established a team in Philadelphia, called the Keystones, put together by future longtime Phillies factotum Billy Shettsline. The team won only 21 and lost 46 before throwing in the towel in August, with losses of $10,000 draining its coffers and its players' enthusiasm. Outfielder Buster Hoover, the only Keystone who was any offensive threat, hit .364. Pitcher Jersey Bakely, a righthander with a predilection for "booze and bad hours," led the league with 30 losses, 25 of them for the Keystones. The Union Association folded after the one disastrous season.[8]

After the dreadful 1883 season, the Phillies had nowhere to go but up. Reach and Rogers were confident that Philadelphians would respond to what they considered the higher quality of National League baseball. Over the next few years, Reach and Rogers made enough moves of the right sort, both on the field and off, that the club could survive hard times when they came along.

For 1884 Reach hired as his new manager the legendary Harry Wright, the former cricketer born in Sheffield, England. Wright was accustomed to winning. As manager of the pioneering Cincinnati Red Stockings, the six-time champion Boston teams in both the National Association and National League, and the powerful Providence Grays in 1882 and 1883, "Uncle Harry" had led only two losing teams in fifteen seasons. The Phillies would test his mettle.

Reach picked up a pitcher named Charley Ferguson out of Charlottesville, Virginia, and an outfielder named Jim Fogarty, to add to his roster of Coleman, first baseman Sid Farrar (the father of future operatic diva Geraldine Farrar), shortstop Bill McClellan, outfielder Jack Manning, and the rest of the crew that won only seventeen games in 1883. With Ferguson winning 21 games (losing 25), the Phillies improved their record to 39–73 in 1884 and moved up to sixth place. For the season, the Phillies made a profit of $6,082.79, divided between Harry Wright, who got 25 percent, and the stockholders, who got the rest.

In 1885 the Phillies did better. The club's hitting was still weak, but Ferguson and a youngster named Ed Daily each won 26 games, and the Phillies finished in third place with a 56–54 record. Charley Ferguson was regarded as one of the coming great stars of the game. In addition to his pitching prowess, he was also the best hitter on the team, batting .306. He played fifteen games in the outfield when he was not pitching.

The club also acquired a stocky lefthanded-throwing catcher named Jack Clements, a local boy who had played with the Keystones in the Union Association. Although Clements hit only .191 that first season with the Phillies, he remained the club's regular catcher through 1897, and his batting improved markedly after his first two years. Clements was also a gate attraction with his unusual southpaw fielding style.[9]

The following year, 1886, the Phillies slipped back to fourth place, even though the club won 71 games and lost only 43, for a winning percentage of .6228. This was unsurpassed by any Phillies team until the identical marks of .6234 in 1976 and 1977. Charley Ferguson had a superb season, winning thirty games and losing nine, with a 1.98 earned run average. Before the season started, Wright traded for a Detroit pitcher named Danny Casey, who came into his own in Philadelphia, picking up 24 wins while losing 18. Ed Daily won 16 more. The Phils' hitting was nothing spectacular, but their pitching was the best in the league. Canadian-born shortstop Arthur Irwin steadied the infield.[10]

Although Chicago, Detroit, and Jim Mutrie's New York club finished ahead of Wright's team in a badly-balanced league, the Phillies were now a respected power, and in Philadelphia they moved ahead of the declining Athletics in popular favor.

So well did the team draw that Reach decided he needed a ballpark with a larger capacity than Recreation Park. He purchased a tract farther out in North Philadelphia, bounded by North Broad Street, Huntingdon Street, 15th Street, and Lehigh Avenue. The property, next to the Reading Railroad tracks, had been serving as a dump before Reach took it in hand. It was soon the site of a modern brick-and-wood structure with double-decked stands between first and third base seating 5,000 and bleachers down the two foul lines holding another 7,500.

The official name of the new facility was The Philadelphia Baseball Park. People usually called it the Huntingdon Street Grounds because the main entrance was at 15th and Huntingdon, or sometimes simply "the Hump." The new ballyard was a bright and shiny addition to the game of baseball and a major step forward in Philadelphia.

The park was quite lopsided, with a 272-foot distance to the right-field fence, about 408 feet to center, and well over 400 feet to the barrier in left field. In the various changes made in the Huntingdon Street Grounds over the years, both before and after it became known as Baker Bowl, this striking bias in favor of lefthanded hitters remained. It was a bias for which the park became notorious, it made a Hall of Famer of Chuck Klein, and it made nervous wrecks of several generations of righthanded pitchers. Ray Benge, who pitched there for five years in the '20s and '30s, said of working in Baker Bowl, "You just had one way to pitch. That was to the righthanded side of the plate, outside to lefthanders, inside to righthanders."[11]

The Phillies' first game in their new home, against New York on April 30, 1887, was an unqualified success. Before a standing-room crowd of 20,000 which spilled over into the outfield, the locals pounded the New Yorkers for a 19–10 victory. Phillies outfielder George Wood hit the first of many home runs in the park.[12]

In their new digs, the Phillies had another good season in 1887, running neck and neck all year with the Detroit Wolverines and the Chicago White Stockings. They eventually beat out Chicago but finished second to Detroit by 3½ games. Casey (28–13), Ferguson (22–10), and former Boston hurler Charlie Buffinton (21–17) handled the mound work for Harry Wright, while Ferguson, who played 38 games in the field (mostly at second base) when not pitching, hit .413, center fielder Ed Andrews hit .354, and Wood smashed 14 home runs. (1887 was the year that bases on balls were scored as hits; with walks excluded, Ferguson's average shrinks to a still-respectable .337 and that of Andrews to .325.) Fogarty, the popular outfielder with a luxuriant handlebar mustache, stole 102 bases. It was a fine team, and hopes ran high for the following year.

These hopes were dashed in the cruelest manner. Charley Ferguson, the club's brightest star, the idol of the city, contracted typhoid fever during pre-season training. He had played in the team's exhibition games through April 11, but on the 13th it was reported that he was ill. Three days later the press said that he was "all right again," but in fact he had suffered a setback on the 15th and taken to his bed again, staying at Arthur Irwin's home. For the first time, typhoid fever was revealed as the illness, and Harry Wright said that "indications are that he will not be able to play for several weeks." Despite several over-optimistic reports of improvement in Ferguson's condition, the young athlete suffered a severe relapse on April 28, aggravated by unseasonably warm weather. Medical science was unable to help him, and on April 30, 1888, the baseball world was shocked to learn that Ferguson, just 25, had died the night before.[13]

In his four Phillies seasons, Ferguson won 99 games, and his batting prowess earned him a spot in the lineup when he was not pitching.

Ferguson even coached the college players at Princeton during the offseason. What this graceful natural athlete had accomplished already was thought to be meager compared with what was to come. His peers considered Ferguson's potential virtually unlimited. There have been many "might-have-beens" in Philadelphia's baseball history — the names of Ryne Sandberg, Nellie Fox, Joe Jackson, and Fergie Jenkins come quickly to mind — but none is as striking as Charley Ferguson, who might have been one of the best of them all.[14]

The Phillies in 1888 and 1889 finished third and then fourth, dipping one game under .500 in the latter season, as Buffinton propped up the team with 55 wins over the two-year span. The club's hitting was mediocre, except for a 20-homer output in 1889 by a big Hoosier outfielder named Sam Thompson. Thompson had played four good seasons for Detroit, and when that franchise folded after 1888, Reach was able to get him. He turned out to be a prize.

In an attempt to fill the void at second base left by Ferguson's death, the Phillies bought a 20-year-old Irishman named Ed Delahanty from the Wheeling, West Virginia, club. One of five ballplaying brothers from Cleveland, Delahanty became an all-time great. It was not as a second baseman, though, but as a slugging outfielder that Big Ed Delahanty would shine. In '88 he hit only .228, and though he raised his average to .293 in 1889, Delahanty failed to hit a home run. His time would come.

Warfare erupted again on the baseball scene in 1890 with the establishment of the Players League, backed by the Brotherhood of Professional Ball Players. An effort by the players to regain control of their own financial and professional destinies, the new organization fought the two older leagues for players and customers. As a result everyone did badly, with the Athletics faring particularly poorly.

The players had considerable support. One of the great early baseball journalists was Philadelphia's Francis C. Richter, who established *Sporting Life* in 1883 and watched its circulation and influence grow. A fervent advocate of players' rights, Richter threw his prestige behind the Brotherhood.

Three of the Brotherhood ringleaders were Phillies Buffinton, Fogarty, and Wood. All National League clubs were hurt by the appearance of the new Players League — some 80 percent of the old league's players defected — but the Phillies managed to contain the damage with a liberal use of cash. Reach and Rogers induced a number of defectors—catchers Clements and Pop Schriver, infielders Joe Mulvey, Al Myers, and Delahanty, and outfielder Sam Thompson — to repudiate their new allegiances and return to the fold.

Unfortunately, when the bidding went up again, Delahanty and Mulvey jumped again, Delahanty to the Brotherhood team in Cleveland and Mulvey to the team established in Philadelphia under Buffinton's direction. The Phillies even went to court to try to keep infielder Bill Hallman from defecting, but the court ruled in the player's favor. Colonel Rogers, on the National League's war committee, was enraged at the treachery of the players.[15]

Nevertheless, with what Rogers and Reach were able to preserve of their team, and with a patched-up pitching staff led by William "Kid" Gleason, a tough little fighter from the Camden docks who won 38 games, the Phillies were able to finish third in the weakened league. The club started well, but in late May manager Harry Wright went temporarily blind, and the team faltered. Clements and Reach himself tried their hands at managing, but astonishingly the best results were gained with 22-year-old rookie shortstop Bob Allen running the club for 35 games. By the end of July, the Phillies were in first place, and Wright resumed command, but Brooklyn soon took control of the race.

During that season, the Phils acquired a light-hitting but very fast outfielder named Billy Sunday, a young Iowan who played 31 games for Philadelphia in his eighth year in the league. After the season, Sunday gave up baseball to become one of the most famous evangelists in America's history, touring the country from coast to coast and peaking in popularity in the years between 1910 and 1920.[16]

The Philadelphia club in the rebel league, called the Quakers, finished fifth with a record of 68–83. The team played at a newly-built ballpark at Broad and Dauphin Streets called Forepaugh Park, and it outdrew the sagging Athletics, who were devastated by the Brotherhood's raids, losing their best players to the outlaw league.

The Phillies were the only National League club to outdraw its Players League opposition in head-to-head confrontation in 1890. At the end of the season, Rogers led his colleagues in putting extreme financial pressure on the Brotherhood clubs; he was entitled to the gloating he indulged in when the Players League threw in the towel.

The Athletics were not so fortunate. The club was in such terrible financial shape after the disastrous season that it was expelled from the Association and replaced by the Quakers franchise from the expiring Players League, now owned by the Wagner brothers. The Quakers kept the name "Athletics" as they played the 1891 campaign at Forepaugh Park.

1891 was the last year for the American Association. In the aftermath of the Brotherhood war, the Association withdrew from the National Agreement in a dispute over the reassignment of contract jumpers. It did not have the financial strength, after the troubles of the year before and with the attendance decline of its Philadelphia franchise, to go it alone. After the season the Association folded. Four clubs were taken into an expanded National League, but the Athletics were not one of them. For the rest of the Gay Nineties, the Phillies had Philadelphia all to themselves.[17]

Chapter 2

The Phillies in the 1890s

After the demise of the Players League, the two established leagues declared a general amnesty for players who had jumped to the Brotherhood league. The Phillies' John Rogers, however, bitterly refused to permit them to return to *his* club. At Reach's insistence, two exceptions were made, for Delahanty, simply because he was too good to let go, and for the very popular Jim Fogarty, because his health was deteriorating. Although the club took Fogarty back, he never played another game, dying of tuberculosis on May 20, 1891. Rogers was especially hostile toward Charlie Buffinton, whom he regarded as one of the main sources of all the trouble, and he refused to consider taking the pitcher back.

The 1891 Phillies could not quite reach the .500 level, finishing fourth with a 68–69 mark. Gleason, with a 24–22 record, and Charley "Duke" Esper, with 20–15, did the best pitching for Wright's team, but the Phillies could have used the banished Buffinton, who won 28 and lost 9 for the Boston Red Stockings as they won the last American Association pennant.

The Phillies have not had many great teams over the years—indeed, few of their squads even qualify as "good"—but every so often they have come up with a player who can arguably be called "the greatest:" the greatest righthanded pitcher in National League history, the greatest third baseman, even the greatest center fielder of the 1950s who did not play in New York. The earliest of these claims to greatness came in the 1890s and was made for a Phillies outfield which arguably was the greatest outfield of all time.

Respected baseball writer Robert Creamer said flatly that "the best outfield ever to play in the big leagues was a remarkable trio that spent five seasons together, a long time as outfields go, on the Philadelphia Phillies in the 1890s, way back in baseball's Dark Ages."[1]

The records bear out Creamer's contention. The members of this storied trio were Ed Delahanty, Big Sam Thompson, and Sliding Billy

Hall of Famer Sam Thompson, part of the Phillies' great outfield of the 1890s.

Hamilton, all three of whom have been immortalized in the Hall of Fame at Cooperstown. Delahanty and Thompson were hard-hitting sluggers, and Hamilton was the quintessential singles hitter, a classic leadoff man who collected a lot of walks and stolen bases. Delahanty was a righthanded hitter, while Big Sam and Little Billy swung from the left side. Hamilton was a mediocre outfielder, but he shone on the basepaths, where he became famous for his head-first slides.

Hamilton, picked up from Kansas City in the American Association, was one of the acquisitions made by Reach and Rogers to fill in the gaps on the 1890 team. He had stolen 117 bases for the Blues, so the Phillies knew he had great speed, and when the Kansas City club went belly-up they went after him. For Harry Wright in 1890, Hamilton played center field and batted in the leadoff spot; he hit .325 and stole 102 bases. The fans in Philadelphia loved "Sliding Billy," who was only 5'6" and weighed 165 pounds. The next year he proved he was no fluke as he hit .340 and stole 115 bases, leading the league in batting, hits, runs scored, walks, and stolen bases.

One old Philadelphia writer remembered "Good-Eye Bill" Hamilton fondly: "He was the ideal man to lead off a batting order. He could out-wait a pitcher better than any other player ... 'Good-Eye Bill' had the patience of Job. He was the thorn in the side of every National League pitcher...." Equally celebrated was "his uncanny habit of getting a tremendous lead off first, his knack of successfully getting back ... and then his quick getaway for second."[2]

The first year the three men played together was 1891, when Hamilton and Thompson had good seasons but Delahanty hit only .243. In 1892, all three hit over .300, with Hamilton leading the way at .330. Only nine players in the league with 400 or more at bats reached the .300 level, and three of them played in the Phillies' outfield.

The next year the whole league's collective batting average climbed 35 points as the pitching distance was pushed back from fifty feet to 60 feet, six inches, a distance which has remained unchanged to this day. Most of the league's hurlers, predictably, had a great deal of trouble in adjusting their pitching motion to the additional ten and a half feet. The hitters flourished, none more so than the Phillies' flycatchers. Hamilton, Thompson, and Delahanty ran one-two-three in the batting race, with marks of .380, .370, and .368. Delahanty led the league in home runs with nineteen, runs batted in with 146, and total bases, finishing just behind his outfield mate Thompson in doubles. Big Sam also led the league in hits and finished second to Delahanty in total bases.

1894 saw another surge of hitting, as the league average reached .309 and the Phillies set a still-standing record for team batting average — an incredible .349. There were five .400 hitters in the National League in 1894, Hughie Duffy of the Boston Beaneaters at .440, and four Phillies outfielders. Delahanty hit .407, Thompson hit .407, Hamilton hit .404 (with 98 stolen bases), and spare outfielder George "Tuck" Turner managed to pick up 339 at bats and hit .416. Hamilton scored a hard-to-believe 196 runs, still the record for runs in a season.

The following year Delahanty piled up an average of .404, second in the league to Cleveland's Jesse Burkett, who hit .409. Sam Thompson was third at .392 and Hamilton was next at .389. Thompson led the circuit in home runs with eighteen, runs batted in with 165, and total bases; he finished second in both doubles (to Delahanty) and triples. Hamilton led the league in runs and stolen bases (97) for the second year in a row.

The Phillies performed in a new facility in 1895, after a disastrous fire destroyed their ballpark on August 6, 1894. The team played a few games at Penn's athletic field, then at the old park after temporary bleachers were set until the end of the season. The new stadium, which opened on the same site at Fifteenth and Huntingdon Streets on May 2, 1895, was the first cantilevered ballpark and was called "the handsomest inclosure ever devoted exclusively to outdoor athletics ... a marvel to visitors, and an object of pride to Philadelphians." Its right field line was shorter than ever, now 272 feet rather than 310.[3]

During the winter Hamilton was traded to Boston after he asked the Phillies for more money, and the great outfield was broken up. It was a magnificent stretch of five years. Over the period, Hamilton hit .368, Thompson .351, and Delahanty .344. The three of them together racked up a collective five-year average of .354. Thompson, at the age of 36, had one more season as a regular before age and infirmity knocked him out. Delahanty put in six more excellent seasons with the Phillies before the appearance of another new league, the American, induced him to jump once again.

Big Ed continued to slug the ball, but marital problems and hard drinking led him to increasingly strange and unpredictable behavior. Delahanty had never been much of a team player. Jack Boyle, his teammate for six years with the Phillies, said that Big Ed never cared much where his team finished; "Del thought [only] of a comfortable winter life on the money he had made in the summer time."[4]

Finally, during the 1903 season, under suspension by Washington for excessive consumption of alcohol, Delahanty was put off a train for disorderly conduct on the Canadian side of the Niagara River. Angry and drunk, he apparently tried to stagger across the bridge after the departing train. He fell into the flood and was swept down the river and over the falls to his death. Big Ed Delahanty, troubled as he was, was batting .333 for the Senators when he perished at the age of 35.[5]

Delahanty's lifetime average is .346, fourth highest of all time, surpassed only by Ty Cobb, Rogers Hornsby, and Joe Jackson. Hamilton's career mark is .344, where he sits in a tie with Ted Williams and Tris Speaker for sixth all-time. Thompson, at .331, is 25th, tied with Stan Musial. Hamilton had 912 stolen bases, a career record for many years until it was surpassed by Lou Brock and then Rickey Henderson.

Hamilton's stolen bases are discounted these days, because the scoring rule for stolen bases has changed; before 1898 a man could get credit for a stolen base by taking an extra base on a careless outfielder, although research indicates that official scorers were reluctant to allow many such steals.

Runs scored are still runs scored, though, and Sliding Billy stands alone at the top of the career list for runs per game, with 1.06, more than anyone who ever played baseball. Thompson is tenth and Delahanty 13th all-time in that category. And Thompson drove in more runs per game over his career — .92 per game — than any other big league player. They were a very productive threesome.

And to what heights did the Philadelphia Nationals rise while they had this trio of superstars on the roster? From 1891 through 1895, the Phils finished fourth, fourth, fourth, fourth, and third. It was, after 1891, a twelve-team league, so the Phillies were definitely in the upper echelon, but they never really challenged Frank Selee's Boston Beaneaters, who won the first three years, or Ned Hanlon's tough Baltimore Orioles, who won in 1894 and 1895.

Gus Weyhing had a couple of outstanding years on the mound for the Phils, winning 32 games in 1892 and 23 more the next year. A little righthander named Wilfred "Kid" Carsey won 81 games from 1892 to 1895. And Jack Clements, the lefthanded throwing catcher, did some fine hitting for Harry Wright and Art Irwin, who managed the team in '94 and '95. Year in and year out, though, the Phillies were known as a team with big bats, the great outfield, and pitchers who just did not measure up.

In 1896, Billy Nash, obtained from Boston in exchange for Hamilton, assumed the reins as manager (still known usually as captain), but the club declined to a record of 62–68, good for only an eighth-place finish. There were few bright spots, mainly the hitting of Delahanty, Thompson, and Dan Brouthers, who hit .344 in his last season, his only one as a Phillie, before leaving the team in a salary dispute.

On July 13, Delahanty had a tremendous game in Chicago. Del hit a home run in the first inning, singled two innings later, blasted another homer in the fifth, and homered once more in the seventh. In the ninth inning, he responded to the cheers of the crowd by smashing his fourth home run of the game, two of which were inside the park. Legend has it that Adonis Terry, who pitched the whole game for Chicago, shook Big

Ed's hand as he crossed the plate the final time. Four home runs, seventeen total bases: a very offensive afternoon![6]

Brewery Jack Taylor, from Staten Island, won twenty games to lead the pitching staff but had 21 losses. A 23-year-old Hoosier named Al Orth, who had won nine out of ten games in his 1895 rookie season, contributed 15 wins in '96; he would win 98 games for the club over seven seasons. The rest of the pitching, though, was decidedly mediocre.

One of the problems the pitching staff had to contend with was the presence, in 73 games, of a lefthanded shortstop named Bill Hulen. Hulen, an indifferent hitter, caused real difficulties in the field, with the awkward adjustments needed for even routine throws. He made 51 errors in those 73 games and had a fielding average of only .874. One wonders why Nash and Reach were unable to come up with some viable alternative to Hulen.

In 1896 the Phillies acquired Napoleon "Larry" Lajoie, who was to become one of the great second basemen in the game's history. Midway through the year Nash turned the reins of the club over to catcher Jack Boyle and departed on a talent search through New England. Watching the Fall River club in the New England League, Nash was impressed by two Fall River players, outfielder Phil Geier and Lajoie, who played the outfield, first base, and caught. Lajoie was widely regarded as an outstanding prospect, and Boston was also scouting him. Pittsburgh's earlier offer of $500 for the big Frenchman from Woonsocket, Rhode Island, had been turned down by Fall River owner Charlie Marston, but he now agreed to sell both Geier and Lajoie to the Phillies for $1,500.[7]

A legend later grew up that Geier was the main target of Nash's pursuit and that Marston "threw in" Lajoie in order to get the Phillies to pay the $1,500 price. This is hardly likely. While Geier was considered a good prospect, Lajoie was banging the ball at a .429 clip in his first professional season, was a fine fielder, and had already been sought by several big league clubs. Nap Lajoie clearly represented a financial asset to Marston, who did not give him away. The price the Phillies paid was a substantial sum for two minor leaguers in 1896.

Lajoie made his big league debut on August 12 in a game at Washington, playing first base and picking up a single. The rookie first baseman played 39 games for the Phillies that year, batting .328 with four home runs. It was the start of a long and glorious big league career, one which began and ended in Philadelphia but was concentrated in Cleveland.

Nap Lajoie played four and a half seasons with the Phillies, and he played them exceedingly well. He never hit under .328; in 1899 he compiled an average of .380, and his overall batting mark for the Phils was .349. In his first full year in Philadelphia, he played mostly at first base, with nineteen games in the outfield, but the following year he was shifted to second base, where his agility and grace made him a natural. It was as a second baseman that he achieved greatness as one of the four or five best at that position in baseball history.

Unfortunately, Lajoie by himself could not push the Phillies into first place. Nor could the hiring of George Stallings as manager in 1897. The Georgia-born Stallings was a peculiar personality. A college graduate with two years of medical school, away from the ballpark he was a courtly gentleman, but in the clubhouse and on the field Stallings was loud, vicious and cruel. He drove his players with sarcasm, obscenity, and derision, and they were not happy with this treatment.

In 1897 the Phillies fell to tenth place (in a twelve-team league) with a record of 55–77, despite Delahanty's average of .377 and Lajoie's .363. Rumors of dissension and players' unhappiness with Stallings swirled around the club, and on June 23 the owners had all the players sign a statement that they "are heartily in accord with Mr. Stallings." It merely delayed the inevitable.[8]

The next year the club was limping along in June at a 19–27 pace when the players reached their limit. They refused to perform any more for Stallings. There was no lack of hardbitten characters on this team, but the manager's vicious tongue was still too much for them.[9]

Outfielder Duff Cooley headed a committee of players which called on Reach and Rogers to unload the manager. Cooley said, "We are fed up with the way Stallings has been riding us and decided we had enough of him.... We may not be the best team in the league but we don't intend to put up with Stallings' tactics." On June 18, the club bought out the rest of his three-year contract and named club secretary Billy Shettsline as the manager.[10]

Shettsline, 35 years old, a native Philadelphian and a resident of Glenolden in Delaware County, had not been a professional ballplayer, but he was a shrewd operator who knew his way around a ballclub. He was a cheery individual and beloved by those who knew him: "a big, portly man," wrote Fred Lieb, "[who] bubbled with good humor, good cheer and a kindly philosophy on life." Shettsline, who had first been involved with the Keystones of the Union Association in 1884, spent nearly four decades with the Phillies, as club secretary, manager, business manager, and president, before his death in 1933.[11]

The most important of Shettsline's characteristics in June 1898 was that he was the exact antithesis of George Stallings. The Phillies, who had been in eighth place when the change was made, played at a .573 clip the rest of the way and climbed to sixth. Wiley Piatt won 24 games, losing 14, and Lajoie, with his modest (for him) .328 average, led the league in runs batted in and doubles. Cooley, Delahanty, and Elmer Flick, a rookie from Bedford, Ohio, had batting averages over .300.

Lieb tells a sad story that the Phillies in 1897 sent a sore-armed pitcher named Con Lucid off to Paterson, New Jersey, in the Atlantic League to check out an infielder, a big Dutchman named John "Honus" Wagner. Lucid watched him in a couple of games and reported back that, while Wagner could hit, he was too awkward to play in the National League. Lucid was more impressed by the other team's shortstop, Norman "Kid" Elberfeld, so the Phils acquired him instead of Wagner, who was then picked up by Louisville a couple of weeks later.[12]

It is hard to tell what to make of this typical Fred Lieb tale. Con Lucid, who had pitched for the Phillies in 1895 and 1896, was *not* on their roster in '97. He pitched that spring for Reading, also in the Atlantic League, and it is possible that he sent reports back to his former team on Wagner and Elberfeld. What is known is that Louisville purchased Wagner on July 16, that a week later the Phillies obtained shortstop Frank Shugart, a hard drinker who had been with four teams in the prior six seasons, from minor league St. Paul, and that they got Elberfeld for the 1898 season, after Shugart was found wanting. And Con Lucid wound up, later in 1897, with the St. Louis Browns.[13]

Elberfeld was certainly a major leaguer, and he had a long career of fourteen years. Only the first and briefest of these was in a Philadelphia uniform. The other guy, of course, proved that he *could* play in the National League, and the rest is history. Not Philadelphia history, unfortunately, though a keystone combination of Honus Wagner and Larry Lajoie would have been something to see.

In 1899, Shettsline had his team in the hunt all the way. They finished third, 8½ games behind Ned Hanlon's Brooklyn Superbas and a game behind Frank Selee's Boston Beaneaters. For a long time the 1899 Phillies were regarded by many as the best team the franchise ever had. They won 94 and lost 58. Three of their pitchers, Piatt, newly-acquired Chick Fraser, and Red Donahue, won more than twenty games. Al Orth won 13 and lost 3.

Delahanty led the league with a .408 mark, also setting the pace in hits, total bases, doubles, and runs batted in. Lajoie hit .380, although he missed much of the season after a brutal collision with Reds third baseman Harry Steinfeldt. Elmer Flick hit .342, and catcher Ed McFarland .333. A rookie center fielder from the University of Pennsylvania and nearby Norristown, Roy Thomas, batted .325 and stole 42 bases. Monte Cross did good work at shortstop.

Thomas, the center fielder, was a paradigm for his position. Small, light and speedy, he made very few extra-base hits and hit only seven home runs over a thirteen-year career. He hit singles, and he walked. With his 5'11" height, a good eye, and an uncanny knack for fouling off pitches (he once fouled off 22 balls in a row before walking), he poked hits between fielders, he beat out bunts, and he walked. Old-timers, many years later, saw in Richie Ashburn the second coming of Roy Thomas. In the nine years he played with the Phillies, Thomas hit over .286 seven times, over .300 five times, and led the league in walks seven times.

The National League was cut back in 1900 to eight teams, at the instigation of New York owner Andrew Freedman. The eight surviving teams put up $100,000 to buy out the Baltimore, Cleveland, Washington, and Louisville franchises.

In the trimmed-down league, the Phillies finished third again, after starting fast. Flick, Lajoie, and Delahanty had big years with the bat, but as so frequently happened Phillies pitching was lackluster. Lajoie hit .346 but missed over a month of activity when he broke his thumb in a clubhouse scuffle with Flick. Flick's .378 average brought him in three points behind that of the new Pittsburgh shortstop, Honus Wagner, picked up from the defunct Louisville franchise.

The 1900 Phillies did score high in chicanery after a mid–September incident in which a Cincinnati infielder discovered an electrical device buried in the third base coaching box at the Phillies' ballpark. The device was connected to the center field home clubhouse, where little-used catcher Morgan Murphy was supposed to have spied out the catcher's signal with a telescope and relayed the pitch to the Phillies' third base coach by way of wires under the coach's feet.[14]

Shettsline and his men denied any such foul play, but the team's hitting declined dramatically after the discovery. All in all, whether aided electrically or not, the Phillies had a good team and a good year. But they were still third.

Baseball had come to the end of an era. From 1892 to 1900, the monopolistic National League had things all its own way. The Brotherhood had been beaten back, and the American Association had drowned in a sea of red ink. With the lack of competition, the League owners forced salaries down, imposed restrictions on players' conduct, and banned black players (informally but nonetheless effectively) from Organized Baseball. They considered enforcing a mammoth trust arrangement upon the game, and they permitted rival clubs to come under common ownership.

The "trust" proposal was dreamed up by New York's Freedman, to make the league one big corporation. In the era of big-business trusts, the idea was not so far-fetched as it may now appear, but Freedman went about pushing it in the wrong way. The New York franchise and Freedman's three allies would, under his scheme, control 66 percent of the stock (New York 30 percent, and Boston, St. Louis, and Cincinnati 12 percent each), while the Phillies and Chicago would receive 10 percent each, Pittsburgh 8 percent, and Brooklyn 6 percent. The moguls not allied with Freedman were furious at the proposal and fought it as hard as they could. The fate of the trust plan was wrapped up in the election of a league president in 1901, with incumbent Nicholas Young enjoying the support of Freedman and his confederates, while the New Yorker's enemies backed the revered Albert G. Spalding. After twenty-five fruitless ballots, Spalding was elected on a parliamentary dodge by Rogers. The election was later ruled illegal, but in the meantime the "trust" plan died.

Just as the League owners played rough with one another, the players of the '90s reveled in a decade of snarling, rough, sometimes vicious play, the style set by Ned Hanlon's Baltimore Orioles. The League had been dominated by Selee's Boston Beaneaters and by the inter-related Baltimore and Brooklyn franchises, but in 1900 Pittsburgh and the Phillies were clearly within shouting range of the Superbas. The League was flying high, and it certainly did not appear as if any kind of a crash was imminent. Yet a collision was on its way, and the epicenter of that collision was to be in Philadelphia.

Chapter 3

The American League Invasion

Nineteen hundred and one marked the debut of the American League as a major league competitor to the old established Nationals. The leader of the upstart organization was a pugnacious former sportswriter named Ban Johnson. Johnson had taken over the old Western League in 1895, changed its name in 1900 to the American League, and after that season announced that his league would not sign the National Agreement, the treaty originally between the National League and the American Association which now served to spell out the relationships between the League and the minor leagues. In fact, what Johnson was saying was that his American League would be a major league in 1901, no longer affiliated with or subordinate to the National League. There were fruitless negotiations between the two groups, but these talks broke off early in December, 1900, when it was recognized that Johnson demanded an equal status which the older league would not accord him.[1]

Johnson caught the Nationals off guard, for they were engaged in bitter internal fighting over Andrew Freedman's "trust" scheme and over the league presidency. In addition, the League moguls were in ill repute with the public; one writer said that, except for Brooklyn and Pittsburgh, "there is not a city in the League circuit in which the magnates are not discredited in the estimation of the sport-loving public," caused "either by the want of the genuine sporting spirit ... or the disreputable, high-handed manner in which they have conducted their dealings with the players and the public." By the time the moguls of the old league looked around to see what was going on, Johnson and his clubs had gotten their feet well within baseball's door.[2]

One of the places where the American League chose to go head to head with its National League rivals was Philadelphia, and the Phillies were not happy. Rogers said no one could expect him and Reach "to consent to a lot of carpet-baggers coming into our territory" and the Phillies "could hardly agree to take the new-comers in on equal terms."[3]

Johnson induced the manager of his Milwaukee club, a tall, thin former weak-hitting catcher named Connie Mack, short for Cornelius McGillicuddy, to come to Philadelphia to run the American League club in the Quaker City. Mack quickly hooked up with an *Inquirer* sportswriter named Frank Hough, who became the Athletics' link to ballplayers in the older league. Hough let them know what Mack would pay those who jumped to the Athletics in the new league. He found a lot of unhappy players who were ready, after a decade of the National League's monopoly, to listen to his siren song.

Local businessman Benjamin F. Shibe was recruited by Mack to put up sufficient cash to give the new club a wholly hometown ownership. When Shibe was announced as the club's new president on February 19, 1901, jaws dropped all over Philadelphia. Ben Shibe was Al Reach's partner in the sporting goods business, and one of his sons was married to Reach's daughter. What was not known at the time was that Reach, wearying of the constant struggles in the National League, had urged Shibe to take the position. He had also signed a contract for the Reach Company to manufacture the official baseball for the American League. With financing assured, the Athletics went on the hunt for ballplayers.[4]

The Phillies' Napoleon Lajoie, already recognized as one of the best players in the game, looked like a glittering prize for the new league. And Lajoie was ripe for an offer. The star second baseman was dissatisfied with the National League and with the Phillies. The National League had, for the past eight years, maintained a salary cap, under which no player could be paid more than $2,400 for a season. Many players were angered by this limitation, and, clubowners being clubowners, there were a number of violations of the cap under the table. Prior to the 1900 season Lajoie and Ed Delahanty had agreed that they would not sign their contracts unless they were paid more than the cap-mandated $2,400. Colonel Rogers agreed to violate the rule, and he induced Lajoie to sign for $2,600, assuring the second baseman that Delahanty would be paid the same. In fact, Rogers signed Delahanty for $3,000.

When Lajoie saw one of Delahanty's paychecks, with Rogers's chicanery clearly revealed, he was furious. Rogers compounded his foolishness by refusing Napoleon's demand for the extra $400. Lajoie played out the season for the Phillies, but when Frank Hough offered him $4,000 to play for the Athletics, there were no bonds of loyalty to keep the star second baseman from signing an American League contract, which he did officially on March 20, 1901.[5]

The Athletics offered the same salary to Delahanty, but the Phillies agreed to equal it, and Delahanty stayed put, at least until the following season, when he jumped to Washington. The Athletics signed three Phillies' pitchers, Chick Fraser, Strawberry Bill Bernhard, and Wiley Piatt, and an infielder named Joe Dolan jumped to the new team after the season began.

John Rogers, who felt he had been through this foolishness before with the Brotherhood, was furious. Connie Mack, in his autobiography, wrote: "Our rivals, the Phillies, were not happy over our invasion of Philadelphia." Rogers, saying that "the American League has come here like a thief in the night," fumed that "the players are our assets, and we will certainly defend our rights to the last ditch."[6]

Asked what he would do about Lajoie, Rogers burst forth in frustration and anger, "What will we do? What can we do? We will bring suit, of course, when we are able to find out who we are to bring suit against. Who are these people, anyway? An unincorporated body, without name, without home or any known quantity! ... Who are these people who come along and steal our players...? Certainly we will bring suit when these people, who have been doing business in hiding and under cover, come out and declare themselves in the open." The Colonel's disposition was not helped when a reporter told him where he could easily find both Shibe and Mack.[7]

Rogers hired John G. Johnson, the city's leading barrister, who filed the Phillies' court actions on March 28, to enjoin the jumpers from playing for the Athletics. Equity suits were brought individually against Bernhard, Fraser, and Lajoie, with Shibe, Mack, and Hough as defendants in each action. In the Philadelphia Common Pleas Court, Judge Robert Ralston and two colleagues heard testimony, argument, and a lot of wrangling for a couple of days, before Ralston threw out the Phillies' case because the standard baseball contract lacked "mutuality," in that the club could terminate it on ten days' notice while the player had no such right. Rogers promptly filed an appeal to the state supreme court, but it soon became time to start the season where it belonged, on the baseball diamond.[8]

The Phillies finished second in 1901 in a severely weakened league, 7½ games behind Pittsburgh. Attendance dropped to 234,000, barely ahead of that of the upstart Athletics. Donahue, Orth, and rookie Bill Duggleby won 60 games among them, and Delahanty and Flick hit .357 and .336 respectively. Late in the season, Colonel Rogers heard that his third baseman Harry Wolverton had signed with Washington in the American League for 1902, so he promptly suspended Wolverton for the rest of the year.

In 1902 Rogers and the Phillies lost most of the team's top players. Connie Mack signed Flick, Duggleby, and shortstop Monte Cross. Washington indeed signed Wolverton, and the capital club also stole away Delahanty, Orth, and pitcher Jack Townsend. The St. Louis Browns signed Donahue. The Phillies faced disaster as they scrambled to find replacements.

They still had the speedy Roy Thomas in center field and the old Orioles' shortstop, Hughie Jennings, on first base. Jennings was near the end of the line. A young lefthander named Guy "Doc" White won 14 games as a rookie in 1901. And they signed a first-year catcher named Charles "Red" Dooin, a young man "bubbling with Gaelic wit, sarcasm and fight," Fred Lieb wrote. Dooin became a beloved institution with the Phillies over the next decade and a half. But all of that was hardly enough to fight off the National League and the Athletics too.[9]

Then, shortly before the season opened, the Phillies won a major legal victory. On April 21, 1902, the Pennsylvania Supreme Court handed down its decision in the club's appeal against Lajoie. Justice William P. Potter, writing for the court, reversed the lower court's holding that Lajoie's contract with the Phillies lacked "mutuality." Potter found merit in the club's contention that Lajoie was unique and virtually irreplaceable: "Lajoie is well known, and has great reputation among the patrons of the sport, for ability in the position which he filled, and was thus a most attractive drawing card for the public." Lajoie "may not be the sun in the baseball firmament," wrote Potter, "but he is certainly a bright, particular star." In conclusion, the court held that it "cannot compel the defendant to play for the plaintiff, but it can restrain him from playing for another club in violation of his agreement."[10]

The baseball world was stunned. Rogers and other National League leaders joyously quoted from the court's opinion, and the Phillies president announced that Lajoie, Fraser, and Bernhard were expected "to report to the club at once." On April 23, the jubilant Rogers applied to Judge Ralston for an injunction against Lajoie's playing for any club but the Phillies. Ralston granted the injunction as to Lajoie, although not as to Bernhard and Fraser, since the Supreme Court opinion dealt only with Lajoie. The judge also asked Rogers how the injunction would affect a player out of the jurisdiction, only to be assured by the Phillies president, incorrectly as it turned out, that it would "be operative ... anywhere else in the United States."[11]

In Baltimore, Larry Lajoie opened the season that day at second base for the Athletics, but when Mack was notified, just before the ninth inning, of the injunction handed down in Philadelphia, he quickly removed Lajoie from the game. On April 28, Judge Ralston issued the injunctions requested by the Phillies against Bernhard and Fraser. Duggleby and Fraser returned to the Phillies, but somehow those two pitchers were all that Colonel Rogers had to show for all his much-vaunted juridical triumphs.

Mack allowed Elmer Flick, who had not been sued but was wary of possible litigation, to join the Cleveland club, and Monte Cross stayed with the Athletics. Rogers never brought any action against his players who jumped to Washington, so there was no question of their rejoining the Phillies. Rogers simply assumed that Lajoie must return to the Phillies, and he met with Larry on May 15 to discuss the terms of that return. When Rogers declared that Lajoie must first pay a substantial fine for jumping the club, the player walked out of the meeting, as anyone with a modicum of sense must have known he would. It then became simply a matter of the Athletics arranging a suitable disposition of Lajoie's contract to another American League club, where he would not be subject to the injunction of a Pennsylvania court. Early in June, Lajoie signed with Cleveland, after saying that Rogers "had his chance to get me, and failed to take advantage of the opportunity."[12]

1902 turned out, in spite of the pyrrhic victory in the Supreme Court, to be just about as bad for the Phillies as it looked before the season began. Shettsline's team won 56, lost 81, and finished seventh. Roy Thomas's .286 was the best average they could muster, and Doc White's 16 wins on the mound were overmatched by 20 defeats.

On top of everything else, the Athletics won the American League pennant and outdrew the Phils, 442,000 to 112,000. Barney Dreyfuss of the Pittsburgh club had to advance a sizable bundle of cash so the Phillies could complete the season. Late in the year, Rogers announced that he was tired of running the club and he thought it was time for Reach to take over again. Reach respectfully declined.

Meanwhile, peace came to the major leagues. After the 1902 season, the National League recognized that it could not continue a war which it was clearly losing, and an agreement between the two leagues was concluded early in 1903. A National Commission, consisting of the two league presidents and Cincinnati president Garry Herrmann, was set up to oversee the operation of the game. Herrmann, while a National League club owner, was actually closer to Ban Johnson, who became the most powerful figure in baseball for many years.

In Philadelphia, there was an upheaval of sorts at 15th and Huntingdon. Rogers and Reach, neither of whom had any further stomach for the operation of the Phillies, sold the franchise in March 1903. The sale price was about $170,000, in a transaction put together by Barney Dreyfuss, who was trying to safeguard his 1902 loan to the Phillies. Rogers and Reach kept the ballpark, which they leased to the new owners, a syndicate headed by socialite James Potter.

Potter knew nothing about running a baseball team. He moved Shettsline back to the club's business office and named Charles "Chief" Zimmer as field manager, at the suggestion of Dreyfuss, who willingly sold his veteran catcher to the Phillies.

The 1903 Phillies were six games worse than the sorry 1902 team, and they finished seventh once again. The team suffered the last casualty of the war with the American League when pitcher Doc White jumped to the White Sox just before the peace agreement was signed. Kid Gleason, who won 62 games pitching for the Phillies in 1890 and 1891, now returned as a second baseman at the age of 37 and batted .284. The pitching was handled by Duggleby, Fraser, Fred Mitchell, and easy-going Tully Sparks.

A noteworthy event was the arrival of John Titus, a quiet lefthanded-hitting outfielder from St. Clair, Pennsylvania. The red-haired Titus, known as "Silent John" and "Tight Pants," wore a handlebar mustache, always had a toothpick in one corner of his mouth, and gave the Phillies ten years of solid outfield play.

Jimmy Hagan, who served in the Phillies' front office from the days of Potter to the time of the Carpenters, said that John Titus was always on the lookout for hairpins, believing them a source of good luck. One day a couple of his practical joker teammates scattered several pounds of hairpins over the street outside the park. The team manager became quite upset when he saw his right fielder nearly get run over by a cab while scooping up hairpins in the middle of Broad Street.[13]

The biggest story of the 1903 Phillies' season was the tragedy of August 8, when the collapse of a balcony on the 15th Street side of the park caused the deaths of twelve fans, with another 300 being maimed or injured. When a disturbance broke out across 15th Street, during the second game of a doubleheader, many of the left field bleacherites rushed over to a three-foot-wide balcony along the street to see what was happening. The balcony's rotted timber supports gave way and precipitated some 500 persons down 25 feet to the street below. The carnage was horrible, as those who fell first were crushed by other fans as well as by broken pieces of the balcony itself.[14]

The 1903 Phillies saw their attendance drop to 140,771, far less than the 512,000 paying customers drawn by the Athletics. And no wonder. For the first time since 1883, the Phillies fell into last place. The team lost 100 games, which it had never done before. The Phils won only 52, and they finished far behind John McGraw's champion Giants.

After Chief Zimmer's unhappy season as manager, he left the job to become an umpire. Future Hall of Famer Hugh Duffy was named manager for 1904, and he had a dismal time of it. The team's hitting was not bad — it seldom was in the Huntingdon Street ballpark, as Titus hit .294, Thomas .290, and a rookie outfielder named Sherry Magee .277 — but the pitching was ineffective and the fielding was atrocious.

The club's best pitcher, Chick Fraser, won 14 and lost 24, while Tully Sparks was 7–18. Duffy's boys committed 403 errors, 55 more than the second-worst team. A 35-year-old rookie pitcher from Easton, Pennsylvania, John McPherson, had one of those records which pops up from time to time in Philadelphia baseball annals: one win and ten defeats, and he had to pitch a shutout for the one victory.

After the 1904 season ended, the front office was reorganized. Potter, obviously out of place, gave up the club presidency to the ubiquitous Billy Shettsline. The new president had broad baseball experience, everywhere but on the playing field, and Phillies followers hoped for something better than the teams produced by the hapless Potter.

A player whom Shettsline had signed in 1904, Sherwood Robert "Sherry" Magee, a righthanded-hitting outfielder from Clarendon, Pennsylvania, helped substantially in producing a much-improved Phillies team in 1905. Fred Lieb called Magee "a blithesome, carefree spirit, with little respect for authority ... [who] found training irksome and never paid much attention to it." Magee was also a bully who, after he became a star, was frequently downright nasty to his teammates, especially youngsters. But the man could hit, and he could run. In his eleven years with the Phillies, he averaged .299 and hit over .300 five times. Magee hit 337 doubles, 127 triples, and 75 home runs, in an era when home runs were not easy to come by. He drove in 889 runs, and for good measure he stole 387 bases. For offensive production like that, the Phillies put up with a few character flaws.[15]

In 1905, Magee hit .299, with 24 doubles, 17 triples, and 48 stolen bases, to contribute a large measure to a team renaissance. Duffy's club rose from the cellar, improving by 31 games to reach fourth place. The other two outfielders banged the ball, with Thomas hitting .317 and Titus .308.

Shettsline made a couple of trades which helped in the club's 1905 improvement. He swapped a rookie to Pittsburgh for veteran first sacker William "Kitty" Bransfield, who took care of the position for the Phillies for the next six years. Shettsline also sent third baseman Harry Wolverton, who had jumped back from Washington in 1902 but was now clearly on the decline, to the Boston Nationals for righthanded pitcher Charles "Togie" Pittinger, who won 23 games for Duffy in 1905. Pittinger, whom local sportswriter Horace Fogel described as "horse-faced," won far fewer

Hard-hitting outfielder Sherry Magee.

than that in his two remaining seasons with the club, but for 1905 he was just what the Phillies needed. Duggleby won 18 and Sparks 14, and the legendary Charles "Kid" Nichols, picked up after being released by St. Louis, won the last ten of his career 360 victories for the 1905 Phillies, losing only six.

The team also came up with a smooth-fielding shortstop named Mickey Doolan, who teamed with Gleason to give Duffy strength up the middle, with the steady Dooin behind the plate and Thomas in center.

The 1905 attendance of 317,932 was the highest in the club's history, but unfortunately there were always those other guys, the ones playing at Columbia Park, whose American League pennant made the Phillies' fourth place finish look like small change.

The Phillies' rivalry with the New York Giants was heating up considerably. Propinquity often breeds animosity, and there was an ill-concealed bitter edge to relations between the two cities, a bare hundred miles apart, with nothing separating them but New Jersey. The swaggering, bullying tactics of John McGraw and the arrogant attitude of his players irritated many in Philadelphia.

In the first series of 1906 in Philadelphia there was a fist-fight on the field between Phils reserve infielder Paul Sentelle and the detested McGraw. The battle was later continued under the stands, and Giant players were mobbed by Philadelphia fans on 15th Street after the game.

Unfortunately, while much of the National League was taking aim at McGraw and his men, Frank Chance's Chicago Cubs roared past the other seven clubs to amass an all-time record of 116 wins. They left everyone in their dust, including the second place New Yorkers. Duffy's Phillies slipped badly in 1906, winning twelve fewer games than the year before, falling eleven games under .500, although holding fourth place. The team's hitting and fielding were both bad. Togie Pittinger's wins fell from 23 to 8, Bill Duggleby's fell from 18 to 13, and Kid Nichols didn't win any, being hit hard in four games before being let go. Tully Sparks won 19 and lost 16. Johnny Lush, a little lefthander who had been signed out of Girard College a couple of years earlier, won 18 and gave the club one of its few highlights on May 1 when he held Brooklyn hitless in a 1–0 victory.

Attendance dropped in 1906, and at the end of the season Hugh Duffy left to take a job with the Providence team in the International League. Hughie found it tough competing against Mack and his Athletics, who were defending their league championship in 1906.

The following year, while the Athletics squared off in a bitter but unsuccessful pennant battle with the Detroit Tigers, the Phillies too had a good season under a new manager, an easygoing Irishman named Billy Murray. The Phillies moved up to third, winning 83 games, a dozen more than the year before. Magee led them with a .328 average and a league high 85 runs batted in, and a youngster named Otto Knabe provided them with sensational play at second base. Tully Sparks compiled a record of 22–8, while Frank Corriden won 18 games.

Toward the end of the campaign, the club brought in two young pitchers who started their big league careers in spectacular fashion. George McQuillan, a righthander from Brooklyn, pitched 41 innings in six games and had a 4–0 record with an ERA of 0.66. Harry Coveleski, a lefty from Shamokin in the upstate hard-coal region, pitched twenty innings over four games and gave up no earned runs at all. The Phillies' attendance of 341,216 was up markedly from the year before, although it fell far short of what the Athletics drew.

Despite setting a franchise attendance record with 420,660, the 1908 Phillies slid to fourth place with a record of 83–71. Kitty Bransfield hit .304, but Sherry Magee tailed off to .283 and only 57 runs driven in. Sparks won 16 and Corriden 14, but the big winner on the pitching staff was one of the late-season phenoms of the year before, George McQuillan. The second-year man won 23 games while losing 17 and had a sparkling earned run average of 1.52 in 360 innings.

When the season was done, though, the big talk around town was about the *other* late-season addition from 1907. Harry Coveleski spent most of the year with Lancaster. Called up again in September, he found himself pitching against the New York Giants on September 29. This was just days after Fred Merkle's famous baserunning blunder had cost the Giants a victory over Chicago in the furious pennant battle being waged by the two teams (along with the Pirates).

All Coveleski did was blank John McGraw's men, 7–0. Then, on October 1, he beat New York again, 6–2, holding them to four hits. Two days later, Murray ran Coveleski out against the Giants once more, and again the young southpaw beat them, 3–2. He outpitched Mathewson, and he escaped unscathed from a second-and-third-with-none-out jam in the ninth. The *New York Herald* wrote, bitterly, "If the Giants lose the pennant, Coveleski deserves the credit for defeating them." McGraw was furious that the Phillies pitched Coveleski out of turn against him.[16]

Phillie fans, of course, became happier and more delighted with McGraw's discomfort the more he screamed and ranted. The Giants were forced into a playoff with the Cubs (actually a replay of the tied Merkle game), and Chicago won it to clinch the pennant. As for Harry Coveleski, he was known ever after as the "Giant Killer." Not as good as his younger brother Stanley, who wound up in the Hall of Fame, Harry Coveleski won 81 big-league games and had three 20-win seasons for Detroit. Nevertheless, his real fame came from those six days in September and October 1908.

1909 was a disappointing year for the Phillies, both because of their own losing record, which dropped them out of the first division, and because of the excitement generated by their American League rivals, who unveiled a brand new ballpark, six blocks down Lehigh Avenue from the Phillies' yard, and then put on a great fight for the pennant. Both the Phils' pitching and hitting were mediocre — Magee dropped off substantially — and the team's record reflected that fact.

Manager Murray expected good work from the Phillies' pitching staff in 1909, but McQuillan's penchant for Philadelphia's night life pulled his record down to 13 and 16, and he dragged the club down with him. "McQuillan found it difficult to resist the good-time Charlies who like to bask in a star's reflected spotlight," Fred Lieb wrote.[17]

Early in the year, a syndicate headed by the city's top political leaders, Israel W. Durham and James P. McNichol, with banker Clarence Wolf, purchased the Phillies franchise from the group originally organized by Potter. Attorney Francis Shunk Brown later told of initiating and consummating the deal in one 15-minute meeting with Charles Ingersoll, Potter's lawyer. James Potter, of course, was by this time very happy to be freed of any further connection with baseball.[18]

Iz Durham, formerly state insurance commissioner and Matthew Quay's successor as the city's Republican boss, ran the city at the time Lincoln Steffens wrote in *McClure's Magazine* in 1903: "Other American cities, no matter how bad their condition may be, all point to Philadelphia as worse — 'the worst-governed city in the country.'" McNichol, a state senator, was Durham's choice to take over the party.[19]

Durham's health was declining, and he hoped that running a baseball team would be less taxing than running the city. He named himself club president, returning Shettsline to business manager. It was not to be; Iz Durham died on June 28, 1909, and McNichol and Wolf let Shettsline and Murray operate the team until November 26, when they sold it again, for some $350,000.

The new president of the Phillies was an astonishing choice — an eccentric 48-year-old former sportswriter named Horace S. Fogel, who had written for the *Philadelphia Item*, the *Evening Telegraph*, the *Bulletin*, and the *Evening Star*. In Fogel's background, curiously, were two brief managerial stints with last place clubs in the National League, Indianapolis in 1887 and the New York Giants in 1902, where he had preceded John McGraw.

Fogel tried to make people believe that he alone had put up the money to buy the club, but few persons in the know subscribed to that idea. Newspapermen were notorious for living a precarious hand-to-mouth existence, with little opportunity to build up any kind of nest-egg. Fogel himself was known to enjoy whiling away his spare time in the company of some of his colleagues and a bottle.

"Just who is back of Fogel," wrote the *Public Ledger*'s correspondent, initially, "or who supplied the money is not known." It was soon common knowledge that the major backing came from members of the Taft family of Cincinnati, closely allied with Charles Murphy, president of the Chicago Cubs.[20]

One of Fogel's first moves was to can Billy Murray, the club's manager, and to replace him with catcher Charles "Red" Dooin, long a Philadelphia favorite. Another move was to change the team's uniforms. The standard black trim on white or gray was changed to green, with a large Old English "P" on the front of the home uniform, and green-and-white striped stockings replacing the old solid black ones.

Fogel also announced the change of the team's nickname from Phillies to the "Live Wires," but, after the laughter subsided, the new name was almost universally ignored. Still, Fogel was well-advised to try to stir things up at 15th and Huntingdon; he was up against stiff competition in the struggle for baseball loyalties in Philadelphia.

Chapter 4

Dooin Takes the Reins

The Phillies were in a tough situation, competing with an Athletics team which won a pennant in 1905, finished a close second in 1907 and 1909, and then won four pennants and three world championships in the next five years. So how did the Phillies do while the guys six blocks down Lehigh Avenue were building a dynasty? Not too badly, actually, although most of the time they did what they did in comparative privacy. In the five years that Red Dooin served as manager, the Phillies achieved three first-division finishes, but they never came close to the Athletics in attendance.

After the 1909 season, the Phillies had a new president in Fogel and a new manager in Dooin. For 1910 the club improved by four games, which put it three games over .500 and moved it up to fourth place. The fans, however, showed little interest, and attendance dropped slightly from the 1909 figures.

Sherry Magee, almost traded away the year before, bounced back in 1910 with a superb season. He hit .331, to wrench the batting title away from Honus Wagner after four years. Magee drove in 123 runs, which also led the league. Dooin got modest hitting from his infield, but the elderly Kitty Bransfield at first base fell off to .239.

In July, the Phillies traded a mediocre hurler named Bill Foxen to Chicago for Fred Luderus, a lefthanded hitting first baseman who had been languishing in the shadow of Frank Chance. In 21 Phils games, the 24-year-old Luderus hit .294 and indicated that Bransfield's days as a regular were numbered.

The pitching staff, from which much was expected, especially with Red Dooin to run it, was a disappointment. Old Tully Sparks, his best days behind him, was hit hard in three games and let go. Early in the season, McQuillan and Earl Moore, a veteran who had been around long enough to know better, were suspended for violating training rules. Moore came back from the suspension to win 22 games, losing 15. McQuillan, whose carousing would eventually cause him to fritter away a considerable talent, was another matter. When he pitched, he pitched well. He led the league with a 1.60 earned run average, although his won-lost record was only 9–6. But he continued to ignore the rules, and in August a disgusted Horace Fogel suspended him for the rest of the season.

After the 1910 season, a bizarre controversy developed, the kind of thing which seemed to crop up around Fogel. On October 26, it was revealed that Dooin had worked out a trade with Cincinnati, sending the troublemaking McQuillan, pitcher Lew Moren, third baseman Eddie Grant, and outfielder Johnny Bates to the Reds for third baseman John Lobert, a speedster with a good bat, outfielder Dode Paskert, and two righthanded pitchers, Fred Beebe and Jack Rowan. Fogel, though, announced that there was no deal, apparently because it leaked to the press before he approved it. The next day an enraged Dooin threatened to resign if the trade did not go through, and Cincinnati president Garry Herrmann said that he regarded the transaction as completed.

On October 27, Dooin's resignation landed in the Phillies' office. Fogel went into conference with the club's legal counsel, who issued a statement that Dooin "had no right to dispose of the players, the transaction not having been sanctioned under the president's signature." Fogel declined to accept Dooin's resignation; he would talk his manager out of it, he said.[1]

When the Reds signed McQuillan and Bates to Cincinnati contracts on October 31, Fogel exploded, accusing Herrmann of "tampering" with his chattels. A reporter learned that McQuillan and Bates had signed for salaries of $3,800 and $3,500 respectively, substantially more than their 1910 figures, and wrote gleefully that "it's no wonder the two Phillies were quick to sign Cincinnati contracts."[2]

There was a lot more bluster, but finally on November 14 Charles Murphy, president of the Cubs and representative of the Taft family interests which owned the majority of the Phillies shares, met with Fogel and advised him to calm down. Fogel did so, and it was soon made clear that Dooin would manage the Phillies in 1911 and the trade with Cincinnati stood.

Paskert and Lobert proved to be valuable additions to the Philadelphia club, and, with the exception of the talented but troublesome McQuillan, the Phillies did not give up much. Even with McQuillan, the judgment that he would never match his promise was correct.

What the commotion about the Cincinnati trade *did* demonstrate was that strange things happened around the Phillies front office with Horace Fogel in command. As a case in point, the green-and-white uniforms of 1910 were ditched after just one season, and the club was clothed for 1911 in red-and-white togs.

Charles "Red" Dooin, a popular catcher and manager.

The 1911 Phillies team finished in fourth place again, with a record almost identical to that of the year before. How they got there, however, was by a totally different route. The Phillies held first place for three weeks in mid-summer, before injuries and other misfortunes sidetracked them, and they unveiled the hottest young pitcher to come along in many a year. As a result, attendance jumped by almost 120,000, to 416,000.

Dooin's three new regulars all paid off. Luderus at first base was weak on defense, but he could hit. He averaged .301, hit sixteen home runs, and drove in 99 runs. Third sacker Lobert and centerfielder Paskert were each fine fielders, and they hit .285 and .273 respectively. Lobert stole his expected 40 bases. Dooin himself batted .328, the highest mark of his career, but broke his leg in late July.

After that, the Phillies used more than a half dozen men behind the plate, one of them a pickup from the Browns named Bill Killefer. Sherry Magee's average fell to .288, although he still hit fifteen home runs and drove home 94. Doolan and Knabe each dropped off about 25 points. John Titus also suffered a broken leg, and his loss combined with that of Red Dooin put a severe strain on the Phillies' offense. When the ill-tempered Magee was suspended for punching umpire Bill Finneran over a called third strike, the club's run at a pennant collapsed.

George Chalmers, a tall rookie righthander born in Scotland, won 13 games and lost 10, and Earl Moore won 15 and lost 19, but otherwise the pitching was rather nondescript. Except for that rookie mentioned earlier.

A tall, sandy-haired righthander out of Elba, Nebraska, his name was Grover Cleveland Alexander, nicknamed "Pete." He had developed great strength growing up on his family's farm. Pitching semi-pro ball on Sundays around his home town, he was spotted by the operator of a minor league team in Galesburg, Illinois, who signed him to a professional contract.

Alexander pitched two good seasons in the low minors, coming back from a serious injury in his first year, when severe double vision resulted from being hit between the eyes by a thrown ball. A few days before the start of the 1910 season, the double vision finally left him, and, pitching for Syracuse in the New York State League, he put up a record of 29–14.[3]

Discovered by Fogel's scout Patsy O'Rourke, Alexander was not purchased immediately by the Phillies. Fogel thought he could save money by waiting for the post-season minor league draft. The Phillies luckily were not burned by this foolish delay and were able to pick up the 24-year-old Alexander for $750. Even so, at the end of spring training, Dooin was going to send Alexander back but backup catcher Pat Moran insisted that

One of the greatest pitchers of all time, Grover Cleveland Alexander.

the rookie be given a final look in a pre-season game with the Athletics. Alexander came through with a superb performance, and his place on the staff was secured.

What came next astounded the Phillies and all of baseball. With his good fast ball, incredible curve, easy motion, and razor-sharp control, Alexander as a National League rookie won 28 games and lost 13, leading the league in victories, complete games, innings pitched, and shutouts. He also piled up 227 strikeouts. It was the greatest first-year pitching season ever. Pete Alexander, appearing out of the blue, was so good it was hard to believe he was real.

A few years later, *Inquirer* columnist S.O. Grauley called Alexander "the ideal boxman [i.e., pitcher] for ease, motion and delivery when hurling. It never seemed to be any exertion for Old Pete to curve them up to the plate. Just a mild sort of arm motion and the ball was on its way to the plate, a twister one time, a drop another and then a straight fast one.... He was as nonchalant as a side show barker. Nothing worried Old Pete. He could fling in any pinch and he never lost his head." Alexander lived on the low and outside part of the plate, either with his sinking fastball or his curve, and batters who happened to hit the ball sent a lot of two-hoppers to the infielders.[4]

Alexander worked quickly (his games rarely took more than an hour and a half), he never complained, and he never criticized his teammates or opponents. He was one of the best-liked players in the game. He was a hard drinker later on, but in his years with the Phillies that was seldom a problem. Phillies fans finally had a pitcher they could compare with the Benders, Waddells, and Planks who had been so prominent with the Athletics since the American League came to town, and in truth Alex was better than any of them.

There was a particularly symbolic game for Alexander on September 7, when he hooked up in a classic duel with Cy Young of the Boston Rustlers at the South End Grounds in Boston. Young was near the end of his career, but he was still not a pitcher to trifle with. Alexander gave Boston only one scratch hit, but his mates could not score against the 44-year-old Young until the eighth inning, when Paskert singled with two out, stole second, and scored on Lobert's hit. Alexander set the home team down in the eighth and ninth to seal his 1–0 victory, in an hour and 27 minutes. It was the first of four consecutive shutouts for the rookie, achieved against one of the all-time greats.

After the excitement and promise of 1911, the 1912 season was a great disappointment. The Phillies' performance on the field was mediocre, paid attendance dropped sharply, and the season ended with the club's president enmeshed in a welter of self-generated controversy. Dooin's team slipped back under the .500 level and dropped into fifth place.

Lobert, Paskert, and Magee all hit over .300, and Otto Knabe boosted his average to .282, but of these players only Dode Paskert put in a full season. Sherry Magee broke his wrist in a pre-season exhibition, and Knabe broke his hand; both missed a lot of games. Lobert incurred various disabling injuries and saw action in only 65 games. Pitchers Moore and Chalmers both were hit by injuries. Alexander, suffering his version of the "sophomore jinx," declined to 19–17, although he led the league in innings and strikeouts.

In all the gloom, there were some bright lights. When the Phillies sent Kitty Bransfield to the Cubs in September 1911 they received cash and Chicago's somewhat cloudy claim upon a righthanded-hitting minor league outfielder named Clifford "Gavvy" Cravath. Cravath, a 30-year-old Californian, had earlier put in two unsuccessful seasons in the American League and returned to the minors. A hot season at Minneapolis, however, turned him into a prospect, and several teams, including the Cubs, claimed that they had acquired options on him.

When the smoke cleared, Gavvy Cravath was a Phillie, and *his* 1912 season was a success. He hit .284 with eleven home runs, taking over left field after John Titus was traded to Boston. What no one in Philadelphia suspected at the time was that over the next seven years Gavvy Cravath, also sometimes known as "Cactus," would become baseball's top all-time home run hitter. (All-time, that is, until the middle of the 1921 season, when he was passed by Babe Ruth.)[5]

Another step forward was the installation of young Bill Killefer as the number one catcher. Red Dooin had done fine work for the Phillies over the years, but he could see that Killefer was an exceptional talent as a receiver. Several pitchers of promise made their appearance at the Hunt-ingdon Grounds in 1912, and Killefer was the man to handle them.

Tom Seaton, another Nebraskan, a fastball pitcher with no change of pace, whose contract had been purchased from Portland, won 16 and lost 12. A 6'5" lefthander named Eppa Jeptha Rixey, from Culpeper, Virginia, came along at the age of 21 to win and lose ten games, demonstrating great raw ability. Another more seasoned southpaw, Addison Brennan, won eleven games. And a young Georgian named Erskine Mayer appeared in seven games, with a 0–1 record, but he would make his mark in the sea-sons to come.

In the meantime, Horace Fogel succeeded in diverting attention from his ballclub to himself. Fogel had been drinking with some of his old news-paper friends on several occasions in August and September, when he offered some opinions on the honesty of the National League and its lead-ers.

With his not-so-secret association with Murphy of Chicago, Fogel was disappointed that the Cubs were going to fall far short in their pen-nant race with New York. On August 12, Fogel told his companions that Roger Bresnahan, managing the Cardinals, had been "pulling" to the Giants, his old team, by seeing that his present team lost games to the New Yorkers.

Fogel stated several weeks later that the race was "fixed," and he made charges against umpire William Brennan. He wrote a letter to league pres-ident Thomas Lynch, attacking the work of several umpires in games between the Phillies and Giants and insinuating that Lynch was behind a plot to make sure New York won. On September 20, Fogel sent a wire to Reds president Garry Herrmann, hinting that the pennant race was "crooked," and on September 28 he wrote an article for the *Chicago Evening Post*, attacking Lynch and his umpires. On October 12 he wrote a letter to the other seven club presidents, elaborating on his charges that the pen-nant race was not an honest one and threatening to make more startling disclosures.

Lynch responded by bringing seven charges of improper conduct against Fogel, and a league meeting was called for November 27 at the Waldorf in New York to hear them. Fogel blustered, stormed, and put up a bold front, but as the meeting date approached it became apparent that he was seeking ways to avoid the confrontation. Stories appeared in the press that several syndicates were attempting to buy the Phillies.

On November 26, as the league magnates assembled for the big show-down, Fogel announced that he had resigned the presidency of the Phillies on November 22 and named Alfred Day Wiler, the club's vice president, in his place. Fogel's attorney took the position that the league had no right to try Fogel, as Horace was no longer an officer in the National League. League officials, however, "generally believed that the move of Fogel in resigning was simply a blind and that after everything blew over he would be re-elected."[6]

On the 27th, the league owners met and, after six stormy hours, found Horace Fogel guilty on five of Lynch's seven charges. He was "expelled forever from the National League." He exited with a defiant statement — "I will sell or represent as I please the Philadelphia Club in the National League as long as I feel inclined to do so, and no one can disturb me from doing so" — but it was clear even to the crushed Horace Fogel that the game was over for him.[7]

Of course Fogel's ouster left the Phillies' front office in a state of considerable confusion. The hapless Alfred Day Wiler retained the unwanted office of president while the owners of the club looked for a buyer. On January 15, 1913, a syndicate headed by William H. Locke, secretary of the Pittsburgh club and right-hand man to Pirates' president Barney Dreyfuss, was announced as the new owner of the Phillies.

Locke was the largest investor in the group. The next biggest was Locke's cousin, William F. Baker, a former New York police commissioner. One little-noticed feature of the sale was that it did not include the 15th and Huntingdon Streets ballpark, which was retained by the prior owners as an investment, graced as it was with a lease binding the Phillies to play there for ninety-nine years.

With the erratic Fogel behind them and the front office apparently stabilized by the arrival of a real baseball man in Locke, the Phillies and Red Dooin jumped off to a fast start in 1913, leading the league most of the time to the end of June. In mid–July, unfortunately, Locke died, to be succeeded by Baker, who did not possess his cousin's baseball savvy. The Phillies were then passed by an outstanding Giants team, but they held on to second place, where they finished, 12½ games behind New York.

The 1913 Phillies had excellent hitting, pitching, and defense. They started to realize what they had in Cravath when Gavvy hit .341, second in the league, and led the circuit with 19 home runs and 128 runs batted in. Luderus was second with 18 home runs, and he drove in 86 runs. Magee hit .306 and added another eleven homers. Lobert played the full season and batted .300, and spare outfielder Beals Becker hit .324 in 306 at bats. The middle of the infield continued to be solid defensively with Knabe and Doolan, and Killefer, now firmly established behind the plate, was widely regarded as the top catcher in the league.

Tom Seaton, in his second year with the Phillies, put together an out-standing season. He won 27 and lost 12, with an earned run average of 2.60, leading the league in innings pitched, wins, and strikeouts. Not far behind Seaton was Pete Alexander, who had a 22–8 record, led the league in shutouts with nine, and was hard on his teammate's heels in strikeouts.

Ad Brennan won 14, and young Eppa Rixey and Erskine Mayer each won nine. Chalmers, though, was ineffective and won but three games, los-ing ten. Still, it was a red-letter year for the Phillies, and their home atten-dance of 470,000 people set a club record. Of course, the other fellows down Lehigh Avenue *did* win a world's championship. But the Phils' prospects for 1914 were bright.

They did not stay that way very long. 1914 saw the start of the Euro-pean war in August, but months before that unhappy event it saw the start of a new baseball war. A minor circuit calling itself the Federal League had operated with moderate success in 1913; it was taken over for 1914 by an ambitious Chicago businessman named James A. Gilmore. Aided by the defrocked Horace Fogel, Gilmore took on the two established leagues in 1914. The Federal League proclaimed itself a major league, and it raided existing big league rosters for manpower.

Baker, the Phillies' frugal new president, declined in most cases to match Federal League offers to his players, so several of them jumped to the new league, most notably Seaton, pitchers Ad Brennan and Howie Camnitz, the longtime keystone combination of Otto Knabe and Mickey Doolan, and outfielder Jimmy Walsh. One Phillie who jumped to the Feds came back. Killefer signed with the Chicago Federal team, whose offer of $17,500 for three years dwarfed his 1913 salary of $3,000. Baker offered the catcher a three-year contract at $6,500 a year, and Killefer jumped back, twelve days after signing the Chicago pact.

When the Chifeds went into federal court seeking an injunction against Killefer playing for the Phillies, the judge found that both ballclubs had "unclean hands" and refused to intervene. He also called Killefer "a person upon whose pledged word little or no reliance can be placed, and who, for gain to himself, neither scruples nor hesitates to disregard and violate his express engagements." When a court of appeals affirmed the lower court, without any further animadversions upon the catcher's char-acter, Killefer was legally free to rejoin the Phillies, which he had already done.[8]

The Federals did not put a team in Philadelphia, but the turmoil caused by a confusing season, the inability of the club to hang onto its play-ers, and a drop back into the second division combined to pull attendance way down, to 138,474. Gavvy Cravath hit 19 home runs and again led the league, and he and Magee were the only National Leaguers to drive in over a hundred runs, Sherry leading with 103. Beals Becker hit .325 as the regular left fielder, and Magee and Luderus hit 15 and 12 home runs respectively.

The club's defense fell off considerably as Dooin tried without much success to reconstruct the middle of his infield. Alexander put together a 27–15 season, leading the league in wins, innings and strikeouts, and Erskine Mayer won 21 while losing 19. The rest of the pitching staff suffered badly, Rixey bringing up the rear at 2–11, with a high earned run average.

Few managers can survive a fall from second place to sixth, with a precipitous drop in attendance, and, shortly after the season, Charlie Dooin was on his way out. The choice of a successor became a problem for Baker, because both Lobert and Sherry Magee promptly let it be known that they were interested.

Ex-Phil Tom Seaton, who won 25 games in his first Federal season, claimed that the choice of either would result in a bonanza for the outlaw league. "It's all off with the Philadelphia club," Seaton said. "Trouble is bound to follow the selection of a manager." He pointed out that Lobert and Magee each headed a faction on the club and, when either was chosen, the other and his followers would likely jump to the Feds. This did not include Alexander, whom the Phillies had taken the precaution to sign to a three-year contract.[9]

On October 20, 1914, Baker announced that Dooin was fired and that his new manager was neither Lobert or Magee but veteran catcher-coach Pat Moran, to whom no one could take offense. Lobert said he was personally disappointed, but he regarded Moran "as a cool, shrewd inside baseball man."[10]

Red Dooin spoke up the next day, saying that he was not fired, he quit. He said he had never had the full support of the club owner, not only Baker but Fogel before him, and that the club's "mercenary attitude" kept him from getting "many a good ball player." Finally, he said, "I am glad I'm free of all the worry of being manager, anyway. I think I would have been a wreck in another year."[11]

Dooin *did* want to continue playing, however, and the Phillies' ownership of his reserve rights was a problem. He tried to negotiate a trade for himself, and he made sure to maintain contacts with the Federals. Magee strengthened the ex-manager's hand by saying that wherever Dooin went he wanted to go too. "Charlie is doing the talking for us both," Magee said.[12]

Moran arranged a deal with the Giants for Dooin, but it fell through when Red demanded a salary of $7,500. In the midst of all this turmoil,

Dode Paskert announced that he was considering a jump to the Federal League. "I like Moran," he said, "but the Feds will give me much more money than the Phillies are paying." A few days later, however, Paskert met privately with Moran and then, appropriately mollified, announced that he was staying.[13]

Finally, the contentions on the ballclub were settled with a quick series of transactions. Early in November, the Phillies sent four players to Portland in the Pacific Coast League in exchange for one of the most coveted men in the minor leagues, a switch-hitting shortstop named Dave Bancroft.

The day before Christmas, Baker traded Magee to the Boston Braves for $10,000 and outfielder George "Possum" Whitted. On January 4, 1915, he dealt Lobert to the Giants for third baseman Milt Stock, righthander Al Demaree, and catcher Jack Adams. And on January 15, after hemming and hawing and saying publicly "nothing doing so far as my going to Cincinnati," Charlie Dooin accepted the Reds' contract offer of $6,000 a year for two years and the Phillies traded him there, in exchange for an infielder named Bert Niehoff.[14]

Baker and Moran had stood their ground, faced down several threats to jump to the Federals, and had a revamped but solid 1915 lineup to take to their first Florida spring training, in St. Petersburg.

Chapter 5

A Pennant for Pat Moran

The year 1915 was as good for the Phillies as it was bad for the Athletics. Connie Mack, shocked that his team lost the World Series in four straight games to the Boston Braves and uncertain that he could fend off Federal League attacks on his roster, astounded the baseball world shortly after the '14 Series by getting rid of Eddie Collins, Chief Bender, Eddie Plank, and Jack Coombs. When a dissatisfied Frank Baker sat out the 1915 season, the bottom fell out for the A's and they plummeted into the American League cellar. The Phillies, on the other hand, had their most successful season ever.

Pat Moran was an Irishman from Massachusetts who had had a lengthy career as a weak-hitting backup catcher (with the Boston Nationals and the Cubs) and (with the Phillies) as a coach. He was good with pitchers, and he ran his club with a firm hand. Moran worked his players hard in spring training, particularly on fundamentals. He worked to instill confidence in his men, to have them thinking and acting like winners. Moran wanted his players to play intelligent ball, and he said that "'inside base ball' will be the Phillies' long suit."[1]

The Phillies got off to a fast start, winning their first eight games, and confirming their self-image as winners, as Moran had insisted. They were a tough bunch, and they backed down to no one. In the early going they were locked in a fight for first place with Roger Bresnahan's Chicago Cubs.

The defending champion Braves were not a factor early in the race; they had lost several key men to the Federals and were not getting good pitching from Lefty [Tyler] and Bill [James], the stars of their miracle run for the 1914 pennant. One writer said flatly, on April 26, "The Phils look to be a lot better team than the Braves. Moran has a bunch that is hustling every minute." On June 8, the Phils overtook Chicago, traded the lead back and forth with the Cubs for another five weeks, and then moved in front.[2]

Luderus, Cravath, Possum Whitted, and Davey Bancroft, the rookie shortstop, supplied most of the offensive firepower. Bancroft, who acquired the nickname "Beauty" from his habit of shouting this word every time his pitcher threw a good pitch, was a revelation. He hit well, he fielded sensationally, and he was an emotional sparkplug for the team.

Bert Niehoff, picked up from Cincinnati in the trade for Dooin, took over second base, where he worked well with the gifted Bancroft. Bobby Byrne and Milt Stock shared third base, and Paskert and Beals Becker took turns in the outfield spot not occupied by Cravath and Whitted. Killefer was simply the best catcher in the league.

It was on the mound that the Phillies established their supremacy. Pete Alexander had an outstanding year; he won 31 games while losing 10, with twelve shutouts and an earned run average of 1.22. Erskine Mayer and Al Demaree, the acquisition from the Giants, pitched fine ball, and Rixey and Chalmers had their moments as well. Even George McQuillan,

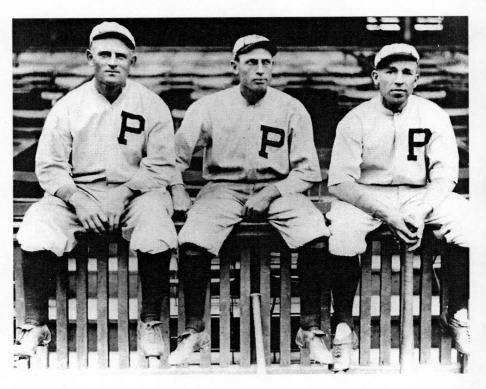

The club's pennant-winning outfield in 1915, *left to right*, the great slugger Clifford "Gavvy" Cravath, Dode Paskert, and George "Possum" Whitted.

erstwhile phenom and bête noire of Red Dooin, contributed after being bought back from Pittsburgh.

By the end of August, the Cubs had faded and the Phillies held a three-game lead over the surprising Brooklyn Dodgers, under manager Wilbert Robinson, and 3½ over Boston. On the final day of August, the Dodgers signed veteran pitchers Larry Cheney and Rube Marquard, putting Robinson's club in what one writer called "a most commanding position for the final dash to the flag with the Phils and Braves." It was not, however, to be for Brooklyn.[3]

With the dependable Alexander, Mayer, Chalmers, and Rixey all winning big games, Moran's men never gave up first place in September. Things looked a bit dicey, though, on the 7th. The club's lead was cut to one game, after three straight losses at Brooklyn, and Killefer damaged his right shoulder, ending his season. His little-used backups, Eddie Burns and Jack Adams, would have to carry the catching load.

The next day, back at 15th and Huntingdon, the Phils behind Chalmers beat the Giants, 9–3, to end their three-game losing streak. Dode Paskert pounded a two-run homer to pace the attack. It was the game they needed to set things straight and avoid the onset of panic. On the 9th, before 22,000, the largest crowd ever at their home park, the Phillies won two from New York, 3–0 behind Alexander, and 9–4 behind Demaree, aided by Cactus Cravath's 20th home run.

On September 10, the Phils and McQuillan beat New York, 7–3, on an eighth-inning grand slam by Cravath, a blast with which Gavvy tied

1915 pitchers, *from left*, Stan Baumgartner, Pete Alexander, Ben Tincup, Erskine Mayer, Al Demaree, Joe Oeschger, and George McQuillan.

the modern (post–1900) single-season home run record at 21, set by
Wildfire Schulte in 1911. At 11:15 that night, the Phillies left Broad Street
Station for their final western trip, holding a 3½ game lead over Brook-
lyn.

The western swing was a great success, as the Phillies won twelve out
of sixteen, with Alexander picking up four of the victories. Mayer won
two and lost a 1–0 heartbreaker to the Pirates, the lone run scoring when
Cravath let a single roll through his legs. Gavvy giveth; Gavvy taketh away.
The Phils were counting "magic numbers" when they headed back east
and into Brooklyn on the 28th.

The *Inquirer*, savoring the steady lead, said: "There is no reason why
the consistent ball playing that has kept the Phils right out front cannot
be maintained…. The Phillies are a hard playing, aggressive lot."[4] On the
28th, they eliminated the Dodgers from the race when Chalmers beat
Robinson's team, 6–4.

The next day, September 29, was "Pat Moran Day" at Braves Field
in Boston, honoring the Massachusetts native and former Braves catcher
who was about to win a pennant in his first shot at managing. After the
festivities were done, the honoree sent Pete Alexander to the mound,
and the good times ended for the home folks. Cravath blasted a three-
run homer in the first inning, and Alex needed nothing more. He held
the Braves to one hit, by Sherry Magee, beat them 5–0 for his 31st triumph, and clinched the first pennant ever for the Philadelphia Phillies.
Quite a day for Pat Moran, his mighty pitcher, and his record-setting
home run slugger.

The Phillies played out the string over the next week, as carpenters
worked to expand the seating at their home park, and the gamblers tried
to figure out how many games Alexander could pitch in the upcoming
World Series with the Red Sox.

The Boston team won 101 games in beating out a tough Tiger squad
for the American League pennant. Its outfield of Harry Hooper, Tris
Speaker, and Duffy Lewis was celebrated as the finest in the game, and the
pitching staff of George "Rube" Foster, Ernie Shore, Babe Ruth, Smoky Joe
Wood, and Hubert "Dutch" Leonard was outstanding. Pitcher Ruth led
the team in home runs with four. Dick Hoblitzell and Larry Gardner
anchored the infield, and Jack Barry, sold by Connie Mack as part of his
housecleaning, played second base with Everett Scott at shortstop.

Boston manager Bill Carrigan told the press, "It seems we must beat
Alexander in that first game and we have devised a means which we think
will accomplish it…. Outside of Alexander I do not think any of the Philly
pitchers compare with my men."[5]

Carrigan was certainly correct to fear Alexander, but a number of other Phillies sported outstanding numbers. Luderus hit .315, second in the league, and Cravath dominated the circuit in the power categories, with 24 home runs and 115 runs batted in. His home run total was one behind the all-time record of 25 set by Buck Freeman of Washington in 1899. After Cravath's near miss, a reporter wrote: "The chances now are that Freeman's record will never again be so closely approached or so seriously threatened as it was by the Phil clouter this season."[6]

The Red Sox were favored to win the World Series, but Pat Moran was not coming to the clash unarmed. Erskine Mayer had won 21 games, Demaree 14, Rixey 11, and Chalmers eight. Moran was disappointed that Killefer could not catch, but Eddie Burns had done a decent job behind the plate. And there was always the great Alexander, who moved *Inquirer* writer "Jim Nasium" to verse:

> Spin me that yarn of their speed on the bases—
> How their base-running tactics will do us;
> Show me the figures thumped out by the maces
> Of Speaker, and Hooper, and Lewis.
> Tell me again they're the fastest team —
> Slip me that same old con;
> But say! What do you
> Think base-runners can do
> When 'Alex' won't let 'em get on?[7]

Baker had turned down Ben Shibe's offer to lend Shibe Park to the Phillies for the Series, and more than 19,000 fans showed up at the augmented National League park for the October 8 opener, some of them sitting in temporary seats placed in front of the fences in left and right field (in the outfield, in other words). Philadelphia's baseball fandom was happy to have the World Series back in town, but while it was something new for the Phillies the city was seeing its fifth Series in six years, thanks to Connie Mack's Athletics. One fan was not happy: Mayor Rudolph Blankenship was irked that he was not furnished a ticket to the game. Such was the lot of a reform mayor in Philadelphia.

Alexander took the mound, opposing big Ernie Shore, Boston's 19-game winner, with Bill Klem umpiring behind the plate. In the home fourth, Paskert led off with a bloop single and was sacrificed to second by Cravath. When Luderus grounded out, Paskert took third, and he scored on Whitted's high-bouncing infield hit over Shore's head. In the eighth inning, Alex walked Speaker with one gone. Dick Hoblitzell grounded to second baseman Stock, whose slight bobble eliminated any chance of a double play. Lewis's single to left brought Speaker around to tie the score.

In the bottom of the inning, Stock walked with one out. Barry made a great play on Bancroft's grounder, which went for a hit when Stock just beat the throw at second. Paskert walked to load the bases. The Phillies regained the lead when Cravath got Stock home with a slow roller to shortstop, and Bancroft scored on a fluke hit by Luderus.

With a 3–1 lead, Alexander came out for the ninth and fanned Barry. Pinch-hitter Olaf Henricksen reached base on an error by the weak-fielding Luderus. Babe Ruth hit for Shore and pulled a ball down to first. Luderus came up with this one for the second out, and he caught Hooper's popup to end the game. Alexander scattered nine hits, fanned six, and walked two. He threw 118 pitches, a total higher than his norm, but he won the game, and the fans carried him off the field on their shoulders.

The next day 20,306 people turned out to see the Red Sox, the Phillies, and President Woodrow Wilson, who made his appearance with Miss Edith Galt, his newly-announced fiancee. Unfortunately, Rube Foster was also there that day, and the 36-year-old Red Sox righthander held the Phillies to three hits, doubles by Cravath and Luderus and a Bancroft single. Mayer struggled but kept his team in the game. In the ninth inning, with the score tied, Foster got his third hit of the game, a single which scored Larry Gardner with the deciding run. The press box pundits felt that Dode Paskert had been playing Foster much too deep, but the run was home in any event and the Series was even.

On to Boston went the two ballclubs, with Game Three scheduled for October 11, in new Braves Field, which the Boston Nationals loaned to the Red Sox for the World Series, just as the Red Sox had loaned the Braves Fenway Park the previous October. 1914–1915 is the only time that the World Series has featured teams from the same cities two years in a row but with the city teams being switched. The exchange of the Boston ballparks just made the oddity a little odder.

A record crowd of 42,300 came out for the game, with Pete Alexander opposing the young southpaw Leonard. The game took only an hour and 48 minutes, and this time Alexander came out on the short end of the 2–1 score. The Phillies again picked up only three hits, a double by Stock and singles by Bancroft and Burns. Bancroft's hit in the third inning gave the Phils a brief 1–0 lead, but they put no one on base after that inning. Boston tied it in the fourth, and Duffy Lewis's hit with two out in the ninth, scoring Hooper, won it for the Sox.

The next day there was more of the same. 41,906 fans watched the Red Sox win their third straight 2–1 game, this time with Shore the winner. Spitballer George Chalmers pitched well for the visitors, but their untimely batting slump did him in. Luderus had three hits and Cravath picked up a triple, but the run that Luderus drove home in the eighth inning was too little and too late.

For Game Five, back in Philadelphia on October 13, Moran hoped to use Alexander again, but as he warmed up the Nebraskan reported that his arm was achy, and the manager was forced to pass him by. The heavy load Alexander had been carrying for the pitching staff finally caught up with him, and Moran could only hope his ace could work Game Six.

Erskine Mayer got the short-notice fifth game assignment, against Foster once again. The Phils started by loading the bases with none out in the first inning. Curiously, Moran then had Cravath bunt, and Gavvy's weak effort, right to the mound, resulted in a pitcher-to-catcher-to-first double play. Luderus salvaged something from the inning with a two-run double to left.

The Sox chased Mayer when they tied it at 2–2 in the third, Eppa Rixey coming in as the first relief pitcher of the Series. In the fourth, Luderus hit a ball over the right field fence for one run, and another scored on a Boston error. The Phils' two-run lead disappeared in the Red Sox eighth when Lewis hit one into the field seats in right-center with a runner on.

In the ninth, Rixey served up a pitch that Hooper hit into the temporary seats, and when Foster retired the Phillies it was all over. The 5–4 Boston triumph clinched the Series in five games, and the world championship stayed in the so-called "Hub of the Universe."

The losers could take what comfort they could find in the fact that all four defeats were by one run, but they could find no consolation at all in the batting figures for the Series. The Phillies as a team hit .182, wasting their good pitching. Luderus hit .438, with seven hits, and Davey Bancroft had five hits for a .294 average, but that was about it. President Baker, too, took a lot of heat for lining the outfield with temporary on-field seats, which turned two Boston fly balls in Game Five into Series-winning home runs.

As always, of course, it is necessary to put things into proper perspective. Despite the World Series loss, the 1915 Phillies won the club's first pennant in their thirty-third season and, with such stars as Alexander, Cravath, Mayer, and Bancroft, seemed entrenched among the league's elite for the foreseeable future.

Chapter 6

For Pickles Dillhoefer???

The National and American Leagues made peace with the Federals on December 22, 1915, declaring victory as the outlaw league went out of business. If it was victory, however, it was most certainly a mixed one. The older leagues permitted jumping players to return without penalty, they allowed Fed owners to buy controlling interests in the St. Louis Browns and Chicago Cubs, and they forked over a large sum of money to pay off the obligations of the Federal League clubs. It was hard to see that anyone had won the war, except perhaps for a few ballplayers who made more money than they would have under normal circumstances.

Coming off the team's most successful year ever in 1915, William Baker and Pat Moran looked ahead with pleasant anticipation to the post-baseball-war world. None of their defectors rejoined the team, but they were not really needed. The 1916 Phillies won one more game than did the 1915 pennant-winners, and they were in the race all the way, finally finishing second, 2½ games behind. The four-way struggle involved New York, Philadelphia, the Brooklyn Robins (named in honor of manager Wilbert Robinson), and Boston, although the Giants faded in September. Brooklyn took over first place in early September and held on, aided by the Phils and Braves playing one another at the end of the season, in effect eliminating each other.

The Phillies' attack was more balanced than the year before. No player hit over .300, but Luderus, Stock, Cravath, Paskert, and Whitted all hit between .279 and .283, and Bert Niehoff led the league with 42 doubles. Gavvy Cravath's home run production fell off to eleven, but this total was still only one shy of the league lead.

Pat Moran's pitching staff did well. Alexander had another superb season, winning 33 and losing 12, with an earned run average of 1.55. Pete's total of sixteen shutouts set a major league record which may stand forever. As usual, Alexander led the league in strikeouts, innings pitched, wins, and earned run average. Eppa Rixey had a fine record of 22–10, with an ERA of 1.85, and Al Demaree was 19–14. Mayer slipped to 7–7, and Chief Bender, returning to Philadelphia as a Phillie after a year in the Federal League, had the same mark. George McQuillan won one, lost seven, and was released.

Alexander did his best to win the pennant by himself. On September 23, he pitched and won both games of a doubleheader against Cincinnati. On October 2, the next to last day of the season, he pitched a 2–0 three-hitter against the Braves in the first game of another doubleheader to put the Phillies in first place. It was Alex's 33rd victory, but winning it all was more than one man could do. In the nightcap, the team fell back to second place, as Milt Stock, at shortstop in place of the injured Dave Bancroft, committed a costly error leading to a 4–1 defeat. The season ended the next day with a double loss to Boston, as the Robins clinched the pennant.

With the spillover from the 1915 championship, a close race, and a spectacular performance by Alexander, the Phillies set a new attendance record of 515,365. It was a mark which would stand unsurpassed for thirty years, until the days of Del Ennis and Schoolboy Rowe.

Although the Phillies finished second again in 1917, McGraw's Giants took control in late June, and Moran's club simply held on for the ride, finishing ten games back. Alexander notched his third straight thirty-win season, with a record of 30–13, and he led the league in just about everything — wins, starts, complete games, innings worked, shutouts, and earned run average, with a sparkling 1.86. His control continued to be excellent, his breaking ball baffled the league's best hitters, and his accomplishments were astonishing.

Gavvy Cravath tied for the National League home run title, with twelve. He and Whitted led the team in batting, at .280, and Killefer hit .274. The Phillies picked up Johnny Evers from Boston, but the 35-year-old second baseman could do no better than .224. Paskert, Niehoff, and Bancroft had disappointing seasons.

Attendance declined sharply to 354,428, and Baker began to worry about money. Philadelphians had already learned, from the experience with Connie Mack and his Athletics, that when baseball owners started to worry about money bad things tended to happen. They waited to see what Baker would do.

During 1917, the United States entered the World War. No one knew what the impact of the war on baseball would be, and the owners' reactions were varied, with some letting servicemen in uniform in free, while others put their players, carrying bats rather than rifles, through marching drills before games. The public observed that there was no surge of players attempting to trade in those bats for rifles.

On December 11, 1917, Philadelphia baseball fans learned what General Sherman meant when he said "war is hell." On that day, Baker announced that the Phillies had traded Alexander and Killefer to the Chicago Cubs for Mike Prendergast, a pitcher with three wins for Chicago in 1917, .126-hitting catcher William "Pickles" Dillhoefer, and $75,000 cash. Baker said he expected to be criticized for the deal "but he was sure that time would show that the move was a wise one." As for Alexander, he said, "I do not think that his best interests would be served by remaining longer in Philadelphia." Sure, he had won thirty games in 1917, Baker said, but "there is no reason for believing that he would be better next year." It all sounded absurd even as he said it, and Baker later admitted, "I needed the money."[1]

Phillies fans were outraged, and with good reason In seven seasons, Alexander won 190 games, an *average* of more than 27 a year. He had 61 shutouts, leading the league in that category five times, five strikeout titles, and three earned run crowns. He worked more than 300 innings every year, led the league six times in innings pitched, and averaged 355 innings a season. This was done pitching his home games in the misshapen Phillies park, now derisively called Baker Bowl, with the right field fence just 272 feet away from the plate.

Old Pete had put in seven incredible years for the Phillies, and Baker gave him away. And for good measure, he threw in one of the National League's top catchers. The fans were horrified, but there was nothing they could do about it. Manager Pat Moran expressed dismay at the trade, but he could do nothing about it either.

Baker could point out later that Alexander was drafted into the army and missed all but three games of the 1918 season. What is also true is that Alexander, when he returned from the war, was never quite the unbelievable hurler of his seven Phillies seasons. What he was, over the remaining eleven-plus years of his career, was a very good pitcher. Tormented after the war by the twin demons of epilepsy and alcohol, as well as by persistent headaches caused by the sound of artillery fire during his time in the trenches, Old Pete won another 183 games, picked up two more earned run average titles, and had three more twenty-win seasons on his way to the Hall of Fame.

The 1918 Phillies team slid from second place to sixth, and attendance dropped to 122,266, once again behind the Athletics. (Allowance must be made, in the attendance figures, for the war-shortened season. When the campaign ended on September 2, the Phillies had twenty-one home games wiped out.) Alexander was gone, Rixey went into the army, Erskine Mayer was traded on July 1 to Pittsburgh, and Bert Niehoff was disposed of before the season to St. Louis.

Fred "Cy" Williams, a 30-year-old slugger who came from the Cubs in a midwinter swap for Dode Paskert, hit .276 with six homers. Cy Williams was a powerful lefthanded hitter for whom Baker Bowl was ideally suited, and he hit a great many home runs for the Phillies before he was through, twelve years later.

Also arriving in 1918 was Emil "Irish" Meusel, a righthanded-hitting outfielder drafted from the Pacific Coast League. He was not a graceful fielder, and his arm was not strong, but Meusel could hit. He batted .279 his first year in Philadelphia and improved every year he was in town.

On July 17, a slender rookie righthander from Louisiana named John "Mule" Watson took the mound for the Phillies against the Cubs in Chicago. He gave up a run in the first inning, but the Phillies matched it in the fourth. Lefty Tyler, the old Braves hero, now with the Cubs, shut the Phillies down after that, but Watson matched him inning for inning until the twenty-first, when the Chicagoans finally pushed across another run. He gave up nineteen hits and four walks, but he kept the Cubs off the scoreboard until three hits and a hit batter finally ended it. No one has ever pitched as long a game for the Phillies as young Mule Watson did that day, but all he had to show for it was a loss—and a very tired arm.[2]

1918, of course, was the war year. Secretary of War Newton D. Baker decreed that fit young men would "work or fight," and this edict resulted in many draft-age baseball players signing up with munitions plants (for whom they often wound up playing on company baseball teams). The government brought the regular baseball season to a close on September 2, with the World Series following soon after. At the end of the year, William F. Baker fired Moran. A four-year record of first-second-second-sixth did not look bad, but Moran had shown himself too independent for Baker's taste. Pat was not unemployed for long. He was quickly hired by Cincinnati as manager and, as in his first year with the Phillies, he led the Reds to the pennant in 1919.

That year 1919 is one that resonates with bad vibrations for baseball. It started with the game trying to get past the image of its players (not all, by any means) hiding out in munitions plants rather than joining the army, and it ended with the stench of the Black Sox World Series, in which seven Chicago players accepted bribes in exchange for conspiring to lose the Series. These seven men, including such stars as Shoeless Joe Jackson and Eddie Cicotte, placed an indelible stain upon their names and reputations which no passage of time has been able to erase.

For the Phillies, 1919 was a very bad year, as they fell into the National League cellar. With the Athletics also in last place, it meant that the city of Philadelphia had exclusive possession of baseball's basement. This had never happened in Philadelphia before, but it would soon become habitual, with the Phillies and A's both in last place in 1919, 1920, and 1921.

Baker named the old Athletics' hero, Jack Coombs, as his manager for 1919. Coombs's tenure at the helm of the Phillies was short and none too sweet. Subjected to constant interference by Baker, who by now fancied himself an expert on baseball, Coombs was fired in early July, after only 62 games, with a record of 18–44. The club was firmly fixed in last place, and there it would stay.[3]

After the departure of Coombs, Baker handed the reins of the Phillies to 38-year-old Gavvy Cravath, apparently reasoning that it would be less costly to employ as manager someone already on the payroll. The club picked up the pace slightly under Cravath, going 29–46 the rest of the way.

Lee Meadows, a short, stocky Carolinian who wore glasses on the field (almost unheard of at the time), came over from the Cardinals. Meadows, a fast worker and a good pitcher, won eight and lost ten for the Phillies, and his earned run average for Cravath was 2.48. Luderus hit .293 and broke Eddie Collins's old record of 479 consecutive games played. Fred's streak would reach 533 games before it ended. Bancroft hit .272, Irish Meusel batted .305, and Cy Williams, with nine home runs, averaged .278.

Possum Whitted hit only .249 and in August was traded to the Pirates for a colorful outfielder named Charles Dillon "Casey" Stengel, who, it was written, "has been in bad in Pittsburgh for some time." Phillies fans had no opportunity to enjoy Stengel in 1919, for he became embroiled in a contract dispute with Baker and sat at home for the rest of the season.[4]

What the fans *did* enjoy was outfielder/manager Cravath. Old Cactus played in only 83 games and had but 214 times at bat, but he banged twelve home runs to lead the league and compiled a batting average of .341. The pitching, aside from Meadows, was bad. Eppa Rixey returned from the service and rang up a 6–12 record, with a high earned run average. The staff ERA was almost a full run higher than any other club's, and it led to the 47–90 record.[5]

In 1920, the Phillies won fifteen more games than the year before and finished only a half game behind George Stallings and his no-longer-miraculous Boston Braves. That half game, unfortunately, was good for last place once again. Cravath got good work from his outfield, with Cy Williams hitting .325 and leading the league with fifteen home runs, Meusel batting at a .309 clip with fourteen home runs, and Casey Stengel (playing for the same $5,300 salary he had scorned the year before) hitting .292.

Gene Paulette, now playing first base after the veteran Luderus was waived, batted .288.

On June 7, however, Baker made a bad trade, one of those deals which cost the club dearly for years. He sent Beauty Bancroft, already the best shortstop in the game and just coming into his prime, to the Giants for 35-year-old shortstop Art Fletcher, pitcher Bill Hubbell, and $100,000 cash. Bancroft, hitting .298 at the time of the trade, was a fine fielder and team leader, and he would get even better after he left the Phillies. "The Philadelphia club is strengthening its infield where it is needed," said Baker, in a statement which made no sense at all. An *Inquirer* reporter said, "Just how the Phillies benefit on this remarkable transaction is hard to imagine," although the cash helped Baker balance the club's books for

Dave "Beauty" Bancroft, a Hall of Fame shortstop traded away by Baker.

1920. Nevertheless, the loss of Bancroft was keenly felt. Fletcher hit .296 in 1920, but his range in the field was greatly reduced by his advancing years. The pitchers certainly could tell the difference between the two men.[6]

On August 31, the Phillies beat the Cubs, 3–0, in Chicago, with Lee Meadows hurling the shutout. Pete Alexander was the loser, and Bevo LeBourveau hit a ninth-inning home run to ice the victory. But there was much more to this particular contest. Shortly before game time, Chicago president William L. Veeck received three telegrams from out of town, telling him that the game was fixed for the Cubs to lose. Claude Hendrix, the Cubs' scheduled starting pitcher, was then scratched and Alexander given the nod. Later, Veeck said, "We knew that Alexander is a man above suspicion, and we felt that with our premier pitcher in the box we were doing all we could."[7]

Veeck asked the Chicago baseball writers to conduct an investigation, and soon there was a Cook County grand jury looking into the fixing and throwing of baseball games. The probe spread from the Phillies-Cubs game to the 1919 World Series, which had raised suspicions all over the place, and on September 28, seven White Sox players were indicted, after Ed Cicotte and Joe Jackson confessed that they had taken money to throw games. Little more was said about the August 31 game, but, significantly, Claude Hendrix pitched no more for the Cubs after that date and at the end of the season his big league career was at an end.[8]

Cravath's playing time was severely curtailed in 1920, and he hit only one home run in his farewell season. As he moves off stage, it is well to remember Gavvy Cravath as a high-quality player who brightened the Philadelphia baseball scene for a number of years. Even with Cravath's reduced production in 1920, the Phillies led the league in home runs with 64; Baker Bowl still had its charms. On the mound, Meadows had a good year, with 16–14 and 2.84.

The veteran Rixey was 11–22. Rixey was now 29 years old, with a career record in Philadelphia of 87–103; he would be gone before the next season got underway. Even with his string of mediocre seasons, it was plain that Eppa Jeptha had good stuff and should have been a winner. One thing he needed, clearly, was a change of scene from Baker Bowl and the Phillies, so he was traded to the Reds, and soon Rixey was doing all the things that had been expected of him for so long.[9]

In 1920, the "dead ball" era came to an end. Babe Ruth, sold by the Red Sox to the New York Yankees, hit 54 home runs for the New Yorkers, and the game was changed forever. The Yankees' attendance climbed spectacularly, to 1,289,000, the first million-customer gate for any team, and the moguls of baseball snapped to attention. Home runs were the key to this surge in attendance, so they would make home runs more abundant. Various steps were taken, including making the ball itself more resilient, banning the spitball and other doctored pitches, and changing baseballs more frequently. The "lively ball" era was underway, and home run production climbed steeply.

In 1921, the two Philadelphia clubs finished last again, but at least they hit a lot of home runs. The A's hit 82 and the Phillies, with the ever-favoring Baker Bowl fences, hit 88. Still, they were bad ballclubs. *Inquirer* writer Jimmy Isaminger said, before the '21 season: "The owners of the Phils ... are finding out that Killefers, Alexanders, Whitteds, Stocks and Bancrofts can't be picked up as easily as sign painters, iron molders and carpenters. They used to sneer at their stars and declare ... that they could fill their place in five minutes if they had to."[10]

Baker did make a couple of changes. One was the trade of Rixey to the Reds. He also fired Gavvy Cravath as manager, replacing the old outfielder with Wild Bill Donovan, a Philadelphia resident who had been a top-notch pitcher for many years.

On March 3, Isaminger wrote that "Paulette at first and Fletcher at short are the bulwarks of the inner works."[11] Whatever comfort Donovan was able to draw from this assurance was short-lived. Late in March first baseman Gene Paulette signed to play with an independent team in Massillon, Ohio. The story soon emerged that Paulette had been summoned to a March 7 meeting with the new commissioner, Judge Kenesaw Mountain Landis, to explain reports which had reached Landis about Paulette's connections with known gamblers. Rather than face Landis, Paulette bolted, and he was barred from baseball. Art Fletcher's father died, and Fletcher left the team to be with his family. His mourning period extended over the full season, and he did not return to the Phillies until 1922. So much for the "bulwarks of the inner works."

In July, Irish Meusel was hitting a lusty .353, with 51 RBIs and twelve home runs, when Baker ordered him benched for "indifference." On July 25, he traded Meusel to New York for three players and $30,000. Baker said he made the deal "for the team's good," but those around the club knew that he had put an unfair tag on Meusel to justify another give-away trade.

While all these diversions were going on around them, the Phillies played at a .287 clip for Donovan, winning 25 and losing 62. In the beginning of August, Baker directed Donovan to depart on a "scouting trip" while the command of the last-place team was turned over to coach Irvin "Kaiser" Wilhelm. It was a clumsy way to fire a manager, but typical of Baker. Donovan appealed to Judge Landis, who made sure that Baker paid Donovan his full salary.

With Wilhelm running the team, the Phillies picked up the pace a little but still finished with a terrible record of 51–103. Cy Williams hit eighteen home runs and batted .320. The leaders of the pitching staff were Meadows, 11–16, Jimmy Ring, with a record of 10–19, Bill Hubbell at 9–16, and Columbia George Smith, who was 4–20. The team earned run average was 4.48, the highest in the league. Before the season, one expert had written that "the infield and pitching staff are as weak as bread," and he was about right.[12]

In 1922, the Phillies led the league with 116 home runs, and the increased firepower helped them to climb out of the basement. They finished in seventh place, four games ahead of the Braves, who with the Red Sox gave the city of Boston a double dose of last place.

Manager Wilhelm's outfield swung big bats: Curt Walker hit .337 with twelve home runs, Cliff Lee averaged .322 with 17 homers, and Williams slugged 26 home runs and batted .308. Catcher Butch Henline hit .316 and 14 homers, and utility infielder Russ Wrightstone hit .305, although his poor fielding kept him from steady work in the infield. As usual, it was the pitching staff which kept the Phillies from advancing further.

As a reward for lifting the Phils out of last place after three years in the cellar, Wilhelm was given the axe by Baker, who replaced him with shortstop Art Fletcher. As it was, that may have been a mercy to Wilhelm after what he had to watch on the afternoon of August 25 at Chicago, a 26–23 defeat which set a still-standing record for total runs in a single game. Wilhelm's pitchers, Jimmy Ring and Lefty Weinert, were pounded for 25 hits, ten for extra bases, his fielders contributed five errors, *and* they stranded sixteen baserunners. The Cubs scored ten runs in the second inning, fourteen in the fourth, and coasted home.

The Athletics also left last place in 1922, and the emergence from the league cellars was significant for the two Philadelphia teams. For the Athletics, it was the beginning of a transformation into one of the great teams of the ages. For the Phillies, unfortunately, under the uncertain, insensitive leadership of William F. Baker and the heavy influence of their strange and misshapen ballpark, it was a promise not to be fulfilled.

Under new manager Art Fletcher, the '23 Phillies dropped back into last place with a record of 50–104. They had no trouble scoring runs: five players, catcher Henline, newly-acquired second baseman Cotton Tierney, first sacker Walter Holke, outfielder Johnny Mokan, and spare flychaser Cliff Lee, hit over .300, and Cy Williams led the league with 41 home runs. Williams drove in 114 runs, second in the National League only to New York's Irish Meusel, who drove home a not-so-indifferent 125. Curt Walker and Russ Wrightstone also contributed their share to the Phils' offense. The club far outstripped everyone else in home runs.

The Phillies' downfall was in its pitching, with the collective staff earned run average of 5.30 more than a run higher than that of any other team. Baker Bowl contributed to that number, to be sure. The "lively ball" era was now in full swing, but somehow the ball seemed a lot livelier when a Phillies pitcher threw it. Some of the pitchers' records were simply awful. Lefty Weinert was 4–17 and 5.42. Charles "Whitey" Glazner, a little Alabamian who accompanied Tierney and a check for $50,000 from Pittsburgh to Philadelphia in exchange for Lee Meadows, won seven and lost fourteen, with a 4.70 ERA. Petie Behan, in his only full season in the majors, was 3–12 and 5.50. Ralph Head, a rookie from Georgia, went 2–9 and 6.68 and soon disappeared from the big time. Amid all this bad hurling, one man stood out. Jimmy Ring, a veteran fastballer, won 18 and lost 16 and kept his earned run average down to 3.77.

At least Fletcher was not forced to drag his 38-year-old body out to shortstop. After the 1922 season, Baker ponied up $40,000 to purchase infielder Henry "Heinie" Sand from Salt Lake City, and Fletcher installed

Fred "Cy" Williams, who won three home run titles in the '20s.

the hustling little rookie at shortstop. Although he hit just .228, Sand performed to satisfaction otherwise. Fletcher never played another game.

The 1924 Phillies climbed out of the cellar, reaching seventh place, to match the 1922 performance. Attendance improved, with the season total exceeding 299,000. Fletcher did a decent job with the team, although he bickered constantly with Baker over the owner's meddling. Cy Williams hit 24 homers and newcomer George Harper 16, while Williams, Wrightstone, and Holke hit over .300. Once again, it was pitching which hurt the Phillies. Jimmy Ring slipped to 10–12 in 1924, and no one picked up the slack for him.

Heinie Sand, the shortstop, was projected into public attention when, on September 27, he was offered a $500 bribe by Giant outfielder Jimmy O'Connell to throw the final weekend series against the New Yorkers. The Giants, in a tight race with Brooklyn, had to win at least one from the Phils when O'Connell murmured to Sand, "It will be worth $500 to you if you don't bear down too hard."

Sand indignantly rejected the offer and promptly reported it to Fletcher, who, after the Giants beat the Phillies that day to clinch the flag, reported the bribe attempt to league president John Heydler. Heydler contacted Landis, and the commissioner promptly got on a train to New York.

When Landis questioned O'Connell, the young outfielder admitted the truth of Sand's story and said that Giants coach Cozy Dolan told him to talk to the Phillie shortstop. O'Connell also implicated three of the Giant stars, Frankie Frisch, George Kelly, and Ross Youngs, all future Hall of Famers; he said, "Kelly spoke to me at the batting cage, asking me what Sand had said, and Frisch and Youngs also spoke to me about it." Dolan refused to admit anything, saying he remembered nothing, and Frisch, Kelly, and Youngs denied any involvement.

With the World Series about to start, Landis placed O'Connell and Dolan on the permanently ineligible list and exonerated Frisch, Kelly, and Youngs. Landis was unable to reach the real culprits behind the clumsy bribery attempt. Certainly Jimmy O'Connell, a promising young player who wound up working on the San Francisco docks, was only a foolish and naive go-between, and Dolan was likely carrying out someone else's orders. What was clear was that the infection of gambling was not yet eradicated from the game.[13]

The 1925 Phillies won thirteen more games than in 1924 but were still only tied for sixth. They did not appear prepared to go much higher. The Phils did some powerful hitting, but their pitching, with an earned run average over five per game, again held them back.

Harper hit .349 and led the club with eighteen home runs and 97 runs driven in. Cy Williams fell off in home runs to thirteen, but he still hit .331. Everybody hit. Utility man Wrightstone batted .346; both the catchers, Henline and young Jimmy Wilson, hit over .300. The new first baseman, Nelson "Chicken" Hawks, hit .322. Utility man Lew Fonseca and spare outfielders Johnny Mokan and Freddy Leach all hit over .300. The team batting average was .295, and the Phillies had no trouble scoring runs. It was when the other team was at bat that the trouble began.

Ring was 14–16, had a high ERA, and led the league in walks for the fourth straight year. Spitballer Hal Carlson was 13–14, and he too had a high earned run average. And they were the stars of the staff. Veteran lefty Clarence Mitchell was 10–17 with a 5.29 ERA, and Art Decatur, obtained in May from the Dodgers, was 4–13 with another unsightly earned run average. And so on. Baker Bowl was a grim place in which to pitch.

It was grimmer in 1926. The Phillies won ten fewer games than the year before, attendance was off sharply, and the club crashed back to last place, costing Fletcher his job. The team's hitting, while still strong, fell off, and the pitching got worse.

The veteran Carlson had a fine season, winning 17, losing 12, and compiling a good ERA of 3.24. But that was it. When Carlson was not on the mound, the tin walls around the Baker Bowl outfield rang with the sound of line drives crashing against them. Jimmy Ring, after five stalwart seasons in Philadelphia, was traded on December 30, 1925, to the Giants for first baseman Jack Bentley and pitcher Wayland Dean. Dean won eight and lost sixteen for the Phillies in 1926, with an earned run average over six. Clarence Mitchell, Jack Knight, Claude Willoughby, Ray Pierce, Dutch Ulrich: they were all bad.

Chicken Hawks was gone, and Bentley replaced him at first base. Bentley hit only .258 in 75 games and by year's end had been sold back to the Giants. Harper hit .314 for half the season before he was laid low by appendicitis. Williams, Leach, Wrightstone, Wilson, and Mokan all hit well, and second baseman Barney Friberg and shortstop Sand did a decent job up the middle, but nothing could overcome the effects of the terrible pitching. Late in the season Fletcher was suspended indefinitely after an altercation with umpire Bill Klem. With his typical class Baker fired Fletcher as manager while he was serving his time.

Baker named another old A's hero, John "Stuffy" McInnis, to manage the Phillies in 1927, and McInnis had a dreadful time. The 1927 Phillies won 51 and fell far short (nine games) of the seventh-place Braves. The only bright spot was Cy Williams's league-leading thirty home runs. A 35-year-old left-hander named Jack Scott, in his only year with the Phillies, lost 21 games,

and he too led the
National League.

Baker traded Geo-
rge Harper, who had the
temerity to hold out for
a better contract, to the
Giants, along with
catcher Butch Henline,
for Scott and infielder
Fresco Thompson. (Har-
per hit .331 for New
York.) The Phils had
high hopes for a young
lefty pitcher named Les
Sweetland. He won two,
lost ten, and had a 6.14
earned run average. It
was that kind of year.

On May 14, there
was another disaster at
Baker Bowl. A heavy
rainstorm hit during a
Saturday afternoon
game, and hundreds of
fans rushed for cover in
the lower deck along the

William F. Baker, who ran a good franchise into the
ground.

right field line. Several innings later, after a grand slam by Russ Wrightstone set off a foot-stamping frenzy among the fans, two sections of grandstand suddenly collapsed under them. One person died from a heart attack
and some fifty others were injured. Luckily, Phillies attendance was so
sparse that there were not more people present to be involved in the accident. The collapse was caused by a rotting main girder.[14]

While Baker Bowl was being patched up, the Phillies moved down the
street and played temporarily in Shibe Park. When observers wondered why
such a sensible move could not be made permanent, they learned that the
Phillies were bound to the old yard by a 99-year lease imposed upon the
club at the time the Taft and Murphy interests sold the franchise in 1913,
retaining the ballpark. The Phillies would return to Baker Bowl for many a
year to come, their landlord the estate of Charles Murphy.

After the season was over, to the surprise of no one, Baker fired Stuffy
McInnis.

Chapter 7

Hitting Isn't Everything

Baker hired a new manager for the 1928 season, a former Browns outfielder and minor league skipper named Burt Shotton. Shotton, a protégé of Branch Rickey, was, as most men trained under Rickey proved to be, a good baseball man and a good manager, although both players and reporters had occasional problems with Shotton's aloof personality. During Shotton's six-year tenure, the Phillies enjoyed surprising success as well as their customary failure.

The 1928 team was even worse than Stuffy McInnis's 1927 crew. It won 43 games, lost 109, and finished 51 games out. The main culprit behind this atrocious record was, as was customary with Baker Bowl Phillies teams, the pitching staff. The big winner was rookie Ray Benge, who won eight games; on the other side of the ledger he lost 18 and had an ERA of 4.55.

The other pitchers were worse. Their earned run averages were all in the fives and sixes. Jimmy Ring came back to town in a December trade; his record was 4–17 and 6.40, and he was dropped. Les Sweetland had a 3–15 record and a 6.60 ERA. A pitcher named Russ Miller was 0–12 and never appeared again in the big leagues. The staff earned run average was 5.52.

There were, however, some notable newcomers on the 1928 Phillies squad. Third baseman Arthur "Pinky" Whitney was drafted from New Orleans for $6,000 when Cleveland, which owned him, got its paperwork fouled up. Whitney turned out to be one of the best third basemen the Phils ever employed. He hit .301 as a rookie, with ten home runs and 103 runs batted in. A fairly good fielder, Pinky made his mark with the club as a solid righthanded hitter who could pull the ball and also hit it to right, off the short fence there. "I hit a bunch of pop flies against it," Whitney said.[1]

A second newcomer was a hefty first baseman picked up from the Cardinals, lefthanded slugger Don Hurst. A classic Baker Bowl player, Hurst was a prime example of a man who thrives performing for losing teams. In 1928 Hurst hit .285 with 19 home runs. The 19 long balls stood as a club rookie record until Richie Allen's 1964 season.

Another newcomer who looked like a keeper was Walter "Peck" Lerian, who hit .272 and took over the regular catching job. He was a gifted catcher and a good handler of pitchers. Tragically, after only two seasons in the majors, Lerian was killed by a truck which struck him as he walked on the sidewalk in his hometown of Baltimore on October 21, 1929.[2]

The most important of the new players with the Phillies in 1928 was an outfielder purchased from the Fort Wayne club in late July for $5,000. His name was Charles "Chuck" Klein, a solidly-built lefthanded hitter, with blonde hair, blue eyes, and freckles. Shotton stuck Klein into the lineup right away, replacing the ancient Cy Williams. "Often an unhymned, obscure minor leaguer can make the grade overnight," wrote Isaminger, "and the little-known Klein seems to be of this type."[3]

Chuck and Baker Bowl were a perfect fit. His picture-perfect left-handed swing drove ball after ball into or over the well-dented tin wall in right field. Klein hit .360, with eleven home runs and 34 RBIs, in less than half a season, and became a favorite of Phillie fans—what there were of them. Attendance for the year, affected no doubt by the spirited pennant race being waged by the Athletics, was only 182,168. It was a Phillies team that hit fairly well, pitched terribly, and lost 109 games.

In 1929, with a team that hit even better and pitched even worse, Shotton got the Phillies up to fifth place, the club's highest finish since Pat Moran's second-place unit of 1917.

The club made a couple of deals over the offseason. Heinie Sand was traded to St. Louis, and outfielder Freddie Leach, who had batted a solid .311 over parts of six seasons with the Phillies, was sent to the Giants for an outfielder named Frank "Lefty" O'Doul and cash. O'Doul, a flop as a pitcher with the Yankees and Red Sox, had converted reluctantly to the outfield, proved to be a solid hitter, and returned to the big time with the 1928 Giants.

Lefty O'Doul far exceeded the high hopes for him. All he did in 1929 was hit .398, tops in the National League, with 32 homers and 122 runs batted in. O'Doul had 254 hits (still a National League record) and tallied 152 runs. But the whole team batted .309; there were a number of other big contributors (besides the ballpark, of course). Chuck Klein, warming up to his surroundings, hit .356, led the circuit with 43 home runs, and drove in 145. On the last day of the season, Klein was tied for the home run lead with Mel Ott of the Giants, whom the Phillies were playing. When Klein hit his 43rd early in the game, Phillie pitchers thereafter walked Ott every time he came up.

Chuck Klein, a mighty slugger in Baker Bowl.

In mid-season, with Klein on a home run tear, the Phillies stuck a 15-foot-high screen on top of the right field wall. People assumed that the stingy Baker did not want Klein to break Ruth's single season home run record because he could not afford to pay Klein what the all-time home run king should receive. On August 2, a letter from Baker appeared in Gordon Mackay's *Record* column, denying that he had any thought of slowing down Klein's home run accumulation. No, the screen went up because of "a number of accidents happen[ing] on Broad Street owing to the balls going over the fence and hitting pedestrians, also damaging automobiles, breaking windshields, etc." The city (and no doubt Klein) surely appreciated Baker's concern for the public safety and the menace his left-handed hitters posed to it.[4]

The other averages on the team were high: Virgil "Spud" Davis, who shared the catching with Peck Lerian, at .342, third sacker Whitney .327 with 115 RBIs, second baseman Fresco Thompson .324, and outfielder Denny Sothern .306. Hurst, the big first baseman, averaged .304, and his power figures showed 31 home runs and 125 runs batted in. With this kind of offensive production, one wonders what could possibly keep the Phillies out of the first division.

Then a glance at the pitching records makes one wonder what kept them out of last place. The team earned run average was 6.13. The ace of the staff was a small righthander from Kansas named Claude Willoughby, in his fifth season with the club. He won 15 and lost 14 but was burdened with an unhealthy-looking ERA of 4.99. In addition, Willoughby led the league in bases on balls. The next most successful hurler was Sweetland, who put together a 13–11 mark, along with an ERA of 5.12. Ray Benge was 11–15 and 6.29, and things went downhill from there.

Unfortunately, the Phillies pitchers were just warming up for 1930. In the "year of the offense," when the swing to the "lively ball" reached its peak, using a baseball with a more resilient core and seams that were sewn down flatter, it seemed only proper that the Phillies, both at bat and on the mound, should produce spectacular numbers. The wonder is that Burt Shotton kept his sanity through the whole mad season.

The team batting average for 1930 was an almost incredible .315, one of the top team seasonal averages in history. The club set still-standing franchise records for hits, singles, doubles, total bases, runs, and runs batted in. Chuck Klein even set a major league record for outfield assists with 44, mostly on ricochets off the Baker Bowl fences.

Yet the Phillies won only 52 games, lost 102, and fell back into the cellar. The Phillies and their opponents combined to bat .350 for the season at Baker Bowl, where Shotton's club put up a mark of 35–42. On the road, though, away from their peculiar ballpark, the Phillies were a horrendous 17–60.

How could they do that? It was easy, given the awful work by the staff. Pitcher Phil Collins, nicknamed "Fidgety Phil" because of his nervous habits on the mound, had a reasonably good season, with a 16–11 won-lost record and the only earned run average under five, at 4.78.

After Collins the pitching went from sad to woeful. Willoughby, the erstwhile staff leader, posted a 4–17 mark, with a hideous ERA of 7.59. Benge was 11–15 and 5.69, Sweetland 7–15 and 7.71, relief pitcher Hal Elliott 6–11 and 7.69 (imagine bringing in a reliever who was guaranteed to give up almost one run *of his own* every inning he pitched, after first scoring all the runners on base when he arrived!), and rookie Roy "Snipe" Hansen was 0–7 and 6.72.

Even Grover Cleveland Alexander, the immortal "Old Pete," contributed to the disaster. The 43-year old veteran signed on with the Phillies for one last crack. It was not a pretty sight. Alex pitched in nine games, three of which he started, won none, lost three, gave up forty hits in 21⅔ innings, and left the big leagues with a 1930 earned run average of 9.14. Alexander was off on the sad road to the barnstorming House of David team, to poverty and obscurity, and to the flea circus on 42nd Street in Manhattan, where he was discovered working two years after his induction at Cooperstown. "It's better living off the fleas," he told an inquiring reporter at the time, "than having them live off you."[5]

The team earned run average in 1930 was an astonishing 6.71. It cannot all be blamed on Baker Bowl, since half of the club's games were played elsewhere. That pitching, combined with a league high 239 errors (23 more than the next worse team), led to opponents scoring 1,199 runs against the Phillies, 644 at home, 555 on the road. No major league team in the twentieth century had ever given up so many runs. No one ever would again.[6]

All of which wasted some very lusty hitting on the part of the Phillies regulars. Klein hit .386 and Lefty O'Doul .383, for starters. Klein hit forty home runs and O'Doul twenty-two. Klein drove in 170 runs (amazingly, this figure did not come close to leading the league, as Hack Wilson drove in 191), and Pinky Whitney drove home 117. Hurst hit .327 with seventeen roundtrippers, Whitney hit .342, utility man Barney Friberg batted .341, and catcher Spud Davis hit .313, contributing fourteen home runs. Even Phil Collins, the pitcher, hit two home runs in one game and a grand slam in another.

Amazingly, the Phillies started the season with Les Sweetland blanking the Dodgers at Ebbets Field, 1–0. After several days of rain, the team moved across the river to visit the Giants, with the press stirring up a rainy day war of words over what the Giants considered Klein's tainted 1929 home run title. Ott was quoted with a derogatory reference to the Phillies' slugger, and Klein lashed back: "He calls me the pop fly home run champ. Say, I can hit a ball farther with one hand than that little runt can with two. Bring on those Giants. I'll eat them up!"[7]

Klein homered but the Giants won the first game at the Polo Grounds, 3–2. On Easter Sunday New York's Carl Hubbell outpitched Alexander for a 2–1 victory, and one reporter wrote that "the ball sounded 'dead' all afternoon as if the boys were swinging at Florida grapefruit." It may be that the leftover baseballs from the year before were being used up, but it seems clear that the supply of 1930 rockets soon arrived. The Phillies' next three games featured scores of 8–6, 6–5, and 16–15, and the slugfest was on. Scores in double figures became commonplace, highlighted by a double-header loss on Memorial Day to Brooklyn, 11–1 and 11–9. Jimmy Isaminger railed in print at the Phils ("The Phillies may have pitchers, but you can't make Burt Shotton believe it"; "Fans here are getting a bit fed up on the futility of the Phillies batting out ten or eleven runs and then losing the game"; "Nine runs are a whopping lot, but mean nothing when cotton-armed pitchers give the opponents sixteen!"), but he was soon resigned to seeing a high-scoring Phillies team lose to higher-scoring opponents. It continued all year.[8]

Despite the losses and the atrocious mound work, attendance climbed to over 299,000. People liked to see hits and runs, and Baker Bowl guaranteed plenty of those. But even more fans might have come out if the Phillies had contrived to win more games and stay up with the rest of the league.

On October 14, 1930, Baker went looking for pitching help. He swapped O'Doul (who had a batting average of .391 for his two full years in Philadelphia) and Thompson to Brooklyn for pitcher James "Jumbo" Elliott, pitcher Clise Dudley, outfielder Hal Lee, and the usual cash sweetener.

On November 6, Baker made another deal, shipping Tommy Thevenow and Willoughby to the Pirates in exchange for scrappy shortstop Dick Bartell, a good hitter and an active, aggressive fielder, who was on the block after a series of run-ins with Pittsburgh owner Barney Dreyfuss. Bartell was to be spared the experience of dealing with William F. Baker, for on December 4, 1930, the Phillies owner died in Montreal, largely unmourned by the baseball fans of Philadelphia, who had watched him turn one of the leading franchises in the National League into a steady loser.

The club's board of directors, meeting on January 5, 1931, named Lewis C. Ruch, who had come into the Phillies picture with Locke and

Baker, the new president of the franchise. Charlie Ruch, 69 years old and not in the best of health, vowed to take an active role in the operation of the team.

During Charlie Ruch's administration, though, the baseball end of things came more and more under the jurisdiction of business manager Gerald P. Nugent. Gerry Nugent was a native Philadelphian, a hero in the Argonne during the Great War, who had courted Mae Mallon, Baker's secretary, in the early 1920s. When Mae introduced her young man to her boss, Baker was so impressed by Nugent's knowledge of the game that he offered him a job with the club. Shortly after Nugent joined the Phillies' front office in 1925, he married Mae Mallon. A year later he was named business manager, succeeding Billy Shettsline, and was soon advising Baker on baseball matters, such as the acquisition of Klein and the trade for Bartell.

When Baker died, he bequeathed 500 of his 1,200 shares of Phillies stock to Mae Mallon Nugent, leaving the balance to his wife. When Mrs. Baker passed away in 1934, she left her shares to Mae and to the couple's son, Gerald P. Nugent, Jr.

The "Nugent Era" chapter of the Phillies' story really begins after the 1932 season, when Ruch retired and Nugent became the club's president. The basic fact which dominated Nugent's ten-year term was a lack of money, which forced him constantly to scratch and scrounge for cash to carry out day-to-day operations.

The two years of Charlie Ruch's tenure as president were comparatively successful ones on the playing field, although attendance slipped in both years from what it had been in 1930, when the club finished last. The Depression was biting ever harder into the American economy, and baseball, essential as it may have seemed to the committed fan, had to take a back seat to the requirements of sustenance and shelter.

In 1931, Shotton got the Phillies up to sixth place, with a 66–88 record, and the next season the Phils finished fourth, winning 78 and losing 76. It was the first time the club made it into the first division since 1917, and it would not again finish in that select group until 1949. Over thirty-one years, the Phillies finished as high as fourth only that once — a dreadful record of consistent futility.

Bartell was a breath of fresh air. He was more than a top-quality ballplayer: he was a winner. He played hard, gave the game everything he had, and expected to win. He was a hustler, he made a lot of noise, and he assumed his teammates would put forth as much effort as he did. The Pirates were winners in the three years Bartell was with them, and he would, later in his career, play shortstop for three championship teams.

What Bartell found when he came to Philadelphia was "these heavy hitters who had finished last and didn't expect to rise any higher." The attitude of a chronic last-place team can be oppressive to one who has been accustomed to winning. Bartell watched Hurst at first base: "Don played for himself and didn't care if we won or lost. I guess when you're used to losing 100 games a year you get that way." Barney Friberg was at second, "a natural athlete ... [who] lacked the drive, ambition, confidence, the belief in himself."[9]

Bartell was not impressed with Pinky Whitney, who "was concerned with himself, too. He was a journeyman third baseman, steady but not aggressive, and a Baker Bowl hitter." In left field, said Bartell, "was Chuck Klein, the ultimate in Baker Bowl hitters and cellar attitude ... always relaxed, laughing and joking." Buzz Arlett was in right field for his only major league season in '31. Arlett was a minor league legend, as Bartell put it, "one of those big, slowfooted outfielders who made a career in the Pacific Coast League." A good hitter always, Arlett hit .313 with eighteen home runs as a 32-year-old rookie, but he was so bad in the field that even the Phillies could not keep him.[10]

Bartell said, "I took charge, trying to shake them up a little. My determination never flagged. I did everything I could to put some spark into them.... At least I kept the fans awake."[11]

It helped that the pitching arose from the horrendous depths of the 1930 season. Jumbo Jim Elliott, acquired in the O'Doul deal, won nineteen games, tops in the league, and lost fourteen, with a 4.27 ERA. Benge, Phil Collins, and Clise Dudley all lost more than they won, but each had an earned run average well under four runs. As a reminder of the immediate past, of course, Shotton used a lefthander named Stew Bolen, in his only full season in the big leagues, for 99 innings worth of work, and Bolen produced a record of 3–12 with a 6.36 ERA.

With better pitching, the Phils could not help but win more. Hurst hit .305, Bartell .289, Whitney .287, and part-time infielder Les Mallon hit .309. Klein batted .337 and led the National League in home runs (31) and runs batted in (121). Catcher Spud Davis hit .326. The team's differential in runs allowed over runs scored shrank from 1930's 255 runs to a more manageable 144.

The next year that differential actually turned around. The 1932 Phillies led the league with 844 runs scored, while their opponents crossed the plate only 796 times. *That*, they learned, is how one finishes in the first division. As usual, the Phillies piled up big numbers in various offensive categories, the most impressive of which was runs batted in, in which Hurst with 143, Klein with 137, and Whitney with 124 finished one-two-three in the league.

Klein hit .348 and led the circuit in home runs with 38 (tied with New York's Ott), in hits, in runs scored, in slugging average, and, surprisingly, in stolen bases. Chuck was voted the most valuable player in the league, both by the baseball writers and by *The Sporting News*.

Hurst batted .339, Spud Davis batted .336, George "Kiddo" Davis, a 30-year-old rookie, hit .309, Bartell hit .308, outfielder Hal Lee hit .303, and Whitney just missed the charmed circle with a .298 average. All of this represented major firepower, and for once it was not all wasted.

Collins was the club's biggest winner, with 14 games, despite an unsightly earned run average. Elliott won 11, lost 10, but had a high ERA. Snipe Hansen was 10–10 with a good ERA, and 30-year-old rookie Ed Holley won another eleven games.

Flint Rhem, picked up from the Cardinals at the end of May, won 11 and lost 7. Rhem, a big South Carolinian, had been with St. Louis since 1924. Flint Rhem, unfortunately, was a world-class drinker. As Bartell said of him, "If he'd ever stayed sober, what a pitcher he could have been. He was the nicest guy in the world, never mean or nasty, never bothered nobody."[12]

It was a good feeling for the Phillies, winning more than they lost, finishing in fourth place, cashing checks for their shares of the World Series proceeds. Hopes were high for 1933, with the new direction under Nugent. But money was a problem; Nugent certainly did not have any, and the first division club of 1932 had lost money. Attendance fell, to 268,914, even as victories increased.

Many ballplayers had invested in the great bull market and saw their nest eggs wiped out in the Crash of 1929. There were even easier ways to lose money. When Flint Rhem came to the Phillies in May 1932, he still had not cashed the World Series check for $4,467.59 he had earned as a member of the winning 1931 Cardinals. His new teammates got on him about this and persuaded Rhem to put it in a bank. So one Friday he opened an account at a Philadelphia bank and deposited his Series check. The bank failed over the weekend, and poor Flint Rhem never saw his money again.[13]

At the beginning of March, manager Shotton predicted that the Phils would win the 1933 pennant. Over the winter they traded Ray Benge to Brooklyn for a scrappy infielder named Mickey Finn. Shotton said he expected Finn to make a difference of about a dozen games in 1933 over the prior season (perhaps confusing Mickey Finn with Frankie Frisch), and he anticipated one of his starting pitchers winning twenty games. Their manager having thus perched himself far out on a limb, the Phillies proceeded to saw it off behind him.

On March 24, Hurst, still unsigned, walked out of camp, vowing never to return. He was going to look, he said, for a job in the movies. He eventually came back, of course, but his season was a pallid imitation of the year before. Hurst hit a soft .267, with only eight homers and 76 runs batted in.

Mickey Finn, the new second baseman, had a stomach ulcer. He underwent surgery at the start of July, but complications set in and the young infielder died in the hospital on July 7. His teammates were stunned at the sudden death, and second base remained a problem.

Spud Davis continued to hit, and Klein had another top-notch season, winning the Triple Crown by leading the league in average (.368), home runs (28) and runs batted in (120). But Bartell declined to .271, Hurst was way off, and Whitney was traded to Boston after 31 games, hitting only .264.

With the overall decline in the team's hitting, the pitching staff could not win. Ed Holley, with 13–15, was the top winner. Collins, Hansen, Elliott, and Rhem all lost a lot more than they won. By the end of May, the team was floundering in last place. They finally managed to nose out Cincinnati for seventh, but it was a sad letdown for the supposed pennant contender.

One of the few highlights of the year for the Phillies was the selection of players for the first (and at the time the *only*) All-Star Game, promoted by Arch Ward, sports editor of the *Chicago Tribune*. In the fans' voting, Klein received the highest number of votes, and a second Phillies representative, Dick Bartell, was named to play shortstop for the senior league.

Unfortunately, putting players in the All-Star Game put no money in Gerry Nugent's pocket. The 1933 attendance of 156,421 was the lowest total for a full season since 1914. After the season, Burt Shotton's limb came crashing down and Nugent let him go, although the problem was hardly the manager.

Chapter 8

Doormats of the National League

The best thing that happened to the Phillies in 1933 was the easing of Pennsylvania's notorious "blue laws," outlawing professional baseball on Sundays. There had been agitation for a long time to do something about the "blue laws," but after the A's played a Sunday game in 1926 as a test case, the state supreme court upheld the law. Now, with Prohibition gone, there was hope finally that the Sunday law would follow. In early 1933, the state legislature sent the necessary legislation, permitting local option, on to Governor Gifford Pinchot, who signed it with some reluctance.[1]

On November 7, 1933, the referendum on Sunday baseball came before the electorate of Philadelphia, which voted to permit the playing of professional baseball on Sundays from 2 p.m. to 6 p.m. The new dispensation was not perfect—experience would demonstrate that it was often not possible to get in a Sunday doubleheader in four hours, with twenty minutes between games—but it was a start.

A later contribution to the gate may have been the inception in 1936 of regular live radio broadcasts of the home games of the A's and Phillies. An announcer named Bill Dyer was the pioneer of play-by-play descriptions to the ever-increasing number of radio owners in the Philadelphia area.

After the Phillies' seventh-place finish in 1933 and the discharge of Burt Shotton, more changes were expected at Baker Bowl. On November 15, Gerry Nugent traded catcher Virgil "Spud" Davis and another player to the Cardinals in exchange for catcher Jimmie Wilson, who was then named the new Phillies manager. Six days later, Nugent sent Chuck Klein to the Cubs in a long-rumored swap, for three inconsequential players and a large chunk of cash.

Wilson, a local man, was considered a prime managerial prospect. "One of baseball's smartest catchers," it was said of him, "he is scrappy, aggressive and knows baseball to his finger tips…. [H]e gets along well with his men, for he has a large fund of common sense and never expects the impossible." The opinion was not unanimous. Dick Bartell called Wilson "the worst manager I ever played for … like a wild man, just couldn't handle the players." In the dugout, Bartell said, Wilson "was highstrung, noisy, openly critical of things you did." Accordingly, the players "didn't respect him."[2]

Under Wilson the 1934 Phillies duplicated the 1933 seventh-place finish. They won four fewer games, but attendance increased slightly to 169,885, perhaps attributable to Sunday baseball, perhaps to fans having a few more bucks in their pockets as the bad times eased somewhat.

Gerald P. Nugent, a savvy operator who ran the club on a shoestring (author's collection).

In early June, Nugent swapped Don Hurst, batting only .262 with two home runs at the time, to the Cubs for rookie first baseman Dolph Camilli. It was a steal for the Phils. The lefthanded-swinging Camilli, after a modest start in 1934, turned into one of the big hitters in the National League, while Hurst hit only .199 in 51 Cub games and was banished to the minors.[3]

The 1934 Phillies had some high-average hitters. Johnny Moore's .343 led the way, followed by outfielder Ethan Allen at .330, catcher Al Todd at .318, Bartell at .310, and freshman second sacker Lou Chiozza with .304. Allen had been picked up from St. Louis, and he was, as Bartell said, "a consistent, steady, reliable player, a great asset to the team," who "gave us a touch of class on the field and off."[4]

The team's pitching leader was an elderly rookie named Curt Davis, getting a crack at the majors at the age of 30, after spending five years in the Pacific Coast League, with big league scouts passing him up as too skinny. A righthander, Davis threw sidearm, and his big curveball was devastating to righthanded hitters. Phillies' scout Patsy O'Rourke liked Curt and had the club buy him. Davis was 19–17, with a 2.95 earned run average, and led the league in games pitched.

Early in the year, the Phillies picked off the waiver wire a Red Sox infielder named William "Bucky" Walters, a native Philadelphian. In parts of three seasons with the Braves and Red Sox Walters had not shown that he could hit major league pitching. Jimmie Wilson put his new man at third base, where Bucky played eighty games, batting .260. But Wilson saw something else. His third baseman had a great throwing arm, so Wilson tried him on the mound in a couple of games. Wilson liked what he saw, and as far as he was concerned, Walters was now a pitcher.

On November 1, 1934, Nugent helped to balance the books for the year by sending Dick Bartell to the Giants. In exchange he got four players and the standard bundle of cash

In 1935, the Phils landed in seventh place for the third year in a row. Camilli hit 25 home runs, and Moore had another good year. Curt Davis had a workmanlike season, at 16–14 and 3.66, and veteran Syl Johnson was 10–8. Bucky Walters, now a full-fledged pitcher, was 9–9, with two shutouts. Walters hurled his first complete game on May 9, beating St.Louis 2–1, and there was no question of his status after that.

The next year saw the Phillies back in last place. They won 54 and lost a hundred, and they were thirteen games out of seventh. With both the A's and Phillies as perennial cellar-dwellers, the third largest city in the country was considered a baseball joke, funny everywhere except around Philadelphia. There was a huge sign on the rightfield wall at Baker Bowl, advertising Lifebuoy, the deodorant soap. "The Phillies use Lifebuoy," the sign proclaimed, and the fans responded, "yeah, and they still stink."

1936 was a year for bringing back heroes from the past. On April 30, Nugent traded shortstop Mickey Haslin to the Braves for Pinky Whitney, who was promptly installed in his old third base job. Pinky, who had been a disappointment in Boston, bolstered his reputation as a Baker Bowl player by hitting .294 with the Phillies and making the All-Star team.

A month after the Whitney trade, the club sent Curt Davis and Ethan Allen to the Cubs for Chuck Klein and a lesser player. The prodigal returned with his credentials slightly tarnished after two and a fraction years in Chicago, where his numbers were not bad but nothing like those of his first six seasons with the Phillies. The pressure got to him with the pennant-contending Cubs, Klein admitted. "With the Phillies nobody paid much attention whether I hit or not," he said in Chicago. "Here they watch you on every pitch."[5]

Back with the Phils, Chuck hit .309 and 20 home runs. Four of these came in one game on July 10 at Forbes Field in Pittsburgh, in the first, fifth, seventh, and tenth innings. Klein was the fourth player (and second Phillie,

Delahanty having accomplished the feat in 1896) to hit four homers in a game.[6]

Bucky Walters now learned the real rewards of pitching in Baker Bowl. He won eleven, lost 21, and posted an earned run average of 4.26. Before the 1936 season, the Phillies picked up another young hurler, a tall, skinny Mississippian named Claude Passeau, in a trade with the Pirates. Passeau put together a rookie season of 11–15, with a 3.48 ERA, and showed promise.

In 1937 both Philadelphia clubs rose to seventh place. The A's beat out a really bad Browns club, while the Phillies were 61–92 and ended up only a game out of sixth. Curiously, the Athletics' seventh-place team increased its home attendance from 285,173 to 430,733, while the improvement of the Phillies was accompanied by an attendance decline from 249,219 to 212,790. Philadelphia was still the A's town.

Wilson's Phillies got major production out of Camilli, Whitney, and Klein. Dolph hit .339 with 27 home runs, while Whitney batted .341 and Klein .325. Walters went 14–15 and was rewarded with a spot on the All-Star team. Passeau was 14–18, and young righthander Hugh Mulcahy put together an 8–18 record. Rookie southpaw Wayne LaMaster was 15–19 and had an ERA of 5.32. The front office was talking seriously of getting out of Baker Bowl, but the crumbling old ballyard was still taking its toll on Phillies pitchers.

1938 saw both Philadelphia teams drop back into last place, a truly dreadful Phillies team at 45–105 trailing seventh-place Brooklyn by 24½ games. Wilson was fired a couple of days before the season ended. 1938, however, marked the end of the Phillies' long tenure in Baker Bowl. On June 25, sportswriter Walter "Red" Smith wrote in the *Record* that arrangements with the Athletics to share Shibe Park were almost completed. The Phillies, he said, were ready to abandon their "fusty, cobwebby House of Horrors," a change which should "lift a burden from the shoulders of Wilson's harassed pitching staff."[7]

On June 30, 1938, the Phillies played their last game in their tawdry, decrepit old home. Fittingly, they absorbed a 14–1 pasting by the Giants. Passeau started, but first baseman Phil Weintraub's error gave the Giants three runs in the second inning, and nine more in the third put the game out of reach. Bill Dooly of the *Record* thanked the Phils for closing the park with "one of their inimitable travesties."[8]

On July 1, in Chicago, the lawyers for the Charles W. Murphy Estate, the actual owner of Baker Bowl, announced that the estate and the ball-club had reached an agreement permitting the Phillies to leave, although it was emphasized that the Phillies were not released from their 99-year lease until payment of an as-yet-undetermined consideration. Gerry Nugent and Connie Mack then signed the lease making the Phillies the tenants of the Athletics in Shibe Park.

Nugent said that "we are definitely through with Baker Bowl. Our contract with the Murphy Estate is now in a suspended state for the next five years," which actually meant the Phillies were to make payments to the Murphy Estate for five more years for the privilege of abandoning the old ballyard. Connie Mack added that "I think the change will benefit both clubs and will make for better baseball in Philadelphia. I am sure the Phils will play better at Shibe Park." Time would tell.[9]

The Phillies made their first appearance at their new digs in a Fourth of July doubleheader before 12,000 fans. In the opener, Hughie Mulcahy was locked in a 5–5 tie with the Boston Bees until the visitors rocked him for five runs in the eighth. Passeau shut down the Bees, 10–2, in the nightcap.

The move came just in time, for Phillies fans were entering a state of terminal disgust. In March, Nugent traded Dolph Camilli to Brooklyn for $45,000 and a nonentity who could not even make the Phillies team, and on June 13, Walters went to Cincinnati for two players and $50,000 cash. Both Walters and Camilli were to win MVP awards within the next three years. Even playing half the season in Shibe Park, the Phillies drew but 166,111 fans, compared to the 385,357 attendance of the Athletics.

The Phils' pitching improved very little with the move to Shibe Park. Passeau led the staff with 11–18 and 4.52. Mulcahy, a steady workman who earned the nickname "Losing Pitcher" because the phrase appeared with his name in so many box scores, was 10–20 and 4.62. Al Hollingsworth was 5–16 after coming over from Cincinnati, and Max Butcher, who came from the Dodgers in a trade for LaMaster, was 4–8 but had a good ERA of 2.94.

In 1938, a young Texan named Byrum Saam came to town and soon became a Philadelphia institution. A broadcaster hired from a Minneapolis station, Saam described both A's and Phillies games to Philadelphia's radio listeners, and after the A's left town he continued with Phillies games from 1955 to 1975.

Saam had a smooth and mellow voice, with no hint of an accent, and several generations of Philadelphians regarded it as the sound of summer and baseball. By Saam employed no frills and no gimmicks, feeling that his listeners simply wanted to know what was going on on the field. He had his moments, however, such as the time he described outfielder Alex Johnson going "back, back, back; he hits his head on the wall, and now it's rolling back toward the infield." In his years of calling Philadelphia baseball, Byrum Saam broadcast more losing games than any other announcer ever.

Nugent hired James Thompson "Doc" Prothro, a part-time dentist and a successful minor league manager, to lead his club in 1939. Eddie Collins, who had become general manager of the Red Sox, called Prothro "one of the ablest developers of young players I know." One of his Phillies pitchers later said that Prothro "was a fine manager who ... was as nervous as a cat in a room full of rocking chairs."[10]

It was Doc Prothro's misfortune to manage three of the worst Phillies teams in the club's long history. In the record book, Prothro's mark as a major league skipper is an abysmal one of 138–320, for a percentage of .301. Yet baseball men all agreed that he was a good manager. The Phillies could do that to anyone.

The 1939 edition of the Philadelphia National League Club ran up a mark of 45–106, 18 games out of seventh place. The team batting average of .261 was last in the circuit, and the staff earned run average of 5.17 was more than a run higher than any other team's. When Prothro took over the club at its New Braunfels, Texas, training camp, he snorted, "That's the worst looking crowd of ballplayers in big league uniforms I've ever seen." That this remark stamped him as an astute judge of talent did not lessen the pain of the season that followed.[11]

Morrie Arnovich led the team with a .324 average, but no one on the club exceeded outfielder Joe Marty's nine home runs. Marty came from the Cubs on May 29, along with pitchers Kirby Higbe and Ray Harrell, in a trade for Passeau. Higbe, a tough, hard-drinking Carolinian with a good fastball, soon established himself as the leader of the staff. He was 10–14 with a 4.86 ERA. Mulcahy was 9–16, and Walter "Boom Boom" Beck, a flop with the Browns and Dodgers, was 7–14.

On June 7, the Phillies released 34-year-old Chuck Klein, who was hitting .191 with one home run. He signed with Pittsburgh and had a decent year for the Pirates. After the season, Pittsburgh released him, and he was signed by the Phillies for 1940. "Chuck has lost the spring in his legs," it was written, "but he can still hit." Another mistake. Klein batted only .218 for the 1940 Phillies, with seven home runs.[12]

The 1940 Phillies were not quite as terrible as their '39 predecessors (50–103 was a slight improvement), but it was all relative: they were still bad, with very weak hitting. Higbe was 14–19 and 3.72 and led the league in strikeouts. Mulcahy was 13–22 and 3.60, and oldtimer Si Johnson was 5–14.

Kirby Higbe started the opening game of the season in the Polo Grounds and beat Carl Hubbell of the Giants, 3–1, on a three-run homer by Gus Suhr. The next six games, including three at home with the Boston Bees, were postponed because of bad weather. When they finally played, Prothro told Higbe, "You pitch the opener here too, Hig. Maybe you can win them all this year if it rains enough." Higbe lost to the Giants, 1–0, and he told Prothro he would decline the offer to pitch them all.[13]

Higbe's contract called for a $1,000 bonus if he won fifteen games. Coming into his last start of the season, he had won fourteen. He lost, 3–1, to the Giants, "when Joe Marty tipped his hat to a line drive to centre [sic]," turning it into a two-run inside-the-park home run for Johnny Rucker. Higbe told Nugent he deserved the bonus. Nugent, who had no money to give away, simply said, "You didn't win fifteen."[14]

In November 1940, Higbe negotiated a new contract with Nugent for $8,500, making him the highest-paid player on the team. Before signing, Kirby said that if the Phillies were going to trade him he would wait to negotiate with his new club. Nugent told him there was not a chance of that, so Higbe went ahead and signed. Driving south from Philadelphia that night, Higbe heard on the radio that he had been traded to Brooklyn for three players and $100,000. When he suggested to Nugent that his bonus could be paid out of the $100,000, the Phillies president told him sadly that that money was already spent.[15]

Sportswriter Stoney McLinn had predicted that Nugent would trade both Higbe and Mulcahy; "the Phils make no bones of the fact that the 1940 season was well-nigh disastrous financially." After the Higbe trade, Nugent said, "It was either sell one of the stars or get out of business." He said the financial loss for the year was more than twice the amount of cash received from Brooklyn.[16]

In the last peacetime season, 1941, both Philadelphia clubs again finished in last place, although the A's improved and the Phillies got worse. Gerry Nugent watched his attendance figures settle once again down near the 230,000 mark, while the Mackmen drew over 528,000. The Phillies' economic picture was becoming desperate, as Nugent was forced to perform never-ending financial juggling tricks just to keep the franchise afloat.

With Higbe already gone, the pitching staff suffered another jolt when Hughie Mulcahy, a good pitcher whose luck was worse than just about anyone else's, became the first major league player taken by the first peacetime military draft in the nation's history. It was only fitting that the draft's initial hit should be absorbed by the team least able to afford it.

Prothro's pitchers were led in 1941 by Johnny Podgajny (9–12) and Tommy Hughes (9–14), both 21-year-old righties who were regarded by Nugent as prospects. ("Prospects," of course, were players who might some day down the line bring a cash consideration.) The records of the rest of

**Connie Mack congratulates Jimmie Wilson on his appointment as manager of
the Phillies, while owner Gerry Nugent looks on (author's collection).**

the staff look grim: Cy Blanton 6–13, Si Johnson 5–12, Ike Pearson 4–14,
Frank Hoerst 3–10, Lee Grissom 2–13, Rube Melton 1–5, and Boom Boom
Beck 1–9.

First baseman Nick Etten (.311) and outfielder Danny Litwhiler (.305)
led the offense, with Litwhiler belting 18 home runs and Etten fourteen.
A tough little Irishman from Chester came up from the minors in mid-
season and took over second base. His name was Danny Murtaugh, and
in his half season he led the league in stolen bases with eighteen.

After the season was over, Nugent let Prothro go and named as his
new manager 60-year-old John "Honus" Lobert, who had spent the previous seven years as a Phillie coach, good-will ambassador, and after-din-
ner speaker. Lobert had sought the job as Phillies manager as far back as
1915, when Red Dooin was fired. At least there could be no surprises for
the new manager, who had suffered with the club through the Wilson and
Prothro regimes. "I'm not satisfied with the team," Honus said, which
showed a commendable sense of reality.[17]

The first thing that happened after Lobert took command was that the club signed Lloyd Waner, a 35-year-old outfielder who had put in many fine seasons with Pittsburgh but had just been released by the Reds. Waner, Dooly wrote, was "a wispy sort of geezer ... who ... may even help our Phils a little, since it is hardly possible for him to hurt them."[18] The second thing that happened was that the Japanese bombed Pearl Harbor and the United States entered the Second World War. It would prove to be an interesting if arduous time for the Phillies.

Chapter 9

The Wartime Phillies

With the entrance of the United States into the war which had started with Hitler's invasion of Poland in 1939, the status of a professional sport like baseball, even though it was called "the national pastime," became very unclear. Gerry Nugent sounded discouraged: "It's going to be harder to keep going from a manpower and playing standpoint with most of the good ballplayers of draft age being called into the service." Of course, Nugent's club was just about broke, and any additional difficulty would likely push his operation under.[1]

There was fear that the game might be shut down altogether, as had happened in 1918, under the decree of the secretary of war, or that some kind of severe curtailment short of closure might be enforced. That concern was alleviated for the baseball magnates on January 15, 1942, when President Franklin D. Roosevelt wrote his famous "green light" letter to Judge Landis, stating "that it would be best for the country to keep baseball going." What was clear, however, from FDR's letter was that baseball should expect no preferential treatment and that the game would have to work its way through the war making the same sort of sacrifices that everyone else was expected to make.

Wartime baseball in Philadelphia, for both the Phillies and their American League counterparts, was just about as bad as it had been in the years leading up to the war. In the four wartime seasons Philadelphia teams finished in last place six times, and several of those wartime squads are considered to be among the worst teams of all time. With the fourteen other big league teams hit with substantial losses through the military draft and munitions employment, it would have seemed logical for the bad Philadelphia teams to gravitate toward the middle of their leagues; for some reason that is not what happened.

It was the Phillies who started the 1945 season with 17-year-old Granville Hamner at shortstop and his slightly-older brother Garvin at second base, an experiment which broke down under a flood of errors and a torrent of boos from the uncharitable but long-suffering Philadelphia fans. It was the Phillies who employed such well-traveled baseball nomads as Babe Dahlgren, Jimmy Wasdell, Jake Powell, and Vince DiMaggio. The fans who came out to Shibe Park to see the Phillies were introduced to such personalities as Hildreth Flitcraft, Bitsy Mott, Mitch Chetkovich, Stumpy Verdel, and Lou "the Mad Russian" Novikoff.

The National League owners met in mid–January 1942 to discuss the upcoming season in light of the nation's entry into the war, as well as their perennial problem, the financial woes of the Phillies. Poor attendance for Phillies home games was also a drag on visiting teams, which seldom made enough from their trips to Philadelphia to pay expenses. The owners were at a loss what to do about it, other than having the league advance Nugent money for operating expenses. What should have been one of the strongest cities in the circuit was a perennial laughingstock.

In February 1942, the club announced the change of the team's name from "Phillies" to "Phils." The reason given was that an unnamed nationally-advertised commercial product was using the name "Phillies." The reference, of course, was to the Bayuk Cigar Company product. It hardly seems possible that a major league baseball club would so meekly surrender its name to a commercial interloper, but Gerry Nugent had more pressing needs for whatever spare cash he had on hand than to file a lawsuit. The new name was spelled out in black block letters across the front of the club's gray road uniforms.[2]

The clubs were then off for spring training. Phils pitcher Rube Melton announced that he was going to Florida early, to absorb everything he could from the club's new coach, the great catching star of yore, Bill Killefer. Unfortunately, the high spot of Melton's spring training was his early March arrest by the Hialeah, Florida, police on charges of disorderly conduct and annoying women. An angry Nugent let the pitcher languish in jail overnight before paying his $300 fine.[3]

The Phillies— or the Phils, as they were for the single season of 1942— were awful. They won 42 and lost 109 and ended 18½ games behind seventh-place Boston. They drew only 230,183, and the wonder is that that many people came to see them. On September 11, only 393 people showed up at Shibe Park to see a loss to Cincinnati.

As the first wartime season opened in April, Mayor Bernard Samuel threw out the first ball, and he and 10,150 watched Alva Javery of the Braves bestow a 2-1 defeat upon the home team. They managed to lose three in a row to the Braves and went on from there to lose 106 more games. Lobert fumed and fussed ("I've stood all the loafing I'm going to.... I want hustlers and fighters, not a lot of mollycoddles"), but none of it did any good. His players had little talent, and the baseball fans of Philadelphia stayed away.[4]

The closest thing the club had to a star was outfielder Danny Litwhiler, who led the team with a .271 average, nine home runs, and 56 runs batted in. Litwhiler did achieve something unprecedented, when he went through the entire season, playing all 151 games, without committing a single error.. His manager was less than impressed with Danny's record: "Danny Litwhiler's perfect fielding record was not a true indication of his fielding ability," Lobert said sourly. "I can remember many an afternoon when I would have given Litwhiler a dozen errors for some of the plays he made, or didn't make, in left field."[5]

Hard-throwing Tommy Hughes led the staff with 12-18 and a decent 3.06 earned run average. Stan Baumgartner called Hughes "just about the best young pitcher in the National League." Melton was 9-20, Si Johnson 8-19, and bespectacled Johnny Podgajny, who never seemed to beat anyone but Chicago, was 6-14. All of them had respectable earned run averages under four, unlike localite Frank Hoerst, who was 4-16 and 5.19. Although the club ERA was the highest in the National League, it was the anemic offensive performance which doomed the Phils to the cellar. The team batting average of .232 was the worst in the club's storied history, and Lobert's men averaged only 2.6 runs per game, hardly enough to win many games even with a much better pitching staff.[6]

With the dreadful 1942 Phillies, the National League had finally had enough. Nugent was in debt to the league and in arrears in the rent owed to the Athletics, and, with an average attendance of less than 3,000 fans per game, no prospect of salvation. The plight of the Phillies was the League's prime concern during the 1942-43 offseason.

Early in November, an owners' meeting was held, at Nugent's request, at which he laid out the Phillies' problems in detail. The Associated Press reported that "sale of the ... [club] now is certain this winter and possibly within a few weeks." League president Ford Frick denied that any definite action had been settled on, but when asked if the league would lend Nugent more money Frick replied, "Absolutely no."[7]

Nugent hoped to receive permission to sell Litwhiler, Tommy Hughes, young Ike Pearson, and Rube Melton for operating cash, a privilege denied to him since the league's loan in the spring of 1942. (Unfortunately, Hughes was soon drafted, cutting off one of Nugent's potential $100,000 escape routes.) When the major league meetings were held in Chicago early in December, the National League devoted one whole day to "threshing out its biggest problem, what to do with the Philadelphia Phils."[8]

Nugent and his attorney, Robert Irwin, sat on a bench outside the meeting room while the other owners deliberated. Then Frick emerged to announce that nothing had been decided. Nugent said he was "willing to sell my stock to a suitable buyer who would have enough capital to build the Phils. As I understand it, no such potential buyer has been uncovered." The problem was dumped back into Nugent's lap; he was in effect told to go back to Philadelphia and find a well-heeled purchaser for his ballclub.[9]

On December 13, the Phillies sold Melton to Brooklyn for $30,000 and elderly pitcher Johnny Allen. Nugent said, "It was a question of cash to operate the Phils." He received $15,000 more and two minor league players from the Yankees for first baseman Nick Etten. Since the club's debts exceeded $300,000, these sales would do little to resolve Nugent's problems. He was truly at the end of the line.[10]

On February 1, Nugent told the press that he discounted the rumors of the league taking the team from him. "Certainly, nobody can come in and take the club without buying it," he said. Another league meeting was called for February 9. It was obvious that no buyer had been located by Gerry Nugent.[11]

On February 8, the *Inquirer* ran an article by Baumgartner analyzing Nugent's situation. Baumgartner said the Phillies owed the league $170,000, two years' rent on Shibe Park to the Athletics, two more years to the Murphy estate on the old Baker Bowl lease, and other debts which brought the total to $330,000. The club's radio rights had been sold for five years, and that money was long gone. "This is really what the Phils owe, and they have nothing with which to meet these bills," he wrote.[12]

It all came to a head at the league meeting on the 9th. The National League purchased "substantially all" of the club stock from Gerry Nugent and other stockholders for whom he acted "at an agreed price" of ten dollars a share for 2,600 shares, plus the assumption of the club's debts. Ed Pollock in the *Evening Bulletin* wrote that the National League had given Nugent "what amounts to a dignified 'bum's rush,'" and Red Smith in the *Record* said "the Phils were sold out from under President Gerry Nugent today." Nugent himself, though, told a reporter that he was "entirely satisfied" with the league's action.[13]

It was during this time period that Bill Veeck, the flamboyant owner of the Milwaukee Brewers of the American Association, attempted, according to his autobiography of twenty years later, to purchase the franchise, intending to break Organized Baseball's long-standing color barrier. Veeck said he made an offer to Nugent to buy the club, planning to "stock it with Negro players," and that Nugent accepted his offer. (Whether Nugent knew of the plan to use black players is not made clear in Veeck's book.) Veeck wrote that out of courtesy he told Judge Landis what he was planning to do and that Landis and Frick then sabotaged his deal.[14]

Close examination of what actually took place in the period from October 1942, when Veeck and Nugent had their one and only meeting, to February 1943, when the National League took over the club and then sold it to William D. Cox, makes it clear that Veeck's story is a fabrication. Veeck, with his right-hand man, Rudie Schaffer, met with Nugent on the way home to Milwaukee after the World Series, talked about the Phillies, and was stopped cold when Nugent mentioned what Veeck called "some large figures." "That was all," Veeck told reporters back in Milwaukee, and in fact that *was* all. There were no further contacts between the two men, at a time when Nugent was eagerly looking for just such a purchaser as Veeck represented himself to be, twenty years later.[15]

Veeck's October meeting was mentioned in the November 12th *Inquirer*, but never again, from that time to the unveiling of the new owner on February 20, 1943, did Veeck's name appear in the Philadelphia papers in speculation about a possible buyer. Branch Rickey was mentioned, until he took a new job as president of the Dodgers, as were former Postmaster General Jim Farley, several Philadelphia prospects, and a couple of groups from Baltimore who wanted to move the franchise there. Bill Veeck was not.

In any event, it was lumber broker William D. Cox, not Bill Veeck, who became the owner of the Phillies in 1943. Cox, a wealthy New Yorker out of Yale, was an owner who meddled constantly in baseball affairs he knew little about and attracted more media attention than his baseball team did. Cox organized a syndicate which put up almost $250,000 for most of the Phillies' stock, including all the club's debt, outbidding a group led by Philadelphia sportsman and brickmaker John B. Kelly, father of the future movie star and princess of Monaco, Grace Kelly.

Bill Cox was only 33 when he took over the Phillies in March 1943, and though he told the press "I'm determined there shall be no interference" with his manager, he found it difficult to restrain himself. He made a wise move in hiring the seasoned and amiable Stanley "Bucky" Harris, who had nineteen years' experience managing in the big leagues. What Cox did not do was leave Harris alone to run his team.[16]

On January 4, 1943, a decree by Judge Landis, in response to a request from the director of War Defense Transportation that baseball curtail its use of the nation's railroad facilities, mandated that all clubs except the Browns and Cardinals must find spring training sites north of the Potomac and Ohio Rivers; the two St. Louis clubs could train anywhere in Missouri.

As a result of this edict, the big league ballclubs found themselves trying to get their players into condition in some very strange northern spots. The Phillies went to Hershey, having been turned down by Swarthmore College.

With the demands of Selective Service, the training camps were not overflowing with ballplayers; the '43 Phillies started with just fourteen men, though the situation improved. The club picked up some proven major leaguers in veterans Ellsworth "Babe" Dahlgren, Jimmy Wasdell, and the former Detroit pitching ace Lynwood "Schoolboy" Rowe. The easygoing Harris got the Phillies off to a good start, with Dahlgren hitting steadily to lead the way. Cox bought newspaper space and radio time to furnish the fans with lots of Phillies news and gossip.

On June 1, though, Cox stunned the faithful with another trade of a popular star when he sent Litwhiler and spare outfielder Earl Naylor to the Cardinals for three outfielders, Elvin "Buster" Adams, Coaker Triplett, and Dain Clay, who was then traded to the Reds for shortstop Charlie Brewster. To Philadelphia fans, the trade of Litwhiler smacked of Gerry Nugent all over again, even though it was not for cash. "The fans will take a lot of convincing," Baumgartner wrote, "and somebody, Triplett or whoever, had better play a dazzling lot of left field."[17]

The fans, though, soon warmed up to the hustling Adams and Triplett, both of whom had been blocked by the glut of outfield talent in the rich Cardinal organization. When the Cubs tried to send roly-poly pitcher Dick Barrett back to the Pacific Coast League, where he had pitched for many years, Barrett balked, so Chicago sold him to the Phillies. The 36-year-old Barrett, known to one and all as "Kewpie Dick," won ten and lost nine for Philadelphia and became a popular favorite. Another acquisition, lefty Al Gerheauser, went 10-19 but had a good earned run average, and Rowe was 14-8 and 2.94.

Cox and his ballclub even earned a write-up in *Time* magazine's July 5 issue, the writer applauding Cox for giving Bucky Harris "free rein." Harris, the article went on, "is working wonders with the material at hand," and through the first 28 home games the Phillies had drawn 253,000, or 23,000 more than their total for all of 1942.[18]

While all this good ink flowed and the Phillies actually approached the first division, trouble was brewing behind the scenes. Cox's regular appearances in the clubhouse to give advice to the players angered Harris and disturbed his men, while Cox blamed Harris for the team's losses and resented the manager not being available to him at any hour of the day or night.

Finally, Cox decided to exercise his owner's prerogative. With the fifth-place Phillies in St. Louis, Cox told the press that the manager's job was being given to veteran hurler Fred Fitzsimmons, just purchased from Brooklyn. Harris learned of his dismissal when a reporter asked him for a reaction. The Phillies players were outraged. They threatened to go on strike unless Harris was reinstated and allowed to resign.[19]

The owner flew to St. Louis to meet with the team behind closed doors, while Harris and Fitzsimmons waited outside. The players, led by Merrill "Pinky" May, shouted and stormed at Cox until he called Harris in and apologized for the way the ouster had been handled. Harris accepted the apology and, pointing out to the players that the game they were going to strike was for the benefit of the Red Cross, urged them to take the field, which they did. Over the next week or so, the public was treated to an exchange of accusations and insults between Cox and his former manager, who called the club president "an All-American jerk."

The Phillies actually improved at first under Fitzsimmons, but after Danny Murtaugh was drafted they slumped to a seventh place finish, still out of the cellar for the first time since 1937. Attendance for 1943, bolstered by the fast start and all the turmoil, was 466,975, double that of a year earlier and the second highest total in team history. Dahlgren hit .287, Pinky May batted .282, and a short, barrel-shaped outfielder named Ron Northey hit 16 home runs, two more than Triplett.

The Phillies' stormy season was to have a stormier aftermath. Bill Cox, it turned out, was a betting man. He had once owned a racehorse and he liked to wager on the ponies. He played cards in high-stake games. And he bet on baseball games. In the bitter recriminations after his firing, Bucky Harris mentioned that Cox bet on ballgames. A reporter asked Judge Landis about this.

Landis began an investigation, and on November 3 Cox told the commissioner that he had booked 15 or 20 bets of from $25 to $100 a game on the Phillies. He said these bets stopped about May 20 when he learned for the first time that baseball had a rule prohibiting such gambling. Landis ordered Cox to appear before him for a formal hearing on December 4. Cox wrote to Landis on November 18 that he had resigned as president and director of the Phillies and was looking for a purchaser for the club. Thus no "useful purpose would be served by my attending any further hearing before you."[20]

Landis, who was unaccustomed to such cavalier responses from his subjects, responded with a public statement on November 23, denying that his scheduled hearing would be of no use, and declaring Cox permanently ineligible to hold any connection with Organized Baseball. That night, Cox went on New York radio to broadcast a maudlin "goodbye to baseball," but a few days later he had a change of heart, retracted his admissions of betting on the Phillies, and asked Landis to hold a hearing.[21]

Cox was represented at the six-hour open hearing by Lloyd Paul Stryker, one of the nation's most eminent trial attorneys. Cox testified at length that his admission of betting had been a sham, to "smoke out" a Phillies director he suspected of disloyalty. Bucky Harris and club employee Nathan "Babe" Alexander supplied damning evidence against their former boss. Harris said he heard a secretary procuring betting odds for Cox over the telephone and she told him she kept gambling records for her boss. Harris said he told her, "If Landis ever hears of that, it will mean the end of Mr. Cox." And so it did. Landis said Cox had failed to convince him that the earlier statements were false, so the permanent suspension of Cox stood. The Phillies were marked as the only club to have two presidents expelled from the game.[22]

With Cox banned from baseball, the Phillies changed owners once again. This time, though, the franchise struck paydirt. Robert R.M. Carpenter, vice president of E.I. DuPont de Nemours, Inc., the giant chemical company, and married to a DuPont, purchased the club for his son, Robert R.M. Carpenter, Jr., for a reported $400,000. For the first time in many years the Phillies had real money behind them.[23]

Young Bob Carpenter, 28 years old when he was named president, was drafted into the army a few months later. Before going off to war, he hired Herb Pennock, the former pitching great, as his general manager. Pennock, from Kennett Square, was a friend of the Carpenter family and had been serving as director of the Red Sox farm system.

Carpenter and Pennock agreed that the key to building a healthy Phillies organization was the creation of a strong minor league system. The Phillies had only a few scouts like Ted McGrew and Jocko Collins, so they would be building almost from scratch, with Joe Reardon in charge. This plan, they knew, would not produce an instant winner, especially during a war in which many young players were unavailable to baseball, but its implementation was crucial to developing a consistent winner. Pennock would have the Carpenter money to use in signing young players and putting together a farm system.

Unforeseen at the time was the effect that the Carpenters' purchase of the Phillies would have on their neighbors and landlords, the Athletics. In the postwar world two-team cities became increasingly less viable economically, and the Phillies were suddenly in a position to outspend the frugal Athletics by a wide margin. Philadelphia, for decades the Athletics' town, with the Phillies the threadbare poor cousins, gradually but inexorably changed its allegiance. When the crunch came, it turned out to be the A's who were in trouble.

In the meantime, though, there was a war on, and Organized Baseball was still struggling with many of its consequences. The 1944 Phillies, under Fat Freddy Fitzsimmons, flopped back into the cellar with a 61-92 record. The Phillies' attendance dropped with their won-lost record, to 369,586. The Phillies got some hitting from Northey, Adams, Wasdell, and first baseman Tony Lupien, a Harvard grad, but the rest of the offense was not very noticeable. Lefty Ken Raffensberger was 13-20, had a good ERA, and was the winning pitcher in the All-Star Game. Rookie Charley Schanz, Kewpie Dick Barrett, and former Cub star Big Bill Lee all won in double figures, but with a weak attack behind them they all lost more than they won.

During the 1944 season the Phillies decided to adopt a new nickname, although whether they intended at the same time to drop their historic one was never clear. From the more than five thousand entries received, many of them derisive and some unprintable, the club chose the name "Blue Jays." This selection elicited a loud complaint from the student body at Johns Hopkins University, where the athletic teams had been called Blue Jays for many years, and the association with the pathetic Philadelphia National League club was not particularly welcomed.

The club seemed uncertain what to do with the new name, since most people continued to use the old one, and the team's uniforms still read "Phillies" across the chest. In 1945, a blue jay was worn on the left uniform sleeve, and someone wrote a fight song called "Blue Jay Jeanne," but the new name never caught on and simply faded away in a few years from disuse and disinterest. A National League club in Philadelphia, the fans and sportswriters seemed to say in no uncertain terms, should be called the "Phillies."

Nazi Germany surrendered shortly after the start of the 1945 season, but the war against Japan continued, and, with a possible invasion of the home islands in prospect, the manpower requirements of the military were greater than ever. Selective Service relaxed its standards in order to get more men into uniform. This change resulted in some ballplayers being drafted who had previously been rejected, including the Phillies' Ron Northey. The game's leaders rolled with the punches and tried to hang on, making whatever accommodations with the war effort were required. Another major change took place on November 25, 1944, when the crusty old commissioner, Kenesaw Mountain Landis, died at the age of 78, after almost a quarter-century of nearly absolute rule.

Life magazine ran a spring training feature on just how bad things seemed to be for big league baseball, with the focus on the Phillies' camp at Wilmington. "The prize 1945 example of a team in trouble is the National League Phillies, managed by Fred Fitzsimmons," *Life* said. Of the 32 players depicted, five were under the age of 21 and nine were over 35. Among those in between the extremes of age were few good ballplayers.[24]

The Phillies were terrible in 1945, finishing 46-108, 52 games out. The Athletics were almost as bad, but this fact was of little comfort. Home attendance for the Blue Jays fell to 285,057. The Phillies were last in batting, fielding, slugging, home runs, earned run average, and complete games. They led the National League in wild pitches, errors, passed balls, and balks. They settled into the cellar the second week of the season and stayed there, never to rise again, insuring that they did not with a sixteen-game losing streak.

The Blue Jays were led by Jimmy Wasdell, who hit .300 right on the nose, and Vince DiMaggio, the oldest and least-accomplished of the DiMaggio brothers, picked up late in March from the Pirates. Vince hit four home runs with the bases loaded to tie a seasonal record. The one-time great Athletics star, Jimmie Foxx, old and portly now, essayed a comeback, but he hit only seven homers in his one-season return to Philadelphia. Toward the end of the year, Foxx tried his hand at pitching, and in nine games, over 23 innings, he turned out to be the most effective pitcher the Phillies had. He won his only decision and had an ERA of 1.57.

Big Charlie Schanz was 4-15 and 4.34. Schanz had kicked around in Tucson and Salt Lake City and San Francisco before the war and his acquisition by Philadelphia. He put up pretty good numbers in 1944, but '45 was another matter. On July 15, in one wild day of sharpshooting, Schanz put himself in the record book by hitting four batters in one game.

In the midst of the Phils' disastrous 1945 season, it was inevitable that the manager would be fired. On June 29, the Blue Jays stood at 17-51, and it was obvious that Fat Freddy Fitzsimmons was not the manager to lift the team. Exit Fat Freddy, with general manager Pennock admitting that "we have been unable to supply Fitz with adequate material because of the scarcity of good players."[25]

The new manager was the former Yankee outfielder, Ben Chapman, a hard-driving Alabamian with rough edges and a nasty mouth. Chapman had returned to the majors as a pitcher with Brooklyn, and the Phillies picked him up from the Dodgers. The club played slightly better for the volatile Chapman than it had for Fitzsimmons, but the difference was hardly discernible. The Phillies welcomed the end of the war with a feeling that things just had to get better. The Carpenter/Pennock regime would have an opportunity to show what it could do.

Chapter 10

Postwar Vistas

The baseball world was a-tingle with anticipation as spring training opened in 1946. The nation was having some difficulty in adjusting to its postwar status, with labor strife, political wrangling, and unforeseen foreign disputes with the Soviet Union, the former ally, but for baseball everything looked rosy. Most of the players who had been in the service were back, and America's baseball fans were looking forward to a better game than they had known before. A new commissioner, Senator Albert B. "Happy" Chandler of Kentucky, had been chosen as Judge Landis's successor, and Branch Rickey's Brooklyn Dodgers had signed two black men, infielder Jackie Robinson and pitcher John Wright, to play for their Montreal farm club. Exciting baseball and full houses were to be the order of the day.[1]

Soon, however, clouds darkened the sunny vistas. Few big league owners had ever heard of the Mexican League, but two brothers who ran that south-of-the-border operation, Jorge and Bernardo Pasquel, suddenly made a major impact on spring training 1946. The Pasquel brothers, in an attempt to boost their league toward big-league levels, began spreading money around the big league camps in sums much in excess of what the National and American League owners were paying. A number of players, including some prominent ones, accepted the Pasquels' offers and jumped their teams for Mexico.

The most lasting effect of the Mexican League affair was the change it made in bargaining positions between players and management. Players quickly became aware that owners were revising contracts or promising bonuses to fend off the Pasquels, and this awareness led shortly to the first attempt at unionization in more than fifty years, an attempt which led directly to the creation of the first baseball pension plan and indirectly to the successful formation of a union some twenty years later. Although the American Baseball Guild failed in 1946, it brought about changes in the basic players' contract as well as fundamental changes in the game's labor-management relations.

The immediate impact of the Mexican League raids varied from team to team, with the Cardinals and Giants suffering the most. The Phillies were hardly affected at all, since the club had no one in whom the Pasquels were interested. The Phillies did not have many big-name players returning from the service, because they had not had many to lose in the first place. When Mulcahy came back, he did not have the same stuff he possessed before being drafted so long before. Similarly, Tommy Hughes and Ike Pearson were no longer the "prospects" they had been. Schoolboy Rowe, even at 36, and Ron Northey were the only Phillies veterans who were of much use.

There was one veteran who had never played with the big-league club before going into the navy but hit well during his one minor league season at Trenton. His name was Delmer Ennis, a 20-year-old outfielder from the Olney section of Philadelphia. Ennis had been a standout in military baseball in the Pacific, but he did not get out of the service until the end of spring training. The Phillies' brain trust did not seem to know a great deal about Ennis—"they had no idea how good I was," he later said—but they were struck by the fact that several other clubs

Delmer Ennis, the consistent slugger from Olney.

expressed a willingness to relieve the Phils of the young outfielder. Pennock kept Ennis around, but he did not regard him as a starter for 1946.[2]

The general manager had a lot of positions to fill, and he was not going to fill many of them with the remnants of the awful 1945 Blue Jays. He and his scouts had already started signing promising youngsters to be groomed in the new farm system, but that would take time. Herb Pennock needed players to put a respectable club on the field in 1946, one that would show the fans of Philadelphia that the Carpenter-owned Phillies were indeed a new organization.

The solution for Pennock was to help out his fellow general managers, many of whom had overflowing rosters, with all the veterans returning from the wars added to the '45 lists. Pennock put in a busy winter. When the Reds offered 35-year-old Frank McCormick, the star first sacker of their 1939–40 pennant winners, Pennock bought him for $30,000. From the Red Sox, he bought slugging third baseman Jim Tabor and shortstop Lamar "Skeeter" Newsome. Pitcher Johnny Humphries came from the White Sox, as did infielder Roy Hughes from the Cubs. Outfielder Johnny Wyrostek and pitcher Al Jurisich were purchased from the Cardinals, who were overstocked at all positions. Thirty-nine-year-old catcher Rollie Hemsley was picked up from the Yankees, who were in the same fix. The selling clubs knew that they had to get rid of some serviceable players, and there was Herb Pennock, with Bob Carpenter's checkbook.

Often in the past, the Phillies had changed their uniform design but kept the same old bumbling baseball players. For the bright new postwar era, the Phillies added a bunch of new players to go with the new uniforms they unveiled on Opening Day. They ditched the old dull uniforms with "Phillies" scripted in blue across the chest. The new outfits combined red and blue lettering with lots of trim and piping of the same colors. The new duds imparted a feeling of excitement that had long been missing from the Phillies' scene.

With all the changes, though, once the season started, the Phillies sank again to last place. Pennock kept up his untiring efforts. He pruned players from his roster and picked up others, trying to find a combination that could win ball games. On May 1, he traded Vince DiMaggio to the Giants for catcher Clyde Kluttz, then turned around and sent Kluttz to St. Louis for smooth-fielding second baseman Emil Verban. With Verban on board to stabilize the infield, Pennock sent second sacker Danny Murtaugh to Rochester and released prewar third baseman Pinky May and infielder Ken Richardson.

He picked up pitcher Al Milnar and outfielder Lou Finney from the Browns, and when Finney said he had a bad leg, that part of the deal was

Owner Bob Carpenter and General Manager Herb Pennock, himself a Hall of Fame pitcher, the architects of the 1950 pennant-winner.

cancelled. Pennock then bought pitcher Charlie Stanceau from the Yanks. In June he got rid of Hal Spindel and Jimmy Wasdell, left over from '45, and brought back outfielder-first baseman Vance Dinges from the minors. And so it went, all season, as Pennock demonstrated that he would keep looking for good players and dropping those who did not produce.[3]

The Phillies in early May had a dismal 2–7 road trip, but *Inquirer* reporter Art Morrow found a ray of sunshine: "[T]he journey was successful if for no other reason than the discovery of a new left-fielder who promises to develop into one of baseball's brightest lights. Indeed, burly Del Ennis … already has begun casting his shadow over rival clubs." One of the two road wins was a 7–1 victory over the Cubs in which Ennis slammed two home runs.[4]

Morrow was right: long after the May 1946 road trip was forgotten, Del Ennis was hitting home runs and driving in runs for the Phillies. Ennis very quickly became one of the most dependable run-producers in Phillies' history. He hit .313 with seventeen home runs and 73 RBIs as a rookie in

1946, and his insertion into the regular lineup, along with that of Emil Verban, got the '46 Phils started.

The victories began to come with more frequency, and on June 21 Schoolboy Rowe's three-hitter over Cincinnati lifted the Phils into seventh place. Two more wins against the Reds the next day moved them into sixth. On Sunday the 23rd, they won the opener of a doubleheader over Cincinnati, 5–4, on Tabor's twelfth-inning home run; the second game ran afoul of the Sunday curfew (the blue laws were not completely gone) and wound up a tie. After a day off, they beat the Cardinals, 5–3, before a huge crowd of 36,356.

Indeed, the Philadelphia fans were turned on by Ben Chapman's hustlers, and big crowds became a regular occurrence. The club's season attendance record was broken on July 24, as the team returned from a long road swing with Rowe's 2–0 shutout of the Pirates. For the year attendance peaked at 1,045,247, the first time any Philadelphia ballclub had drawn more than a million spectators.

The Phillies finished fifth in 1946, with a record of 69–85. They made money, and they unveiled some real talent. Ennis and Verban had excellent years, and they were joined on the National League All-Star squad by Frank McCormick, who set a fielding record for first basemen with one lone error all season.

Northey hit sixteen home runs, and Johnny Wyrostek batted .281 while playing a graceful center field. The pitching after Rowe, who was 11–4 and 2.12, was shaky, but southpaws Oscar Judd and Ken Raffensberger had good earned run averages despite losing records. Andy Seminick, who had struggled to hit wartime pitching while learning how to catch, showed signs of progress in 1946 and became the team's regular backstop. Coaches Benny Bengough and Cy Perkins, both old catchers, worked diligently with Seminick. Herb Pennock was starting to fit some of the pieces together, and 1946 represented real progress.

1947 was a watershed season in baseball, the year that Brooklyn's Jackie Robinson overcame the unwritten but quite effective ban against black players. Robinson led the way, but before the season was out he was followed by teammate Dan Bankhead, Cleveland's Larry Doby, and Henry Thompson and Willard Brown of the St. Louis Browns. Rickey's gamble on Robinson had paid off, and baseball was changed for the better.

The Phillies had a troubling season. Ben Chapman and some of his players became the objects of much criticism for the rough way they treated Brooklyn's Robinson when they first played the Dodgers. The team opened a series at Ebbets Field on April 22, and Chapman directed a stream of racial insults and taunts at Robinson. "At no time in my life have I heard racial venom and dugout abuse to match the abuse that Ben sprayed on Robinson that night," wrote Brooklyn columnist Harold Parrott. "Chapman mentioned everything from thick lips to the supposedly extra-thick Negro skull ... [and] the repulsive sores and diseases he said Robinson's teammates would become infected with if they touched the towels or combs he used."[5]

Three or four of the Phils players, along with trainer Dusty Cooke, joined in Chapman's abuse throughout the three-game series, much to the discomfort of first baseman Howie Schultz, newly acquired from the Dodgers, who had gotten to know and like Robinson during spring training.

Robinson later wrote that "this day of all the unpleasant days in my life, brought me nearer to cracking up than I ever had been." He knew that Chapman was a Southerner with a reputation for bigotry from his playing days, but he almost let it get to him. He thought, "To hell with Mr. Rickey's 'noble experiment.'" He felt he "could throw down my bat, stride over to that Phillies dugout, grab one of those white sons of bitches and smash his teeth in with my despised black fist," and then walk away from it all — just the kind of reaction Chapman was trying to provoke. But he contained himself, said nothing, and went on to play.[6]

In the meantime, Chapman's conduct did not go unnoticed. Spectators sitting near the visiting dugout wrote letters to Happy Chandler, protesting Chapman's behavior, and syndicated columnist Walter Winchell excoriated the Phillies manager on his national radio broadcast. Chandler notified Carpenter that the conduct of his manager was out of bounds and must cease.

Chapman defended himself, asserting that bench jockeying based on players' personal characteristics, ethnicity, and religion, was an old and established tradition; he wanted to see whether Robinson could take it. Chapman drew some isolated support for his position, but the general consensus was that the abuse poured on Robinson was unacceptable. In addition, it brought the white members of the Dodgers together in support of Robinson. One Phillie, infielder Lee Handley, apologized to Robinson.[7]

When the Dodgers made their first visit to Philadelphia, in early May, Robinson was turned away from the Benjamin Franklin Hotel, where the Brooklyn team was staying. Pennock had attempted to dissuade Rickey from bringing Robinson to Philadelphia, saying, "[You] just can't bring that nigger here with the rest of your team, Branch. We're just not ready for that sort of thing yet." When Pennock suggested that the Phillies would boycott the games, Rickey said the Dodgers would gladly accept forfeits.

Instead, they decided to have a conciliatory photograph taken of Robinson and Chapman together, one of the most uncomfortable-looking pic-
tures in baseball's gallery.[8]

The Phillies went on from this unsavory start to fall back into the cellar. They started off well enough, but by mid–June they had dropped to
seventh and soon were last. In September, only a late-season collapse by
Pittsburgh enabled the two Pennsylvania clubs to share seventh and eighth
place.

The highlight of a dark season came on May 3, when Pennock swapped
outfielder Ron Northey, hitting a disappointing .255, to the Cardinals, in
exchange for outfielder Harry Walker, who was poking along at a .200 clip.
Walker caught fire with the Phillies and never stopped hitting. In 130 games
with Philadelphia, Walker hit .371, and his season average of .363 led the
league by 46 points over the runner-up. Walker's 16 triples also topped
the National League. Walker fascinated the local fans with his habit of
backing out of the box after every pitch, removing his cap, and smooth-
ing back his thinning hair, and they were soon calling him "Harry the
Hat." His was the first batting title for the Phillies since the early Chuck
Klein days.

The club's attendance dropped to 907,332, and it would undoubtedly
have fallen much further without Walker's hitting heroics and the large
numbers of black people who came to the ballpark to see the Dodgers and
Jackie Robinson. On May 11, 41,660 spectators— the largest baseball crowd
ever in Shibe Park — showed up to see a doubleheader with Brooklyn.

Wyrostek, Ennis, Verban, and Seminick provided some batting
backup to Walker, and two elderly veterans, Rowe and knuckleballer Emil
"Dutch" Leonard, from the Senators, were the team's most effective pitchers, often combining to pitch the two games of the usual Sunday doubleheader. Late in the season, three youngsters, third baseman Willie Jones,
shortstop Granny Hamner, and second baseman Ralph "Putsy" Caballero,
made brief appearances, signs of things to come, and in the last game of
the year Chapman gave a start to 18-year-old southpaw Curt Simmons,
who responded with a 3–1 five-hitter over the Giants.

Simmons, from nearby Egypt, Pennsylvania, had been the object of
a spirited bidding war among a number of teams, and Pennock won his
rights with a $60,000 bonus offer. The Phillies and scout Chuck Ward
signed another young pitcher with promise, a graduate of Michigan State
named Robin Evan Roberts, giving the righthander a $25,000 bonus for
signing. More pieces were falling into place.

On June 14, 1947, however, Pennock made a terrible trade, sending lefty
Kenny Raffensberger and another player to Cincinnati for a lumbering

backstop named Al Lakeman, who hit .159 and .162 in his two seasons in Philadelphia. Raffensberger, who had been a good if unlucky pitcher in a Phillies uniform, won 89 games for the Reds during his six-plus years in Cincinnati. Pennock did not have much chance to make up for the Lakeman trade, for he died on January 30, 1948, just shy of his 54th birthday. He missed by a few weeks learning of his election to the Hall of Fame, and he obviously never saw the fruits of his labor in Philadelphia. Nevertheless, it was universally recognized that the Phillies' 1950 pennant-winner was Herb Pennock's creation.[9]

One of the most unexpected occurrences in postwar Philadelphia was the collapse of the long-entrenched Republican organization. In the fall of 1947, a vigorous young Democratic attorney, a Yale-educated ex-Marine named Richardson Dilworth, ran a hard-hitting campaign for mayor against the incumbent, the bleak and uninspiring Bernard Samuel, naming names and citing cases in the corrupt city administration. The creaky machine was able to eke out one last victory, electing Samuel to another term, but it was the last time.

It had long been maintained, without any empirical evidence, that Republicans were A's fans while Democrats, what there were of them in Philadelphia, supported the downtrodden Phillies. Now, as the Phillies rose in popular favor, the Democratic party prepared to take over the city. Cause-and-effect, or sheer coincidence? No one could say, of course, but the fact of both these developments taking place soon became evident.

Dilworth and his close associate Joseph Sill Clark, Jr., like Dilworth an Ivy League product from a major Center City law firm, resuscitated the Democratic party, so long submerged in Republican Philadelphia. The Democrats, usually happy to receive whatever crumbs the dominant party threw to them, rose up and captured the city. In 1949, Dilworth was elected city treasurer and Clark controller, and two years later, after the approval in 1950 of a new City Charter, Clark became the first Democratic mayor in many long decades. A combination of patrician reformers and savvy politicos put the Democrats on top, and a half century later they were still there. An early *Daily News* comment decried the possibility of "Silly and Dilly [ruling] over Philly," but as the calendar turned over to the year 2001 many observers and historians rated Richardson Dilworth Philadelphia's man of the 20th century.

The Democratic takeover, though, was still in the future in 1948, and the Phillies, too, seemed to be marking time. They finished sixth, with a 66–88 record, but in fact more of the pieces of the team of the future fell into place. Over the winter, two trades with Cincinnati procured versatile Bert Haas and Eddie Miller, long one of the National League's premier shortstops. With Miller at shortstop, young Granny Hamner at second, and third base shared by Caballero and Haas, the infield was in fair shape. Dick Sisler, son of the immortal George, was picked up in a trade with the Cardinals and installed at first base, where he hit .274 with eleven home runs.

Defending batting champion Harry Walker's brief holdout forced Chapman to bring in a replacement outfielder from the Utica club. The newcomer was a 21-year-old, towheaded Nebraskan named Richie Ashburn, only 5'10" but fast, faster by far than what Philadelphia fans were used to. He had no power and choked way up on the bat, but he beat out bunts and infield grounders, he poked hits through the infield, and he dropped little line drives in front of the outfielders. "He was very aggressive, competitive, and intense," said Andy Seminick, "although off the field he was a funny guy with dry humor." Ashburn started the year in left, but when Walker slumped and was benched Richie moved to center field. Walker, when he got back into the lineup, played left and Ashburn was in center for good. He covered all of center field and half of right and left, and as he skittered and dashed around the greensward, oldtimers said the Phillies hadn't seen anything like him since the days of Billy Hamilton, or perhaps Roy Thomas.[10]

The fans fell in love with Ashburn, a devotion which continued to the day he died in 1997, more than thirty years into his tenure as a broadcaster for the club. In his freshman year, Richie batted .333, put together a 23-game hitting streak, and led the league with 32 stolen bases, even though his season came to a premature end late in August when he broke a finger sliding into second base. For his achievements, Ashburn was named "Rookie of the Year" by *The Sporting News.*

Del Ennis hit .290 for the '48 Phils, with 30 homers and 95 RBIs, and Walker batted .292 in his curtailed season. The veteran pitchers Leonard and Rowe were 22–27 between them, although both hurled fairly effectively. Nineteen-year-old Curt Simmons, still learning to pitch, went 7–13, and silver-haired lefty Ken Heintzelman was a loser at 6–11.

Young Robin Roberts, the bonus baby from Michigan State, started the year in Wilmington, where he was 9–1, and joined the Phillies in June. He lost his first start, 2–0 to the Pirates, but he impressed all who watched him with his good stuff, his control, and his poise. Seminick said of Roberts, "There was something special about him. He had a lot of velocity and his control was fantastic.. You put a glove here and there and he'd hit it, even as a rookie." For the season, Roberts was 7–9, with a 3.10 earned run average.[11]

During the All-Star break, Bob Carpenter decided it was time for a change in the leadership of the club. The volatile Chapman was not the

Hall of Fame outfielder and longtime broadcaster Richie Ashburn.

man to manage a team of promising youngsters, so Ben was fired. (Chapman's vicious treatment of Jackie Robinson did not place his job in jeopardy; he was released for the more grievous sin of losing, with a 37–42 record at the end.) Carpenter announced the change with the enigmatic averment that "there is a difference between firing a man and concluding business with him."[12]

Coach (and former trainer) Dusty Cooke ran the team for thirteen games before Carpenter's new selection arrived. He was 37-year-old Eddie Sawyer, a biology teacher at Ithaca College in the off-season who never played in the big leagues but was well-known to the team's younger players, many of whom had played for him when he managed Phillies farms at Utica and Toronto. Del Ennis said, "Sawyer was a very different type of manager than Ben Chapman. He was mild-mannered, a professor. He grew on us. We learned a lot of baseball under Eddie Sawyer." The Phillies won 23 games and lost 40 for Sawyer the rest of the year and remained in sixth place.[13]

The '49 Phillies, though, moved into the first division and demonstrated that they were indeed a coming contender. Over the offseason, the team made several deals with the Chicago Cubs which resulted in pitchers Hank Borowy and Russ Meyer, first baseman Eddie Waitkus, and outfielder Bill Nicholson coming to the Quaker City in exchange for Harry Walker, pitchers Dutch Leonard and Walt Dubiel, and some cash. The trades strengthened the pitching staff, put a top-notch performer on first base, and gave the outfield added punch with slugger Nicholson and Dick Sisler, moved from first.

The farm system produced a number of players, Willie "Puddin' Head" Jones, who took over as the regular third baseman, a big strong catcher named Stan Lopata, and outfielders Stan Hollmig and Jackie Mayo. The aging Eddie Miller was moved to second base and Hamner took over at shortstop, where he was soon acknowledged as one of the league's best. Sawyer made Jim Konstanty, a veteran picked up from the minors near the end of the '48 season, his main man in the bullpen.

Konstanty, who had disappointed in earlier tours with the Reds and Braves and had been mediocre when Sawyer had him at Toronto, took hold of the relief job and posted a 9–5 record in 53 games in 1949, with seven saves (although the latter statistic had not yet been invented as a means of measuring relievers). And Konstanty was just warming up. His repertoire, which featured a palm ball, slow stuff, and impeccable control, baffled the big swingers of the National League. Konstanty had a friend back in his home town of Oneonta, New York, an undertaker named Andy Skinner, whom he would consult when his pitching was going badly, and Skinner seemed able to straighten him out every time.

Meyer, who bore the nickname "Mad Monk" because of a fiery temper which sometimes boiled out of control, ran up a 17–8 record, while Heintzelman was 17–10. Young Robin Roberts, showing unmistakable signs of potential greatness, was 15–15, and Borowy was 12–12. Simmons, still just 20 years old, struggled to a 4–10 record, and ancient Schoolboy Rowe posted a 3–7 record in his final season.[14]

Ashburn slipped to .284, admittedly full of himself and learning for the first time that baseball will bite you as soon as you start to take it for granted. But the rookie Jones hit 19 home runs, and Ennis hit 25, with 110 runs batted in and a .302 average. Andy Seminick, gradually becoming a quality catcher, banged out 24 fourbaggers.

Three of Seminick's circuit clouts came in one game against Cincinnati, on June 2. In the eighth inning of that game, the Phils exploded for a record five home runs, teeing off on Ken Raffensberger and two relievers. Seminick hit two of his three that inning, along with blasts by Ennis, Jones, and Rowe.

Waitkus, the acquisition from the Cubs, quickly became a favorite with Phillies fans, with his graceful play around first base and his timely hitting, and trouble seemed the last thing to be heading his way. On June 15, however, with the club in Chicago, Waitkus received a note at the Edgewater Beach, the team hotel, asking him to come to the room of a young woman named Ruth Ann Steinhagen. Waitkus promptly did so, but his reception was not what he expected. When he arrived, the lady shot him in the chest with a .22 rifle. The slug ripped through Waitkus's chest and lung and came to rest near his spine.

The 19-year-old Ruth Ann, mentally unbalanced, turned out to be a worshipper (literally) of the ex-Cub; in her room at home she had created a shrine to Waitkus, and the trade of her idol to Philadelphia pushed her over the edge. If she could not have the 29-year-old bachelor, she apparently reasoned, no one else could either. Ruth Ann Steinhagen was placed in a mental institution, while the seriously-wounded first baseman underwent five operations before starting a rehab program. His 1949 season was over, and Sisler moved back to first base, contributing solid .289 hitting to the team's attack.

The team, promising as it appeared with its mixture of veterans and fuzzy-cheeked youngsters, was poking along in fifth place in mid–August, the players getting into sloppy and careless habits, when Sawyer read the riot act to them at the Polo Grounds, chewing them out for their lackadaisical play, their unfocussed thinking, and their conduct off the field. He imposed a curfew and a daily meal allowance limit. The unexpected scorching by the softspoken Sawyer had its intended effect. The club won 16 of its last 26 games for an 81–73 record and a third-place finish. The Phillies convinced themselves they could play with anyone in the National League.

Chapter 11

Jubilee

Nineteen hundred fifty was the fiftieth season of Connie Mack's tenure as manager of the Athletics, and the year had been designated his Golden Jubilee. The A's expected to have a contending team in 1950, especially after making several major trades. Instead, the club bombed, and it was the Phillies for whom 1950 was particularly memorable.

After many seasons of broadcasting only home games, with occasional road games done through telegraphic reconstruction (what were called "ticker-tape games"), the Athletics and Phillies decided to broadcast all their games live, both home and away. The A's games would be on radio station WIBG, long the town's baseball station, while the Phillies would be carried by WPEN. The longtime voice of Philadelphia baseball, Byrum Saam, with his sidekick Claude Haring, elected to stick with the A's, so the Phillies signed on Gene Kelly, a tall, colorful West Virginian, to cover their games. Kelly, with his country expressions and exhortations to his listeners, was something different for Philadelphia fans, who were accustomed to the mellow voice of By Saam telling them what was happening with no fancy frills added. "Tug on your caps, boys and girls," Kelly would say, "rub your noses, and let's get our Fightin' Phils some runs!"

The Phillies looked forward to the new season with eager anticipation. Eddie Waitkus was back in harness, and the doctors told club officials the first baseman would be physically as good as ever. His return freed Dick Sisler for duty in the outfield. There was a question mark at second base, where rookie Mike Goliat had been brought up from the minors and given the job the last couple of months of the '49 season, though second base was not his natural position. Goliat hit only .212, but this was still better than the fading Eddie Miller had done. Miller was waived to the Cardinals in early April, so Goliat, from Yatesboro out in western Pennsylvania, was the second baseman.

The rest of the infield was set, with rising stars in Hamner and Willie Jones. To go with Ennis, Ashburn, and Sisler in the outfield, Sawyer had Bill Nicholson, the former Cub home run slugger, and Dick Whitman from the Dodgers. Seminick and Stan Lopata, a hulking youngster from Detroit, would take care of the catching, while Roberts, Heintzelman, Meyer, Simmons, and reliever Konstanty would handle the bulk of the pitching. Things looked promising, the biggest anxiety was taken care of with Waitkus's return, and Eddie Sawyer was hopeful.

Spring training gave encouragement to the Phillies, particularly when Curt Simmons had a great camp. The Phillies knew that Simmons had all the makings of a fine pitcher, but control problems and immaturity had hindered him his first two seasons. If these problems could be overcome, as appeared likely in Florida, there was no telling what Simmons might do.

The Phillies opened at home. Before a healthy throng of 29,074, Eddie Sawyer's men unveiled their new red and white pin-striped uniforms and their dashing style of play. Robin Roberts took the mound against Brooklyn's giant hard-throwing righthander, Don Newcombe. These were the Dodgers of Robinson and Reese, of Snider and Hodges, the mighty arm of Carl Furillo and the magic glove of Billy Cox, of Campanella and Preacher Roe, the defending champions, and as they emerged from the visitors' dugout, loose and confident, Philadelphians who were predicting a flag for the home team began to feel a bit presumptuous.

The psychological lump was the first obstacle, and Roberts took care of that on Opening Day. He showed that he threw as hard and as accurately as Newcombe, and he made it appear easy. He throttled the Dodgers while his teammates, led by unsung Mike Goliat, pounded Newcombe for a 9–1 Phillies victory. After the Phillies had scored five runs against Newcombe, Jackie Robinson came to the plate and asked Seminick, "What do you guys think you're going to do, win the pennant?" "You bet," said Andy. The new uniforms looked good, and so did the players wearing them. The Dodgers? They could be beaten, though Newcombe and his mates would be heard from again.[1]

Through April the Phils played only .500 ball, and they were handicapped by a seven-day suspension drawn by Russ Meyer, the result of a wild argument with umpire Al Barlick. But with May came good times. On May 10 the Phils were rained out in Pittsburgh but moved into first place when Ken Raffensberger of the Reds shut out Brooklyn. The next night, Roberts beat the Pirates, 3–2, forcing slugger Ralph Kiner to pop up with the game on the line, and the team came home to Philadelphia leading the league.

They received a rousing welcome from their fans at the old B&O station, and Eddie Sawyer said, "I feel we'll be hard to beat." Still, from mid–May to October was a long time. The young Phillies, now being called the "Whiz Kids" for their combination of youth and enthusiasm, would be tested. Sawyer was just the right kind of manager for them. Coach Maje McDonnell said, "Sawyer was tremendous with the young ballplayers, very patient. He was a good man, knew the game, and just let the boys play. And they played relaxed…. He was a leader of men."[2]

In his next outing, Roberts hooked up with Ewell Blackwell of the Reds, one of the league's premier pitchers, a side-arming righthander with a wicked buggy-whip motion and a nasty disposition on the mound, on a night when both pitchers were at their best. Ashburn and Hamner led off the first inning with scratch hits and Waitkus walked. When Del Ennis grounded into a double play, Ashburn scored, but the Phillies got nothing more from Blackwell. Roberts, though, gave up only two hits and made one run stand up to win. The Phillies now had supreme confidence in Roberts and in themselves; they began to believe they really could win a pennant.

When Simmons pitched a 7–1 three-hitter over the Giants, aided by Sisler and Ennis home runs, the Phils had won six in a row and stretched their league lead to a game and a half. Sisler, at .372, was second in the league in hitting and was one of five Phillies over .300 at that point, Jones, Ennis, Waitkus, and Ashburn the others.

The Dodgers were not playing dead, however, and neither were the Cardinals. On May 20, Brooklyn beat the Pirates twice while Bob Rush of the Cubs stopped the Phillies, and Burt Shotton's Dodgers went back into first place. Through late May and early June, the Phils see-sawed back and forth with the Dodgers and Cards.

Memorial Day was a particularly bad day for Sawyer's men. They lost both ends of a doubleheader at Ebbets Field, 7–6 in ten innings and 6–4. They left fifteen men on base in each game. Duke Snider hit three home runs and Robinson and Campanella one each as the Dodgers demonstrated that they were still the power team in the National League. By the end of the day the Phillies were in third place. The pressure of playing every game with first place at stake was maturing the Whiz Kids very quickly.

As the summer moved on, the Phillies were involved in all manner of excitement. On June 7, rookie righthander Bob Miller won his fourth straight game, beating the Reds, 4–0, to move the Phillies to within a half game of first-place Brooklyn. One week and a few bad games later, the Phils were 3½ games behind the Cardinals. By June 20, as the seesaw continued, they were only a half game behind the Cards but the Dodgers were another game in front.

On the 27th Simmons, with help from Konstanty, beat Boston's Warren Spahn, 3–2, to take over first place. The next day Johnny Sain of the
Braves beat them, but on the 30th Konstanty beat Brooklyn's Newcombe,
8–5, before 31,000 fans at Shibe Park, and Sawyer's men moved back into
the lead. On Sunday July 2, with 35,000 in the stands, the Phils took the
first game of a doubleheader from the Dodgers on a home run by Bill
Nicholson, only to have an 8–0 second game lead slip away, resulting in a
frustrating 8–8 tie in a game halted by the Sunday curfew.

On the 4th of July, the Fightin' Phils, as they were now being called,
split with Boston and at that traditional milestone of the baseball season
were in second place, 1½ games behind St. Louis. The Braves were 2½ out,
the Dodgers four. It was anyone's pennant race. Through the early weeks
of July the Cards, Braves, and Phillies took turns in first place.

Simmons won key games for Sawyer, Konstanty was steady and solid
in relief, Roberts was a big winner, and Nicholson, Ennis, Goliat, Hamner, and Jones took turns coming up with big hits. Two freshman pitchers, Bob Miller and Bubba Church, were welcome surprises. Richie
Ashburn seemed to be on base all the time. On July 18, Sawyer put Waitkus in the leadoff spot, moved Ashburn to second, and dropped Hamner
to sixth. With these switches, everything came together. The team won
consistently, took first place for good on July 25, and soon built a substantial lead.

Konstanty was fabulous. His appearance on August 15, when he helped
Simmons stop Sain and the Braves to stretch the lead to six games, was
his 53rd of the season. At a time when starting pitchers were expected to
complete their games, Konstanty was carving out a new role for the relief
specialist. Game after game the big reliever came on to stop the opposition with his assortment of junk and tight control.

Nicholson, asked about Konstanty's palm ball, said, "It comes up to
the plate, looks you in the eye, stops, waits until you drop your bat, and
then goes on." Konstanty called himself a "mushball pitcher," but he
admitted that in his own mind, "every hitter I face is in a slump."[3]

The city was alive with the Phillies. When Roberts beat the Braves on
August 16 to run his record to 16–5 and drop second-place Boston seven
games back, City Council decided to look into the possibility of playing
the World Series at huge (and for baseball, oddly-shaped) Municipal Stadium. Nothing came of that idea, fortunately, but it suggests the pennant
fever which had gripped the town.

On August 22 the Phils left on a western swing, and Roberts got them
off on the right foot, stopping the Reds, 4–3, on a Del Ennis hit in the
ninth inning. The lead was 5½ over Brooklyn. They lost a couple, but

Konstanty pulled them out of it with his finest effort of the season, giving up only five hits in nine relief innings as the Phils beat the Pirates at Forbes Field 9–7 in fifteen innings. When rookie Bubba Church won in Boston on September 1, the lead over the Dodgers was back up to seven games. Simmons beat Sain, 2–0, the next day, and a mob of fans jammed the Philadelphia airport to welcome the team home with its big lead.

Labor Day at Shibe Park, though, was a semi-disaster. Jim Hearn and Sal Maglie of the Giants shut the Phillies out twice, but Brooklyn lost two to Billy Southworth's Braves, so the margin stayed at seven games. When the Dodgers lost to the Giants the next day, they fell 7½ back.

On the 6th, the Phillies lost another doubleheader, Church and Simmons going down to the Dodgers, 2–0 and 3–2. When Roberts lost to Carl Erskine the next day, 3–2, the club's lead was cut to 4½ games and uneasiness set in, especially as it was learned that slugger Bill Nicholson had been hospitalized with diabetes and was lost for the season.

On September 8, Russ Meyer beat Brooklyn, 4–3, to restore a 5½ game lead. On the 9th, Konstanty beat the Braves 7–6 on a clutch hit by Willie Jones, and Maglie's shutout of the Dodgers made the gap 6½ games again.

The game on the 9th was Curt Simmons's last appearance. To keep their young southpaw out of the draft, the Phillies had arranged for Curt to join the Pennsylvania National Guard. When the North Korean attack on South Korea earlier in the summer resulted in the Guard's call to active duty, Simmons had to report to Camp Atterbury, Indiana.

Both the Phils and Dodgers lost on September 10. Two days later, Roberts came up with a gem, beating the Cards' Max Lanier 1–0 on a Seminick homer. On the 14th, Jones singled home the winner in the ninth as Konstanty beat St. Louis, 3–2.

The next night the Phils won a twi-night doubleheader from Cincinnati, but they did it the hard way. In the third inning of the opener, Ted Kluszewski, the mammoth first baseman of the Reds, smashed a line drive at Bubba Church that hit the young pitcher in the face just under his left eye and caromed all the way down the right field line. Church spun around before falling to the ground. Russ Meyer, one of the first to reach him, said, "I thought Bubba was dead. It was really scary." Church never lost consciousness, though, and he was carted off by Jimmy Bloodworth and trainer Frank Wiechec. Ken Heintzelman was called in hurriedly, and he stopped the Reds the rest of the way, winning 2–1 on a Seminick home run.[4]

In the nightcap the Reds took an early 5–0 lead over Roberts on loose play by the Phils and a couple of big hits by Joe Adcock. The Phillies fought back and eventually tied it on Hamner's ninth-inning double. Konstanty came in to pitch the tenth. As the night wore on, Konstanty and Reds pitcher Herman Wehmeier matched scoreless innings until the 18th, when the weary Phillies ace suddenly lost his control, walking the bases loaded and yielding a two-run single to Kluszewski. The Whiz Kids came back. Ennis doubled, and Sisler singled. Hamner's fly scored Ennis from third, and Stan Lopata slashed a triple to tie the game again.

In the 19th, after reliever Blix Donnelly retired the Reds in the top of the inning, Waitkus and Ashburn singled, Jones walked, and Ennis singled home the run that ended the marathon evening. Though the Phillies had two wins to show for their twenty-eight innings of work, the loss of Church further weakened Eddie Sawyer's mound staff.

The next afternoon the tired Phils were no match for Blackwell, who beat them 2–0 with a three-hitter. Bob Miller pulled a muscle in his right shoulder to load more woes onto the pitching corps. On Sunday the 17th, Russ Meyer hurt his ankle in a winning 5–3 effort over the Pirates. Hamner's three-run home run won that one, and Konstanty saved it. The lead was still 7½, over Boston now, but the Phillies were in danger of running out of able-bodied pitchers.

On Tuesday night, Frank Hiller of the Cubs beat Roberts, 1–0, on a Hank Sauer four-bagger, and the lead fell to 6½ games. On the 20th, Konstanty beat the Cubs, 9–6, in relief of Meyer, for his 16th win of the year, with the help of two homers by Mike Goliat. It was big Jim's 68th appearance of the year, and the lead over the Dodgers and Braves was up to 7½ games again. It looked as if the Whiz Kids were in, and the 100,000 people who swamped the front office with World Series ticket orders on the 20th obviously thought so, too.

On the 21st, the Braves and Dodgers each won. The Phils were idle both that day and the next, and on the 23rd Newcombe and the Dodgers came into Shibe Park and beat Roberts 3–2 on a three-run home run by Gil Hodges. It was Newcombe's 19th win, and Robbie's third failure in his try for his twentieth. The next day Bubba Church had his first outing since the Kluszewski liner. It was a disaster. Erv Palica worked for Brooklyn, pitched a two-hit shutout, and hit a grand slam home run. The 11–0 loss cut the Philadelphia lead to five games.

The next day the Phillies went to Braves Field for two with Boston. Heintzelman won the opener, 12–4, but Konstanty, though tying the old record for most games pitched in a season with 70, was hit hard and lost the second game, 5–3. Infielder Gene Mauch, with a single, two doubles, and a sacrifice, led the Braves. The Dodgers split a pair with New York, so the lead stayed at five. On the 26th, Ennis had four hits including his 31st homer to beat the Braves, 8–7, and eliminate them from the race.

On September 27, the Phillies' slide became serious. They lost two to the Giants at the Polo Grounds, 8–7 and 5–0. Roberts was hit hard in the opener, and Church was routed in the first inning of the nightcap on Bobby Thomson's grand slam. The Dodgers split with the Braves to cut the Phillies' lead to four games.

In the tenth inning of the first game at New York, Monte Irvin slammed into Phillies catcher Andy Seminick as he scored the winning run, and in the collision a bone in Seminick's ankle was broken. Several incidents, all involving Seminick, had soured relations between the two teams, but the tough, baldheaded catcher would not give the Giants the satisfaction of putting him on the bench. He played the rest of the season on Novocain, grimacing through the pain but staying in the lineup. Ennis said, "Andy was really a hard-nosed, aggressive catcher. He was strong like a bull … he played so tough and was so good at blocking the plate."[5]

On the 28th the Whiz Kids lost two more at the Polo Grounds, both by the score of 3–1. Heintzelman and Roberts (starting for the second day in a row) both pitched well, but Maglie and Sheldon Jones pitched better. The Dodgers split another doubleheader to cut the Phils' lead to three games, but their loss in the second game clinched a tie for the pennant for the Phillies. All Sawyer's boys had to do was win one or the Dodgers lose one and it would be all over. But when?

The next day the Dodgers won two games from Boston in their third successive twinbill, while the Phillies were idle. The Phils brought a two-game lead into Ebbets Field for the last two games of the campaign. The young Philadelphia players, few of whom had ever faced pressure like this, were going head-to-head with the defending champions. Two Brooklyn wins would bring on a three-game playoff for the pennant. The battered Phillies' pitching staff would stand little chance in that situation.

On Saturday, Sawyer sent sore-shouldered Bob Miller to oppose Palica, but Brooklyn chased him with four runs in the fifth. The Whiz Kids battled back with three runs in the sixth, but Roy Campanella hit a home run with two on in the eighth off Konstanty, and that was it. It was Jim's 74th game of the year, and he was visibly losing effectiveness.

Stan Baumgartner of the *Inquirer*, who had pitched for the club's only pennant-winner in 1915, wrote: "Only Robin Roberts, young righthanded hurler from Michigan State College, stood between the Phillies and the most colossal collapse of a pennant aspirant in the history of the National League."[6]

To face Roberts, going with two days' rest, Burt Shotton, the ex-Phillies skipper who now managed the Dodgers, sent out Newcombe, who had opposed the Phillies' ace so often that season. 35,073 Dodger fans, the year's largest crowd at Ebbets Field, packed the stands. If the Dodgers' fireballer beat the Phils, all the cards would be stacked in Brooklyn's favor in the playoff games to follow.

Both pitchers had their good stuff and dueled on even terms through five innings. In the sixth, hits by Sisler, Ennis, and Jones gave the Phillies a one-run lead. In the bottom of the inning Pee Wee Reese hit a fluke home run, a fly ball that hit the screen in right field and lodged on the shelf at the top of the fence. The ball just sat there, and the Phillies could do nothing but watch Reese circle the bases.

With the game now tied, Roberts pulled himself together and retired the Brooks in the seventh and eighth innings. In the bottom of the ninth, trouble came quickly. Cal Abrams led off with a walk, and Reese singled to left. Men on first and second with none out, and the fat part of the lineup coming up. Then came the play that saved the season. Duke Snider smashed a hit to center. Ashburn, playing shallow with the winning run on second, picked up the ball almost as it landed and fired an accurate one-bounce shot to the plate. Third base coach Milt Stock sent Abrams home, but catcher Stan Lopata had the ball in plenty of time to tag out the astonished runner. "I had Abrams by maybe 20 feet, if not more," Lopata said. The Dodgers were stunned.[7]

Roberts, still in a tight situation, walked Robinson intentionally and then got another huge out when Carl Furillo hit a pop foul to Waitkus. Hodges flied to Ennis, a ball which Del lost in the sun but which hit him in the chest and then landed in his glove, for the final out of the inning. The Phillies were still in the ballgame.

Buoyed by their narrow escape, the Phils came to bat in the tenth. Roberts led off with a single to center, and Waitkus followed with another hit to the same area. Ashburn bunted, but Robbie was forced on a close play at third. Newcombe got ahead of Dick Sisler in the count, one and two. The big Dodger righthander came in with a fastball on the outside part of the plate, and Sisler lashed it on a line into the left field stands. The Philadelphia bench erupted as Waitkus, Ashburn, and Sisler crossed the plate.

There was no way Robin Roberts would cough up a three-run lead in that situation, and he made quick work of Brooklyn in the bottom of the tenth. Campanella flied to Jack Mayo, who had gone in to play left field. Jim Russell batted for Billy Cox and struck out, and Tommy Brown, hitting for Newcombe, fouled out to Waitkus.

As Brown's ball nestled in the first baseman's mitt at 4:39 p.m., the unthinkable had happened. The Philadelphia Phillies, perennial doormats of the National League, had won their second pennant, their first in thirty-five years. On the gutty pitching of Robin Roberts, the fantastic throw by Richie Ashburn, and the clutch home run by Dick Sisler, the Whiz Kids made good all the earlier heroics of Simmons, Ennis, Konstanty, Hamner, Church, Jones, Waitkus, Miller and the rest.

They came home from New York that night to the welcome of 30,000 fans at Thirtieth Street Station, and thousands of others at North Philadelphia Station and outside the Warwick Hotel, where the team buses brought the players. A warm and wonderful night it was, as Philadelphia celebrated its first championship since that of the A's of 1931. Factory whistles, ships' foghorns, auto horns, and firecrackers went off, and, the *Inquirer* noted, "the wild celebration lasted all night." The nosedive, the errors and the batting slump of the last week, the fears and tensions of the last few days, the horrors of the doubleheaders at the Polo Grounds— all was forgotten but the great and courageous play of the final game, when the Phillies, their backs to the wall, responded like champions and won their championship.[8]

After this, the World Series was an anticlimax — "almost an aftermath," Ennis called it. Not that the Phillies planned it that way. Worn out emotionally (*Newsweek* called "the last week of the baseball pennant race ... a psychological torture chamber"), physically tired, they were unable to match a Yankee team which was not really much better than they were.[9]

With Roberts having pitched ten tough innings on Sunday and Simmons in the army, there was much speculation about Sawyer's starter against Vic Raschi in the Series opener on Wednesday, the first World Series game in Philadelphia since 1931. On Tuesday, the Phils' skipper astounded the baseball world by announcing that the starting pitcher would be his great relief ace, Jim Konstanty.

It was a good gamble, except for one thing. The Phillies scored no runs at all against Raschi, picking up only two singles, by Jones and Seminick, and Konstanty lost, 1–0. He gave up a run in the fourth on a double by Bobby Brown and two outfield flies by Hank Bauer and Jerry Coleman, but he certainly justified Sawyer's faith in him, yielding only four hits in eight innings. 30,746 fans showed up, ready to shout for their Whiz Kids, but there was little to shout about.

Roberts lost the second game, 2–1, in ten innings, when Joe DiMaggio hit one out of the park. Again, it was difficult to fault the Phillies' pitching, but their hitters seemed to have died completely, except for Gran Hamner, who had a double and triple, and Ashburn and Waitkus with two hits each, against Yankee hurler Allie Reynolds.

On Friday October 6, the teams moved to Yankee Stadium, but the story was much the same, a 3–2 New York win, before 64,505 spectators, with shaky infield play the culprit in the Phillies' loss. Kenny Heintzelman squared off against New York's Ed Lopat in a battle of lefties, and the Phils led 2–1 going into the eighth. When Heintzelman ran out of gas and walked three in a row, Konstanty came in and got Brown to hit an easy grounder to short for what should have been the third out. Hamner fumbled it, and the tying run scored.

In the ninth, Hamner doubled off reliever Tom Ferrick and went to third on a sacrifice bunt, but he was thrown out at the plate on pinch-hitter Dick Whitman's infield roller. Russ Meyer got the first two outs in the home ninth before second baseman Jimmy Bloodworth misplayed Gene Woodling's grounder into a base hit. Phil Rizzuto hit one which Bloodworth knocked down but could not hold, and Jerry Coleman singled to left center to win the game.

In Game Four Sawyer sent Bob Miller against Whitey Ford, before 68,098. The Yanks roughed up the Phillie righthander for two runs in the first inning and added three more off Konstanty in the sixth, while the Phillies were unable to touch Ford. Down 5–0 in the ninth, the Phils scored two runs, with the help of a fly ball dropped by Woodling, to chase Ford before Allie Reynolds came on to close it out.

Four in a row is never a good way to lose a World Series, even when the first three games are by one run each. Time after time the Phils "were in a position where one hit — the softest sort of single — would have turned the tide." Not once did that all-important hit materialize. Even worse was the thought that the Phillies lost nine of their last ten games. The one they won, however, the pennant-clincher at Ebbets Field, was enough to assure their place in the books.[10]

It was a very satisfying season. Robin Roberts became the first pitcher to win twenty games for the Phillies since Pete Alexander, with his 20–11. Del Ennis led the league with 126 runs batted in. Ennis and Ashburn both batted over .300, and Simmons was 17–8 in his abbreviated season.[11]

Jim Konstanty, relief pitcher extraordinary, with his 74 games, 16–7 record, 2.66 ERA and 22 saves, was an easy choice as Most Valuable Player in the league, finishing well ahead of Stan Musial. Waitkus made a fine comeback from his gunshot wound. And Rich Ashburn, Dick Sisler, Granny Hamner, Andy Seminick, Willie Jones, Curt Simmons, Bob Miller, Mike Goliat, Stan Lopata, Bubba Church, Ken Heintzelman, Russ Meyer, Ralph Caballero, Dick Whitman, and the rest of the Whiz Kids carved out their special place in Philadelphia's baseball history. Not the best Philadelphia team ever, the 1950 Phillies club may well be the most beloved.

Chapter 12

Middle-Class Baseball

One can only guess just how much the Yankee sweep of the 1950 World Series took out of the young Phillies. The record shows that the promising Whiz Kids, winning their pennant probably a year ahead of reasonable expectations, performed at little better than a .500 pace for the next seven years, as they grew old. As a partial explanation of this, the record shows as well that the Phillies were one of the last major league clubs to employ black ballplayers. When their rivals were putting such men as Roy Campanella, Willie Mays, Henry Aaron, and Monte Irvin on the field, what the Phillies did was tantamount to fighting with one arm tied behind the back.

Certainly, 1950 was the high point of what Herb Pennock accomplished and, with Bob Carpenter foolishly trying to operate the club without a baseball man as general manager, the failure to remain a contender was to be expected. Yet, although Philadelphia fans had no more flags to contemplate, they had the pleasure of watching quality players like Robin Roberts, Del Ennis, Curt Simmons, Richie Ashburn, and Gran Hamner through the decade.

The 1950s were known as a time of gray conformity, as the country became accustomed to prosperity after the trials and trauma of the '30s and '40s, with their depression, war, and recovery. It was a time when the poison of McCarthyism spread across the land, and the Republican party under Dwight Eisenhower regained power after long years of wandering in the Rooseveltian wilderness. Conversely, Philadelphia became Democratic, with Joe Clark's election as mayor in 1951. Suburbia exploded in the '50s, as "white flight" started to undermine America's cities. Ownership of a television set became almost universal, and rock-and-roll displaced the old pop music. It was the Fifties, the age of tail fins on cars and "the sack" on women, and for a great many Americans it seemed like "the good times."

For Robert R.M. Carpenter and his Phillies, it was not the best of times but not, certainly, the worst. 1951 was bad, because the club came into the season as defending champion and plunged into the second division. With Simmons in the service, Eddie Sawyer knew that he would have to scratch for pitching, but he had Roberts, veterans Meyer and Heintzleman, second-year men Church and Miller, promising youngsters like Ken Johnson, Niles Jordan, Leo Cristante, Paul Stuffel, Lou Possehl, and Jocko Thompson, with Konstanty to bail out a lot of mistakes. The rest of the lineup that won the pennant was intact, so the Phillies expected to do well.

Instead, they were terrible. They won eighteen fewer games than the year before, finished in fifth place, and were never a factor in the race. Roberts won 21 and established himself as one of the premier hurlers in the game. Ashburn hit .344 and finished second to Musial in the batting race. There were few other bright spots. Konstanty, no miracle worker in 1951, was 4–11 with an ERA over four. Meyer and Heintzleman were little more successful than in 1950, and Bubba Church's improvement, to 15–11, was offset by Miller's arm trouble, which restricted him to just 34 innings of work. None of the youngsters came through, and Simmons was sorely missed.

Ennis fell way off from his 1950 performance. The rest of the team, with the exception of Ashburn and Willie Jones, followed suit. Waitkus, Sisler, Seminick, and Hamner all declined, and second base was a disaster area. Goliat hit poorly, went to the minors, and was finally shipped to the Browns. At different times, the Phillies' second baseman was Goliat, Putsy Caballero, Jimmy Bloodworth, veteran American Leaguer Eddie Pellagrini, Dodger castoff Tommy Brown, and a rookie named Dick Young. None of them hit much, and second base was as much a problem at the end of the season as at the beginning.

1951, of course, was the year of the Miracle of Coogan's Bluff, the incredible rush of the Giants which overcame a 13½ game Brooklyn lead in mid–August to set up the memorable playoff series ended by Bobby Thomson's historic home run. The Dodgers came into Shibe Park for the last three games of the season holding a scant half-game lead over Leo Durocher's Giants. On Friday night, Carl Erskine was unable to hold a three-run lead and Seminick's home run in the ninth won it for the Phils, 4–3, dropping Brooklyn into a tie for first. Saturday night Newcombe scattered seven hits in a 5–0 victory, but the Giants also won.

On Sunday, the last day of the season, the Giants won their game early while the Dodgers and Phillies were locked in a tense battle. The Phils took an early 6–1 lead against Preacher Roe, but the Dodgers battled back. They tied it at 8–8 in the eighth, and a great catch by Andy Pafko saved it in the ninth.

On and on it went, until the twelfth inning, when the Phillies loaded the bases against Newcombe with two outs. Eddie Waitkus slashed a low line drive over second base, a shot that had the death of Brooklyn's hopes written all over it, until from nowhere came Jackie Robinson, diving and perhaps catching the ball inches from the ground. Robin Roberts to this day maintains that the ball hit the ground and umpire Lon Warneke simply missed the call. Robinson knocked himself out momentarily on the play, but a couple of innings later he smashed a home run off Roberts to keep his team alive for greater heartbreak to come.

After the season, to rectify the second base problem, the Phillies negotiated a seven-player trade with Cincinnati, bringing them veteran second sacker Connie Ryan, along with pitcher Howard Fox and a short, round catcher named Forrest "Smoky" Burgess, a deeply religious man who neither smoked nor drank. The Phillies gave up Niles Jordan, Eddie Pellagrini, and two of the heroes of 1950, Seminick and Sisler.

Ryan was a help. He hit .241 with twelve homers and played consistently in the field. Ashburn slumped to .282, but Ennis rebounded to knock in 107 runs, Waitkus and Hamner hit much better, and Johnny Wyrostek, reclaimed from the Reds in a May 23 trade for Bubba Church, batted .274. Curt Simmons came back from the army and pitched very well, going 14–8 and 2.82.

The big story was Roberts. In 1952, Robbie won 28 games and lost only seven; he had an earned run average of 2.59, and he pitched 330 innings. He was a superb player, pitching the club back into the first division, dominating the league with his nervous mannerisms on the mound, his easy delivery, hard fastball, and uncanny control. In one of the great miscarriages of baseball justice, a big, slow Chicago outfielder named Hank Sauer, who hit .270 with 37 home runs for the fifth-place Cubs, edged out Roberts for the Most Valuable Player award.

From 1951 through 1957, Phillies teams tended to blend into one another. The Phils constituted the great middle class of the National League during these years. Over this period, Richardson Dilworth became mayor, defeating a former Princeton football star named Thacher Longstreth, while Joe Clark moved on to the U.S. Senate. Antoine "Fats" Domino sang "Blueberry Hill" in Pep's, at Broad and South, hometown favorites Eddie Fisher, the Four Aces, and Bill Haley ground out one hit record after another, and a popular saxophonist named Mike Pedicin led his group at Bay Shores in Somers Point, at the Jersey shore. A beautiful dark-haired stripper named Julie Gibson performed her "Dance of the Bashful Bride" at the Wedge, a nightclub at Broad and Ridge, Horn & Hardart's restaurants still promised "less work for mother," and Billy Kretchmer played at his jazz club on Latimer Street.

This was Philadelphia in the Fifties, a decade celebrated as one of blandness, of anxiety over The Bomb, when even moments of excitement were somewhat restrained. So it was with the Phillies. Over the span of seven years through 1957 the club won exactly eight more games than it lost. In two of these years it finished right at .500. The excitement *was* restrained, as the gaudy promise of the Whiz Kids became the cold reality of fourth or fifth place.

The town got better acquainted with the heroes of 1950 as the decade wore on. With Robin Roberts, for one. Robbie won twenty or more games for six years in a row and in 1956 lost in the last game of the season, to wind up at 19–18. What fan of the time

A great favorite and a great pitcher, Robin Roberts.

can forget the picture of Robin Roberts standing on the mound, pulling on his pant leg, tugging on the bill of his cap, moving into his smooth delivery and whistling a fastball over the outside corner of the plate. With it all, as the victories piled up, he was a quiet, moderate individual, the perfect picture of a baseball hero, and a pitcher who did not believe in throwing at batters. Ralph Kiner said that, while Roberts did not throw "the fastest fastball in the National League ... he threw the best. It had the most movement."[1]

Ashburn was a consistent .300 hitter, and twice he led the National League in batting. Because he did not hit home runs nor play in New York, Ashburn was always overshadowed by Willie Mays, Mickey Mantle, and Duke Snider, but his career batting average is higher than all of theirs, and six of the top ten seasons for outfield putouts are his. Ashburn was steady and predictable, "a great contact hitter," as Roberts described him, "choking up on the bat and spraying the ball to all fields." He took his customary closed stance in the lefthanded batter's box, watched the outfielders shorten up and the infielders come in, and then poked another single into an open spot. It was a way of life for the blond Nebraskan. Sometimes he bunted his way on or beat out an infield hit with sheer speed. However he did it, Ashburn piled up 2,217 hits over his twelve seasons with the Phillies, more than any Phillie before him and more than any after him until Mike Schmidt. Richie's lifetime average was .308.[2]

Year after year Ashburn led National League outfielders in putouts, and he holds a major league record of nine separate seasons with more than 400 putouts. With his speed, he covered all of center field and part of wherever Ennis was playing.

Ennis, the strong boy from Olney, was a big hitter. From the start of his career, which spanned managerial tenures from Ben Chapman to Mayo Smith, Del was the man the manager counted on to drive in more runs than anyone else. Invariably he did so, and he hit for average as well, batting over .300 in three of his eleven years with the team. Ennis was booed by the Shibe Park customers, in part because of his so-so fielding, in part as a function of being the big hitter on a team which habitually doomed its followers to disappointment. Curt Simmons said, "They needed someone to pick on and they picked on him. They expected him to drive in all of the runs." Nevertheless, Del Ennis produced. His 259 home runs and 1,124 runs batted in were both club records before the arrival of Mike Schmidt.[3]

Granny Hamner played good shortstop, or sometimes second base, through the '50s, hit in the clutch, served as the club leader, and was appreciated. Willie Jones, the tall, homely third baseman from down in South Carolina, played almost ten years of third base for the Phils, complaining about his sore feet ("mah dawgs," he called them), a prodigious drinker and womanizer, erratic at bat but steady in the field.[4]

Curt Simmons was constant in his inconsistency, pitching very well when he felt healthy, pitching poorly when his left arm or shoulder troubled him. Simmons had another misfortune, too, when he sliced off a portion of a toe with a power mower while cutting his lawn in suburban Meadowbrook. At his best, though, Simmons was one of the toughest lefthanders in the league, and the big lefthanded sluggers like Duke Snider tried to avoid him. Like Roberts, Curt Simmons never intentionally threw at hitters; "the reason I don't throw at guys is that I don't want to put them on base," he said.[5]

One thing that could be counted on was the regularity with which the Phillies changed managers. Nobody stayed around long. Sawyer was let go in the middle of the 1952 campaign, with the team in sixth place, in favor of old-timer Steve O'Neill, formerly with Cleveland, Detroit, and the

Red Sox. O'Neill got them to play at an excellent 59–32 clip the rest of the way to finish fourth, and he brought them in third in 1953, tied with the Cardinals, despite losing Simmons to the lawn mower for part of the season. They were third on July 15, 1954, with a mark of 40–37 when the easy-going skipper was unexpectedly fired for no very good reason by new general manager H. Roy Hamey.

O'Neill's replacement was Terry Moore, the former star center fielder of the Cardinals. Moore had no experience as a manager; even Hamey admitted that "the appointment of Moore is a shot in the dark." Actually, it was the Phillies shooting themselves in the foot. Moore showed little aptitude for his job, and he clashed with some of his key players, notably Hamner, who was having a fine season. When Granny discovered that he was being tailed by a private detective employed by the club, he was incensed. Then it developed that the inept private eye was supposed to be following Jones, who, as Ashburn later wrote, "didn't break training rules; he destroyed them."[6]

The Phillies played at 35–42 for Moore and slipped back to fourth. At the end of the season, the front office decided another manager would be easier to find than another shortstop, so Moore was turned loose.

The job then went to Yankee farm club manager Mayo Smith. The fans, who had at least heard of Terry Moore, wondered who the new man was. Investigation turned up a big league playing career of 73 undistinguished games with the 1945 A's. Mayo Smith proved to be a calm and relaxed type, a manager who kept the team playing at its accustomed "win one, lose one" level for three years. In '55, he brought the team in fourth, at 77–77, and in 1956 its record of 71–83 was good for fifth. The Phils were fifth again in '57, with another 77–77 mark. The Phillies players were not wild about Smith; Ennis said, "Smith was a bad manager — the worst. He lacked confidence, never stuck up for the team, and didn't do anything positive on the field." Frankie Baumholtz said that Smith "wasn't very good."[7]

In 1958 the Phillies were at 39–44 when Smith was fired, to be replaced by Eddie Sawyer, whose second coming was marked by a collapse into last place. Perhaps the front office was a little quick with the hook on Mayo Smith.

The Phillies during these years were an interesting team to watch, even after it became clear that the Whiz Kids had been a one-year wonder. They had pitchers like Roberts and Simmons, Murry Dickson, Herman Wehmeier, and Harvey Haddix. For six years in succession, from 1950 through 1955, a Phillie pitcher was the National League starter in the All-Star Game — Roberts five times and Simmons once. Smoky Burgess played three years for them, never failed to hit well, and in 1954 batted .368. Smoky was a line-drive hitter who, despite poor speed, got a lot of doubles on balls hit to the farther reaches of the outfield.

Early in 1955, Hamey traded Burgess back to Cincinnati, along with two other players, for Seminick, now very near the end of the line, and two outfielders, Glen Gorbous and Jim Greengrass, a big slugger for the Reds the prior two years. Gorbous had a great throwing arm and little else, and Greengrass was a major disappointment. He suffered from phlebitis in his leg, and he gave the Phillies two mediocre seasons before they let him go. Meanwhile, Smoky Burgess went on for twelve more years, hitting line drives, compiling a lifetime average of .295, and becoming one of the all-time great pinch-hitters.

In 1956, catcher Stan Lopata put together a super year for the Phillies. As a part-time player off and on since 1949, the big backstop had frequently shown power, and he belted 22 home runs in 1955. The next year, when Rogers Hornsby suggested he change his stance at the plate to an exaggerated crouch, Lopata hit 32 home runs and drove in 95 runs. "After I changed my stance," Lopata said later, "I kept hitting line drives and pulling the ball, and it was just one of those fabulous years ... I just hit everything hard."[8]

Spots on the club's roster through the '50s were often occupied by "bonus babies," so called because they had signed out of high school for more than a specified limit, usually $4,000, and under the rules had to be carried with the big league club for two years. The Phillies had hit it big with Roberts and Simmons, so they were willing to play the bonus game, signing such youngsters as Tom Qualters, Mack Burk, Tom Casagrande, Hugh Radcliffe, Ted Kazanski, Charlie Bicknell, and Paul Penson. Kazanski played with some regularity over several seasons, but he was a poor hitter (.217 lifetime) and too slow afoot to cover the ground necessary for a major league infielder. The others never contributed much of anything.

Things did change with the Phillies as the decade passed. After the A's moved to Kansas City, following the 1954 season, Carpenter bought the ballpark, which had been renamed Connie Mack Stadium in 1953, for $1,657,000. He had no desire to *own* the facility, but he really had no choice at the time, because he had to have a place for his team to play.

Del Ennis's run production dropped in 1956 to 95 and his batting average to .260, and Hamey decided it was time to move him on, though after eleven seasons Del was still one of the most consistent sluggers in the league. While Bob Carpenter was off on a hunting trip, Ennis was traded to the Cardinals for outfielder Rip Repulski and infielder Bobby Morgan. Morgan was soon sent to the Cubs, and Repulski had a mediocre year for the Phillies, while Ennis drove in 105 runs and batted .286 for the Cards. It was not Roy Hamey's best trade, though far from his worst.

Hamner's left shoulder gave him trouble, hampering his batting, so in '56 and '57 he tried to make it as a pitcher. Smith put him into several games, and Granny tried valiantly, but a big league pitcher he was not. A bad knee disabled him through most of 1958, and the next spring he was sold to Cleveland, to play out the string. Hamner had come a long way from the nervous teenager out of Richmond who first appeared with the Phillies in 1944, but in the interim he had been one of the National League's class shortstops, sharing the distinction with Marty Marion, Pee Wee Reese, and Alvin Dark.[9]

In 1957, Mayo Smith had the benefit of a fine crop of rookies, and the club's home attendance for the year soared over the million mark, to 1,146,230, only the third time a Philadelphia team had done that. Two of the freshman favorites were pitchers from the Boston area, Dick Farrell, a big righthander with a slightly game leg from a childhood polio attack, and a stocky, 27-year-old blond named Jack Sanford. Both of them threw hard and believed in keeping hitters loose at the plate. Sanford won 19 games, lost eight, led the league in strikeouts, and was named the league's best rookie pitcher.[10]

Smith made Farrell a relief pitcher because he was tough and mean coming into situations with the game on the line. He was 10–2 and did everything the club asked of him. Bob Uecker tells the story of a game several years later in which manager Gene Mauch tired of the Dodgers' Don Drysdale dusting off Phillies hitters. "Knock him down," Mauch shouted to Farrell, who soon had Drysdale sprawling in the dirt. On the next pitch, Drysdale doubled off the wall and, standing at second, shouted, "There's your knockdown pitch, Farrell." Farrell then made an ostensible pickoff throw to second, nailing Drysdale squarely on the hip. "There's your two-base hit, Drysdale," Farrell said.[11]

It was a good thing Smith had his freshman hurlers, because Simmons and Haddix had disappointing records, while Roberts suffered through a disastrous 10–22 season. Robbie's fast ball lost a little of its edge after seven straight seasons of 297 innings or more, and enemy batters, relying on his dependable control, whaled away at it.

The other good first-year men with the Phils in 1957 were outfielders Harry Anderson and Bob Bowman and first baseman Ed Bouchee. Bouchee and Anderson each hit 17 home runs, and Bouchee with his .293 average was named National League rookie player of the year by *The Sporting News*. It looked like the second coming of the Whiz Kids.

Over the winter, however, Bouchee got in trouble back home in Spokane. He was arrested and charged with exposing himself to young girls, and after he pleaded guilty the best that Carpenter could do for him was to have him placed in a psychiatric institution. While there, the doctors who worked on ridding Bouchee of his behavioral problems apparently also cured him of his natural high-average batting stroke. He was allowed to rejoin the club in mid–1958, but the best he could do was .257. Although Eddie stayed in the big leagues for several more years, he never fulfilled his early promise, winding up with a .265 lifetime mark.

Anderson, a handsome young man from nearby West Chester State College, did even better his second year, hitting .301 with 23 homers and 97 runs driven in. The future looked bright for Harry Anderson. Yet he too faded (to .240 in '59) and in a couple more years was out of the majors. Bowman, who hit well and dazzled the fans with a great throwing arm in 1957 and 1958, hit nothing in 1959 and was soon gone.

Roberts came back in 1958 to win 17 games, and Richie Ashburn won his second batting title with .350, getting three hits in the last game to nose out Mays. Farrell was sensational in the first half of the season, and he threw two overpowering innings in the All-Star Game. Then he seemed to lose something; he was just an ordinary pitcher the rest of the year as the Phillies slid into last place under Sawyer.

Sanford, too, slipped in his second season, and in December Hamey shipped him to San Francisco for screwball pitcher Ruben Gomez from Puerto Rico and catcher Valmy Thomas from the Virgin Islands. It was Roy Hamey's worst deal. Sanford was a fine pitcher for the Giants, pushing them to a pennant in 1962, while Gomez won only three games (losing eleven) in two years with the Phils, and Thomas hit a weak .200 in his only Philly season.

A few days after the Sanford transaction, Hamey struck again, this time to solve the Phillies' persistent second base problem. He traded Rip Repulski and two pitchers to the Dodgers for a weak-hitting minor league second baseman named George "Sparky" Anderson. Hamey never dreamed he was getting a future Hall of Famer, but when Anderson was voted into Cooperstown in 2000 it was not for anything he did with the Phillies. Anderson hit a meek .218 in one Phillie season and then disappeared, to surface years later as a manager at Cincinnati.

In January 1959, when Roy Hamey's contract as general manager expired, Carpenter let him go, replacing him with John Quinn, who had built a powerhouse at Milwaukee. Quinn took over a club at the bottom of the league, a team which had died over the last two months of the '58 season.[12]

One of the first tasks Quinn set for himself was the dispersal of the remaining Whiz Kids. Before the new season started, he traded Stan Lopata for Braves pitcher Gene Conley, a 6'8" pro basketball player. Pitcher Bob Miller was cut loose. Quinn sent Hamner and Jones to Cleveland early in the season, and when Ashburn slumped at bat he was traded the next winter to the Cubs. Only Roberts and Simmons were left.

Another reason for the breakdown of the Phillies, besides the overlong reliance on the survivors of the pennant-winner, was the club's failure to sign black players. Not until 1957 did the first player of African descent appear in a Phillies uniform in a league game; he was a brown-skinned Cuban shortstop of modest abilities named Humberto "Chico" Fernandez, obtained from Brooklyn for four players and $75,000. Fernandez played three progressively poorer seasons with the Phils before being traded to Detroit.[13]

In 1959, with Gomez and Thomas added to Fernandez, the Phillies had not one mediocre black Latin but three. Then, for Hamner, the Phils got a Panamanian pitcher named Humberto Robinson, whose only achievement of note in two seasons in town was an allegation to the police that a gambler had approached him to throw a game. With the 1959 Phillies, that constituted overkill of the rankest order.

In any event, twelve years after Jackie Robinson entered the league, the Phillies had still not employed a single quality black player. Responsibility for this state of affairs must be laid at the feet of the owner, Bob Carpenter, and it is hardly surprising that some years later, when pitcher Grant Jackson departed the team, he accused Phillies' management of being anti-black.

1959 was another bad year. Roberts pitched well, going 15–17 with a poor team, but Simmons had arm trouble and appeared in only seven games without a decision. He was farmed out to Williamsport in the Eastern League for a couple of weeks to see if some minor league work might help his aching left arm. Farrell was hit around, and he too suffered a minor league exile. Gene Freese, a former Pirate and Cardinal infielder, played third for the Phils in '59 and hit 23 home runs, a lone high spot.

Sawyer's team finished last again, well behind the seventh-place Cards. The team had no spark, no personality, to arouse the fans. As the fifties came to a close, the Phillies, alone in town now, had managed to work their way down from first place to last.

Chapter 13

The Coming of
Gene Mauch

John Quinn continued to deal after the sad 1959 season. He traded Ashburn to the Cubs for Alvin Dark and rookie Jim Woods, sent Fernandez and pitcher Ray Semproch to Detroit for veteran infielder Ted Lepcio and outfielder Ken Walters, and swapped Gene Freese to the White Sox for a highly-touted young outfielder named John Callison. Freese returned the favor by saying that leaving Philadelphia was like "getting out of jail." Quinn drafted Bobby Malkmus, a light-hitting ex-Senator infielder, and a catcher with the elegant name of Clayton Errol Dalrymple. He dealt catcher Carl Sawatski to St. Louis for two guys named Smith.

The club even changed its play-by-play man, dropping Gene Kelly, so closely associated in the public's mind with the Whiz Kids, in favor of a young man named Frank Sims, who would work for three years with Byrum Saam and Claude Haring.

The team looked terrible in spring training. Sawyer did not agree with some of Quinn's moves, and he wondered what other changes might be in store. Some onlookers wondered about Eddie Sawyer. One day Sawyer told the writers that Lepcio was the worst looking big league ballplayer he had ever seen. (Lepcio, who had already logged eight years in the American League, was not overjoyed by this assessment.) In a strange experiment that left everyone puzzled, Sawyer put rookie slugger Pancho Herrera at second base. Herrera had never played second and thought he was coming to the majors as a first baseman. He was 6'3", weighed 220 pounds, and was not considered either fast or graceful.

On Opening Day, 1960, the Phillies took a 9–4 licking from the Cincinnati Reds. After the game, Sawyer announced that he was quitting. "I'm forty-nine years old," he said, "and I want to live to be fifty." Ed Bouchee commented, "I'm sure it wasn't just because of his players but because of his frustration with the front office." Coach Andy Cohen ran the club in the second game of the season, and then John Quinn's new manager came to town. His name was Gene Mauch, and he came from Minneapolis in the American Association, where he was widely regarded as the brightest young manager in the minors.[1]

Mauch had been an infielder with Rickey's Dodgers, a scrapper who could make the plays but was never much of a hitter. With limited talent, Mauch put together a big league career on intelligence, hustle, and what are called, in baseball parlance, "the intangibles." A careful student of the game, with a prodigious memory, he had a keen imagination and little hesitation in putting into effect the unusual maneuvers his fertile brain conjured up.

Mauch was a man of courage as well, as was apparent to anyone who looked at the sad bunch he inherited from Eddie Sawyer in April 1960. Spoken of for some time as a future major league manager, Mauch at 34 could certainly have waited for a more promising situation than the mess in Philadelphia. Over time, as Gene Mauch became a sort of institution in Philadelphia, the mention of his name often provoked violent arguments between those who thought he was the best in the business and those who felt he overmanaged outrageously. In 1960, it was conceded that nothing Mauch might do could have helped very much.

It was quite a crew. The catching was handled by two rookies, Jim Coker, who could catch but not hit, and Dalrymple, who hit all right but could not throw, and a veteran named Cal Neeman, who was a little shy in all those areas. Herrera, after they rescued him from second base, played first most of the year and hit fairly well; unfortunately, he also established a new league record by striking out 136 times.

At second, Quinn came up with a winner. On May 13, he swapped Eddie Bouchee and pitcher Don Cardwell to the Cubs for Neeman and second sacker Tony Taylor. Taylor, a short, speedy Cuban, hit well, fielded sharply, and stole a lot of bases. He played a long time in Philadelphia, always performed dependably, and became a great favorite.

The shortstop was either Joe Koppe, or Malkmus, or a smooth-fielding Mexican named Ruben Amaro. It was an unsettled position. So was third base. Young Jim Woods played a few games there, and so did Alvin Dark, who was traded to Milwaukee in June. The fellow they got from the Braves was third baseman Joe Morgan, who figured in one of the saddest stories of the year.

On July 21 at San Francisco, Robin Roberts cranked up a game in which, for one of the few times all season, he looked like the Roberts of old. Robbie won 12 and lost 16, but the year was a struggle. This day,

though, he had it all going, and he should have achieved a feat which
eluded him throughout his illustrious career, a no-hitter. The only Giant
hit given up by Roberts was a fifth-inning smash down the third base line
by Felipe Alou. There was Joe Morgan. Joe fielded the ball cleanly enough,
but the impact knocked him onto his rear end. By the time he scrambled
to his feet, there was no play. The official scorer had no choice but to rule
it a hit, and Robbie's no-hitter was gone. Shortly thereafter, so was Joe
Morgan, although he returned years later as manager of the Red Sox.

The outfield was revamped in mid–June when Quinn traded the fading Harry Anderson and Wally Post, a top slugger with the Reds but a bust
in Philadelphia, to Cincinnati for outfielders Lee Walls and Tony Gonzalez. Walls was a disappointment at bat, but he was a steady fielder and could
even play third base. Gonzalez, a little Cuban and a good outfielder with
lefthanded power, made it a profitable trade.[2]

The other outfielders, used mainly in lefthanded and righthanded
platoons, were Callison, the erstwhile "Golden Boy" of the White Sox, still
learning how to play the game, much-traveled Bobby del Greco, Bobby
Gene Smith, Ken Walters, and a young Bahamian named Tony Curry.

Curry hit well with the Phillies' lower farm teams, so Quinn decided
to force-feed him to the majors. Tony did not hit badly, finishing at .261,
but he was a calamity in the outfield. Philadelphia fans had seen bad
outfielders over the years, but it is doubtful they ever saw one quite like
Tony Curry. Every baseball hit toward him was an adventure, with the
outcome in question until the last second. Just because Tony looked ready
meant little. When he threw the ball, no one, least of all Curry, had any
idea where it might land. "When he picked up a baseball," Clay Dalrymple remembered, "the whole stadium scattered." Gene Mauch's hair started
turning gray in 1960, and Tony Curry had a lot to do with it.[3]

The pitching in 1960 was none too good. Roberts struggled, as his
stuff deserted him and his pride kept him from changing his style. He and
Mauch did not see eye to eye on how he should pitch. The manager, who
had always had to scrap and improvise with his limited skills, could not
understand the great pitcher; if a man could no longer throw a fastball,
then he should rely on his slider or a change-up or a trick pitch like a
knuckleball. Roberts kept throwing his moderate-speed fastball, and the
hitters belted it.

The sore-armed Simmons was released, considered washed up by
John Quinn, a verdict the Phillies would regret many times as Curt won
73 more big league games over the next seven years, many of them against
Philadelphia. Conley had a middling kind of season, 8–14 and 3.69. A couple of rookies from Delaware, righthanded Dallas Green and lefthanded

Chris Short, showed promise but took their lumps. John Buzhardt, highly touted by *Sports Illustrated* in the spring, compiled a record of 5–16. Another rookie, a tall, dark-eyed righthander named Art Mahaffey, was brought up from the minors at midseason and pitched well, winning seven and losing only three, with a 2.32 ERA.

The rest of the pitching staff was the Dalton Gang, the sobriquet conferred on a group of Phillies pitchers by pitching coach Tom Ferrick, because of their night-time escapades, high living, and disregard of curfew and training rules. The members were Turk Farrell, Jim Owens, and Jack Meyer.

Another pitcher, chunky lefthander Seth Morehead, had been a member before going to the Cubs in 1959. Morehead, 2–9 in parts of three seasons with the Phillies, was perhaps the worst fielding pitcher ever seen. (In the two full seasons he pitched for the Phils, Morehead's fielding average was .793.) Seth did not pitch often, but when he did the opposition was sure to lay down a few bunts. Seth Morehead could no more handle a bunt than leap over City Hall. It was a fatal flaw.

Even without Morehead, there were enough Daltons to go around. And go around they did. Turk Farrell boasted that he held the record for barroom fights. Farrell was tough and sometimes hostile, but he got the job done on the field, where he was 10–6 as Mauch's main reliever. Owens and Meyer were less successful on the mound, so their extracurricular activities were less tolerable.

Jack Meyer was a curly-haired blond who had been a reliever with the club since 1955. Jack, a local boy from Penn Charter School in Germantown, came to the majors with a blazing fastball, and in his first couple of years with the club he gave several spectacular performances. By 1960, though, he was slipping, and after several misadventures, Meyer was gone.

Owens had apparently come into his own in 1959, when he went 12–12 and 3.22 for a bad team. But he never even made it through spring training in 1960 before getting into trouble. He got into a barroom brawl in Florida and was fined. Owens, resentful, told reporters that he was the kind of pitcher who could drink all night and throw a shutout the next day. Philadelphia had seen pitchers like that in the past, but a Pete Alexander or Rube Waddell he was not. Owens went 4–14 and 5.04 for Mauch in 1960. His style of play was not Gene Mauch's; the young manager could not abide a player squandering his talent.

In June, *Sports Illustrated* published an article by Walter Bingham entitled "The Dalton Gang Rides Again," detailing the exploits of the Philadelphia pitchers and concluding, "Unlike some of the storied hellraisers of old, the members of the Dalton Gang aren't really good enough to be so bad." The hurlers filed a libel action against the magazine which was later quietly withdrawn; truth is a defense to a libel claim.[4]

His first year showed Mauch that he had the Dalton Gang, a few quality players, and a lot of bad ones. The time had come to rebuild the Phillies. Unfortunately the process meant that the 1961 team was even worse than that of 1960, which had finished last at 59–95, just a game behind the Cubs. The '61 model came in at 47–107, 17 games behind Chicago. Attendance dropped sharply, to 590,039; even the sorry 1960 team drew 862,205.

But Mauch persevered. From the minors he brought in a red-haired reliever named Jack Baldschun, who threw a screwball as his money pitch and got people out with it. Mauch stuck with Dalrymple behind the plate, and Clay now showed that his throwing problem of the year before had been only temporary. At the same time his batting average fell sharply. Regardless, he was Mauch's catcher, and his thought processes began to mirror those of the skipper.[5]

Mauch played Callison and Gonzalez in the outfield, and he got Wes Covington from Kansas City. Covington, a former Braves slugger, was no fancy dan in the field and he had trouble with lefthanded pitching, but he was murder on righthanders.

Early in the season Farrell was traded to Los Angeles for Don Demeter, a big righthanded outfielder who hit well for the Phils, and a third baseman named Charley Smith. Taylor played regularly at second, and Amaro was installed at shortstop.

Short, Mahaffey, and Buzhardt lost a lot of games, but they were learning how to pitch. On April 23, Mahaffey fanned 17 Cubs in one game, to set a new club record. Frank Sullivan came over from the Red Sox, pitched in bad luck all year, and had a record of 3–16.

The saddest story was that of Roberts. The great pitcher was a shadow of his former self, and his disagreements with the manager became public knowledge, particularly when Mauch said that Robbie was "throwing like Dolley Madison" (or perhaps Betsy Ross; the quotes were mixed, but the meaning was clear enough). Roberts won one game, lost ten, had a 5.85 earned run average, and pitched sparingly the latter part of the year. After the season, Bob Carpenter arranged to sell Roberts, the last of the Whiz Kids, to the New York Yankees, so that he might have a shot at pitching in another World Series.[6]

Midway through the season, the 1961 Phillies dug themselves an historic hole in the record books. On July 28, John Buzhardt beat San Francisco 4–3 in the second game of a twin-bill. From then until August 20, the Phils lost twenty-three games in a row, something no other baseball team in the twentieth century ever managed to do. They lost at home, and they lost on the road. They lost close games (eight by one run) and they lost blowouts. Finally, on August 20, in the nightcap of a doubleheader in Milwaukee, they beat the Braves, 7–4, again behind Buzhardt.

Bad as the streak was, Mauch maintained that it made this disparate group of players think of themselves for the first time as Phillies, rather than as ex-Braves or ex-Indians or ex-something else. It was still a low point in Philadelphia baseball.

Nineteen hundred sixty-two saw the Phillies heading up. Two brand new teams, the Houston Colt .45s and the New York Mets, came into existence with the National League's expansion to ten teams, the first change in the league's size since the cutdown of 1900. The Phillies finished seventh, ahead of both expansion teams and the Chicago Cubs, who ended up behind Houston. The Phils had their first winning record since 1953, at 81–80. Some of the promising young players gathered in the prior two years started to realize their potential. The lineup was fitting together.

Mauch was maturing as a manager, a big factor in the club's improvement. Gene Mauch thought deeply about baseball. No part of the game or the way it was played was too insignificant for him. He knew the rule book inside and out, but that was just the beginning of what was in his mind. Bob Uecker said that he "would sit on the bench with his arms folded and his eyes never stopped moving. He didn't miss a thing."[7]

Mauch was always on the alert for that little edge which could make the difference between winning and losing a game. For years, the Phillies and A's had maintained their home bullpens in the left field corner. The reason for this was lost in antiquity, but no one thought about it until Mauch came along. He switched the home and visiting bullpens, putting the Phils' relievers in right field. He had observed that his team was losing extra bases to opposing right fielders pretending they were going to catch drives which instead hit the wall. Runners would hold up and barely make the next base instead of going hard for extra bases. Mauch had his bullpen occupants wave towels when it was obvious that a ball was headed for the wall, a visible signal to runners and coaches alike. The Phillies fell victim to a right fielder's decoy no more.[8]

Mauch knew his percentages. Over the years, conservative, predictable managers have often been called "good percentage managers." They know what will happen in a given situation most of the time and base their strategy on this. Gene Mauch, on the other hand, frequently astounded fans, opponents, and reporters with bold and unexpected moves, but when asked about them, Mauch always had a logical explanation. He knew the percentages better than most other managers: he had pondered the probabilities for long hours, analyzed the various things that can happen in a given situation, and determined in advance what he would do if that situation arose, with all the variables frozen into a specific set of factors. What set Gene Mauch apart was that he included in his thinking more of the variables than other managers did. It gave him an edge.

He was single-mindedly devoted to winning. He was not bothered by criticism from the press or the fans if he was convinced that what he was doing would help the club to win. When he went through a string of relief pitchers, each facing one or two hitters, he did not care that the spectators jeered, since he knew the percentages better than they did.

A frequently-booed decision was pinch-hitting for Wes

Gene Mauch, the manager from 1960 to 1968.

Covington with a lefty on the mound. Covington was very popular. Wes had a certain flair to his game, he gave lots of colorful quotes to the writers, and he hit the ball hard — against righthanders. Mauch knew that Wes did not hit lefties at all, but the fans refused to believe it. Mauch knew the figures on Covington against lefthanders, and he was familiar with the picture of Wes's futile swing against a southpaw with a dinky slider. So, most of the time, when Covington was scheduled to hit against a left-handed pitcher, out he would come, though the spectators roared their disapproval.

In the turnaround season of 1962, Baldschun pitched tireless relief ball, had a record of 12–7 and 2.95, and baffled hitters with his screwball. Mahaffey won nineteen games, and Chris Short won eleven, as he finally brought his fastball under control. Demeter, Gonzalez, and Callison all hit .300 or better, and each hit at least 20 home runs, Demeter with 29. When Callison got his average to .300 on the next-to-last day of the season, Mauch sat him down for the final game so that the youngster would have a whole winter to think of himself as a .300 hitter.

Dalrymple, Covington, and Taylor were established major leaguers at their positions, and two veterans from the American League, first baseman Roy Sievers and pitcher Calvin McLish, added a dash of seasoned experience to the club. Sievers hit 21 homers and drove in 80 runs, while McLish went 11–5.

Another pitching find was a breezy lefthander brought up from Buffalo in midseason, Dennis Bennett, who won and lost nine games but pitched with the confidence of a veteran. A rookie shortstop, a rifle-armed fielding whiz named Bobby Wine, added strength to the infield. Wine was not a good hitter, but he had more power than Ruben Amaro. Amaro ran better and hit for a higher average than Wine, and both were excellent fielders. Shortstop was a pleasant puzzle for Mauch.

Mauch was named the league's manager of the year for 1962. After the season ended, he got rid of the last member of the Dalton Gang. Owens won only two games in 1962, being used sparingly and pitching badly when called upon. Mauch had had enough of Jim Owens, and the pitcher was traded to Cincinnati for a little Cuban infielder named Octavio "Cookie" Rojas. The *Inquirer* headlined the story, "Phils Trade Owens to Reds for Unknown." When reporters asked him why he would trade for an undersized utility man who hit only .221 for the Reds, Mauch, unaware of the real prize he had captured in the transaction, calmly answered, "Sometimes you add by subtracting."[9]

Another off-season trade brought Don Hoak, a pugnacious third baseman, Mauch's kind of player, from the Pirates, even though he was now thirty-five and had shown signs of aging.

Major adjustments were made in the radio and television broadcast crew for 1963. Gone were Sims and Haring. On board, working with Byrum Saam, were Bill Campbell, whose eight years with the Phillies would be a brief interlude in a very long career in Philadelphia sports broadcasting, and Richie Ashburn, retired as a player after hitting .306 for the woeful 1962 New York Mets. The fans were happy to have him back, because Richie Ashburn always seemed to mean good things for the Phillies.

Trouble struck early, however. Pitching coach Al Widmar went down to Puerto Rico to check on some of his boys playing winter ball. He and Dennis Bennett and minor-league prospect Joel Gibson were in a serious auto accident, in which the driver of their car was killed. Gibson's pitching arm was broken, Widmar's ribs were cracked, and Bennett's ankle was badly torn up. Gibson never did make it to the majors, and Bennett was out of action until late June, returning then only because of a grueling and courageous training regimen.

Without Bennett, though, the pitching was suspect. The situation became more serious as Art Mahaffey, after a great Opening Night performance, lost his control, his confidence, and a bundle of ballgames. Mahaffey's shoulder hurt, and it showed in his work. Short pitched well but had little luck. In the early going Cal McLish — or Calvin Coolidge Julius Caesar Tuskahoma McLish, to give the part–Indian pitcher his full handle — did the best mound work for Mauch. McLish, 37 years old, had first come to the majors with the Brooklyn Dodgers back in 1944. But he knew how to pitch, and he won 13 games for Mauch in '63, giving him 209 innings of work.

The other pitching savior in the early part of the season was rookie Ray Culp, a chunky righthander from Texas whose good high school fastball had won him a big wad of Bob Carpenter's bonus dollars several years earlier. The Phillies' minor league people soon had Culp throwing curveballs to go with his hummer, and he developed a persistent sore arm. He kicked around at Asheville and Des Moines and Williamsport, but his arm ached and his pitching was not very good. Culp showed signs of coming out of it in 1962, and the Phillies took him to camp in '63. The real reason they did so, however, was that under baseball law they either had to bring him to the majors or let him go.

Spring training at Clearwater in 1963 was the last shot for Ray Culp. He had a couple of good outings, so Mauch took him north with the club. He was used in relief several times in the first couple of weeks, and he came through. Soon Mauch had him starting, and Culp became a mainstay of the staff. It had been a close-run thing, but Culp's staying in the majors was a break for the Phils and made up some for the loss of Bennett. For the year, Culp was 14–11, with an ERA of 2.97.

Still, the Phillies started slowly. Hoak's batting average almost disappeared, Sievers was hurt, Demeter faded after a fast start, neither Wine or Amaro hit a lick, and Johnny Callison struggled at the plate. But in late June, at about the same time as Bennett's gutty return to action, the Phils started to play good baseball and headed toward the first division.

Baldschun, John Klippstein, and Ryne Duren shored up the relief staff, while McLish, Culp, Short, and Bennett took most of the starting turns. Callison got straightened out and wound up with .284 and 26 home runs. Dalrymple had a solid year behind the plate, and Sievers eventually drove in his 82 runs. Tony Taylor had a fine season, and Wes Covington, batting mostly against righthanders, hit .303. Gonzalez, playing against everyone, hit .306, although his home run production fell mysteriously from twenty to four. His RBIs were up, however, and he did the job in center field, so Mauch was happy with him.

Toward the end of September, the Phils lazed into Houston for a weekend series in Colt Stadium. They were in fourth place, and a good season was assured. There would be no pennant, though, and their attitude verged suspiciously on that of "playing out the string." Gene Mauch never played out the string, and his players were about to have that fact brought home to them very graphically.

The team split the first two games, but there seemed to be no spark. On Sunday, a one-run lead was lost, and the game went with it with two out in the ninth, when Klippstein flopped up a bad curve to a raw rookie named Joe Morgan. Morgan, the future Hall of Famer, stroked his first big league hit and won the game with it, 2–1. The Phillies fell to fifth place.

A seething Gene Mauch gathered his players together in the clubhouse and lectured them on the evils of lackadaisical play. As he warmed to the subject, he lost his temper and started shouting. Finally, spotting a table full of snacks and delicacies prepared by the clubhouse attendant, Mauch overturned the whole thing. Food spattered around the lockerroom, and greasy spare ribs landed on suits belonging to Covington and Gonzalez. The tirade ended immediately; the players sat stunned, while the manager retreated to his cubicle.

The story soon got out, and back in Philadelphia it furnished ammunition both to the pro–Mauch and anti–Mauch legions. It was an uncivilized thing to do (though Mauch bought new suits for his two outfielders and apologized for the outburst to the players and the clubhouse man), and it demonstrated that the man had a nasty temper. On the other hand, the Phillies were shown in a memorable fashion that Gene Mauch, while he was their manager, would not tolerate less than one hundred per cent effort.[10]

That message came across. The Phillies won five of the remaining six games, all on the west coast, finished fourth, only a game behind the Giants, and wound up with a fine 87–75 record for the year. The spare ribs helped.

Chapter 14

Tote'm Home Pennant

Hopes were high for 1964. With the best young manager in baseball, with a blend of excellent youngsters and heady veterans, the Phillies expected to go somewhere in '64. It was too soon, probably, to expect a pennant, but there was every reason to anticipate Mauch's club establishing itself among the National League's elite.

Only one trade was made over the off-season, but it was a big one. Quinn sent Don Demeter, the tall, gangling outfielder who had slumped badly in the latter half of 1963, to Detroit with pitcher Jack Hamilton for catcher Gus Triandos and Jim Bunning, a slim, no-nonsense righthander who had piled up a lot of victories and strikeouts in eight years as a Tiger. Bunning appeared to have outlived his usefulness in Detroit; at 32, a change of scenery seemed to be in order.

Don Hoak was still around, but a powerful rookie named Richie Allen was counted on to play third base. Allen, a young black man from western Pennsylvania, had received a healthy bonus to sign with the Phillies. After two and a half years with farm teams in northern towns, he had been sent in 1963 to Little Rock, to the Phillies' triple-A Arkansas club. Distressed at the racism he encountered there and resentful of the Phillies for sending him south, Allen still led the International League in triples, home runs, and RBIs, and became a favorite of the Little Rock fans. Allen was not a good fielder, but he hit so well, both for average and for power, that some place had to be found for him. "Third base is not as demanding a position as short or second," said Mauch.[1]

Sievers, the old pro, was the first baseman, Taylor was at second, and Wine and Amaro shared shortstop. Callison, whom Mauch called "just about the complete ballplayer," was in right field, Gonzalez in center, with Covington and others in left. Cookie Rojas could fill in anywhere he was needed.[2]

Dalrymple was the catcher, backed by Triandos, while Bunning, Short, McLish, Mahaffey, Bennett, and Culp furnished the nucleus of a good starting staff, with the dependable Jack Baldschun in the bullpen.

Philadelphia was ready for a winner. The Clark-Dilworth era of municipal government, probably the best the city ever had, was over, and the president of the city council, James H.J. Tate, a tall, handsome ward leader, had succeeded Dilworth when the latter resigned to run for governor in 1962. The Democratic party was still in firm control of Philadelphia politics, from Fishtown to West Oak Lane.

The city, like many other big cities, experienced the racial turmoil that plagued urban America in the mid-sixties. At the end of August, North Philadelphia's black ghetto, primarily along Columbia and Ridge Avenues, suffered several nights of rioting and looting. With the help of Frank L. Rizzo, a tough deputy police commissioner, Tate managed to keep a lid on. Philadelphia did not blow up, and this was important to the Phillies, whose ballpark was in the midst of an increasingly black area.

Everything seemed to break right for the Phillies. When the season started, they began winning and stayed near the top of the league. Bunning pitched good ball, and so did Dennis Bennett. On May 18, Jim Wynn got the only Houston hit in a 4–0 victory for Bunning, pitching as well as he ever had.

Allen, the rookie third baseman, hit the ball hard, fielded erratically but acceptably, and made it possible to let Hoak go. Callison played very well, and Cookie Rojas, appearing all over the field, wherever Mauch needed to plug a hole, did everything that was asked of him and astounded the league by hitting solidly and often. For the year Cookie hit .291, and repeat performances in later years proved that this was no fluke. Gus Triandos, looking at the strange and exciting things that were happening, called it "the Year of the Blue Snow."[3]

There were some dark spots. Roy Sievers at 37 could not get untracked with the bat, and first base became a trouble area. A former Michigan fullback named John Herrnstein played there some, but he was not a consistent hitter. Cal McLish had arm trouble and never did win a game, Mahaffey and Culp were unsteady, and Klippstein was shipped to the Minnesota Twins in June.

On the whole, though, things were fine. Allen, Callison, Covington, and Gonzalez led the way, and Rojas, Taylor, and Amaro were right behind. Dalrymple did not hit much, but he was a dependable catcher and handled the pitching staff the way Gene Mauch wanted. Wine covered shortstop almost flawlessly. Jack Baldschun worked his wonders out of the pen, backed by veteran Ed Roebuck, and Chris Short blossomed into a dominating southpaw.

Allen was not the only rookie contributor. Outfielders Danny Cater, Alex Johnson, and John Briggs and pitcher Rick Wise, used sparingly at first, more later, helped out over and over again. Cater, an engaging 24-year-old, hit .296 before breaking his ankle in late July.

With it all, there was Mauch, juggling, shifting, finding an edge here, a little-known rule there, encouraging a youngster, goading a veteran, extracting from his team a little more than anyone else could have gotten. Even Richie Allen, who had his troubles with Mauch over the years, said in his autobiography, "I learned more about baseball as a chess game under Gene Mauch than I did from anybody else in baseball. The man's a master of the little game — when to bunt, how to steal a sign, what base to throw to, all the ways to outthink your opponent."[4]

Through the early weeks of the season, the Phillies contended with the west coast teams, primarily San Francisco, for the league lead. In April, May, and June, the Giants of Mays and Marichal and Cepeda, of Jim Ray Hart and Gaylord Perry, were the major opposition. Then, as the weather warmed up, the Phils put Alvin Dark's Giants away and took the league lead.

The high point of this surge came on Father's Day, June 21, a hot, sunny Sunday at Shea Stadium, the new home of the New York Mets. In the first game of the doubleheader, Bunning had good stuff, and he looked sharp in the early innings. Allen drove in a run in the first inning and Triandos one in the second, and the Phils took an early 2–0 lead.

In the fifth, the Mets' Jesse Gonder smashed a ball in the hole between first and second, but Taylor made a diving stop, knocked the ball down, and threw out the slow-moving catcher. The Mets still had not gotten anyone on base. The next inning, Callison hit a home run, Bunning himself doubled home two runs, and the Phils held a 6–0 lead. Mauch inserted Wine at shortstop in the Mets' sixth, moving Rojas from there to left field in place of the unsteady Covington.

The Mets went out quickly in the sixth, and in the seventh Bunning struck out two of the three hitters he faced, getting the other on a hard grounder at Allen. In the eighth, as the fans realized that Bunning had still not allowed a baserunner, tension increased, and the crowd roared with each batter.

Bunning appeared to be getting stronger as the game progressed. He struck out Joe Christopher to start the eighth, then watched as Gonder grounded once again to Taylor at second. Bob Taylor ran the count full, then took a called third strike. Jim Bunning had retired twenty-four straight batters. He drew a standing ovation from the New York fans when he batted in the ninth. In the bottom of the inning some of them were rooting for him.

Charley Smith, a former Phil, ran the count to two-and-two, then hit a foul pop down the third base line. Wine raced over and gathered it in.

Two to go. George Altman, a veteran lefthanded outfielder, a tough out, came to bat as a pinch-hitter. Altman hit two foul balls out of play and then missed a curveball for Bunning's ninth strikeout.

Manager Casey Stengel, with one out left, sent catcher John Stephenson to hit for the pitcher. The first pitch, a curveball, Stephenson missed. Bunning then put another curve over the plate for called strike two. He missed with two pitches just wide of the plate, as the huge holiday crowd groaned. Finally, another curveball flashed over the plate, Stephenson swung and missed it, and Jim Bunning of the Phillies had pitched a perfect game, only the ninth perfect game in major league history (including Harvey Haddix's losing 13-inning effort of 1959) and the first in regular season play since 1922, except for the Haddix game. Indeed, it was the first perfect complete game in the National League since 1880, when the pitching rules were altogether different.[5]

Clearly, it was the Phillies' year. Bunning, Short, and Callison were selected for the All-Star Game at Shea Stadium. Bunning pitched two scoreless innings, and in the bottom of the ninth, Callison came to the plate with two outs, two on, and the game tied at 4–4. Facing big Dick Radatz, the relief ace of the Red Sox, Johnny belted one out of the park to win the game.

As the summer rolled on, the Phils stayed at the top of the league, and Mauch's inventive maneuvering continued to pay off. They had trouble from time to time, though, with lefthanded pitching, which tended to neutralize the strength of Callison, Gonzalez, and Covington, and emphasize the decline of Sievers.

One night early in June, L.A.'s lefthanded ace Sandy Koufax pitched a no-hitter against them, facing only twenty-seven batters as the lone recipient of a base on balls was erased trying to steal. It was not only Koufax who gave the Phillies problems. Every once in a while a club would drag out an unknown rookie southpaw, like a Cardinal pitcher named Gordon Richardson who came from nowhere to stop the Phils one day. Finally, the Phillies moved to solve this problem.

In early August, Quinn sent two unneeded players and cash to the Mets for Frank Thomas, a big righthanded slugger who had been in the National League for years. Thomas was to fill the first base hole left by the slump and ultimate departure of Sievers, and he was to punish clubs which persisted in feeding lefthanders to the Phillies. In his first at-bat, Thomas pulled a double down the left field line against the Mets' Al Jackson, and he kept on hitting, driving in 26 runs in 34 games.

August and early September were glorious for Mauch's team. Mahaffey and Bennett won a few games, and Bunning and Short hardly ever lost.

Callison was probably the best player in the league, hitting the ball often and with power, driving in key runs, and playing right field as well as it was possible to play it. Allen was just behind Callison in offensive production, and the surprising Rojas continued to hit and play all over the infield and outfield. Thomas did everything he was supposed to do and was a key factor in several come-from-behind victories.

On August 20, the Phillies won two from Pittsburgh, the first game a 2–0 Art Mahaffey two-hitter, the nightcap a 3–2 victory on a two-run sacrifice fly. Callison's 420-foot fly ball to center field scored Rick Wise from third *and* Tony Gonzalez, catching relay man Dick Schofield by surprise, from second. The play

Popular outfield star of the 1960s, Johnny Callison.

symbolized the way the '64 Phillies made things happen.

The Ballantine beer people, who sponsored the broadcasts of the club's games, had a big sign on the top of the right field scoreboard reading "Tote'm Home Plenty," the brewery's current advertising slogan. When the Phils came home in September, the sign had been changed to read "Tote'm Home Pennant," in honor of the impending triumph. The Phillies had the National League lead, and their fans, who had suffered through a 23-game losing streak just three summers earlier, were about to reap the reward for their faith.

On September 8, Frank Thomas broke his thumb sliding into second base against the Dodgers. A tough break, but the writers figured that Thomas would probably be ready to play again by the World Series. Just to be on the safe side, and hoping that lightning might perhaps strike twice,

Quinn purchased the veteran Vic Power from the Angels to fill in at first, but there would be no Cinderella story here. Power hit poorly for the Phils, .208 in 18 games, and the vulnerability to lefthanded pitching was back.[6]

Still, the Phillies were ahead. Short in St. Louis and Bennett with a 1–0 beauty over the Giants in San Francisco provided solid wins to maintain the lead at six games. They lost a tough game in Los Angeles on September 19, when Willie Davis stole home in the sixteenth inning for a Dodger win. It was not a smart play by Davis: there were two outs and two strikes on the batter, and all pitcher Morrie Steevens, who had just joined the Phillies, had to do was throw a strike. Instead he threw the ball to the backstop and the Phils lost. The next afternoon, though, Bunning pitched his tired teammates to a 3–2 win over the Dodgers for his 18th win, and they came home for a seven-game stand.

The Phillies had a 6½ game lead with twelve games to play, two numbers which Phillies fans of a certain age can never forget. Neither the Reds nor the Cardinals, the teams behind them, were going anywhere. Gussie Busch, the owner of the Cards, made no secret of his plan to replace manager Johnny Keane with Leo Durocher as soon as the season ended, and the Reds were playing for interim manager Dick Sisler, who had taken over when Fred Hutchinson had to step aside with the cancer that would cause his death in November. For Gene Mauch's Phillies, the pennant appeared won.

In the first game of the homestand, against second-place Cincinnati, Mahaffey, going for his 13th win, pitched superbly in a torrid duel with the Reds' John Tsitouris. In the sixth inning, with two out and a strike on the Reds' best hitter, Frank Robinson, utility man Chico Ruiz took off from third base on his own, trying to steal home. Manager Sisler was stunned when he saw Ruiz heading for the plate; after the game, he said, "If Chico hadn't scored, he'd still be running — all the way to San Diego," a Reds' farm club. (Ruiz later told reporters, "I was hoping to be safe. I didn't want to think of what the manager might say.") In the batter's box Robinson was startled, and Mahaffey could not believe his eyes. "At the exact fraction of a second that I'm going to throw the ball, I see him running," Mahaffey said; "I was in shock for a split second." It was a bonehead play by Ruiz, but it worked. Mahaffey threw the ball in the dirt, Ruiz scored, and the Phillies lost, 1–0. Dalrymple later said, with the benefit of hindsight, "When you lose one like that, the whole world starts to crumble around you pretty quickly. That's when we started to crumble."[7]

The next night, Short was bombed early, lefty Jim O'Toole had it all together for the Reds, and Cincinnati won, 9–2. It was a solid loss for the Phillies, and nothing could be done about it. People started getting nervous, though. Some of the fans remembered the horrendous skid of 1950, ended just in time by Sisler's home run on the last day.

The third Cincinnati game was a hard one to lose, because Dennis Bennett, working with a sore arm, was endowed with a 3–2 lead going into the seventh on Alex Johnson's two-run sixth-inning homer. Then Bennett and reliever Ed Roebuck gave up four runs to put Cincinnati ahead. The Phils loaded the bases in the seventh on three walks, but Reds' reliever Sammy Ellis struck out Callison on a checked swing and Taylor looking. He then breezed through the next two innings to save a 6–4 Cincinnati win.

By now the Philadelphia fans had started coming apart. "[T]he entire city," wrote *Sports Illustrated*, "was in a state of shock." Jim Bunning said the players were not bothered by the pressure, "but the fans! They all want to know what's wrong with us. They're the ones that can't handle the pressure."[8]

The Milwaukee Braves came to town after the Reds. The series gave the Braves, going nowhere themselves, a chance to salvage some self-respect out of a mediocre season. The first game matched Bunning against rookie southpaw Wade Blasingame. Leading off and playing center field for the Phils was Adolfo Phillips, a young Panamanian just up from Little Rock. Mauch put him in the lineup because he understood that Phillips hit Blasingame very well in the minors. It later developed, when it was too late, that there was some confusion on this point.

In the second inning, Bunning walked Eddie Mathews and gave up Joe Torre's line drive hit to center which Phillips overran and played into a triple. 1–0 Milwaukee. In the fifth, two-out hits by pitcher Blasingame and Felipe Alou scored two more runs. 3–0 Braves. In the seventh, the Phillies had two baserunners, first Allen and then Johnson, tagged out when they overslid second base. The Braves scored two more off Baldschun before the Phillies rallied for three ineffectual runs in the eighth. Adolfo Phillips was 0-for-3 against Blasingame.

The club's four losses in a row were magnified by the fact that neither Cincinnati or St. Louis had lost a game since the Phils' streak started. The Cardinals' Dick Groat said, "The Phillies must have thought they were entitled to lose a game now and then, but every time they lost, we won." The lead was shrinking fast. Richie Allen, irritated with the panicky reactions of the fans, said, "I think we'd be better off on the road."[9]

The next game was devastating. Chris Short, pitching with two days' rest and clearly not suffering for it, took a 1–0 lead into the seventh. He fanned Mathews, but Denis Menke was awarded first base when catcher Dalrymple tipped his bat. Mike de la Hoz doubled, and a sacrifice fly and a base hit produced two runs. Short left in the eighth when the Braves scored another run, but Johnny Callison hit a two-run homer in the bottom of the eighth to tie the game.

In the tenth, with righthander Bobby Locke pitching for Philadelphia, Ty Cline singled and Torre homered on a hanging curve to give Milwaukee a 5–3 lead. The Phillies fought back. Rojas singled, and with two gone Allen hit an inside-the-park home run off the scoreboard catwalk to restore the tie. Despite the reprieve, reliever John Boozer gave up two runs in the twelfth, when a possible double-play ball bounced off the glove of first baseman Frank Thomas, who had taken the cast off his thumb just so he could get back into the lineup. One run scored, and another came home on a double steal, and that was it. The gloom was thick over Philadelphia after this game. The once-commanding lead was only a game and a half.

On Saturday afternoon, before a crowd of 26,381, it appeared as if the Phillies' fortunes had finally turned. In the opening inning, Rojas singled, Allen tripled, and Alex Johnson belted a long home run. The Phils built up an early 4–0 lead for Mahaffey. Milwaukee picked up one run in the sixth and two in the seventh, but the Phillies had a 4–3 edge going into the ninth. Hank Aaron and Eddie Mathews started the final frame with singles and, with the bases loaded, the Braves' Rico Carty slammed a triple off reliever Bobby Shantz, the old A's star who was winding up his career with the '64 Phils. After this 6–4 loss, the sixth in a row, the Phillies' lead was down to a slim half game.

Bunning asked Mauch to let him pitch on Sunday with two days rest, but it was not his day. The Braves built up a big early lead, although curiously they did not hit Bunning hard. There was a steady stream of ground balls just eluding the infielders and bloopers dropping in front of the outfielders, but they all counted and they all put men on base, most of whom scored. Callison hit three successive home runs that day, but the early Milwaukee runs were too much to overcome, as the losing streak reached seven.

The 14–8 loss dropped the Phillies out of first place for the first time since July 16. They still had five games left, on the road against the two teams with which they were contending, the Cards and Reds. Cincinnati had the lead now, but it treated it as much like a hot potato as the Phillies had. The Pirates shut the Reds out twice, one a 16-inning 1–0 game.

Unfortunately, the Phillies were not finished losing. The local writers were by now criticizing Mauch for the team's play during the disastrous streak and for pitching Short and Bunning with insufficient rest. Of course, the team lost four games before the first use of a starter on short rest, and it did not lose the fifth game because of Short's pitching. The

Perfect game hurler Jim Bunning.

critics were also after Mauch for not using Ray Culp, who had a sore arm but seemed to be in the doghouse, too. The Phillips-Blasingame routine had not gone down well, either.[10]

But Mauch was operating the same way he had all season as the club built up the big lead. Besides, he was suffering more than anyone. Managing during this stretch, Mauch said, was "like watching someone drown." Asked by a *Bulletin* writer on September 27 what he could do to stop the losing, he replied, "Well, I never could hit and I never tried to pitch."[11]

The pitching was the problem. With Culp unavailable and Bennett hurting, throwing Bunning and Short in on limited rest was probably the best option Mauch had. There is some difference of opinion on Mauch's behavior during the slump. Allen said, "Once we really started to skid, Mauch became a wild man." Dalrymple, on the other hand, said, "Mauch was the quietest that I had ever seen him during that ten-game streak. He was absolutely silent." The one thing Mauch did not do was something, anything, to make his players relax, to loosen them up. It was not Gene Mauch's way.[12]

Short, again pitching with two days rest, going on guts and control, worked the opener in St. Louis, where the Cardinals, who had written off the season earlier, were now coming on strong. They scored a couple of quick runs, and that was all Bob Gibson needed to breeze to a 5–1 victory. The Phillies suddenly found themselves in third place. A shaken Gene Mauch cleared the press out of the clubhouse after the game, barking to reporters, "You S.O.B.s get the hell out of here," although he then met with them quite calmly twenty minutes later.

The next night, Bennett was hit hard early, and St. Louis won 4–2 as knuckleballer Barney Schultz saved the win for Ray Sadecki. It was the ninth loss in a row for the Phillies. There was a sad moment in this game when Callison, out of the lineup with the flu, pinch-hit a single. Shivering on first base, he called for his warmup jacket, but his fingers were shaking so badly he could not button it up. Bill White, the Cardinal first baseman, had to snap up the buttons for him. Allen's two strikeouts broke the National League seasonal record.

Wednesday night the Phils' defense collapsed behind Bunning, once more going with short rest, making four errors in the first four innings. Bunning did not have good stuff, and the Cards built up a lead of 8–0 behind Curt Simmons, who ran his career record against his original team to 16–2 with the win. The Phillies eventually rallied for five runs to knock out their former star, but the final of 8–5 was their tenth straight loss.

Nothing but a miracle could resurrect the Phillies, who were practically in a state of catatonia as they journeyed on to Cincinnati. Before they played the Reds they finally had a day off, the first in six weeks. A much-needed chance to regroup was long overdue. The rest of the season showed two games between the Phils and Reds, while the Cardinals had three games with Casey Stengel's hapless Mets. St. Louis had a record of 92–67, a half game ahead of the Reds at 92–68, and 2½ games ahead of the Phils, who were at 90–70 and could do no better than tie for first if they won both their games while the Cards lost all three.

On Friday night in Crosley Field, the Reds led the Phils, 3–0, when Short grazed Leo Cardenas with a pitch in the seventh inning. Cardenas, upset, tried to get at Short to retaliate, but his teammates stopped him. The next inning, Frank Thomas hit a popup behind second that Cardenas, still seething, failed to catch. The Phillies went on to score four runs and win the game, with an Allen triple the big blow. The awful streak was over, and the Mets beat the Cardinals to keep the race alive.

On Saturday the Mets beat St. Louis again, while the Reds and Phillies had the day off. Going into the last day of the season, St. Louis and Cincinnati were tied for first with the Phillies one game behind. Either the Cards or the Reds could win the flag outright, there could be a tie between the two, or a Philadelphia victory coupled with a Cardinal loss could create a three-way tie.

For this last pressure game, Mauch selected Jim Bunning, and his ace responded magnificently. He pitched a six-hit shutout and, backed up by good support from his teammates, including a double and two homers by Allen, beat the Reds, 10–0. The Phils put the game away quickly and then watched the scoreboard for the Mets-Cards action. New York led 3–2 in the fifth inning and hopes soared, but the Cardinals knocked out Galen Cisco with three runs in the fifth. Bill White hit a two-run homer in the sixth, Bob Gibson came in from the bullpen for St. Louis, and the Cards went on to win, 11–5, to nail down the 1964 pennant. The pennant that should have been Philadelphia's.[13]

It was a devastating end of the year for Gene Mauch and his players. They had much individual recognition to show for the season. Mauch won managerial plaudits, and Richie Allen, whose fine season included 29 home runs, 91 runs batted in, a league-leading 125 runs scored, and a .318 average, was named the league's top rookie, although he was jeered by the Philadelphia fans for his forty errors and 138 strikeouts, also tops in the National League.

Bunning finished at 19–8, with a 2.63 earned run average; he was voted "comeback of the year," though this miffed him somewhat since he thought he had been pretty good the year before. Short was 17–9, with an ERA of 2.20. Callison hit 31 home runs and drove in 104 runs. He was certainly the league's most valuable player in 1964, although the late-season debacle, for which little of the blame could be attached to him, cost him that honor, which went to Ken Boyer of the champion Cardinals.

With all the individual kudos, however, the 1964 Phillies were marked for posterity as perpetrators of one of the greatest and most ill-timed collapses in the game's history. No one who followed Philadelphia baseball in 1964 will ever forget that dreadful end to the season, and it is the first thing most fans think of whenever they hear Gene Mauch's name.

Mauch years later said of his '64 club, "I've had more talented clubs. But I've never had a smarter, more unselfish club than this one." His players, most of them, recognized the kind of job Mauch had done in 1964, although Mahaffey, Culp, and Covington were openly unhappy with the manager. Bunning said later, "Everybody blamed Gene for what happened, but to this day and until I die I will never blame him." Ed Roebuck, a veteran relief pitcher, said, "Gene did a tremendous job that year. He got the most out of us ... [W]e were a good club that wasn't good enough, and the fact that we got so close was a tribute to him." Close enough to create a legend in Philadelphia. Cookie Rojas summed it up at the time: "It was like swimming in a long, long lake," Cookie said, "and then you drown."[14]

Chapter 15

Last Years of an
Old Ballpark

The years between the searing heartbreak of 1964 and the departure from Connie Mack Stadium can be divided for the Phillies into two general periods: the three and a half seasons during which Gene Mauch continued as manager and the club tried desperately to win the pennant so cruelly snatched away by the baseball gods, and the years after in which the team sank heavily back to the bottom of the league. Another possible division is of seasons coping with the presence of Richie Allen and those in which they tried to cope without him.

These were the years of the final decline of Connie Mack Stadium and the delayed move to the new ballpark in South Philadelphia. They were not happy years for the Phillies, just as they were not happy years for Americans generally. Grim division spread across the land, generated by the horror of Vietnam, marked by the bitter alienation of youth and the black man from mainstream America, and symbolized by Grant Park, My Lai, and Selma. Lyndon Johnson's administration collapsed amid inflation, ineptitude, and a mammoth credibility gap, to be succeeded by that of Richard Nixon, who made divisiveness a calculated policy. The Phillies kept pace with LBJ: 1964 was their high point, and it was all downhill afterwards.

In preparation for 1965, John Quinn and Gene Mauch made several moves which showed that they were ready to trade the future for a current pennant. With only two pennants in the club's history, it is hard to be too critical of this policy, but the sad fact that the deals produced no championship laid Quinn and his manager open to fearful second-guessing.

Quinn swapped young Danny Cater, who became a fine player in ten American League seasons, to the White Sox for used-up pitcher Ray

Herbert, who went 7–13 in two undistinguished Philadelphia campaigns. He sent two youngsters to the California Angels for the cocky and over-rated Robert "Bo" Belinsky, who had become famous in L.A. for (a) pitching a no-hitter and (b) being seen in public with a succession of sexy Hollywood starlets. Bo's act did not play well in Philadelphia, where he was 4–9 with a high earned run average. He later claimed that Mauch ruined his arm by making him pitch relief, but he also admitted that "I think I have gotten more publicity for doing less than any player who ever lived."[1]

Quinn also traded Dennis Bennett to Boston for the weird but colorful first baseman Dick Stuart. Stuart, a mighty slugger whose weak and nonchalant fielding had earned him such nicknames as "Stonefingers" and "Doctor Strangeglove," hit 28 homers for the Phils but his influence on the team was so deleterious that Quinn practically gave him away to the Mets the following winter.

The Phils had a winning mark of 85–76 in 1965 but fell to sixth place, 11½ games behind the pennant-winning Dodgers. Bunning and Short were again superb pitchers, going 19–9 and 18–11 respectively, with earned run averages under three. Callison slammed 32 homers with 101 RBIs, Gonzalez and Alex Johnson both hit well, and Cookie Rojas batted .303 in 142 games.

Allen's hitting fell off slightly, to .302 and 20 home runs, and an incident in early July led to a serious impairment of relations between Richie and the Philadelphia fans.

On July 3, Allen, Callison and several other players were needling the veteran Frank Thomas during batting practice. Thomas had lost his job to Stuart and was seeing infrequent action. In the previous game, he had struck out trying to bunt in a key situation. Allen threw this failure up to him, and Thomas shouted back, "You're getting just like Cassius Clay — Muhammed Clay — always running off at the mouth."

Allen challenged him, and when Thomas said he did not intend to hurt the young black man's feelings, Allen answered, "That don't go with me," and took a swing at him, hitting him in the chest (Allen says he hit his jaw). Thomas, who had just left the batting cage, swung the bat he still had in his hands and hit Allen hard on the left shoulder. The enraged Allen then went for the veteran, as teammates struggled to break up the fight.[2]

Thomas's attempt to apologize before the game was rejected by Allen, while Mauch told the press, "It's the kind of thing that could happen between two people in any business." In the game that followed, Allen had two triples, a single, and four RBIs, while Thomas, pinch-hitting in the eighth, hit his first home run of the year. After the game, though, the team placed Thomas on irrevocable waivers "for the best interest of the club," and he was claimed by Houston.[3]

Allen, for his part, was directed by the Phillies to say nothing about the fight. The team's handling of the affair was about as maladroit as could be. Thomas was very popular with the local fans, who saw him as the guy who came in when needed and almost won them the '64 pennant. When Thomas was released after the fight, Allen was blamed. Allen never got to tell his side of the story, but Thomas was quoted extensively in the press and on the radio with his version of the fight. When Thomas told an *Inquirer* reporter, "Certain guys can dish it out but can't take it," fans all over the Delaware Valley nodded knowingly.[4]

Finally, Richie Allen was black and Thomas was white, and this too made a difference, especially in the atmosphere of the mid–'60s around Connie Mack Stadium, where the average white fan was nervous in any event coming to a ballgame in what was now a solidly black neighborhood. Allen had never concealed his racial consciousness, and this was something to which the man in the grandstand was unaccustomed. Henceforth, Allen was booed regularly in Philadelphia, and it was not the good-natured booing to which Del Ennis and the A's Gus Zernial had been subjected. It was mean and nasty, freighted with racial animus, and it changed Richie Allen.

Still, Allen could rip the ball, and Callison was one of the league's superstars. Ray Culp bounced back in 1965 (14–10), and there were still Bunning and Short. Quinn felt the Phillies could win it all in 1966, so he made some more trades. He dealt Mahaffey, Alex Johnson, and reserve catcher Pat Corrales to St. Louis for half of the Cardinals' championship infield of 1964, first baseman Bill White and shortstop Dick Groat, along with catcher Bob Uecker, whose specialty was funny stories. Groat was 35 and White 31, but it was hoped they had some good ball left. Baldschun went to Baltimore for veteran outfielder Jackie Brandt and young reliever Darold Knowles.

Then, shortly after the season started, Quinn talked the Cubs out of veteran pitchers Larry Jackson and Bob Buhl; "these two," said Quinn, "give our pitching staff a lot of status." To get them, he gave up Adolfo Phillips, John Herrnstein, and a young relief pitcher from Canada named Ferguson Jenkins, about whose fastball there seemed to be some question. Buhl was near the end of the line, but Mauch got several seasons of valuable work from Jackson. Phillips was moody and erratic for the Cubs, and neither he nor Herrnstein lasted long in the big leagues.[5]

But Jenkins, unfortunately for Quinn's reputation, soon became one of the top pitchers in the game, a consistent, year-in year-out twenty-game winner in Chicago and Texas, who won 284 games on his way to a place in the Hall of Fame. It was a disastrous trade.

Nevertheless, for 1966 it was a success. Larry Jackson won 15 games for the Phillies and was a big help. Knowles pitched well out of the bullpen. Groat and White both had good years. Bunning won 19 for the third year in a row, with a 2.41 ERA, and Short was 20–10.

Allen hit .317 with forty home runs and 110 RBIs, but stories were starting to circulate around town about the slugger's heavy drinking. Allen was a loner and an individualist — a man who "felt a powerful resistance to having his mind made up for him," as Bob Uecker, his best friend on the club, wrote — and signs of trouble were sprouting around him.[6]

Mauch's problems were compounded by a mysterious power slump by Callison. The slim outfielder, though raising his average a few points, dropped in home run production to eleven, after averaging 28 over the prior four seasons, and his RBIs, in which he averaged 91 over the same period, fell off to 55. He finished the year wearing glasses.

The 1966 Phils climbed a couple of notches, to fourth place, and had their third straight million-plus attendance. They were still eight games behind pennant-winning Los Angeles.

Over the winter, Bill White tore his Achilles' tendon playing handball, and the pattern was set for a series of crippling injuries. White was never again the player he had been before the injury. Groat hurt his ankle, could hardly function at all, and was sold to the Giants in mid–June. Short injured his knee and then his back and won only nine games. And on August 24, Richie Allen cut his hand.

Allen's injury was strange. He was pushing an old car when he slipped and his right hand broke the headlight, severing two tendons and the ulnar nerve. Allen said the hand "looked like it had been blown off by a land mine." He underwent two and a quarter hours of surgery at Temple University Hospital and was through for the year.[7]

The fans, suspicious now of anything having to do with Allen, thought the car-pushing story, an odd one at best, sounded fishy. Who pushes a car by the headlight, anyway? All sorts of theories floated around town, from the familiar drunken-brawl one to the ever-popular jealous-husband scenario. The severe nature of Allen's injury made his future doubtful, but he worked hard to rehabilitate the hand and only his throwing was affected. When he came back in 1968, Allen played left field, with shortstop Bobby Pena running deep into the outfield to get the ball from him.

With all the injuries, Mauch had a tough time keeping his club in the first division. Before the season, Quinn made a couple more of his youth-for-age deals, getting outfielder Don Lock from Washington for reliever

Knowles and making a straight pitcher swap with the Cubs, Ray Culp for lefty Dick Ellsworth. Neither trade helped much.

Far more useful were two aging relief pitchers picked up for next to nothing, Dick Hall and the returning Dick Farrell. Both were marvelous coming out of Mauch's bullpen. Bunning pitched very well, leading the league in innings and strikeouts, posting a 2.29 ERA, but only 17–15 in wins and losses. He set a record by losing five 1–0 games, indicative of the type of support he was getting. The hitting slump was general, as Callison continued to struggle. Only Tony Gonzalez, who finished second in batting with .339, helped much, although Allen hit .307 with 23 homers in his abbreviated season.

The decline of the Phillies was now apparent. The personnel was over-aged, and too many good young players had been shunted off to other teams. Callison had unexpectedly burned out as a high-quality player, and Richie Allen's psyche and extracurricular activity seemed of more interest than his exploits on the field. In the Age of Aquarius, baseball seemed very traditional and establishment-oriented. Philadelphia was certainly not immune from this feeling.

Attendance dropped markedly, down to 828,888 in 1967, after three years of well over a million, and the ballpark had become shabby and down at the heel. The neighborhood around the park had changed, too, with the working-class whites who had been there since it was built moving out and black people moving in. With the change in the neighborhood came stories of cars stolen from the streets, robberies along the sidewalks, muggings in the men's rooms during games.

The old scam of car-watching ("Watch your car for a quarter, mister!") had seemed amusing and innocent back in the 1940s when practiced by young white boys; it seemed more sinister and threatening to white fans a generation later when the car-watchers were a couple of black youths.

Whether the stories of crime around Connie Mack Stadium were true or not hardly mattered. White people who used to come to 21st and Lehigh without giving it a thought believed they were true, so they stayed away from the Phillies. It was a dilemma for Bob Carpenter along with his sagging ballclub, and the political machinations involved with Philadelphia's building a new stadium made that project seem interminable.

Over the next two seasons the Allen problem became acute. Richie squabbled with Quinn over money, he fought with the manager over club rules, he asked repeatedly to be traded, he failed to show up for games, and often he was under the influence of alcohol when he made his appearance in the locker room. "I began to hit the sauce pretty good," Allen said, "and I didn't care who knew it." Mauch tried to get his attention with a series of heavy fines for drinking before a game, for missing batting practice, for showing up late. Nothing worked. Mauch even benched Allen for a couple of weeks. Little changed.[8]

The skipper was given several days off to visit his sick daughter in California and, while he was gone, on June 14, 1968, he was fired. It was a shabby way of making a change, although Mauch surely suspected it was coming. Management had decided on a course of appeasement: Allen and Mauch did not hit it off, so Allen would be mollified by the discharge of Gene Mauch. Bob Skinner, from the Phils' San Diego farm club, was named manager.

Mauch managed the club for over eight years, unheard of

Controversial slugger Dick Allen.

in Phillies annals, and was their most successful leader in the twentieth century up to that time. He was colorful, confident, and controversial, a center of attention since he had come to town. Now he was gone, although he would not remain unemployed for long. He was soon hired to run the new Montreal club.

In the meantime, 1968 was a bad year. The club won as often as it lost for Mauch, but it nose-dived under Skinner. Short won 19 games, but he was the only high spot. Larry Jackson was 13–17, and a tobacco farmer from Kentucky named Woodie Fryman was 12–14, although both of them joined Short with earned run averages under three.

Bunning had been traded to Pittsburgh during the off-season, for Fryman, infield prospect Don Money, and two pitchers. Gonzalez slumped, the team did not hit, and its final standing was a tie for seventh place. Attendance fell again, to 664,546; there were better things for folks in the Philadelphia area to do than come out to Connie Mack Stadium to boo Richie Allen.

The next year was worse. Even with two more expansion teams in the league, San Diego and Montreal, the Phillies finished 37 games out of first place, fifth in their six-team division. They won 63 and lost 99, and home attendance fell to 519,414, the lowest total since wartime 1945. Chris Short was idled all season with a back injury, and the pitching burden fell on young Rick Wise (15–13), left-hander Grant Jackson (14–18), and Fryman (12–15). Allen pounded 32 home runs and rookie outfielder Larry Hisle hit 20, but the team was dispirited and dull.

The only thing to keep anyone's interest was seeing what Allen would do next. He missed team flights, missed games, arrived late for games. He moved out of the team's locker room and into a nearby storage room, in hopes of having more privacy.

On June 24, when Allen was not present at Shea Stadium for the start of a twi-night doubleheader, Skinner announced his suspension. Allen heard the news on the radio as he was driving to Shea, with the first game already underway, so he turned around, went back to the hotel, packed his bag, and disappeared for two weeks. Finally, after a private meeting with Carpenter in which the owner promised to trade him after the season, he reported back to the team and was reinstated.

When Allen refused to play an early August exhibition game with the club's Reading farm and was supported by Carpenter, Skinner quit. Coach George Myatt took over as manager for the rest of the season and answered the first question of the press this way: "I don't think God Almighty Himself could handle Richie Allen, so all I can do is try."[9]

Now playing first base, where his fielding deficiencies did the least damage to the team, Allen amused himself by drawing words with his spikes in the dirt around his position. Finally he started drawing numbers, representing the games he had left in a Phillies uniform.

Shortly after the '69 season ended, the Phillies started making changes. They hired Frank Lucchesi, a successful manager in their farm system, as the team's new field leader. Lucchesi, an emotional, empathic man who helped the club's public relations immeasurably, visited hospitals, met with youth groups, spoke to service clubs, and appealed to the Italian neighbors of the new ballpark being built in South Philadelphia.

On October 8, the Phillies finally solved their Allen problem, only to find themselves with a new one. They traded Richie to St. Louis, along with Rojas and pitcher Jerry Johnson, for the Cardinals' Curt Flood, Tim McCarver, reliever Joe Hoerner, and Byron Browne, a marginal outfielder. The key players were outfielder Flood, a quality center fielder for twelve years, and McCarver, the Cards' regular catcher since 1963. They had played on three championship teams in St. Louis and were proven winners.

Flood, however, threw a monkey-wrench into the works, when he announced that he was not coming to Philadelphia. A black man, Flood decried what he perceived as the racist atmosphere of Philadelphia and the Phillies organization, and he said he would not be bought and sold as a chattel. Flood referred to Philadelphia as "the nation's northernmost southern city" and the "scene of Richie Allen's ordeals."[10]

As Flood litigated the validity of the reserve clause in the federal courts over the next couple of years, eventually losing his case in the U.S. Supreme Court, the Phillies traded his rights to Washington and also received two more players from St. Louis as compensation. Significantly, no one asked the Cards to send Allen back.

One of the most controversial individuals ever to play baseball in Philadelphia, Allen certainly appeared to be finished with the town. Yet, over six full seasons, even with the cut hand and suspensions and drinking and sulks, Richard Anthony Allen hit an even .300, with 177 home runs, 544 runs batted in, and, for good measure, 64 stolen bases. Allen was an immensely talented offensive baseball player, one who could have made the Hall of Fame had he not been so self-destructive.

The other big trade the club made for 1970 sent John Callison to the Cubs for relief pitcher Dick Selma and outfielder Oscar Gamble. This was a trade with which no one was happy, although Callison, fed up with dealing with John Quinn, had insisted upon being moved. The modest and soft-spoken Callison was very popular with the fans, who remembered fondly the four fine seasons he had put together from 1962 through 1965. He hit 112 home runs over those four seasons, drove in 366 runs, twice led the league in triples, and, with his great arm, led all outfielders in assists all four years. He established himself as one of the best hitters in the National League at 26, with a very bright future.[11]

Something happened, though, in 1966, and the bright future never materialized: Johnny Callison became just a journeyman ballplayer. But for four years he could do it all: hit for average, hit with power, hit in the clutch, run, play the outfield, and throw. Callison was an exciting ballplayer to watch, and he made things happen. The fans loved him, and they made allowances for him long after his talents began to fade, long after the power left his bat. They wanted so much to believe in the Johnny Callison of those four years.

For 1970, everything was refurbished. In addition to the trades and the new manager, the Phillies unveiled new uniforms and coined a slogan, telling the world that "It's a new ball game." This was all predicated on the move to the stadium in South Philadelphia, a move which never took place in 1970. Building delays, political charges, and typical

Philadelphia bad luck prevented the stadium's completion. The Phillies, all dolled up in their brand-new uniforms, were forced to spend a last year in rundown Connie Mack Stadium.

1970 was better than the year before. The team won ten more games, and attendance was up, to 708,247. Tony Taylor, having one of his finest years, hit .301. Don Money hit a solid .295, with 14 homers. First baseman Deron Johnson, the ex-Reds slugger who had come to the Phillies in 1969, whacked 27 home runs and drove in 93 runs. Selma and Hoerner pitched well in relief, and a rookie keystone duo of second baseman Denny Doyle and shortstop Larry Bowa played very well.

The pitching was shaky. Rick Wise put up a 13–14 record, Jim Bunning, re-acquired from Los Angeles at 38, went 10–15, Chris Short was 9–16, and Grant Jackson posted a mark of 5–15. In one awful inning on May 2, both catchers, McCarver and Mike Ryan, broke their hands, and Lucchesi had a disaster area behind the plate, with a steady stream of minor league backstops coming and going after that.

On October 1, 1970, the last game was played in Connie Mack Stadium, known for most of its history as Shibe Park. Carpenter, who had been forced to buy the park when the A's moved out, had sold it at a loss in 1961 to a developer, and it had been sold again, to Jerry Wolman, the then-owner of the football Eagles, in 1964. The Phillies had reverted to their old status as tenants while awaiting the completion of a new facility. Still, the last game brought back a flood of memories, and it was in itself a night not to be forgotten.

There was a big crowd, later announced at 31,822, for which the ticket-sellers, ushers, and vendors were totally unprepared. In a concession to the historic nature of the occasion, the Phillies management handed out to the first few thousand persons coming through the gates red wooden boards, supposed to represent seat slats, apparently on the theory that these would satisfy souvenir-hunters. These boards made useful tools in breaking apart the real seats; they were also used to bash other fans' heads.[12]

The game, against Montreal, was a good one, even a meaningful one to some extent (the loser finished last), but few of the spectators paid much attention to it. "Souvenir hunters nearly ripped old Connie Mack Stadium apart last night," the *Bulletin* reported. From the start there was a constant clanging, banging din: the noise of people hammering the old seats apart. A bunch of young men drew a big cheer when they hoisted over their heads a whole row of seats, still connected but unbolted from the floor. Another man paraded through the stands holding aloft a seat from a men's room toilet.[13]

Soon people started running onto the field, first singly, then two, three, four at a time. Most of them wanted to shake hands with Tony Taylor, though some preferred sliding into bases. It was a good-natured crowd, but the umpires were getting nervous. Out on the field, the sound of a ballpark being dismantled must have been unsettling.

Finally, after the Expos had tied the score at 1–1 in the ninth, scoring when outfielder Ron Stone was unable to catch John Bateman's line drive because a fan had grabbed his arm, the umps announced that the next intrusion onto the field would cause the forfeiture of the game to Montreal. Gene Mauch, the Expos' manager, who knew Philadelphia fans well, exploded out of the dugout to tell the umpires that he wanted no part of any forfeit, which could easily touch off a riot. Luckily, in the tenth, McCarver singled with two out, stole second, and scored on Gamble's single the last run ever in the old park.

The crowd erupted onto the field, and souvenir-hunting began in earnest. The Phillies were forced to cancel the planned post-game ceremony, as fans wrestled the groundskeepers for the bases, planks were stripped off the outfield walls, huge swatches of sod were torn up, thousands of seats were wrenched loose, and anything not bolted or chained down was carted off.[14]

Thus did baseball leave old Connie Mack Stadium. It was not one of the biggest parks, except in its infancy, and it certainly was not one of the fanciest. Poles blocked vision, and winding staircases made it difficult to leave when there was any kind of a crowd. It had inadequate automobile parking, and it was slightly unbalanced, favoring righthanded hitters over lefties, because of the high right field wall.

Yet it was a place with character, a personality of its own, and generations of Philadelphia youngsters grown old had a considerable emotional investment in the old yard. Its time was past, of course, by 1970, and it had to be replaced, but there was many a pause of regret and nostalgia at the passing of a storied landmark in Philadelphia baseball. Bob Carpenter expressed the sentiments of many when he said, "Progress. I guess that's what you'd have to call it. But damn, I hate to leave this place."[15]

Chapter 16

The Vet

On a cold and windy April 10, 1971, before 55,352 people, the largest baseball crowd ever in Pennsylvania, 39-year-old Jim Bunning stood on a pitcher's mound in South Philadelphia and prepared to pitch to a Montreal outfielder named Charles "Boots" Day. When Bunning delivered the ball, which Day hit right back to him, Veterans Stadium became officially a major league ballpark. Bunning threw the ball to first baseman Deron Johnson for the stadium's first out and went on to notch a 4–1 win in the first game played in the Phillies' new digs.

How Veterans Stadium came to be is a story in itself and one which, in Philadelphia, was bound to have tortuous twists and turns. Mayor Richardson Dilworth had talked about a new stadium for Philadelphia's sports teams as far back as 1953, and over the ensuing years studies were made and conjectures floated about how and where such a facility could be erected. In 1964 the voters approved a $25 million bond issue for a new stadium, but that was just a start. To pay its way, the stadium would have to have both the Phillies and Eagles as tenants, and the Eagles were none too anxious to sign on. The pro football club had a comfortable arrangement with the University of Pennsylvania for the use of Franklin Field, a football-only horseshoe with excellent sight lines all around, and agreed to leave it most reluctantly.

The shape of the new facility remained a matter of dispute between the Phillies and the Eagles. Even harder to settle was the question of where to locate it. Among the suggested sites were Fairmount Park, Torresdale on the Delaware River, Cedarbrook in suburban Cheltenham Township, even the air space over the tracks at 30th Street Station. With the city dragging its feet in the mid–60s, Bob Carpenter bought eighty acres of undeveloped land on Route 70 in Cherry Hill, New Jersey. This purchase, when it became known, served to focus the city's attention on the problem. "I didn't buy the land expressly to use as leverage," Carpenter said later, innocently, "although I was certainly accused of that."[1]

The city finally decided on a 74-acre site near the foot of Broad Street in South Philadelphia, at Pattison Avenue. Architect Hugh Stubbins designed a stadium in the form of an "octorad," an eight-radius shape that is something between a square and a circle and seemed the best that could be done to satisfy the requirements of the two sports. In 1967, another bond issue, for 13 million, was approved, to meet rising costs, and on October 2, 1967, Mayor Tate broke ground at the Broad and Pattison location.

It took more than three years to bring the project to completion, with labor problems, weather problems, design problems, money problems, grand jury investigations—all the usual ills to which a public project in Philadelphia is subject. There were disputes over what to name the place, although Paul D'Ortona, the president of City Council, took care of those by hammering a bill through that body to have it called Philadelphia Veterans Stadium, no matter what the fans and taxpayers might prefer. The final cost amounted to 52 million dollars, but it was done.

What did Philadelphia get for its money? It got a huge concrete structure, enclosed all the way around with two tiers of seating, its floor covered with Astroturf. The place held some 56,000 seats for baseball and more for football, thanks to movable grandstands. There was parking for 12,000 cars. The playing field was symmetrical, with distances of 330 feet down the foul lines and 408 feet to centerfield. And, even with Hugh Stubbins's "octorad," the shape of the playing surface was still an unhappy compromise between the needs of a baseball diamond and those of a football field, with the seating areas pushed far back from the playing area.

Philadelphia got a building with none of the character or the feeling of involvement in the game of its predecessor. An architectural critic, comparing the Vet to similar stadiums built at about the same time in Pittsburgh, St. Louis, Atlanta, and Cincinnati, wrote, "The Vet shares the structural expressionism of most recent stadiums where circulation ramps, elevators, and columns are the sole elements of composition," part of "a generation of frontless, scaleless, placeless behemoths seemingly cast adrift in a sea of parking lots." In this regard, he wrote, "the Vet is little better or worse than most of its peers."[2]

The Astroturf, which covered most of the playing surface — all but the four bases and the pitcher's mound — was controversial from the start. In its favor was the fact that the rug drained better than did a grass field, so that rainouts became less frequent. The plastic grass was also said to be cheaper to maintain, although the necessity of replacing the whole carpet every seven or eight years cuts into those savings. It was claimed that artificial turf was a necessity with both baseball and football teams using the field, since grass would be torn up by the steady use.

The drawbacks of artificial turf, however, are substantial. Because it sits on a hard subsurface and has little give to it, artificial turf contributes to more numerous and more serious injuries than are incurred on natural grass. On a sunny summer day, it can heat up to 120 degrees or more, sapping the energy of even the best-conditioned athlete.

Worst of all for baseball, artificial turf changes the nature of the game. Because the surface is so fast, bunting becomes more difficult, ground balls scoot through the infield (and between the outfielders) more quickly, and middle infielders now customarily play back on what used to be called the outfield grass. An outfielder who gets too close to a ball dropping in front of him risks the ball bounding over his head.

For 1971 Lucchesi's Phillies had their shiny new ballpark. They had a new voice in Harry Kalas, an import from Houston who replaced Bill Campbell on the broadcast crew and was soon regarded as one of baseball's best announcers. The team was pretty much the same one which had stumbled to 88 defeats the year before. For '71 the Phils won only 67, lost 95, and finished last, sixth place in the divisional setup.

With the new facility, this bad team set a Philadelphia season attendance record, with 1,511,223 customers coming through the gates. What they saw was not very exciting. McCarver had the highest batting average, .278, and Deron Johnson hit 34 home runs. Willie Montanez, one of the replacements obtained from St. Louis for the no-show Flood, had a fine rookie season with 30 home runs and 99 RBIs. Rick Wise led the pitching staff with a record of 17–14 and 2.88. Fryman was 10–7, Short 7–14, and Bunning was 5–12 in his final year.

The high point of the Phillies' year, aside from the opener at the Vet, came on June 23 at Cincinnati. Wise pitched a no-hit, no-run game against the Reds, allowing only one baserunner when he walked Dave Concepcion in the sixth inning. There have been lots of no-hitters over the years (although not many by Phillies pitchers), but no one ever did what Rick Wise did in his. He hit two home runs, to make it just about a perfect day, especially when third baseman John Vukovich caught Pete Rose's line drive for the final out.

In November 1971, Philadelphia chose a new mayor and began a new era in the city's history. Frank L. Rizzo, a large and imposing ex-policeman, was elected in '71 and re-elected in '75, then rebuffed by the voters when he attempted to have the City Charter amended to permit him to run again. Rizzo switched from the Democratic party to the Republican to run again in 1987, losing to W. Wilson Goode, the city's first black mayor. Win or lose, Frank Rizzo was a presence in Philadelphia civic life until his death in the summer of 1991, in the midst of another run for the mayoralty. A blunt, tough-talking, charismatic figure, Rizzo was adored by ethnic groups and by those who felt he would not be deterred by legal niceties in fighting street crime and violence. Similarly, he was anathema to liberals and blacks, who deplored his methods and decried the fiscal and labor policies which shredded the city's credit rating. In Philadelphia, no one was neutral about Frank Rizzo.

Before the '72 spring camp opened, Rick Wise and general manager John Quinn reached a stalemate over the pitcher's contract. When he learned that the Cardinals were having the same problem with one of their top pitchers, Quinn proposed a swap of the holdout hurlers. On February 25, 1972, Wise was traded to St. Louis, even up for lefthanded pitcher Steve Carlton, who had been 20–9 for the '71 Redbirds. Carlton, 27 years old, had already won 77 games for St. Louis in five full and two partial seasons and was considered one of the league's premier pitchers. But then Wise was a year younger and had won 75 games. It looked like an even trade, but it haunted the Cardinals for years. Carlton's 1972 performance with a terrible Phillies team was to be the stuff of legend.

The Phillies were awful. They won 59 games and lost 97. They scored fewer runs than any other team in the league. And they might have finished in the Sally League without Carlton. He compiled a record of 27 and 10, winning an astounding 46 per cent of his team's victories, unmatched by any pitcher of modern times. He led the league with an earned run average of 1.97, with 310 strikeouts, 30 complete games, and 346 innings. He threw eight shutouts. He won fifteen games in succession at one stretch, and he was the unanimous winner of the Cy Young Award as the league's best pitcher. Rick Wise was 16–16, with a good 3.11 ERA for the Cardinals, but Steve Carlton's 1972 season may have been the greatest pitching performance of all time, given the calibre of his teammates.

Since the rest of the staff had a combined record of 32–87, there is not much point to dwelling very long on the other performances, like the 2–15 record of southpaw Ken Reynolds, the 4–14 of Billy Champion, or the 4–10 of Woodie Fryman. The leading hitter on the team was a powerfully-built rookie outfielder named Greg Luzinski, soon to be called "the Bull," whose .281, 18 home runs, and 68 RBIs all led the club. Bowa, the scrawny-looking shortstop, led the league with 13 triples. Montanez paced the NL in doubles and outfield assists, but his average and power numbers were down. In September, the club called up a red-haired minor league infielder named Michael Jack Schmidt and played him in eleven games at third base. He hit .206, with one home run.

Schmidt was the discovery of Tony Lucadello, perhaps the best talent scout baseball has ever known. Lucadello worked for the Phillies for thirty-three years until his suicide in May 1989. He started scouting in 1942 for the Cubs and joined the Phillies in 1957. Lucadello's territory was Ohio, Michigan, Indiana, and Illinois, and he signed fifty players who made it to the big leagues, a number never approached by any other scout. One of Tony's boys, Ferguson Jenkins, went into the Hall of Fame in 1991, and Schmidt's 1995 election gave him a second, although Lucadello had to sweat out the 1971 draft until the Phillies picked Schmidt in the second round.[3]

Attendance was down in 1972, to 1,343,329, and the team was terrible, so on June 3, the Phillies retired general manager John Quinn, replacing him with farm director Paul Owens, known as "the Pope." They felt the game had passed Quinn by; he sometimes drank more than he should have, and his parsimonious manner was no longer appropriate in the dawning new era of owner-player relations. Still, John Quinn's last trade, the Wise-for-Carlton swap, was certainly one for the ages. On July 10, with the team still floundering except on days when Carlton pitched, Owens relieved Lucchesi as manager and took on that job too. Lucchesi wept when he faced the press, his anguish at losing a job he loved aggravated by Owens's lack of candor about the club's intentions.[4]

Assumption of the managerial position by Paul Owens was not the case of self-aggrandizement it appeared to be at first blush. The Pope wanted to take a closer look at the team, particularly its young players, so that as general manager he would have a better idea of the club's potential strengths and weaknesses. As the former farm director, Owens knew that there were good times coming, with the players then in the minor league system, but he wanted to have a look at those already in the majors, like Doyle, Bowa, Luzinski, outfielder Mike Anderson, and reliever Mac Scarce.

After the '72 season mercifully ended, Paul Owens looked for a manager. There was talk of former Cincinnati manager Dave Bristol, and there was hard lobbying for former pitching great Jim Bunning. In fact, both men believed that the job was to be theirs. When Owens called a press conference on November 1 and introduced as the new manager of the Phillies a sad-eyed and virtually unknown Dodger coach named Danny Ozark, it was a stunning surprise. Ozark had never played in the major leagues, and few in Philadelphia had noticed him while he was serving as Walter Alston's long-time third base coach.[5]

Three weeks later, on November 22, Bob Carpenter convened a press conference of his own, to state that he was leaving the club's presidency and turning the job over to his son, Robert Ruliph Morgan Carpenter III, who had played football and baseball at Yale. Ruly Carpenter was 32 at the time, and he had been working for the Phillies, in the front office and in player development, for nine years. He became the youngest club president in the big leagues, and one of the best prepared.

Chapter 17

The Ozark Years

Danny Ozark was not a brilliant strategist or an innovator; as it turned out, he had some problems as a communicator. What he was was a solid, fundamental baseball man, typical of the Brooklyn/Los Angeles organization since the days of Branch Rickey — just what the bedraggled Phillies needed after the sorry '71 and '72 seasons. When the players reported for spring training in 1973 they learned that fundamental baseball was what was in store for them. As Bill Conlin of the *Daily News* once wrote, "Danny Ozark's early camps were colored Dodger Blue. Baseball was taught the Dodger way...."[1]

There were new faces for 1973. The day before he named his new manager, Paul Owens swung a major trade with Milwaukee, giving up Money, Vukovich, and Champion to get four hurlers from the Brewers, the key figure being Jim Lonborg, the former Red Sox ace who had come back from serious injuries to pitch well.

A month later Owens traded for Minnesota handyman Cesar Tovar and Cleveland outfielder Del Unser. He also expected rookies Schmidt, catcher Bob Boone, and pitcher Dick Ruthven to contribute in 1973. Indeed, it was his belief in Schmidt's potential that allowed him to trade the talented Don Money for Lonborg.

With his emphasis on fundamentals, Ozark brought the 1973 edition of the Phillies home a much improved team. They put together a record of 71–91, winning twelve more games than the '72 crew, and they drew 1,475,934, up more than 130,000. They still finished sixth, but they were actually in contention for part of the year in an evenly-balanced Eastern Division.

They did this despite a major slump by Carlton. Steve had been the toast of Philadelphia after his spectacular 1972 season, and he spent the off-season going to banquets, giving speeches, and making commercials. The resulting lack of focus led to a 13–20, 3.90 record in 1973. Where

Carlton had been free in discussing his philosophy of life with the local writers in 1972, he found them ridiculing him and his philosophy as a loser in 1973. Carlton still led the league in games started, complete games, and innings pitched, but he led as well in losses.

Lonborg, too, was a disappointment, as his 13–16 record was matched by a high 4.88 earned run average. But the slack was picked up by Ken Brett, a throw-in in the big trade with Milwaukee, and righthander Wayne Twitchell. Brett won 13 and lost nine, put together an ERA of 3.44, and startled everyone with his hitting. He had always hit well, and for the Phillies he had an amazing streak of home runs in four consecutive games. Twitchell, a skinny 6'6", was also 13–9 and had an earned run average of 2.50. Ruthven, in part-time duty, was 6–9.[2]

With Money gone to Milwaukee, rookie Mike Schmidt was given the third base job. The Ohio University graduate fielded well but his batting average was a feeble .196, with an alarming 136 strikeouts. Just when he seemed to be overmatched by National League pitching, though, Schmidt would rip one into the seats. He hit 18 home runs, so better days were expected.

Boone, the freshman catcher, batted .261 and looked fine behind the plate. Doyle hit .273 at second, but Bowa slipped badly to .211, while still playing an excellent shortstop. Unser in center field hit .289 with eleven home runs, and big Greg Luzinski walloped 29 home runs, drove in 97 runs, and averaged .285. Tovar was a disappointment, hitting only .268. On the whole, though, 1973 was a year of progress, especially if Carlton's bad year was viewed as an aberration.

A lot more progress was made in 1974. In the off-season, Owens traded Brett to Pittsburgh for Dave Cash, an up-and-coming star at second base. Ozark's Phillies won nine more games than in '73, finishing with a record of 80–82, good for third place in the East. The team was in the hunt for a good part of the year, staying up with the first-place Pirates into August before falling back and slipping behind the Cardinals.

The big change for the Phillies was in second-year man Mike Schmidt, who blossomed into one of the league's top sluggers. Schmidt hit 36 home runs to lead the league, and he drove in 116 runs with his .282 batting average. The red-haired third sacker paced the National League in slugging percentage, although he was also on top of the circuit with his 138 whiffs.

Willie Montanez at first base hit .304, and Cash batted .300 while providing hustling leadership. Luzinski missed a good chunk of the season with a torn-up knee, and his numbers were way down. Bowa hit an encouraging .275, and spare outfielder Jay Johnstone, picked up from the

Toledo Mud Hens after eight years in the American League, batted .295 and became a fan favorite with his slightly off-center personality.

Carlton and Lonborg rebounded from their off-years, Carlton going 16–13 and leading the league in strikeouts and Lonborg putting together a 17–13 record. Ron Schueler, a tall righthander obtained from the Atlanta Braves, Ruthven, and Twitchell filled out the rotation. For the bullpen, the Phillies picked up Gene Garber, a bearded righthander with an odd motion which saw him face completely away from the batter just before delivering the ball. Garber pitched in 34 games and had a low earned run average of 2.06.

The '74 Phillies were still a couple of games under the .500 level, but it was clear that with young stars like Schmidt, Carlton, Luzinski, Boone, Bowa, and Cash they were on their way to becoming legitimate contenders. A new attendance record of 1,808,648 showed that the sometimes-skeptical fans of Philadelphia and South Jersey were convinced of this as well.

Owens made a big trade over the winter, sending Unser, Mac Scarce, and catching prospect John "Bad Dude" Stearns to New York for free-spirited Frank "Tug" McGraw, the bullpen star of the '73 Mets champions, and two lesser lights. The Mets were worried about McGraw's nagging shoulder problem, but it cleared up after he reported to Clearwater. The pieces were falling into place for the best team over a period of years in the club's history, and the won-loss record started to show it.

In 1975, the Phillies were in the race most of the way, as they went 86–76 to finish second behind the Pirates. Indeed, according to Danny Ozark, they were still in the race after they were out of it. On September 22, Pittsburgh's Bruce Kison defeated the Phillies to take a seven-game lead with six games to play. In most people's book that combination spells "mathematical elimination," but never-say-die Danny told a reporter that night after the game, "We aren't out of it if we win every game and they lose every game." Told that his club was mathematically done, Ozark said, "That's disheartening."[3]

It made no difference, of course, since the Pirates were in. What it did, unfortunately, was turn Danny Ozark into a figure of fun, a mathematical buffoon, in Philadelphia, and he found it hard to be taken seriously thereafter. Which was a shame, because he as field manager, Owens as general manager, and ex-pitcher Dallas Green, the farm director who was turning out a number of quality ballplayers, had taken a bad team and made it a good one in a relatively short period of time.

Schmidt repeated as home run champion, with 38, and he drove in 95 runs. His average slipped to .249, and his strikeout total, already the highest in the league in '74, ballooned to an alarming 180. He also had a tendency to sulk when things went poorly, and the fans started to get on him, overlooking his excellent fielding.

The right field platoon of Jay Johnstone (.329) and Downtown Ollie Brown (.303) hit very well, and Luzinski, his knee better, hit 34 round-trippers and led the league in RBIs with 120, while batting .300. Both parts of the keystone combination, second baseman Cash and shortstop Bowa, hit .305 and did the job in the field. On May 4, Owens traded the popular Montanez to San Francisco for Garry Maddox, a fine center fielder who hit .291 the rest of the way for Ozark.

Another trade three days later brought Richie Allen, now known at his request as "Dick," back to Philadelphia from Atlanta. Allen told the White Sox that he was retiring after the 1974 season, so the Sox peddled his contract to the Atlanta Braves. Allen declined to report to the Braves, viewing the thought of playing again in the Deep South with distaste, but surprisingly he agreed to come to the Phillies when a deal was put together.

The convincer for Allen was a couple of visits to his home by Phillies people, first by Schmidt, Cash, and outfielder-turned-broadcaster Richie Ashburn, then by Ashburn and Robin Roberts. As a result of these meetings, Allen believed that the Phillies wanted him and that the atmosphere around the club was different from what it had been during his earlier stay. After the trade, Ruly Carpenter told Allen in no uncertain terms that he was wanted, and that was the clincher.[4]

Allen seemed a different man now, the Phillies were a different team (utility infielder Terry Harmon was the only player remaining from the 1969 Phils team Allen had left), and the Philadelphia fans were different, too. They cheered Dick Allen when he returned, they cheered him when he got a single his first time up, and they continued to cheer him even when he sloughed off to a .233 average, with only twelve home runs. Allen felt that Ozark put him in the lineup before he was in shape, but the season was moving along and Danny needed some clout at first base.

Underneath, Allen was not so different after all; he still nursed his feelings of mistreatment, still cherished his grudges. The potential for trouble with the manager was there, too, because Ozark, a coach with the Dodgers the one year Allen played for L.A., did not want him on the team. During the previous winter, when the possibility of acquiring Allen first surfaced, Ozark said that though he wanted to win very badly "there would have to be a lot of sacrifices made by me and by the players on this club if we got Richie Allen. We'd have to shut our eyes to a lot of things."[5]

Carlton led the pitchers with 15–14, and Tom Underwood had a 14–13 record. Rookie right-hander Larry Christenson posted a mark of 11–6, while Lonborg, troubled with a groin injury, was 8–6. McGraw teamed with Garber to give the Phils an effective bullpen, each reliever picking up fourteen saves.

At the end of the '75 season, By Saam retired from the broadcast booth. Saam, troubled with vision problems, stepped down a year before the Phillies' division title, just as he had elected to go with the A's rather than the Phillies in 1950. In his long career behind the mike, Byrum Saam never had a championship baseball team. Nevertheless, his voice was the sound of summer to countless thousands of Philadelphians.

The 1975 club set another new attendance record, with a total turnout of 1,909,233. It was not enough. The Phillies had been close to the top for parts of two seasons now. With their young stars maturing, they felt it was time to get there in 1976.

On December 10, Paul Owens traded Ruthven and a couple other players to the White Sox for veteran pitcher Jim Kaat. Thirty-seven years old, the left-handed Kaat was still in top form, having won 41 games in the 1974–75 seasons. He was a perennial winner of the Gold Glove for fielding excellence among pitchers, and he had been a productive hitter in the American League before the advent of the designated hitter.

Nineteen hundred seventy-six was the nation's Bicentennial Year, and it should have been a great year in Philadelphia, too. When Mayor Rizzo publicly called for armored vehicles to help him repel the protesters he expected to mar the city's celebration, he managed to keep the protesters away but the anticipated tourists stayed away too. The All-Star Game was staged in Veterans Stadium, with President Gerald Ford tossing out the first ball, and a capacity crowd watched as local heroes Luzinski, Cash, Schmidt, Boone and Bowa performed for the National League.

The Phillies started out like gangbusters in 1976, and they had a ten-game lead at the All-Star break. They had been inspired by an unbelievable victory on April 17, at Chicago's Wrigley Field. The fabled Wrigley wind was blowing out, and the Cubs had their hitting shoes on early. They battered Carlton and several relievers to take a 13–2 lead. The Phillies started a comeback with a two-run Schmidt homer off Rick Reuschel in the fifth, and Michael Jack nailed Reuschel again in the seventh. In the eighth Schmidt banged a three-run shot against reliever Mike Garman, and Bob Boone led off the ninth with a home run to tie the score. In the tenth inning, against Rick's brother Paul Reuschel now, Schmidt hit his historic fourth straight home run for two more runs to put the Phils up, 18–16. In the bottom of the tenth, Lonborg finally got the Cubs out to tie it down.

From then on, Ozark's crew was hard to beat. By late August their lead was up to 15½ games. A September slump cut it dramatically and at

Steve Carlton, the best left-handed pitcher the Phillies ever had.

one point they were only three games ahead of Pittsburgh. Panic set in, and all over town people said, "It's just like '64!" Then Larry Christenson won a big game over the Mets, the talk about 1964 subsided, and the club righted itself to win the division by a comfortable nine games over the Pirates.

On September 26, a 4–1 Jim Lonborg win over Montreal clinched the division title. Home attendance hit a new high of 2,480,150, as Phillies Fever swept the Delaware Valley, and the club won 101 games, the most in franchise history.

Mike Schmidt once again led the majors with 38 home runs. He batted .262, drove in 107, and cut his league-leading strikeout number down to 149. Luzinski hit 21 homers and drove in 95 runs, while Allen had 15 home runs and 49 RBIs. Maddox hit .330, Johnstone .318, Luzinski .304, and catcher Bob Boone, valued most for his defensive skills, batted a tidy .271. Cash and Bowa tied the infield together, Bobby Tolan and Ollie Brown were valuable spare outfielders, and veteran Tim McCarver did a good job spelling Boone behind the plate, especially in catching Carlton, his old Cardinal batterymate.

Carlton had an excellent year, with a 20–7 tally, and Lonborg was back to his old form with a record of 18–10. Christenson was 13–8, Kaat was 12–14, and Underwood went 10–5. Ron Reed, a 6'6" righthander who had played pro basketball, came from the Cardinals in a trade for the disappointing Mike Anderson. Reed, mostly a starter in his eight earlier seasons, became a reliever for the Phillies and did a fine job. With the continuing good work of Garber and McGraw, his contribution gave the Phillies an outstanding bullpen.

Danny Ozark was named Manager of the Year by *The Sporting News* and the National League's top manager by both the major wire services. Part of the recognition coming to Ozark, of course, was for his relatively successful use of Dick Allen. Early in the season, he was forced to scratch Allen from the starting lineup when the player showed up in no condition to perform. Danny was able to keep things together to the point that Allen contributed offensively, although at a pace far from his earlier standards.

The years, the turmoil, the drinking, the business of simply being Dick Allen, had taken much of the sting from his bat. Toward the end of the season, too, there were signs that Dick Allen was turning back into Richie Allen, as he started having problems with the manager, with other players like Larry Bowa and Tug McGraw, and ultimately with the fans. Allen sulked when Ozark took him out of the lineup, and he soiled the Phillies' celebration of their first championship of any kind since 1950 when he declined to take part in the locker-room festivities in Montreal after the clinching, instead sitting most visibly by himself in the dugout while the whooping and hollering were going on inside.

Allen accused management of racist motives in both roster and on-field playing decisions. He threatened to boycott the playoffs if the Phillies, who had to take someone off the roster to get down to the 25-player limit, did the obvious and removed 40-year-old Tony Taylor, who had had just 23 at-bats all season. And the fans started to get on him again.

Allen wrote that just prior to the playoff series with Cincinnati "both Danny Ozark and Ruly Carpenter made it clear to me that there wouldn't be a place for me with the Phillies in '77." Dick Allen was learning the hard truth that a .268 hitter was not given as much leeway to be confrontational as was a .317 hitter.[6]

For the league championship series, the Big Red Machine, the Cincinnati club managed by onetime-Phillie Sparky Anderson, was the betting choice to win the series. For the first game, though, Steve Carlton gave the Phillies an apparent edge. The Phils drew first blood, scoring in the first inning against the Reds' Don Gullett on a Dave Cash double, an infield out, and a sacrifice fly by Schmidt. The roaring crowd of 62,640 in Veterans Stadium was wild with excitement.

Then Gullett settled down, allowing only one more hit in seven more innings, while the Reds pecked away at Carlton. A run in the second tied the game, and Schmidt's error set up two Cincy runs in the sixth. Gullett doubled home two more in the eighth to put the game out of reach. The 6–3 victory put the Reds in the driver's seat. Cincinnati's Pete Rose said, "Steve Carlton is their best. We beat their best, and that's got to make them think a little."[7]

In the second game, Lonborg held the Reds hitless through five innings. The Phillies took a 2–0 lead on an RBI single by Boone and a mammoth home run by Luzinski. In the sixth, Lonborg came unstrung. After a walk and two hits produced one Cincinnati run, Ozark relieved him with Gene Garber, who walked Joe Morgan intentionally to load the bases. Tony Perez then hit a line drive toward first base. Allen, breaking toward the bag for a pickoff play, got his glove on the ball but did not catch it. Two runs scored on what was ruled an error, and Morgan scored the fourth run of the inning on an infield out. The Reds coasted to a 6–2 win.

Naturally, the major preoccupation of the media after the game, other than the sudden unraveling of Jim Lonborg, was the ball that Allen failed to catch. If he had caught it, he would easily have doubled Morgan off first. Perez and Sparky Anderson thought it should have been ruled a hit, but Danny Ozark said, "I think the ball was catchable, yes." Allen said he was not surprised it was ruled an error; "you have to take into consideration that this is Philadelphia," he said, overlooking the fact that the two official scorers were reporters from Camden and Cincinnati.[8]

Two days later, the Phillies and Reds went at it again in Cincinnati's Riverfront Stadium, with the home team holding a two-game lead in the best-of-five series. Kaat held the home team to one hit in six innings while the Phils built up a 3–0 lead. In the seventh the Reds rallied for four runs against Kaat and Ron Reed, but the Phillies regained the lead with two in the eighth. In the top of the ninth, a Rose error and a Jay Johnstone triple gave the Phils a 6–4 lead.[9]

The 55,047 on hand grew hushed as their Reds came to bat. Leadoff hitter George Foster crushed a 2–2 fastball into the left field seats, and Johnny Bench followed with a game-tying homer over the left-center field wall. Garber relieved the shocked Ron Reed, and Concepcion greeted him with a base hit. Underwood came on to give up a walk and a sacrifice bunt to move the winning run to third. After an intentional walk to load the bases, Ken Griffey chopped a high bouncer which glanced off first sacker Bobby Tolan's glove for a single as Concepcion scored the pennant-winning run.

The Reds celebrated their return to the World Series they had won the year before, while the Phillies trudged off the field, still not having won a post-season game since the first game of the 1915 World Series. They thought they could go head-to-head with the Big Red Machine, but when the chips were down they were not up to it.

After the 1975 season, a ruling by arbitrator Peter Seitz had upheld the challenges of pitchers Andy Messersmith and Dave McNally to baseball's venerable reserve clause. A lockout by the owners wiped out most of the 1976 spring training, but out of the turmoil came new procedures to deal with the unprecedented problems and opportunities of free agency. After the 1976 season, the Phillies were to have their first exposure to the new regimen.

They lost second baseman Dave Cash, who, after three successful seasons in Philadelphia, took advantage of his new status to sign a contract with Montreal, but they picked up a free agent of their own in 29-year-old Pirate third baseman Richie Hebner. The Phils clearly did not sign Hebner to play third base, not with Schmidt around, but they thought, correctly, that he could take over first base from the departed Dick Allen.

With Cash gone, Paul Owens got together with the Dodgers, trading for veteran second baseman Ted Sizemore. The last piece to the puzzle fell into place on June 15, 1977, when Owens sent Underwood and two rookies to the Cardinals for Arnold "Bake" McBride, a speedy outfielder who had been a consistent .300 hitter with little power in his four years in St. Louis. McBride was not happy with the Cards, and his knees were bad, but he was the lefthanded slasher Owens was seeking. Bake McBride became a complete player with the Phillies.

Many baseball experts believe that the 1977 Phillies team was and still is the best team in the history of the franchise. There was the superb 1899 team, but it finished third. The 1915 and 1950 pennant winners must be considered, as well as the 91-game-winning 1916 club. The 1964 team won 92 games, but it broke the city's heart. Obviously, the 1980 team is the only Phillies world champion, and the 1983 and 1993 squads came through with pennants. However, the only Phillies teams ever to exceed one hundred wins in a season were those of 1976 and 1977, with identical 101–61 records. In a comparison, the '77 team looks far superior. What happened in the post-season is another heartbreak, but that comes later.

Of the regulars, Mike Schmidt's .274 was the lowest batting average, and he walked 101 times to go along with his 38 home runs and 101 runs batted in. Schmidt did not even lead the team in the slugging categories, as Luzinski had a great season, hitting 39 homers and driving in 130 runs, with a .309 average.

At first base Hebner hit .285 with 18 home runs. Sizemore batted .281 and Bowa .280. Maddox hit .292, Johnstone .284, and Bake McBride, "Shake and Bake," as he soon became known, hit .339 with eleven home runs as a Phillie (.316 with his Cardinal record thrown in). Bob Boone batted .284, with eleven home runs.

The Phillies reserves did some lusty hitting, too: infielder Davey Johnson, signed by Owens upon his return from Japan, hit .321 with eight homers, Tim McCarver hit .320, and first baseman-pinch-hitter Tommy Hutton hit a healthy .309. The club easily led the league in batting, in slugging, and in runs scored. Even outfielder Jerry Martin, used primarily as a late-inning defensive replacement for the ponderous Luzinski, hit .260 with six round-trippers.

The 1977 Phillies were not all offense, either. Carlton won his second Cy Young Award with a 23–10, 2.64 record, and young Larry Christenson put up a mark of 19–6, although his ERA was a bit high at 4.07. Lonborg was 11–4 although troubled by shoulder problems, and Randy Lerch, known as "the Blade," a rookie lefthander, 6'5" and 195 pounds, won ten and lost six.

Once again the Phillies' bullpen was great, leading the league in saves. Garber, Reed, McGraw, and rookie Warren Brusstar all had earned run averages under three, and Garber and Reed had 19 and 15 saves, respectively.

Curiously, the '77 Phillies did not take over first place until August 5. They started slowly while the Chicago Cubs set a hot pace. With the catalyst of the deal for McBride in June, Ozark's men put increasing pressure on Chicago, and once they caught the Cubs in early August they never looked back. Chicago eventually faded to fourth, and the Phils finished five games ahead of second-place Pittsburgh, setting a new attendance record in the process with 2,700,070.

The Dodgers, under manager Tom Lasorda, a product of nearby Norristown, easily beat the Reds for the West title. The playoff series opened in Los Angeles in 1977, and the Phillies were ready, hardened by their 1976 experience.

Steve Carlton started against L.A.'s Tommy John, and the Phils busted out to a sizable lead. Luzinski hit a two-run home run in the opening inning, and Davey Johnson drove John from the game with a two-run single in the fifth. The Dodgers got one run in the bottom of the fifth, but Carlton singled home McCarver in the sixth to make the score 5–1. In the seventh, though, third baseman Ron Cey hit a Dodger grand slam to tie the game, 5–5, and Garber relieved Carlton.

But these Phils did not fold as the '76 team had. With one out in the ninth and the score still tied, McBride and Bowa both singled, and Schmidt then drove home the go-ahead run with a base hit. Dodger pitcher Elias Sosa balked home another run, and McGraw made the 7–5 score stand up for a Phillies win.

The next night, Dodger pitcher Don Sutton breezed to a 7–1 victory over Lonborg. The only blow of consequence for the Phillies was McBride's third inning home run, which was more than matched by Dusty Baker's grand slam in the home fourth. The two teams departed for Philadelphia tied at one game apiece.

The game these two teams played on Friday, October 7, 1977, at Veterans Stadium was one of the wildest, most controversial baseball games ever played in Philadelphia. It started out with Burt Hooton on the mound against Larry Christenson. The Phillies had a record of 60–21 in their home park, and their fans liked to think they were a part of that.

63,719 of them turned out for Game Three, and after the Dodgers scored two runs in the top of the second the fans got into the action. In the bottom of the inning, Hooton, the L.A. pitcher, had control problems. He felt that umpire Harry Wendelstedt was squeezing the strike zone on him, and the more visibly upset Hooton got, both at Wendelstedt and himself, the louder the fans roared at him. He became so unnerved that, with the bases already loaded, he walked Christenson, McBride, and Bowa to bring in three runs, and Lasorda had to yank him.

The Dodgers tied the game in the fourth, but in the eighth inning the Phillies scored two runs to take the lead. Going into the ninth with a two-run lead, Ozark curiously neglected to make the move he had been making all year, replacing left fielder Luzinski with Jerry Martin for defense. When Gene Garber retired the first two Dodgers, the omission seemed academic. Lasorda sent up 38-year-old Vic Davalillo as a pinch-hitter, and Davalillo beat out a perfect drag bunt to the first-base side of the pitcher's mound.

Lasorda's other pinch-hitting specialist, 39-year-old Manny Mota, came to the plate. Garber got ahead of him 0-and-2, but Mota hit a ball deep to left field, a ball which Jerry Martin could have caught without much difficulty. Luzinski lumbered back, got his glove on the ball, but trapped it against the fence. When he threw it to second base, the ball got away from Sizemore for an error. Davalillo scored and Mota went to third.

The next batter was Davey Lopes, whose hot smash toward third hit a seam of the Astroturf, bounded up to hit Schmidt on the knee, and caromed into the hands of shortstop Bowa. Bowa, as if he practiced this play all the time, fired the ball to first to retire Lopes and end the game. Except for one thing. First base umpire Bruce Froemming, obviously never expecting Bowa to make the play, was out of position and called Lopes safe as the tying run scored. The 5–4 victory which the Phillies had earned on Bowa's sensational play was down the drain because of an umpire's bad call.

Things got worse. Garber made an errant pickoff throw to first, and Lopes moved up a base. He scored the winning run on Bill Russell's single, as the shocked Phillies and their equally shocked fans stared in disbelief. Danny Ozark, sitting later in his office, said, "I don't know why. I don't know why. I go to church, too." He knew the unused Jerry Martin would haunt him for the rest of his tenure in Philadelphia.[10]

There was still one more to go for Los Angeles, and Tommy John took care of it the next night. Before 64,924 unhappy fans, in a game that never should have been played because of a steady rainfall, John scattered seven hits in a 4–1 victory over Steve Carlton. Baker's two-run homer in the second inning was all John really needed. Chub Feeney, the National League president, sat unconcerned in the downpour, as if to indicate that the rain was really nothing, but everyone knew the game was going on because it was a television network's prime-time Saturday night show, Conditions were not really fit for playing baseball, but, as they say, they were the same for both teams, and the Dodgers won.

So, in a weird and wild playoff series, the best Phillies team ever, perhaps, went down, three games to one. No one on the team, except Bob Boone and Richie Hebner and a couple of the relievers, had played up to expectations. The team lost, and it hurt.

The 1978 Phillies were anxious to atone for the playoff loss to the Dodgers, and they won the division once again. They were in front most of the way, but it was not easy, and they had to hold off the Pirates at the end to win it. A Pittsburgh sweep of a twi-night doubleheader at Three Rivers Stadium on the last Friday night of the season narrowed the Phils' lead to a game and a half, but the following day, in the next-to-last game of the year, the Phillies clinched with a 10–8 win over the Bucs.

The '78 club won eleven fewer games than its predecessor, going 90–72, and attendance dropped to 2,583,389. Almost everyone hit more poorly than in 1977, except for Bowa and Boone. Schmidt, plagued by knee and hamstring injuries, fell to 21 home runs and only 78 RBIs, with a .251 average, and the hometown fans were on him all season. Luzinski hit 35 homers and drove in 101, but his batting average also suffered.

Carlton was 16–13, although he pitched well all year, and Christenson was 13–14. At the June 15 trading deadline, Owens brought back Dick Ruthven from the Braves, in a trade for Gene Garber. Ruthven was unhappy in Atlanta, where he disliked pitching for volatile Braves owner Ted Turner, and he pitched very well for the Phillies, winning 13, losing five, and putting together a 2.99 earned run average. Reed, McGraw, and Brusstar gave the team a top-notch bullpen.

The league playoff opened on October 4 at the Vet, with the Dodgers again offering the opposition. 63,460 fans turned out for the opener, hoping for retribution against their '77 tormentors, but they were sorely disappointed. Christenson gave up a three-run homer to Steve Garvey in the third inning, yielded two more runs in the fourth, and was gone when another run scored in the fifth. Jerry Martin's late home run and Bowa's three hits were the most the Phillies could muster against Hooton and winner Bob Welch, as the Dodgers cruised to a 9–5 win. The fans made their displeasure known quite vocally.

Ruthven started Game Two, against Tommy John, and for three innings it was all even. Lopes led off the visitors' fourth with a home run, and two more L.A. runs in the fifth chased Ruthven. John scattered four singles, by Schmidt, Maddox, Luzinski, and Boone, and the Dodgers won again, 4–0. The 60,643 on hand for this letdown booed loudly as the game wound down.

Carlton started the third game of the series, Friday night, October 6, in Los Angeles, upset that Ozark had not used him in either of the two games in Philadelphia. "I felt I was ready, more or less at the peak," he said of his condition at the time of the opener. But he was ready still when he took the mound against Don Sutton in Game Three, pitching a complete-game 9–4 victory, the first routegoing job in the Phillies' three years of playoffs. To add to his evening, Carlton hit a home run and drove in four runs. Luzinski also hit a roundtripper, and a Lopes error led to three sixth-inning runs.[11]

The Phillies were still down, two games to one, but their ace made sure they were still alive. The fourth game, though, was destined to be another one of those ruefully remembered for a long time to come. The Phillies got two early runs on a home run by Luzinski, but Randy Lerch fell behind by 3–2. McBride, pinch-hitting for Brusstar in the seventh, homered to tie the game, 3–3. It continued tied at the end of regulation play, and the Phillies failed to score in the top of the tenth.

In the bottom of the inning, Tug McGraw got two quick outs before he walked Ron Cey. Dusty Baker hit a soft line drive to center, where the man known as the best centerfielder in the game, Garry Maddox, moved in on the ball — and dropped it. Russell hit a single and Cey scored, and it was all over. Once again, the Phillies had all winter to think about what had happened. Maddox, of course, had the opportunity to think about it as soon as the reporters were able to get to the visitors' clubhouse. "The ball was right in my glove," Garry said. "It was not a tough play, just a routine line drive. It cost us a shot at being World Champions."[12]

After the third straight playoff defeat, despite having talent equal or superior to that of the teams that beat them, the Phillies organization felt someone was needed who knew how to win, someone who possessed that indefinable something which made the difference between winners and also-rans. In a stroke of luck, they came up with such a player.

After the 1978 season, the Reds were unable to sign their star infielder-outfielder Pete Rose, the three-time batting champion and former MVP. Rose and his agent conducted a barnstorming tour of big-league cities, entertaining offers for his services in 1979 and beyond. Rose was 37 years old, but he kept himself in top condition, and his performance in 1978 had given no hint that he was anywhere near the end of the line. An average fielder at best, Rose was an offensive wonder.

The Phillies were one of the numerous clubs to make an offer to Rose, but Owens and Ruly Carpenter understood that their proposal was not close to the top. What they did not know was that Rose, a close friend of Bowa and Schmidt, wanted to play for the Phillies. So, with some reworking of the club's offer, with the addition of more cash thrown into the pot by the team's television station, Pete Rose became a Phillie, with a four-year contract for $3,200,000.

On February 23, 1979, Owens, faced with the decline of second baseman Ted Sizemore, worked out a trade with the Cubs for their second sacker, Manny Trillo. He gave up Sizemore, Jerry Martin, spare catcher Barry Foote, and a couple of minor leaguers, and he got with Trillo catcher Dave Rader and Greg Gross, a high average/low power hitter. Trillo, a Venezuelan who had been developed in the Phillies' system but had gone on to play for Oakland and the Cubs, was a respectable hitter, but he was an excellent fielder at second base, blessed with a strong throwing arm.

Even with their additions, the Phillies floundered in 1979. Early in the year, on May 17, the Phillies and Cubs hooked up in a legendary battle at

Wrigley Field. The wind was blowing fiercely to left field on one of those days when no lead was safe. Indeed, the Phillies had leads of 7–0, 17–6, and 21–9, but the score was tied at 22 at the end of nine innings. The Cubs had six home runs and the Phillies four. Finally, in the tenth, Schmidt hit a monstrous home run over the left field bleachers, his second roundtripper of the day, and reliever Rawly Eastwick retired the Cubs for a 23–22 victory. The win put the Phils in first place, but it was their season's high point. Everything after that was downhill.

Rose hit .331, and Schmidt rebounded to hit 45 home runs, with 114 runs batted in, but otherwise the offense was off. Schmidt's home run total erased Chuck Klein's long-standing club record of 43, set in 1929. Trillo missed forty games after a pitch broke his arm in early May. Carlton and Nino Espinosa pitched well, but Lerch, Ruthven, and Christenson struggled, the latter two with serious physical problems. The work out of the bullpen was ragged, as McGraw, Eastwick, and Brusstar had tough seasons, and Reed did not pitch well despite a 13–8 record.

A bright spot was provided by Del Unser, brought back primarily for pinch-hitting duties. At the end of June and start of July, Unser set a major league record with home runs in three consecutive pinch-hitting appearances.

On the last day of August, with the team 12½ games out at 65–67, Paul Owens announced that Ozark was being fired as manager, to be replaced on an interim basis by farm director Dallas Green. Ozark showed up for the press conference ("I haven't backed away from a situation yet, and I never will," he said) as Owens said the words so often used by general managers of losing teams: "we felt that something had to be done."[13]

So the Ozark Era was over. Despite the great success the club had enjoyed — Ozark's record of 594–510 is one of the best for any Phillies manager — there had always been disappointment at the end, and the team's fans had never really warmed to the easygoing Danny Ozark. There was little reaction in Philadelphia to the news of his dismissal, and life went on, although the players knew things would be different with the intense, hard-driving Green. Infielder John Vukovich later said, "From Ozark to Dallas was the most drastic change I've ever seen."[14]

The team played better baseball for Dallas Green, winning nineteen out of thirty games, and pulled itself up a notch in the standings. Indeed, attendance in 1979, boosted by the three earlier division titles and the signing of Rose, reached an all-time record of 2,775,011. Still, they finished fourth, fourteen games behind the flag-winning Pirates, and the fans writhed in frustration.

Chapter 18

The Team That Wouldn't Die

The fans of the Delaware Valley looked at the Phillies' lineup, with such stars as Bowa, Rose, Schmidt, Luzinski and the rest, and wondered why their team was continually denied the ultimate reward, the trifecta of the division title, league championship and World Series. The Phillies, with the core of this team intact through the late '70s, had not been able to get past the playoffs. They were regarded as being too cool, too laid back, too spoiled, too much concerned with their individual records.

Dallas Green, who had been high in the club's organization during these frustrating times, thought he had the answer. Whether it was the right answer or not, Dallas Green and time would determine. For he and the front office came to a meeting of the minds, after the '79 season, agreeing that Green would continue on as manager in 1980. Paul Owens, who had been grooming Green to succeed him as general manager, promised the ex-pitcher that his position in the front office was secure when he was no longer field manager of the club.

So, on October 18, they held a news conference to announce that Green was the man for 1980. There was some criticism. Frank Dolson of the *Inquirer* suggested that "the Phillies have the kind of club that needs a proven manager, a man with a track record that the Bowas, the Carltons, the Roses, the Schmidts, the Luzinskis, can look up to," inferring that they would not respect Green. Specifically, Dolson was disappointed that the job did not go to Dorrell "Whitey" Herzog, former skipper of the Kansas City Royals. Owens chose to stay within the organization, and Dallas Green was his man.[1]

Green's first test was in spring training. He took command from Day One, and there was no doubt who was boss. He stressed fundamentals, all those little things which had to become automatic when they came up during the long season ahead. One of Green's slogans, one his players wearied of hearing, was "grind it out," a shorthand way of stressing that baseball is a tough game, that there are no easy roads, and that success comes to those who persist and work. The grinding started in Clearwater. One jaded reporter said that Green's training camp was perhaps "the best anybody has ever seen down here." He called it "professional, efficient, intelligently planned, impartial, executed without flab or dead spots."[2]

In addition to the physical aspects of the game, Green emphasized that baseball is first and foremost a team game. "We, not I," became the motto which Dallas Green tried to implant in each Phillie's brain, and signs bearing this motto were posted around the locker room. Green was an unsubtle man, with a voice which could carry into the next county, and it was without subtlety that he let his players know they would win or lose as a team. Danny Ozark had not screamed at his players, and they had settled into a comfortable niche below the game's top level. Time was running down for some of the Phillies' best players, and if they were to get beyond the disappointments of the Ozark years it would have to be with Dallas Green's loud voice sounding in their ears.

The 1980 Phillies gave little indication as the season progressed that they were to be anything special. They stayed near the top of the division, but this was no more than their predecessors in the mid–'70s had done. Steve Carlton pitched well and won a bushel of ball games, including a one-hitter against the Cardinals on April 26, the sixth of his career, a National League record. For May, Carlton was the N.L. Pitcher of the Month and Mike Schmidt the league's Player of the Month. Michael Jack led the majors at the end of that month with 16 home runs and 41 RBIs.

But good things from Schmidt and Carlton had happened before, and the Phils were still a game behind Pittsburgh. Manny Trillo contributed with both his glove and his bat, and Bake McBride hit high for average and drove in a lot of runs. Christenson was having trouble with his elbow, and at the end of May he underwent surgery. To take Christenson's place in the rotation Paul Owens summoned from the Oklahoma City farm a 23-year-old righthander named Bob Walk, soon to be nicknamed "Whirlybird" for his sometimes goofy antics. Walk pitched well and won a few games.

The largely veteran squad was aided by a couple of other rookies, outfielder Lonnie Smith and backup catcher Keith Moreland, each of whom contributed offensively. Smith was erratic in the outfield and so unsteady on the bases that he was called "Skates," but he was a good hitter. The team bounced around in the standings, reaching first place for a couple of days in May and again in mid–July, then dropping back.

In June, an article in the *Trenton Times* caused a stir, alleging that authorities in Pennsylvania were investigating a drug scandal involving Dr. Patrick Mazza, the club physician for the Reading farm team, and several members of the Phillies. Published reports indicated that Mazza had distributed amphetamines to team members without giving required medical examinations and without keeping proper records. Rose, Carlton, Luzinski, Christensen, and Lerch were mentioned as being under scrutiny.

The players issued denials of any wrongdoing, while Ruly Carpenter acknowledged that certain members of the team had been questioned but were "not suspected of any criminal involvement." Vice-president Bill Giles said of Doctor Mazza, "I've never heard his name. I have no knowledge of him," which was odd, since Mazza had been Reading's team physician since 1969 and had been a key figure in a 1976 lawsuit brought against the Phillies. Management played the story down, hoping it would go away.[3]

The Mazza flap faded for a time, but it was an unwelcome distraction in the midst of a pennant chase. The manner in which the story played in the newspapers confirmed in the minds of many Phillies players their belief that the press was their enemy. Players who felt little affection for their teammates now shared a common foe. Many of the players had been cool toward reporters before this incident, and this chill now turned to a resentful hostility which made the Phillies' clubhouse a tense and unfriendly place.

Greg Luzinski's average was way down. The Bull was still hitting home runs but his RBI production fell with his batting average. His knee hurt, and he did not get along with Dallas Green. Rose was under .300, and that was an unfamiliar neighborhood for him. Boone was coming back from knee surgery, his average was near .220, and the fans booed him regularly, although he did his customary solid job behind the plate.

Randy Lerch disliked Green, and he was a disappointment on the mound. Tug McGraw was mediocre coming out of the pen. Christenson was lost when he went under the knife, and McGraw went on the disabled list in July with tendinitis.

Through it all, Dallas Green managed his way. He shouted and screamed at players who made mistakes, he was blunt with the press about players who were not performing well, and he was impatient with anyone who did not go along wholeheartedly with his message of "We, not I." Green allowed later that the season was not great joy for him, "having Greg Luzinski calling me Hitler or listening to Bowa pop off on his radio show or having Garry Maddox pout all the time. I just felt it was the way to go. I could have backed off, but … I think we would have lost again."[4]

Players such as Maddox were troubled by Green's approach, while others seemed to thrive on it. In mid–July Luzinski gave vent to his feelings about Green, saying, "I think he's hurting us ... You get the feeling sometimes that he doesn't think we're trying. He says 'We' when we win, but he says 'they' when we lose." The fiery Bowa went head-to-head with Green, giving as good as he got, while others were uncomfortable with the charged atmosphere.[5]

On August 10, following Friday and Saturday defeats at the hands of the Pirates, the club lost both games of a Sunday doubleheader in Pittsburgh, to fall six games out of first place, behind both the Pirates and Dick Williams's Montreal Expos. Between games, Green ripped into his team in a closed clubhouse meeting, although with the manager's high-decibel voice no one in the corridor outside the locker room was left in any doubt as to what was taking place. Green, Conlin wrote in the *Daily News*, could be "heard through bolted steel doors."[6]

During the second game, Green and reliever Ron Reed almost went at it in the Phillies' dugout. The team had a players-only meeting in Chicago, at which they vowed to "win it for us." Whatever it was, it worked. The Phillies started winning consistently, taking two out of three from the Cubs and sweeping five games from the Mets. They quickly moved up on the leaders.

On September 1, in an effort to end the internal carping and the mini-war which his players were waging with the media, Paul Owens laid down the law in another clubhouse meeting, this one in San Francisco. After the meeting, Carlton beat the Giants for his 21st victory to put the club in first place by percentage points over Montreal and Pittsburgh. The last month would see ups and downs, but the Phillies would, as Dallas Green exhorted them, "grind it out."

Tug McGraw was magnificent down the stretch; indeed, after coming off the disabled list on July 17, McGraw pitched the best baseball of his life, yielding but three earned runs over 52⅓ innings, or an earned run average of 0.51.

When the rosters expanded on September 1, Owens brought up a tall, red-haired righthanded pitcher named Marty Bystrom from his farm system, and Bystrom was touched with magic that month. He started five games, won all five, and put together a 5–0, 1.50 record for his brief time in the big show. On September 13, the Texas Rangers sold the Phillies Al "Sparky" Lyle, a former standout relief pitcher who had been showing signs of wear and tear. Lyle gave the Phillies ten games out of the bullpen the rest of the way, with two saves and a low ERA.

By mid-month, the Expos were up by 2½ games, while the Pirates were settling back into third place. The Phillies fought back and on the

22nd took a half game lead as Carlton beat the Cardinals. The lead see-sawed through the next week, with Montreal going a half-game up before the Phils won two tight games against New York.

When the Expos came into the Vet the next weekend and took two out of three, despite a dramatic game-winning ninth inning homer by Bake McBride on Friday night, they left town with a half-game lead. Montreal manager Dick Williams said, "I think we're in the driver's seat." The Expos had three games left with St. Louis while the Phillies played four with Chicago, before the two leaders met for a final set of three in Montreal.[7]

On Monday, the Expos beat the Cards, 5–2, while the Phillies had a nailbiter with the Cubs. When Green kept Maddox, Luzinski and Boone out of the starting lineup, Maddox and Bowa had things to say about that to the media. With the score tied 3–3 going into the fifteenth inning, Chicago scored two runs against Dickie Noles and Kevin Saucier, and the disappointed Philadelphia fans booed. The Phillies came back in the bottom half of the inning. Smith and Rose walked and moved up on a wild pitch. Smith scored on McBride's ground ball, but Schmidt popped out. Maddox, inserted into the game in the twelfth, singled to tie the score, and hits by Keith Moreland and Trillo brought Maddox home for an improbable 6–5 victory.

Schmidt later called this game "the catalyst for the Phillies' magic in October." Nevertheless, in the clubhouse afterwards Larry Bowa screamed about "the worst fans in baseball." What this outburst assured Bowa was being booed in every game thereafter in Philadelphia, the remaining three with the Cubs, the playoffs, and the World Series. If it bothered the fiery little shortstop, who also had problems from time to time with his teammates, he never showed it.[8]

Montreal gave the Phillies no room to relax. On Tuesday, the Expos won again, 7–2, and Marty Bystrom hurled the Phillies to a 14–2 romp over the Cubbies. The next day, the Expos blanked the Cards to keep their tiny lead, while Carlton pitched a two-hitter to beat Chicago, 5–0, aided by home runs by Schmidt and Luzinski. On Thursday, with Montreal idle, rookie Bob Walk beat the Cubs, 4–2, as Mike Schmidt broke his own team record with his 46th home run. The three-game set in Montreal was ready to go, with the two teams dead even.

Schmidt, the team's offensive leader, was weakened by a touch of the flu as Dick Ruthven faced off against the Expos, but Schmitty was strong enough to hit home run #47 and drive in a second run with a sacrifice fly. Ruthven made these scores hold up for a crucial 2–1 victory, his 17th of the season, with sterling relief help from Lyle and McGraw, who struck out five of the six batters he faced. One more win in the two games left would clinch the division. The win would come in one of the strangest games ever played.

Saturday afternoon was wet in Montreal. Steady rain delayed the game for three hours and ten minutes before it began at 5:25. Bowa said, "The field was worse than it was for that 1977 playoff game with the Dodgers." The Phillies' five errors and four baserunning mistakes confirmed that judgment.[9]

The Expos took an early one-run lead, although they missed out on another run in the first inning when Rodney Scott missed home plate. In the seventh, with the bases loaded and no outs, Luzinski banged Steve Rogers's 3–0 pitch up the middle for two runs to put the Phils ahead. Hopes for more were dashed when Schmidt was trapped and then tagged out between second and third, and the Bull was run down between first and second. In the bottom of the inning, Trillo's rare muff of a one-out popup led to two Expo runs, and the Phils were behind 4–3.

In the eighth, Montreal relief ace and ex-Phillie Woodie Fryman came in with Phillies on first and second to fan Garry Maddox, but he walked Rose to start the ninth. McBride forced Rose at second but beat the throw at first base. Schmidt then appeared to beat out an infield scratch toward third, only to have umpire Dick Stello call him out. Down to the last out, Bob Boone, slumping and batting a soft .228, singled sharply up the middle to tie the game.

McGraw relieved in the ninth, struck out Larry Parrish and Jerry Manuel, and popped Tim Wallach up to send the game into overtime. After the Phils were retired in the tenth, Jerry White led off with a single and went to third on a sacrifice and a ground-out. Green gave McGraw his choice of Andre Dawson or Gary Carter, who followed, and the Tugger chose Dawson, whom he struck out.

Rose led off the eleventh against Stan Bahnsen with a single, and McBride fouled out. Even though rookie catcher Don McCormack was waiting on deck for his first big league plate appearance, the veteran Bahnsen somehow gave Mike Schmidt a 2–0 fastball over the plate, and Schmidt whaled it deep into the left field seats to put the Phillies up, 6–4. His 48th home run set a new record for major league third basemen.

McGraw, going out to pitch the bottom of the eleventh for the division title, found himself pitching to young McCormack, a September callup seeing his first major league action because Dallas Green had run out of catchers. "I was so tense," McGraw said, "but then I looked at our catcher, Don McCormack… He gets into the biggest game of the year by accident. He's sitting behind the plate, smiling, in total control, having a good time.

I looked at him and how could I not pitch well?" With McCormack handling him, McGraw set Montreal down in order to set off a wild champagne-drenched celebration in the visiting locker room. Bowa said, "Everybody was saying we didn't care. Well, we care. You better believe we care."[10]

If the Phillies thought Montreal was tough, they would find the Western Division champion Houston Astros tougher. Many consider the five-game National League playoff in 1980 the best such series ever played. The set opened in Philadelphia on October 7, the day after the Astros, under manager Bill Virdon, won a one-game division playoff against the Dodgers.

Carlton opened against Ken Forsch, always hard on the Phillies. A playoff-record crowd of 65,277 settled back to watch the proceedings. The Astros picked up a third-inning run, but Luzinski slugged a two-run homer on a 3-and-2 Forsch fastball in the sixth to put his team ahead. Pinch-hitter Greg Gross hit for Carlton in the seventh and singled home a third run, and Green then turned the game over to Tug McGraw. The relief ace retired the Astros without a hit in the eighth and ninth, and the Phillies had a quick one-game lead.

An even larger crowd turned out the next night, a new record of 65,476, but these fans were subjected to a painful evening. Ruthven pitched seven good innings, but the score was tied at 2–2 when he left for a pinch-hitter. The Phillies loaded the bases in the seventh with one out, but lefty Joe Sambito struck out McBride and righthander Dave Smith came in to get Schmidt looking at a third strike.

In the ninth, with the score still tied, McBride, Schmidt, and Lonnie Smith got consecutive one-out singles to load the bases. Frank LaCorte then fanned Trillo and retired Maddox on a foul pop fly. In the top of the tenth Houston rocked Ron Reed for four runs, with a two-run triple by Dave Bergman the key hit. The Phils came back with a run but lost 7–4. The series was tied, with the remaining three games to be played in Houston's Astrodome, where the home team seldom lost in 1980.

Game Three went to Houston in eleven innings, when Joe Morgan tripled to lead off and Denny Walling's short sacrifice fly to Luzinski scored the only run of a 1–0 game. Later Green asked, "How far did that fly go? Fifty-sixty feet? Hell, Bull wouldn't have thrown him out from forty-five."[11]

Christenson held the Astros to three hits in six innings, and relievers Dickie Ray Noles and McGraw kept the home team under control until the eleventh. Joe Niekro pitched ten strong innings for Virdon before Smith won it. The Astros suffered a costly loss in the sixth inning when Cesar Cedeno, one of their best hitters, tore a ligament in his foot lunging toward first base and was lost for the rest of the playoff. The Phillies were now backed to the wall, needing to win both remaining games in Texas.

The fourth game was another strange one, and Bill Virdon said, "The things that occurred have happened at one time or another, but never all in the same game."[12] Well, most of them had. In the top of the fourth, with no score, no outs and Trillo and McBride on base, an absolutely unique play took place. Garry Maddox hit a ball back toward pitcher Vern Ruhle, who dived and came up with it at the dirt edge of the pitching mound. No one really knew whether Ruhle caught the ball in the air or not, and plate umpire Doug Harvey, his view obscured by Maddox, signaled "no catch." Ruhle threw to first, apparently to retire Maddox, but the Astros contended this doubled up Trillo.

Harvey conferred with his fellow umpires, who convinced him that Ruhle had caught the ball in the air, so Harvey ruled a double play. With McBride standing at third, the Astros tagged second and claimed a triple play, but Harvey said his "no catch" call had induced McBride to leave second. He denied the triple play and put Bake back at second. A twenty minute argument resulted in both managers protesting the game.[13]

In the bottom of the fourth, Carlton gave up a long fly to left to Astro Enos Cabell. Lonnie Smith, playing left field, turned to face the wall and play the carom and was astonished to have the ball drop on the warning track, just a few feet behind him. Cabell got a double out of it and later moved up to third. Art Howe hit another fly to Smith. Lonnie caught this one and wound up to throw home as Cabell tagged up. Unfortunately for Smith, the ball slipped from his hand and bounced a few feet in front of him as Cabell scored the game's first run and the fans roared with laughter.

The Astros scored again in the fifth, and Carlton left in the sixth with Gary Woods on third and one out. Noles came in and got catcher Luis Pujols to fly to McBride in right, scoring Woods, or so it seemed. When the Phillies appealed, Woods was ruled out for leaving third too soon.

The Phils got three runs in the eighth against Ruhle and Smith, when Greg Gross, Smith, Rose, and Schmidt singled in succession to tie the score before Trillo's line drive to right dropped in front of outfielder Jeff Leonard. Umpire Bruce Froemming called Trillo out, even though television replays indicated clearly that Leonard had trapped the ball. The Astros then doubled Schmidt off first to end the inning, although Rose tagged up and scored before the last out was made.

The Astros tied the game again in the bottom of the ninth when Terry Puhl singled in a run off Brusstar, and it was extra innings for the third game in a row.

In the Phillies' tenth Rose scored from first on Luzinski's pinch double against Sambito, knocking Houston catcher Bruce Bochy off the plate with a vicious forearm shiver to the face. Trillo doubled Luzinski home for an insurance run, and McGraw came on to snuff out the Astros in the tenth. Paul Owens said simply, "I never saw a game like that."[14]

With one game to play for the pennant on Sunday, October 12, Virdon sent the future Hall of Famer, Nolan Ryan, to the mound against Phillies rookie Marty Bystrom, although Dick Ruthven could not understand why he was not given the ball. The sensational September star was in the postseason series only because the Phillies came up with a fortuitous injury to Nino Espinosa and were able to replace him with Bystrom on the eligible list.

Houston scored a first-inning run, and the Phillies reached Ryan for two in the second. The Astros tied it with a run against Bystrom in the sixth and then scored three in the seventh against an ineffective Larry Christenson. With Ryan throwing smoke and a 5–2 lead in the eighth inning, it looked like Houston's pennant. But Bowa led off the eighth with a base hit, and Boone's bouncer to the mound was deflected by Ryan and went for an infield single. Gross dropped a perfect bunt toward third and beat it out for another hit to load the bases. Ryan went to three-and-two on Rose and then walked him to force home a run.

The score was 5–3 Houston, and Ryan departed in favor of Sambito. Moreland got another run home on a force-out at second. Ken Forsch came in to strike out Schmidt, but pinch-hitter Del Unser singled to right center to tie the game. Manny Trillo's triple down the left field line brought in two more Philadelphia runs.

Houston was not done. In the home eighth, hits by Rafael Landestoy and Jose Cruz off McGraw drove in two Astro runs to deadlock the game once again. The Phillies went out in the ninth, and Ruthven came in to retire Houston in order in the bottom of the inning, to require extra innings once again.

Frank LaCorte fanned Schmidt to open the tenth. The amazing Del Unser then smashed a ball that bounded crazily over the head of first baseman Bergman, winding up in the right field corner for a double. Trillo flied out and Unser took third, and Garry Maddox, notorious for swinging at the first pitch, did it again, lining the ball to center where it was just out of Terry Puhl's reach. Unser crossed the plate, and the Phillies had an 8–7 lead.

Ruthven returned to the mound in the bottom of the tenth, retired the first two hitters, pinch-hitter Danny Heep and Puhl, the hottest hitter on both teams with ten hits in the series, and then got Enos Cabell to hit a three-and-two pitch in the air to center field. When the ball settled into Maddox's glove, the Phillies were the 1980 National League champs. But they were humbled by the intensity of the battle with the Astros. Said Rose, "I'm not sure the better team won."[15]

Once the celebrating in the Astrodome ended, the Phillies headed for home and their date to meet the Kansas City Royals in the World Series. The Royals were similar in many ways to the Phillies. They too had lost playoff series in 1976, 1977, and 1978, before breaking through in 1980 with a first-year manager, former Orioles' coach Jim Frey. And they were led by a superstar third baseman, George Brett, who had flirted with the .400 mark before settling for a magnificent .390.

There was a danger that the Phillies would be emotionally exhausted by their series with Houston and come up short in an anticlimactic World Series, as had happened in 1950, the team's last appearance in the inter-league classic. But they were calling this 1980 Phillies squad The Team That Wouldn't Die, and the players roused themselves for another great effort.

Dallas Green's first problem was finding a starter for Game One. The games in the Astrodome had shredded his pitching staff, and the only one to whom he could turn was rookie Bob Walk. Whirlybird Walk had put together a record of 11–7 after coming up from Oklahoma City, and Green felt that he could give the tired pitching staff some innings. Walk had not pitched in twelve days and was so loosely wound that he would probably not feel the pressure.

On the mound for the American League champions was a bearded redhead named Dennis Leonard, who had in 1980 become a twenty-game winner for the third time. It looked like a mismatch before the Veterans Stadium crowd of 65,791, and things appeared dark when Amos Otis in the second inning and Willie Aikens in the third hit two-run homers off Walk.

But a four-run deficit was nothing to these Phillies. In the bottom of the third, Bowa singled and stole second. Boone doubled him home and scored himself on Lonnie Smith's base hit, although Smith was nailed when Brett went to second base with the relay throw. Rose then took a pitch on the calf, and Schmidt walked. When Bake McBride slammed a Leonard sinker over the right field fence, the Team That Wouldn't Die was suddenly up, 5–4.

Boone doubled home another run in the fourth inning, and Maddox scored one in the fifth on a sacrifice fly. Walk settled down and held K.C. scoreless until the eighth, when Aikens hit another two-run home run to make it 7–6 Phillies.

McGraw came in to shut the Royals down for the last two innings, and the Phillies had their first World Series win since 1915. Bob Walk joined Grover Cleveland Alexander as the only Phillies pitchers to win a World Series game, a distinction which would last one day.

Game Two saw Carlton on the mound against Larry Gura, a southpaw winner of eighteen games for Jim Frey, but most attention was on George Brett, who was suffering from a painful case of hemorrhoids. The Phils picked up two fifth-inning runs, driven in by Maddox and Bowa, but the Royals reached Carlton for a run in the sixth and three more in the seventh.

Ahead 4–2, Frey brought in his closer, Dan Quisenberry, a sidearming submariner, who retired the Phils in the seventh. In the eighth, Boone walked and scored on Unser's pinch double to the left-center alley. When Unser moved to third on a groundout and McBride singled on an Astroturf bouncer over second sacker Frank White, the score was tied. Schmidt doubled to the right-centerfield gap, and it was untied. Moreland scored Schmidt with another hit, and Ron Reed saved the win for Carlton with a scoreless ninth.

Brett had two hits and a walk before leaving the game in pain in the sixth inning, while the sportswriters cranked out a spate of bad puns and tasteless one-liners. Carlton threw 159 pitches in his eight innings, striking out ten while yielding ten hits and six walks. It was not a vintage Carlton performance, but it was good enough, and the Phillies headed for Kansas City with a two-game lead. "You can't believe the juices that are flowing in this dugout," said Schmidt.[16]

The off-day between the second and third games was good news for Brett, Frey, and Kansas City. A proctologist alleviated Brett's hemorrhoid problem, and the third baseman confidently announced, "The pain is behind me."[17]

In his first at-bat in Game Three, George hammered a Ruthven fastball for a home run. The Phillies scored one in the second off starter Rich Gale, K.C. went ahead again in the fourth, and Schmidt homered into the Phillies bullpen to even the score in the fifth. Otis hit a four-bagger in the seventh to make it 3–2, but Rose singled home a run in the eighth.

After both sides were retired in the ninth, the game went into extra innings, and the Phillies nearly won it in the tenth. With one out and Rose and Boone on base, Schmidt hit a screaming liner toward right-center which was speared by second baseman White, who easily doubled Boone off second. Without White's play, two Philadelphia runs probably would have scored. In the bottom of the tenth, Aikens singled home a two-out run against McGraw to give K.C. its first-ever World Series win.

The fourth game went to Kansas City, 5–3, but it may have decided the Series in the Phillies' favor. Christenson started against Leonard, and Larry did not have a thing. By the time Green got him out of the game, the Royals had a 4–0 lead with only one out in the first, on five hits including a Brett triple and another two-run home run by Aikens. Dickie Ray Noles relieved and gave up another Aikens homer in the second, for a 5–1 K.C. lead. The Royals looked free and easy, and they were swinging the bats with confidence, digging in and whaling away at the Phillies pitchers.

In the fourth inning, though, Noles knocked Brett down with an 0-and-2 fastball right at his head. Brett sprawled on the ground and a furious Frey sprinted out of the dugout, screaming at the umpires and Noles and anyone else within earshot. Soon the Royals' skipper was in a shouting match with Pete Rose. Umpire Don Denkinger let Noles stay in the game, and Brett struck out. Dickie later denied throwing at the Royals' star, but Mike Schmidt said, "I believe that pitch had a great deal of purpose behind it — it was a pitch meant to intimidate."[18]

In any event, whether the knockdown had anything to do with it or not, the Royals stopped hitting and the Phillies' swagger returned. Even though Kansas City won Game Four to even the Series, the Phils soon took command.

For the fifth game, Green sent Bystrom to the hill, while Jim Frey, still steamed, countered with Larry Gura. In the fourth inning, with McBride on base, Gura tried a changeup to Schmidt. Mike slammed it over the center field fence, 410 feet away, and it was 2–0 Phils. K.C. got a run in the fifth and two more in the sixth, as Reed replaced Bystrom.

In the seventh Quisenberry came on for the Royals, and Dan was still protecting a one-run lead as the ninth began. Schmidt, the leadoff hitter, had surprised Brett the day before by bunting for a hit down the third-base line, so to prevent a recurrence Brett played up, even with the bag. As a result, he was able only to knock down Schmidt's hard line drive, and Mike had a base hit.

Del Unser batted for Smith and pulled a shot just past the diving Aikens at first and down into the corner, as Schmidt scored the tying run. Moreland sacrificed Del to third, but Maddox grounded out to Brett. Quisenberry got his glove on Trillo's hard shot, and the ball rolled behind the mound. Brett scooped it up and threw late to first, while Unser tallied the go-ahead run.

It was not over yet. Tug McGraw, in his third inning of work, had a few thrills left. He walked White but got Brett on a called third strike. He walked Aikens and then got Hal McRae to force pinch-runner Onix Concepcion at second, but not before McRae smashed a ball just foul into the left field stands, with the Tugger patting his heart in relief as the foul call was made.

Then he walked Amos Otis to load the bases. One-time Phillie Jose Cardenal was the next hitter, and he fouled off a pitch, took a ball, and then fouled off two more. On the fifth pitch, Cardenal swung and missed a fastball inside. McGraw leaped and thrust his arms into the air. The Phillies were going home with a one-game lead, needing one more victory.

Game Six, on Tuesday, October 21, matched Steve Carlton against Rich Gale for Kansas City, before 65,838 fans in Veterans Stadium. Carlton was at his best, which was bad news for the Royals. Rose and Schmidt drove runs home in the third, and the Phillies built the lead to 4–0 with single runs in the fifth and sixth. In the eighth, a walk and a hit to the first two batters brought McGraw in to relieve a tiring Carlton. McGraw got White but walked Willie Wilson to load the bases. A sacrifice fly scored a run, and Brett beat out an infield single to reload them. Tug got the dangerous McRae to ground to Trillo to retire the side.

In the ninth, it was more of the same. As a troop of mounted police ringed the field, matched by more policemen with dogs from the K-9 Corps, McGraw struck out Otis, walked Aikens, and gave up hits to John Wathan and Cardenal to load the bases. The tying runs were on base as Frank White came to bat, and Green visited the mound for a quick word with his pitcher.

After the manager left, White hit a foul popup near the dugout on the first base side, and Boone and Rose converged on the ball. Boone called for it, but the foul clanked off his mitt. Then, as if they practiced the play every day, Rose calmly caught the ball before it hit the ground.

At that moment, with one out still to go, the fans of Philadelphia, the survivors of 1950 and 1964 and 1977, knew for the first time that the Phillies were really going to win. That play, unbelievable as it was, meant that this time the baseball gods were smiling on the Phillies.

When McGraw went to one-and-two on Willie Wilson, who had already fanned eleven times in the Series, all Philadelphia knew what was coming. Wilson swung through the next fastball, McGraw leaped high in the air, and the Philadelphia Phillies were, for the first time in their 97-year history, the champions of all baseball.

The fans, the 65,000 in the stands and the uncounted millions watching on television, looked on as the world champion Phillies, the Team That Wouldn't Die, began their celebration on the field, with Mike Schmidt, always the picture of detached coolness, leaping onto the pile of white-and-red-pinstriped players near the pitcher's mound. The people stood and shouted and cheered, and they cheered some more when Dallas Green led his players back out onto the field from the clubhouse.

The next day, hundreds of thousands of them stood around City Hall and along South Broad Street and jammed into the old Sesqui stadium in South Philadelphia to cheer and appreciate and express their feelings as the Phillies rode in their victory parade on flatbed trucks to the city's celebration.

Larry Bowa told the crowd that it was the greatest moment of his life "and I'm glad I can share it with the greatest fans in baseball." The fans, most of whom had been booing the shortstop for a month, roared. Mike Schmidt told them to "take that world championship and savor it because you all deserve it."[19]

And Tug McGraw, who had been the "You Gotta Believe" inspiration for the 1973 Mets but was getting tired of New York writers ripping the Phillies players for their demeanor and attitude, drew a huge cheer when he said, "All through baseball history Philadelphia has had to take a back seat to New York City. But New York City can take *this* world championship and stick it!"[20]

The crowds dispersed and the players went home and their wives planned how to spend the winning Series share. And a week or so later, a New York writer named Pete Axthelm, one of those critics McGraw was talking about, published a full-page column in the November 3 *Newsweek* entitled "Those Malevolent Phillies," attacking McGraw, the '80 team, individual players, and the franchise itself. "The Phillies," Axthelm wrote, "celebrated as they had played against Kansas City, in bullying and abrasive style," and he asked if the new champions could "really be as joyless, juvenile and obnoxious as they seem?"[21]

Philadelphia ignored the screed, leaving Pete Axthelm to stew in his own bile. The fans of the Quaker City waited for the honors they knew their Phillies were going to win. First, of course, was Mike Schmidt's designation as the most valuable player of the World Series. Later on, Michael Jack was named the National League's Most Valuable Player, the first Phillie to win that award since Jim Konstanty in 1950, and the Major League Player of the Year by *The Sporting News*. The same publication named Lonnie Smith Rookie of the Year and Carlton as the Major League Pitcher of the Year.

The numbers were something to enjoy as well. Schmidt batted .286 and led the league with his 48 home runs and 121 runs batted in. Lonnie Smith hit .339 and Keith Moreland .314 in their rookie seasons. McBride batted .309, and his 87 RBIs were second on the team. Manny Trillo hit .292 and was named the most valuable player of the league playoff with Houston.

Carlton, the Cy Young award winner, was 24–9, with a 2.34 ERA, and he had league highs of 304 innings pitched and 286 strikeouts. Ruthven was 17–10, and McGraw had twenty saves, most of them after his return from the disabled list in July. Tug's earned run average was 1.47.

All in all, it was quite a year for the "malevolent" Phillies. They may not have been the sweetest bunch of ballplayers ever assembled, and they may have taken on more of the personality of their manager than anyone ever expected, but on the field, between the white lines, they made up a great baseball team.

Chapter 19

Another Flag

The Team That Wouldn't Die was followed by The Team That Died of Labor Trouble. The 1981 Phillies, a team of great promise, turned it off when the players' strike hit and never turned it back on. Schmidt and Carlton each had another fine season, but they were not joined by many teammates in 1981.

Before the season started, the Phillies made a couple of major player moves. On March 30, Greg Luzinski went to the White Sox. The Bull's numbers were down in 1980, his weight was up, his knee injury took away what little running speed he previously possessed, and he was no favorite of Dallas Green. During the World Series, in which Luzinski was 0-for-9 in three games, a reporter told Green that Luzinski was complaining about not playing. "I love Greg," Green said sarcastically. "I'd love to play him. But I'm not the one who hit .228 this year."[15]

Coming into spring training, Green said pointedly, "You can't continually live on the past ... I don't think he [Luzinski] is assured of a job unless he works at it." The Bull answered that "maybe it's best that I move on." So Greg Luzinski took his bat off to Comiskey Park, to be a designated hitter.[2]

On the 25th of March Owens sent Bob Walk to the Braves for outfielder Gary Matthews, a veteran of eight solid seasons with San Francisco and Atlanta.

On March 6, Phillies owner Ruly Carpenter shocked Philadelphia and the baseball world when he announced the family's intention to sell the ballclub. Four months and a few days after what he called "the greatest day of my life, more awesome, more emotional than I ever dreamed it would be," Carpenter said he was going to get out of the game that had been his life. "Some deeply ingrained philosophical differences exist between the Carpenter family and some of the other owners as to how the baseball business should be conducted," he said, so they had decided to sell.[3]

Carpenter was tired of labor negotiations, contract hassles with agents, and the huge amounts of money being thrown around in the game. The final bit of lunacy was the outlandish contract which Atlanta's Ted Turner had just recently given journeyman outfielder Claudell Washington. Carpenter suggested to Bill Giles, the club's executive vice-president and the son of former Cincinnati Reds and National League president Warren Giles, that he put together a syndicate. The Carpenters would entertain offers.

Another tough moment for the team came in January, when the state pressed charges against Dr. Patrick Mazza for illegally prescribing drugs for, and against a Reading machinist named Robert L. Masley and his son for delivering them to, Phillies players at Veterans Stadium. Testimony at the preliminary hearing beginning on January 7 in Reading indicated that the amphetamines and diet pills in question were issued in the names of several players and their wives. The Phillies' stonewalling continued, with Larry Christenson and Jean Luzinski testifying that they could not remember anything about receiving such pills, and Rose denying knowledge of amphetamines.

At the continuation of the hearing, however, the stonewall collapsed. Randy Lerch admitted under oath that he had indeed received antidepressants prescribed by Mazza and delivered by Masley. The Masleys followed with testimony about their deliveries to players in the Phillies' Vet Stadium locker room. Doctor Mazza confirmed that he had written the prescriptions at the request of the players.

Charges against Mazza and the Masleys were dismissed. The players in question came out looking bad, for their obviously untruthful testimony before Lerch's admission, for the apparent use of amphetamines (although no one pretended that this was not widespread in baseball at the time), and, most of all, for their readiness to let Mazza and the Masleys "take the rap" in order to keep their own skirts clean. It was not a shining moment in Philadelphia's baseball history.[4]

Even with the shock of Ruly Carpenter's bombshell and the Doctor Mazza mess, the defending world champion Phillies started off well. There were rumblings of trouble to come, as the players threatened a midseason strike over the lack of a labor agreement with the owners.

On the evening of June 10, Rose rapped a single off Houston's Nolan Ryan, the 3,630th hit of his career, tying Stan Musial's National League record for hits. Ryan fanned Rose the next three times at bat, and Pete did not break Musial's record that night.

Before another game was played, the strike began, and major league baseball came to a sudden halt, the first time that had happened since the secretary of war brought a premature end to the 1918 season. The Phillies beat Ryan in that last game before the stoppage, and the strike found them leading the Eastern Division by 1½ games, with a 34–21 record. Carlton was a superb 9–1, and Schmidt, Rose, Matthews, and Trillo were all hitting the ball well.

They all had to hang up their spikes while the owners' negotiators and the union leaders engaged in mostly fruitless labor negotiations. The strike continued for fifty days, validating most of what Ruly Carpenter had said in March, before a settlement was reached and the season resumed on August 10.

The owners capped the series of blunders which had caused the strike in the first place with an ill-conceived split-season playoff scheme. Designed primarily to make up lost revenue, the plan matched the winner of the first half of the season (before the strike) in a best-of-five playoff with the team in each division with the best record after the strike, to determine the division winners. Never mind that no one in the early days of June realized they were winding up a mini-pennant race, or that the scheme rendered the post-strike period irrelevant for teams like the Phillies which were guaranteed a spot in the playoff because they happened to have been in front when the strike started. Business was business.

After the regular season ended, the Phillies played Montreal and the Dodgers played Houston for the division titles, even though, for the whole season, St. Louis and Cincinnati had the best records in the two divisions. The Phillies, their playoff spot already won, went 25–27 after the strike, for a season's record of 59–48. Veteran scout Jocko Collins said of the post-strike Phillies, "These guys look sluggish."[5]

A number of Phillies continued to perform well when the season resumed. Rose, in his first game back, got the hit which broke Musial's record. Pete finished the year with a .325 average and led the league in hits; he was not one to permit a few labor troubles to divert him from his game.

Schmidt won his second straight MVP award, on the strength of 31 homers, 91 runs batted in, 228 total bases, and a .644 slugging percentage, all major league highs, and his .316 batting average, a personal high. There is no telling what totals he might have posted if fifty-five games had not been lost to the strike.

Carlton finished at 13–4, with a 2.42 ERA, and might have won another Cy Young award were it not for the highly-publicized Fernando-mania which swayed the voting to the Dodgers' rookie Valenzuela. Gary Matthews wound up at .301, Lonnie Smith batted .324 as a part-timer, Trillo hit .287, and Bowa hit .283.

Mike Schmidt, the greatest third baseman in baseball history.

Some Phillies let themselves get badly out of shape during the layoff, and there was a certain something missing from the club's performance after the strike. With a playoff spot assured, the Phillies treated the second part of the year as an exhibition schedule.

Green's team was flat coming into the mini-playoff with the Expos, and its performance in Montreal showed it. In the first game, Steve Rogers outpitched Carlton, 3–1, with Keith Moreland's three hits including a second-inning homer the only offense for the Phils. The next night, Dick Ruthven was touched for three runs early, and Bill Gullickson and Jeff Reardon stifled the visitors for another 3–1 Expo victory.

The Phillies came home to Philadelphia down two games, to read in the papers that manager Dallas Green had agreed to take a job as general manager of the Chicago Cubs. A disappointing crowd of 36,835 turned out at the Vet to see Christenson win the third game, 6–2, with relief help from Sparky Lyle and Ron Reed. Matthews had three hits, and Schmidt, hitless in the games at Montreal, a single and a double.

For the fourth game, with 38,818 in attendance, Dickie Noles started against Scott Sanderson. The Phillies were ahead, 4–2, when Noles left in the fifth, but the Expos tied it against Brusstar in the sixth. The Phillies scored a run in the sixth, but the Expos made it 5–5 in the seventh. Tug McGraw pitched three strong relief innings, and pinch-hitter George Vukovich won it for the Phillies with a leadoff home run in the tenth.

For the final game, on Sunday the 11th, a larger crowd of 47,384 watched Carlton face off against Rogers again. The two pitchers worked a scoreless game until Rogers himself singled home two runs in the fifth inning. Larry Parrish of the Expos drove in a third run in the sixth. The Phillies could do little against Rogers, who won the game and the division title, 3–0. The playoff never really piqued the interest of Philadelphia's fandom, perhaps because the second half of the sundered season never did either.

Ruly Carpenter dropped the second shoe on October 29, announcing that the team had been sold to Giles and the group he put together for the price of $30,175,000. The thirty-eight year tenure of the Carpenters was over.

There had been both good and bad features to the Carpenter Era. The Carpenter money was the deciding factor in the Phillies, not the Athletics, surviving in the city when two-team towns were being winnowed out, a development that would have astounded generations of fans who always regarded Mack and his A's as top dogs in Philadelphia.

Even with the money, of course, Bob Carpenter and his front office were not always too generous in spreading it around, and this fact, coupled with his clear reluctance to employ black ballplayers, meant that the Quaker City's fans had to endure more decades of mediocrity. The one area, it must be said, where the Phillies under the Carpenters did not stint was in scouting and player development, and their minor league operation, under directors Cy Morgan, Gene Martin, Owens, and then Green, was one of the best.

Dallas Green did in fact take the job in Chicago, so the Phillies named Pat Corrales, who had caught for them in the mid-'60s, as their new manager. Corrales, known as a quiet but tough man, had put in two so-so seasons in 1979–80 as manager of the Texas Rangers.

Between seasons, the Phillies were active in the trading market. On November 20, they made a three-way trade with the Cardinals and Indians, sending Lonnie Smith to the Cardinals and receiving catcher Baudilio "Bo" Diaz from Cleveland. On December 8, they traded Moreland, Dickie Noles, and pitcher Dan Larson to the Cubs for right-handed starting pitcher Mike Krukow.

On January 27 the club made a deal which should for all time establish a rule to "Never Trade with Your Former Farm Director." Owens picked up shortstop Ivan DeJesus from the Cubs in exchange for Larry Bowa and an infielder from the farm system named Ryne Sandberg. Sandberg had been in thirteen Phillie games in September 1981, with one hit in six at-bats. He was clearly a prospect, but Dallas Green suspected he could be much more than that. DeJesus-for-Bowa was basically a standoff— even though DeJesus was eight years younger, Bowa lasted longer with the Cubs than Ivan did with the Phillies— but Ryne Sandberg became a potential Hall of Famer.

Another consequence of Green's departure for Chicago was a major turnover in the Phillies' minor league and scouting operation. During the years when Dallas ran the show, from 1972 to 1979, opposing scouts used to say, "There are three sure things in life — death, taxes, and two Phillies scouts behind you every time you turn." The Carpenters spent what was necessary on scouting and the draft.[6]

When Green took the manager's position, Jim Baumer and Jack Pastore took over the minor league and scouting operation. (Green felt that mistakes in the player development area started almost as soon as he left for the dugout.) With the concurrent departures of Green and the Carpenters, the Phillies' scouts did not know where they stood, and Baumer, the head of the minor league system, did not know where the scouts' loyalties lay. As a result, several of the club's top scouts left to go with the Cubs, and they were not replaced by the new regime, which was more cost-conscious than Ruly Carpenter and his father had been. Bill Giles, the new president, came from a marketing and promotion background, and he was less concerned with player development than his predecessor had been.

One of the scouts who went to Chicago was former infielder Ruben Amaro, who had been responsible for a stream of good Latin talent flowing into the organization. This particular source dried up, and the reduced scouting capabilities and some unwise decisions resulted in several years of bad drafts by the Phillies. These, of course, had serious consequences down the road.

Another noteworthy transaction was the sale in early December of Bob Boone to California. Boone, operating on a bad knee, had been unsuccessful in throwing out base-stealers in 1981, although Phillies pitchers, with the exception of Carlton, were deficient at holding runners close to first. The Phillies made a judgment, faulty as it turned out, that Bob Boone was no longer a premier catcher, and so they went after Bo Diaz. Finally, on February 16, Owens swapped Bake McBride to Cleveland for reliever Sid Monge.

With good work from Diaz, who hit .288 with 18 homers and 85 runs batted in, with a splendid 23–11, 286 strikeout season from Carlton, and 19 home runs and 83 RBIs from Matthews, the Phillies were in the race most of the way and finished second with a record of 89–73. Schmidt missed several weeks with a pulled muscle in his rib cage, but he still hit .280, slugged 35 round-trippers, and drove in 87 runs. DeJesus hit only

.239 but played an acceptable shortstop, and rookie outfielder Bob Dernier stole 42 bases.

Rose and Trillo both sloughed off to .271 averages, but Trillo had a splendid season in the field, playing 149 games with only five errors. McGraw had an off-year, but Reed and Monge pitched well out of the bullpen, and Mike Krukow proved to be a good acquisition, with 33 starts, a 13–11 record, and a 3.12 ERA.

The National League East developed into a struggle between the Phillies and Whitey Herzog's Cardinals, who opened a three-game series on September 13 at the Vet tied for first place. Carlton won the first game to put the Phillies ahead. The next night the Cards won, beating Krukow, when reliever Bruce Sutter threw his fabled split-finger fastball to Schmidt with the bases loaded in the eighth and got him to bounce into a pitcher-to-catcher-to-first double play. When newly-acquired John Denny lost to St. Louis the next night, the Cardinals had a lead they would not relinquish. The Phillies finished three games back.

Paul Owens made a couple of major trades during the off-season. On December 9, 1982, he traded five players, Manny Trillo, outfielder George Vukovich, infield prospect Julio Franco, pitcher Jay Baller, and minor-league catcher Jerry Willard, to the Cleveland Indians for a young left-handed-hitting outfielder named Von Hayes.

The fans were stunned by the deal, especially at the departure of the popular Trillo. Manny was asking for a big-money long-term contract, which Owens was reluctant to give. The other part of the public's reaction was, "Who is this guy we're giving up five players for?" Hayes, at Cleveland, had certainly not been overpublicized, but Owens knew that he was a tall, slender versatile player with speed, a quick bat, good power, and a great deal of potential. The demanding press and fans of Philadelphia expected to see that potential realized sooner rather than later, in 1983, to be precise, and when it was not, they let the young outfielder know it. Philadelphia never warmed to Von Hayes.

Several days later, Owens traded Krukow, young southpaw pitcher Mark Davis, and a minor leaguer to the Giants for Joe Morgan, the great second baseman of the Astros and the Reds, and reliever Al Holland. Morgan was 39 and far past his prime, but Owens was confident that he could fill the time gap between Manny Trillo and minor-league second base prospect Juan Samuel.

When the Phillies signed free-agent Tony Perez, they suddenly possessed, with Morgan, Rose, and Perez, three of the top stars of Cincinnati's Big Red Machine of the mid-'70s. The only trouble was that it was now closer to the mid-'80s, and the Phillies were soon being called "the Wheeze Kids."

The 1983 National League East race was a peculiar one, with no one apparently able to take charge of it. The Phillies were in it, with Pittsburgh, Montreal, and the Cardinals, but they impressed nobody.

Schmidt continued to supply most of the power, with a league-leading forty home runs and 109 runs batted in. The others in double figures in homers were Morgan (16), Diaz (15), and Matthews (10). Spare outfielders Greg Gross and Joe Lefebvre hit over .300. Morgan's average was way down, though, as was Pete Rose's. Rose hit .245 and Morgan .230.

Hayes, the phenom from Cleveland, was a disappointment. Apparently spooked by the loudly-expressed expectations of the fans as well as by the nickname Rose hung on him, "Old Five for One," Hayes seemed tentative and edgy. He hit .265 with six home runs and only 32 RBIs. When the pennant race was being won in September, he rode the bench. Another who did so, surprisingly, was Rose. First base in September belonged to rookie Len Matuszek, who responded well to the challenge with .275, four home runs, and 16 runs batted in in 28 games.

Steve Carlton won fifteen and lost sixteen, led the league in strikeouts, and put up a 3.11 ERA, but it was not a great year for Lefty, and others had to take up the slack. Christenson could not, as he was only 2–4 in nine games in an injury-wracked season, and Ruthven was traded to Chicago. The man they received for Ruthven, relief pitcher Willie Hernandez, was one of those who took the pressure off Carlton. Hernandez was 8–4 with seven saves in 63 appearances. Rookie Charles Hudson started 26 games and compiled an 8–8 record. Another rookie, Kevin Gross, posted a 4–6 record in 17 starts.

The main men on the staff were John Denny and Al Holland. Denny, who came from Cleveland late in the '82 season with a reputation for surliness, had put in five years with the Cards and two with the Indians. Owens hoped Denny, now a born-again Christian, would be a useful addition to the staff, but no one expected him to come through as he did, winning the Cy Young Award with a record of 19–6 and 2.37.

Holland, a burly left-handed relief pitcher with a scowl and a Fu Manchu mustache, was nicknamed "Mr. T" after the then-popular television character of that name. Holland won 8, lost 4, had an ERA of 2.26, and 25 saves. In 91⅔ innings, he rolled up 100 strikeouts and became a popular favorite.

On July 18, Owens relieved Pat Corrales of the manager's job and took it on himself again. Corrales had impressed few with his overmanaging and questionable strategy on the field, but the timing of his release was odd, because the Phillies were in first place at the time — albeit with a record of 43–42.

Rose said that with Corrales, "Nobody knows who the regulars are on this team." More to the point was that the team was not performing anywhere near its potential. Peter Pascarelli of the *Inquirer* wrote that "there were a lot of fingerprints belonging to a lot of Phillies players on the ax that fell on Corrales."[7]

Owens was reluctant to take the job, but the change was insisted on by new president Giles. Owens was the antithesis of Corrales as a manager. Joe Morgan said he was "a nice enough man but a guy who had absolutely nothing to say about anything — especially what was going on in the field." The Pope was quoted as saying that "the toughest thing about managing is standing up for nine innings." Coach Bobby Wine actually ran the club for Owens in the Phillies' dugout.[8]

The Phillies did not immediately play better for Owens, but things settled down somewhat. It was a difficult team to manage, with all of the veterans, including five potential Hall of Fame candidates. Owens and Wine did a lot of righty-lefty platooning, and this did not sit well with some of those platooned, particularly older players like Maddox and Matthews.

When September rolled around, the Phillies were still in a race which was up for grabs among four possible claimants, in spite of an interview Mike Schmidt gave over Labor Day weekend. Schmidt said, "We're the least likely of the four teams to get hot in September, because we don't have any kind of a foundation for the guys to build on.... We got a team full of guys that are capable of turning on a switch, and you wouldn't know it's the same ballclub two weeks later. But we've got an organization ... full of soap-opera problems that are cutting into the chances of that happening." As it turned out, he was right about the team's capability and wrong about what was shortly to happen.[9]

With Matuszek supplying punch at first base and Joe Morgan suddenly playing like the Morgan of old, it was the Phillies who ran off and stole the division crown. On September 14, they swept a Veterans Stadium doubleheader from Montreal to take first place by a game over the Pirates, 1½ over the Expos, and 2½ over the Cards. Schmidt's home runs and a shutout from the forgotten Marty Bystrom, 25 days after his last appearance, led the Phillies in the sweep.

The Phillies never looked back. They won eleven in succession and 14 out of their final 16, clinching the division in Wrigley Field on September 28. One of those victories was Steve Carlton's 6–2 win over the Cardinals at St. Louis on September 23, the 300th victory of his great career. He was the sixteenth pitcher in history to win that many. The club's final margin over Pittsburgh was six games. Suddenly, no one was laughing at "the Wheeze Kids."

Tommy Lasorda's Dodgers were the opposition in the league playoffs, and this was a concern because they had beaten the Phils eleven out of twelve games in the regular season. The series opened in Los Angeles on October 4, and the Phillies hoped to throw regular-season records out the window.

Carlton opposed Jerry Reuss, and Schmidt teed off on the Dodger left-hander in the first inning for a center field home run. There were no other runs scored, and Carlton picked Dodger speedster Steve Sax off first base twice. The closest the Dodgers came to scoring was in the eighth, when they loaded the bases with two out. Holland replaced Carlton, retired Mike Marshall on a fly ball, and set the Dodgers down in order in the ninth for the 1–0 victory.

The next night Denny faced southpaw Fernando Valenzuela, and the Dodgers picked up a run in the first, matched by Matthews's tying home run in the second. Two Dodger runs in the fifth and another off Reed in the eighth gave Los Angeles a 4–1 victory to even the series, which headed for Philadelphia.

53,490 people showed up at the Vet on a beautiful Friday afternoon for Game Three, with rookie Charles Hudson on the mound against Bob Welch. The Phillies put two on the board in the second inning and another in the third on Joe Lefebvre's sacrifice fly. Marshall closed the gap with a two-run shot in the top of the fourth, but Matthews hit another four-bagger in the bottom of the inning. Schmidt called the Matthews homer "the biggest hit of the series," because it demoralized the Dodgers after Marshall had pulled them close. In the fifth inning, Matthews drove home two more runs with a single, and brought in the run that made it 7–2, the final score, in the seventh. Hudson went all the way and limited the visitors to four hits.[10]

With 64,494 in attendance on Saturday night, October 8, Gary Matthews struck again in the first inning, this time with a three-run home run off Reuss. It was more than enough for Steve Carlton, who pitched six innings and left with a 7–1 lead. Reed gave up a run in the eighth, but Holland blanked the Dodgers for the final five outs, three of them on strikes. It was time to pour the champagne in the clubhouse for the fourth National League pennant in Phillies' history, this one coming in the franchise's centennial season.

In the World Series the Phils met the Baltimore Orioles, a club which had posted a storied record of success since arriving in Crabtown in 1954 as the sorry and disheveled St. Louis Browns. Joe Altobelli had brought his team home on top in his first season in Baltimore. The Orioles were led by first baseman Eddie Murray, shortstop Cal Ripken, catcher Rick

Dempsey, and pitching stalwarts Mike Boddicker, Scott McGregor, Mike Flanagan, and the aging Jim Palmer.

"The I-95 series," so called for the highway linking the two cities, opened on a rainy October 11 at Baltimore's Memorial Stadium. Denny opposed McGregor, with President Ronald Reagan among the 52,204 onlookers. Jim Dwyer hit a long home run for Baltimore in the first inning, and that run was the only marker in the game for the first five innings, as both pitchers hurled effectively. Denny, the *Inquirer* reported, "just got stronger as the rain fell ... and the wind gusted."[11]

Morgan drilled a curveball over the right field fence in the sixth to tie the score at 1–1, and Maddox put the Phillies ahead 2–1 with a left field home run on McGregor's first pitch of the eighth inning. When little Al Bumbry doubled off Denny with two outs in the bottom of the inning, Owens brought in Holland. The burly lefthander gor Disco Dan Ford to end the inning and Ripken, Murray, and Gary Roenicke in the ninth to preserve the win for Denny. The Phillies collected only five hits against McGregor and two relievers, but they were enough.

In Game Two, they picked up only three hits off soft-throwing rookie Mike Boddicker, and they were not enough. The Phils scored one in the fourth inning, on a sacrifice fly by Joe Lefebvre, but the O's came back with three in the fifth against Hudson on a homer by outfielder John Lowenstein, three hits, and a sacrifice fly. Another run in the seventh made it 4–1 Baltimore, and that is how it ended, with the Series moving to Philadelphia tied at one game apiece.

The Phillies' lack of hitting in the first two games had been accentuated by the fine control of the Baltimore pitchers, who had yielded no bases on balls. Schmidt was 0-for-8 and Rose 1-for-8 in the two games, so Owens decided to bench Rose. Pete had not been hitting in the late season anyway. With Matuszek ineligible because of his September callup, Owens put Tony Perez in the lineup at first base. The self-centered Rose, not exactly the perfect team player, chose to make an issue of his benching, complaining to sportscaster Howard Cosell on national television before the game that he was hurt and embarrassed.[12]

In the second inning of the game, before 65,792 at the Vet, Matthews bombed a home run off Mike Flanagan. Morgan led off the third with another roundtripper, and the Phils led, 2–0. Carlton had four strikeouts through three innings, with no hits allowed, and appeared to be in command. In the fourth inning, however, the lower back problems which he had recently been experiencing reappeared, and his back started to tighten up. The Phillies' brain trust kept him in the game.

In the sixth inning, Ford hit a homer to cut the lead to 2–1. In the bottom of the inning, with Palmer pitching in relief for the Orioles, Bo

Diaz singled with two out, took second on a wild pitch, and watched DeJesus walk to put two men on. Owens came out to the on-deck circle to ask Carlton, the next hitter, if he could go another inning. The pitcher gave an ambiguous answer, but Owens eschewed the use of a pinch-hitter and let Carlton, who was pitching in pain, bat for himself. It was not a wise decision. The team had gotten as much from the great southpaw as it could reasonably have expected that evening. When Steve fanned, the inning was over.

In the seventh, Carlton got the first two outs before Rick Dempsey doubled and advanced on a wild pitch. Benny Ayala, batting for Palmer, singled to left to tie the game and knock Carlton out. Holland came on to give up a hit to John Shelby before Dan Ford hit a hard ground ball to DeJesus. The ball bounced off the shortstop's glove for an error as Ayala scored the tie-breaking run.

Sammy Stewart threw two strong innings and Tippy Martinez one as Altobelli's bullpen held the 3–2 lead for Palmer. It was the fourth World Series win for the future Hall of Famer and the last victory of his illustrious career.

As the Phillies fell behind in the Series, writer Allen Lewis said that the team had to be concerned with Schmidt's hitting in the Series: "Their leading RBI man not only has not driven in a run, but he also has not collected a hit."[13]

Storm Davis started Game Four against Denny, a Saturday afternoon contest before 66,947, and the Orioles scored two early runs. In the bottom of the fourth, Lefebvre doubled after singles by Rose and Schmidt (his only hit of the Series) to score a run. The Phils took a 3–2 lead in the fifth on Diaz's double, Denny's single, and Rose's double, but Baltimore came right back in the sixth with two runs to regain the edge. In the seventh, the O's notched another run on Rich Dauer's third hit, while reliever Sammy Stewart held the Phillies scoreless through the eighth, though aided in that inning by Tippy Martinez. In the ninth, pinch-hitter Ozzie Virgil drove home a Phils run, but the team fell short to lose, 5–4.

The Series ended on Sunday, October 16, as Scotty McGregor blanked the Phillies, 5–0, on five hits. With the largest crowd in history for a baseball game in Philadelphia, 67,064, the Phillies were never in the game at all. Murray touched Charles Hudson for two home runs and Dempsey hit one. McGregor took it from there. It was, said the *Inquirer*, "a depressing ending to what had been a glorious fall."[14]

The World Series was certainly a disappointment for the Phillies, whose bats were stifled by Oriole pitching for a .195 average. Owens said, "We're better than the way we played," and Joe Morgan said, "I believe we were the better club — but we lost." Schmidt was 1-for-20, and his slump clearly hurt the team's offense. "I tried as hard as I could," Mike said, "but it just didn't work out. I apologize for my performance, but not for my effort." Lost in the gloom, perhaps, was the realization that it was only the fourth World Series appearance ever for the Phillies, and there were twenty-four other clubs who did not get that far in 1983.[15]

Chapter 20

Michael Jack
and the Dude

Paul Owens decided to stay on as manager for 1984, even though it meant relinquishing his job as general manager — a clear case of a man leaving a position for which he was well qualified for one in which he was in over his head. Nineteen hundred eighty-four was not a happy year for the Phillies or for the Pope.

The changes made to the National League champions of 1983 were not on balance good ones. Bill Giles believed, having been told so by his minor league people, that the players being developed by the Phillies would work out as the Luzinskis, Bowas, Boones, and Schmidts of the 1970s had. But John Russell, Jeff Stone, Rick Schu, Juan Samuel, and the rest were not in the same class as their predecessors.

The Phillies quickly dismantled the 1983 pennant-winner. Rose was released the day after the World Series, having left a bad taste in everyone's mouth with his public whining about being benched in Game Three. Morgan was cut loose, primarily because Samuel was thought ready to take over second base full time. Tony Perez was sold back to Cincinnati. Ron Reed was traded to the White Sox for veteran southpaw Jerry Koosman.

Two major trades were made in late March. One deal sent Willie Hernandez and just-acquired Dave Bergman to the Tigers for outfielder Glenn Wilson and catcher John Wockenfuss, while the other brought in reliever Bill Campbell and a minor leaguer from the Chicago Cubs, at the cost of Gary Matthews, Bob Dernier, and reliever Porfirio Altamirano.

The trades worked out badly for the Phillies. Hernandez had a sensational year for the Series-winning Tigers, receiving both the Most Valuable Player and Cy Young awards, while Matthews hit .291 with 82 runs batted in, leading the league in on-base percentage, to help the Cubs win the National League East. Pouring more salt into the Phillies' wounds, the National League MVP was Ryne Sandberg.

The Phillies began well but soon dropped off the pace. A ten-game winning streak, including a sweep of its California rivals, put the club back in contention, as the hitting of Schmidt, Samuel, and Hayes, and the pitching of Koosman, Carlton, Holland, and Shane Rawley, obtained at the end of June from the Yankees, sustained it. The team faded badly in September, losing its last nine games. At season's end, with the Phillies finishing in fourth place at 81–81, Owens announced that he was returning to the front office as a special assistant to Giles. Coach John Felske, previously a farm system manager, was named skipper.

As usual, the team's offensive leader in 1984 was Mike Schmidt. Michael Jack hit 36 home runs, which tied him for the league lead with Atlanta's Dale Murphy, and he and Gary Carter of Montreal shared the RBI crown with 106. Von Hayes batted .292, hit 16 homers, and stole 48 bases as he began to show the talent which led the Phils to give five players for him.

Samuel hit .272, led the league with 19 triples, hit 15 home runs, and stole 72 bases. He was an exciting player to watch at the plate and on the bases, although a lack of discipline caused 168 strikeouts, tops in the league. He was not a good second baseman, and his thirty-three errors (Manny Trillo had six for San Francisco) led the league as well.

If better things were expected for 1985, that hope was dashed early, as the club under new manager Felske got off to a terrible start from which it never recovered. With a record of 75–87, the Phillies finished in fifth place, far behind the division-winning Cardinals.

Going into the season, the Phils were touted by their public relations people as a bunch of speedburners, with clusters of stolen bases to be expected from Samuel, Hayes, and quasi-rookie Jeff Stone, who had stolen 27 bases in 51 games in '84, batting .362 in the process. It never happened. Hayes's total fell from 48 to 21, and his batting average slipped to .263. Samuel's thefts dropped to 53, his average declined to .264, but he still led the league in strikeouts. Stone hit .265 and stole only fifteen bases.

Glenn Wilson, after a disappointing year in 1984, became a fan favorite. He hit .275, drove in 102 runs, and displayed a great throwing arm, leading the league's outfielders with eighteen assists. Schmidt played most of the season at first base, so rookie Rick Schu could be worked into the lineup at third. Mike showed some good moves at first, and he hit 33 home runs with 93 RBIs for another good year of power production. His tour at first brought an end to his streak of nine Gold Glove seasons at third base, although he would win the honor again when he went back to third in 1986.

Schmidt's hot-and-cold relationship with the fans took a dip in late June, when the *Montreal Gazette* printed an interview which Mike had given on April 29. Asked about the fans in his home city, Schmidt said, "They're beyond help. It's a mob scene, uncontrollable." He elaborated: "I'll tell you something about playing in Philadelphia. Whatever I've got in my career now, I would have had a great [deal] more if I'd played my whole career in Los Angeles or Chicago, you name a town — somewhere where they were just grateful to have me around." Questioned about the boos he had received over the years, Schmidt said, "In the past it has affected me. I was bleeped off. I tried too hard. I couldn't understand it and I felt sorry for myself."[1]

When the team returned home on July 1, Schmidt braced himself for the storm to come after the publication of these thoughts. Taking the field for infield drill, he wore a long black wig and sunglasses, courtesy of pitcher-humorist Larry Andersen, and the fans responded with laughter and forgiveness, mixed perhaps with a trace of chagrin at the treatment which had caused Schmidt's feelings.

The Phils' pitching in 1985 was not what they hoped for. Steve Carlton, on the far downhill side of his great career, won only one game and lost eight, completing none of the sixteen games he started. Denny was 11–14, Koosman was 6–4, and Hudson was 8–13. Kevin Gross's 15–13 helped, as did Shane Rawley's 13–8. Holland was traded to Pittsburgh early in the year for submarining Kent Tekulve, long one of the league's premier relief pitchers, and Tekulve became the main man in the bullpen.

On June 11 the Phillies trounced the New York Mets by an amazing 26–7 score, piling up nine runs in the first inning and seven more in the second. Von Hayes wrote himself into the record book in the first inning explosion with two home runs, the second with the bases loaded. One of the astonishing features of the game was the difficulty the team's starting pitcher, Hudson, had in staggering through the required five innings to pick up the almost-guaranteed win.

Late in the '85 season, the Phillies made what might have been one of the great trades in their history, if only they had recognized it. They sent rookie pitcher Rick Surhoff, who had pitched in two games for the Phils, to Texas for Dave "Smoke" Stewart, a pitcher who had worked four and a fraction seasons for the Dodgers and Rangers. He had long impressed the Phillies as the possessor of a great arm but was not doing well when they got him. After going 0–6 for the Rangers, Stewart pitched in four games for the Phillies in 1985, worked in eight games at the start of the '86 season, failed to excite Felske or pitching coach Claude Osteen, and was released on May 9. Picked up by Oakland, Stewart won 116 games for the A's in seven years, including twenty wins or more for four straight seasons.

The team made a couple of trades in preparation for the 1986 season. Catcher Ozzie Virgil and a minor leaguer went to Atlanta for pitcher Steve Bedrosian and outfielder Milt Thompson, and Cincinnati gave up outfielder Gary Redus and reliever Tom Hume in exchange for Denny and a minor leaguer. Despite the newcomers, the Phillies played poorly and landed in the division basement by the middle of May.

Garry Maddox, troubled by persistent back problems, retired in May, after ten-plus years as a major contributor to the Phillies. A timely hitter, with a .285 lifetime batting average, Maddox was noted primarily for his defense. Known widely as "the Secretary of Defense" and the winner of eight Gold Gloves, it was said of him that "two-thirds of the earth is covered by water, the other third by Garry Maddox."

Another painful departure took place in June, when the Phillies released Steve Carlton. They urged the great left-hander to retire, but he refused to do so. The victim of bad investments, Carlton needed the money he could make as a big-league pitcher, and he refused to believe that his ineffectiveness—he was 4–8 with a 6.18 ERA when the Phillies cut him loose — was anything but temporary.

In a sad end to a great career, Carlton hung on for almost two more years, going from San Francisco to the White Sox to Cleveland to the Twins, winning 11 and losing 21, before running out of teams that would hire him. Lefty's final record was 329 wins, second only to Warren Spahn among lefthanders, 244 losses, an earned run average of 3.22, and second place all-time (to Nolan Ryan in each category) in both strikeouts and bases on balls. All this plus four Cy Young awards.

For the Phillies, Steve Carlton won more games (241), started more games, and struck out more batters than any other pitcher. His 39 shutouts rank him second among Phillies pitchers to Pete Alexander, and his total games and innings pitched for the club are surpassed only by Robin Roberts. Carlton is certainly the greatest southpaw ever to pitch for the Phillies, and he must be ranked with Alexander and Roberts as the best pitchers the team ever had.

With all of his accomplishments, Carlton was not really well known by the people of Philadelphia. Early in his tenure in the Quaker City, Carlton's resentment of things written by the local press led him to stop talking to reporters altogether, a position he maintained consistently thereafter. The public was occasionally told what a swell fellow Lefty was, if only the public could get to know him better, and many stories were written about the strenuous and even brutal conditioning routines he followed, with the aid of martial arts guru Gus Hoefling.

What the fans really had to go by in assessing Carlton was his work on the mound. And that was enough. A power pitcher with a devastating slider, Steve Carlton at his best was unhittable, and he was just slightly less than that even when not at his best. Willie Stargell, the Pittsburgh slugger, once said of Carlton, "Hitting him was like trying to drink coffee with a fork." The tall southpaw entered the Hall of Fame in 1994.

When Carlton was let go, the Phillies brought up a young lefthander named Bruce Ruffin, who turned in a 9–4 record, with a 2.46 ERA; his sinkerball had batters beating the ball into the ground. With Ruffin, Rawley, young Don Carman, and Kevin Gross handling most of the starts, and Tekulve and Bedrosian forming an effective bullpen, the team came alive in June.

Schmidt, back at third base, had another great year, both at bat and in the field, and Von Hayes had the best season of his career, batting .305, hitting 19 home runs, driving in 98 runs, and leading the league in runs scored and doubles. Redus, one of the league's top offensive producers at Cincinnati, was a disappointment, hitting only .247 with but 33 RBIs. Felske's team moved into second place in August, and there it finished, with a record of 86–75. Second place was fine, of course, but the Phillies were 21½ games behind the first place New York Mets, who won 108 games.

When the season was over, Mike Schmidt was rewarded with his third Most Valuable Player award, based on his .290 average and his league-leading totals of 37 home runs and 119 runs batted in. His fielding excellence was recognized with his tenth Gold Glove. The Philly fans, who had so often given Schmidt a hard time, were coming to realize what a treasure they had in the red-haired third baseman from Dayton, Ohio.

Hopes were high for 1987, since it was unreasonable to expect the Mets to have as good a season as in '86, and the Phillies felt that they improved their squad considerably. In off-season deals, the club traded Hudson to the Yankees for outfielder Mike Easler, a good batter whose nickname was "The Hit Man," and Redus to the White Sox for righthanded pitcher Joe Cowley, who had won 32 games, including a no-hitter, in three American League seasons. Cowley always walked quite a few hitters, but he had a good arm and the Phillies hoped that he was coming into his prime at 28.

The most important acquisition, though, was catcher Lance Parrish, signed as a free agent after ten years with Detroit in which he had established himself as one of the top receivers in the game. This was the first winter of the clubowners' "collusion" in refusing to sign other teams' free agents, and Giles brought some displeasure down upon himself in signing Parrish.

It was hardly worth it. Lance Parrish was a flop as a Phillie, batting only .245 with 67 runs batted in. He appeared to be performing with less than enthusiastic zeal, and it did not take long for the Philadelphia boobirds to target him. Easler hit .282 in 33 games, but he drove in only ten runs and on June 10 was traded back to the Yankees.

Even more of a bust was Joe Cowley. He could not find the plate at all, and he was soon gone. Cowley pitched in five games, starting four, and they were games that the fans who were present found hard to forget. He was 0–4 in his brief tenure as a Phillie, with 17 walks and 21 hits in the twelve total innings he worked. His earned run average was a hideous 15.43. After Cowley's second start, in which he gave up four hits, four walks, and five runs in one-plus innings against the Mets, pitching coach Osteen said, "If you need a comment after watching that performance, then, well, I don't know." Sent to the minors, Cowley found he could not throw strikes there either, and he never made it back to the big leagues.[2]

With these disappointments, the club had a losing year, finishing fourth in its division with an 80–82 record. Disappointed with the phlegmatic, unemotional John Felske, who came to be known as "the Wooden Soldier" for his unchanging demeanor, the Phillies' brass fired him in June, replacing him with former Cubs manager Lee Elia, a Philadelphia native who had grown up in the Phillies' organization. The team played a little better for Elia than it had for Felske, winning one more than it lost, but it all still added up to fourth place.

Schmidt led the way once again, batting .293 with 35 homers and 113 RBIs. On April 18, Mike became the fourteenth player in major league history to hit five hundred home runs, and No. 500 was particularly meaningful, a three-run ninth-inning blast at Three Rivers Stadium which brought the Phillies a come-from-behind victory over the Pirates.

Von Hayes fell off from his '86 performance but still hit 21 homers with 84 RBIs. Samuel hit 28 home runs, drove in 100 runs, and led the league with 15 triples. Shane Rawley was the top starter, with a 17–11 record, and Bedrosian had a spectacular year coming out of the bullpen. Bedrosian was 5–3 with a 2.83 ERA, and he rang up forty saves to win the Cy Young Award in what was admittedly not a year of outstanding pitching. (No one won more than 18 games, and Nolan Ryan, the ERA leader, had an 8–16 won-lost record.) Bedrosian was ably assisted by setup man Tekulve.

Pitcher Kevin Gross was suspended by the league when he was caught with sandpaper in his glove. He protested his innocence of doctoring the ball, but as he was engaged in no construction projects at the time he was hard-pressed to come up with a legitimate explanation of the sandpaper.

The Easler-Cowley-Parrish bombs finally convinced club president Bill Giles that running the team by front-office committee, the so-called "Gang of Six" who conferred on most decisions, was not working. Early in the season, Mike Schmidt talked to reporters about the decline of the organization: "We've gone from having the best of everything ... to what I consider rock bottom.... The minor league system is depleted.... The field is the worst field in the league. The dugouts are filthy. The clubhouse is dirty. The pride factor is not what it used to be."[3]

The club's executives had a hard time denying Schmidt's statements. Things had to be turned around. So, after the season, Giles hired as his new general manager William Frederick "Woody" Woodward, a former utility infielder with the Braves and Reds. Woodward had prior front-office experience with the Yankees under the always-meddling George Steinbrenner, so presumably he would be able to handle whatever problems the Phillies might present.

Woodward made two trades, neither very successful, in a tenure with the Phils which came to a premature and astonishing end. He sent Glenn Wilson and a promising young reliever named Mike Jackson to Seattle for outfielder Phil Bradley, and he traded Stone, Schu, and Keith Hughes to Baltimore for outfielder Mike Young and a minor leaguer. Bradley put together a moderately-good season, but he was sullen and withdrawn in the clubhouse and was traded away after the season. Young batted .226 and went to Milwaukee in August.

In the meantime, the '88 Phillies were a bad ballclub. They lost eight of their first eleven games and never recovered, ending with a record of 65–96, in last place. Schmidt suffered a rotator cuff injury and missed a large part of the season; he hit .249 with twelve home runs and 62 runs batted in over 108 games. Hayes had a bad year, Samuel had a bad year, Parrish had a terrible year, batting .215, and shortstop Steve Jeltz, playing in 148 games, hit only .187. No one on the pitching staff had a winning record, and Bedrosian was hard-pressed to find the 28 games he saved.

Woodward, the new general manager, was fired on June 8. "It just didn't work out," said Giles, as Woodward, who may have learned the wrong things from Steinbrenner, could not get along with many of the Phillies' people. It was said that "Woodward had alienated himself from virtually everyone in the organization to such an extent that he left Giles with almost no choice but to fire him."[4]

When Woodward was axed, farm director Jim Baumer was removed from that job, in recognition of the fact that the once highly-productive

Phillies farm system was in disarray. Several weeks after the discharge of Baumer, Giles hired Lee Thomas, director of player development for the St. Louis Cardinals, as his new general manager. Thomas played eight years in the '60s as a power-hitting outfielder, and after his playing days, he put in eighteen years in the Cardinal organization. Thomas was well-grounded in most aspects of the game when he arrived, and he set out immediately to shake up an organization that was badly in need of it.

There was not much that Thomas could do about the '88 Phillies, although he made the trade that disposed of Mike Young. Nine games before the end of the season, he let Elia go, naming coach John Vukovich interim manager for the last few days. The team finished last, 35½ games out of first place.

For 1989, Thomas dipped into the Cardinal organization and selected a Redbird coach named Nick Leyva as the Phillies' manager. Leyva was 35 years old, totally unknown in Philadelphia, a man who had never played in the majors but had managed several St. Louis farm clubs.

Leyva, Thomas made sure, would have some interesting new players to manage. As soon as the '88 season ended, Thomas traded Parrish to California, getting rid of a big salary. Later in October, he sent Rawley to Minnesota for second sacker Tommy Herr and two supernumeraries. On December 6, Thomas swapped Kevin Gross to Montreal for relief pitcher Jeff Parrett and starting pitcher Floyd Youmans. Youmans was 24 and had experienced moderate success with the Expos, but most baseball people thought he had a great arm and could do well if he could get his head into the game.

A couple of days later, Bradley went to Baltimore for pitchers Ken Howell and Gordon Dillard. Howell was expected to be a starter for the Phillies. A week later, Thomas made a trade with his old employers, giving St. Louis outfielder Milt Thompson in exchange for catcher Steve Lake and outfielder Curt Ford. Thomas added another seasoned infielder with the free-agent signing of shortstop Dickie Thon.

A problem for Thomas was Mike Schmidt. Based on his '88 performance, the 39-year-old superstar was clearly near the end of the line. Mike's knees had been problems for him from the start, and now he had shoulder miseries as well. Schmidt himself was not yet convinced that he was done, and Thomas as a new general manager was not anxious to be known as the man who let the best player in the club's history go to another team. As a result, Schmidt was signed by the Phillies for another year.

The team got off to a good start, with Schmidt hitting two home runs in the first game, but reality soon settled in, both for Schmidt and for the Phillies. Floyd Youmans was a flop; he was 1–5 in ten games, with a 5.70

earned run average, and he appeared to have little interest in his job. Howell pitched well, and Bedrosian and Parrett were effective in relief, but their use was limited by the fact that the team seldom had a lead to protect. By mid-season, the Phillies were back in last place.

On May 29, Mike Schmidt called a news conference at Jack Murphy Stadium in San Diego, to announce his retirement. He told the reporters, "Over the years of my career, I've set high standards for myself as a player. I've always said that when I don't feel I can perform up to those standards, that's when it would be time to retire." Pointing out what had become apparent, Schmidt said, "My skills— to do the things on the field, to make the adjustments needed to hit, to make the routine play on defense and run the bases aggressively — have deteriorated." And then this great ballplayer, the man who had always seemed to epitomize cool and unemotional detachment, broke down and cried.[5]

With that it was over. The greatest third baseman of all time, the finest player ever to play for the Philadelphia Phillies, was no longer an active baseball player. There was a press conference for Schmidt back at the Vet, a ceremony later in the season to retire his uniform number "20," a surprising tribute from the baseball fans of America, who voted him the starting third baseman for the National League All-Star team, even though he had retired and would not play. But the hard reality was that Mike Schmidt was gone, and many a long day would pass before Philadelphia would see his like again.

As Schmidt passed from the scene, what Philadelphia could do was look back over his remarkable career, in fond remembrance and appreciation of a player who was not always treated so fondly by the fans and press as that career progressed.

Michael Jack Schmidt played sixteen full seasons and parts of two others for the Phillies, 2,404 games, more than any other player. He held the club record for hits with 2,234, at bats with 8,352, and extra base hits with 1,015. He scored more runs, drove in more, and had more total bases than any other Phillie. His 548 home runs, seventh highest of all time, dwarf the 249 of Del Ennis, second in team history. He was second only to Ed Delahanty in doubles, and he even stood eighth in Phillies history in stolen bases.

Schmidt won eight home run titles and four RBI crowns, and he led the league in slugging percentage four times, in total bases three times, and in runs scored once. Eight times he hit ten or more home runs in a month, and 44 times he hit two or more roundtrippers in a game, including the fabled four home runs at Wrigley Field on April 17, 1976. His seven career grand slams are a club record, as are his nine extra-inning home runs, capped by the one against Stan Bahnsen that clinched the division in 1980.

And Mike Schmidt was a complete ballplayer. A great fielder at third base, with exceptional range, he won ten Gold Glove awards, leading the league in assists seven times and in double plays five times. He was deadly charging topped balls headed toward third, grabbing the ball barehanded and firing across his body to retire the batter. Schmidt even perfected a variation on that play, for use in situations where there was already a runner on first. He would fake the throw to first, then rifle the ball to second to nail an unwary runner rounding the bag. It was for Schmidt's fielding brilliance added to his mighty slugging that he won his three MVP awards and the consensus of being the best ever at his position.

Gradually, too, over the years, despite occasional troubles with the fans and the press, with blunt and candid statements revealing his true feelings, the people of Philadelphia came to realize that Mike Schmidt, in addition to being a great baseball player, was an unusual young man as well. He could be surly to youngsters who waited to see him, but he could be charming as well. He was intelligent and articulate, and he did not leave people in doubt as to what was on his mind.

With Schmidt's departure, there was a void on the team. Chris James, by trade and training an outfielder, was told he was the regular third baseman, and the Phillies headed into the post–Michael Jack era. James's tenure was about as brief as could be. On June 2, four days after Schmidt's retirement, Lee Thomas started shaping the new Phillies team. He traded James to San Diego for outfielder-first baseman John Kruk and infielder Randy Ready.

Kruk was a portly lefthanded swinger from West Virginia with a round, expressive face and an elfin and self-deprecating sense of humor. *Chicago Tribune* columnist Mike Royko wrote of Kruk: "He was pudgy, unshaven, unwashed and in need of a haircut. He had a goofy batting stance, wore a uniform that didn't fit, and he walked funny." Catcher Charlie O'Brien once told Kruk that the Mets' book on him was to pitch him "under your belt where you can't see it." But John Kruk could hit: he had batted over .300 in his first two Padre seasons and then slumped to .241 in 1988. He was hitting only .184 at the time of the trade, and San Diego management apparently came to the conclusion that he had forgotten how to hit. With the Phillies Kruk batted .331, and the fans came to appreciate his eccentricities.[6]

With Kruk and Ready in the fold, Lee Thomas was prepared for his big moves. On Sunday June 18, he announced the trade of Bedrosian to the San Francisco Giants, with a minor leaguer, for two young lefthanded pitchers, Dennis Cook and Terry Mulholland, and third base prospect Charlie Hayes. The departure of Bedrosian had been rumored for some time, since the possession of a top-notch closer was a luxury the last-place Phillies could hardly afford.

Moments later, Thomas announced another deal, one which was not anticipated. Juan Samuel, the Phillies' offensive catalyst, was traded to the New York Mets for outfielder Lenny Dykstra and reliever Roger McDowell. The key to this trade, Thomas admitted, was Dykstra, "the kind of guy I always hated playing against, and now we've got him." Dykstra, a pesky hustler, was not happy as a platoon player with the Mets, and the Phillies promised him a lot more action.[7]

The Phillies' clubhouse had changed measurably from the cool laid-back place it had been with Schmidt as its leading citizen. Kruk, Ready, Cook, and McDowell were flakes, and the intense Dykstra was said to be "one of those athletes with his mental VCR on permanent fast-forward."[8]

The Phillies improved considerably in the second half of the season, although they were unable to escape last place. Von Hayes hit 26 home runs and drove in 78 runs to lead the team in power production, while Ken Howell, with 12–12 and 3.44, led the pitching staff. The acquisitions from the Giants, Cook and Mulholland, were given plenty of work, and they went 6–8 and 4–7 respectively.

The club's top 1988 draft choice, southpaw Pat Combs, was called up in September and put together a strong 4–0 record in six starts, with a 2.09 ERA. One sour note was the play of Dykstra, who batted only .222 in 90 games as a Phillie, far below his performance in New York, as he appeared to be unhappy with the fates that had moved him to Philadelphia.

In 1990, though, the Phillies found out what they had really gotten with Lenny Dykstra. The brash young outfielder, who customarily called everyone "Dude" and thus picked up the nickname for himself, had a super season, hitting .325, fourth in the league, and tying for leadership in hits with 192. He had a sensational start and was hitting over .400 in June. Although Dykstra cooled off and eventually finished behind Willie McGee in the batting race, he showed himself to be the dominant figure on the Phillies team. The club's leadership had finally passed from the cool Mike Schmidt to the red hot Lenny Dykstra.

With Dykstra leading the way, the Phillies got off to a rare good start which had them near the top of the division before they faded in June. They finished at 77–85, a ten-game improvement over 1989 and good enough to tie Chicago for fourth place. There were other heroics beside those of Dykstra. John Kruk hit .291 and became a favorite for his endearing if somewhat goofy ways. Von Hayes hit 17 home runs and drove in 73 runs, and catcher Darren Daulton, who had been with the team since 1983 with very little success, had a great second half after being installed by Leyva in the second slot in the batting order, winding up with a .268 average with twelve home runs. The .268 mark may not sound like much, but Daulton had batted .194, .208, and .201 in his three prior seasons.

The pitching was shaky in 1990. Rookie Pat Combs, with 10–10, was the only double-figure winner. Terry Mulholland was 9–10, with a 3.34 earned run average, and he posted the greatest achievement of all on August 15 when he held his former teammates, the Giants, without a hit in a 6–0 victory. Only the seventh no-hitter in club history, it was the first pitched for the Phillies at home since that of Red Donahue in 1898.

Dennis Cook was 8–3 for the Phillies, but he was traded away to Los Angeles in September for backup catcher Darrin Fletcher. Bruce Ruffin, whose pitching had worsened since his 1986 rookie year, fell to 6–13, with an unimpressive 5.38 ERA. Righthander Jose DeJesus, obtained from Kansas City just before the season for the weak-hitting Steve Jeltz, was a pleasant surprise with a 7–8 record in 22 starts.

Lee Thomas made two other noteworthy deals during the 1990 season. On August 3, he received 36-year-old Dale Murphy and pitcher Tommy Greene from Atlanta for Parrett and two minor leaguers. Murphy, a two-time MVP with the Braves, was clearly in the decline phase of his career, but he could still swing the bat with authority. The surprise was the young right-hander, Greene, who impressed everyone with a good, live major league arm.

The other trade came on August 30, with the Phillies sending journeyman outfielder Carmelo Martinez to Pittsburgh for three minor league outfielders, Wes Chamberlain, Tony Longmire, and Julio Peguero. The Pirates had inadvertently put Chamberlain, one of their top prospects, on the wrong waiver list, where the Phillies alertly spotted him and put in a claim. In order to get something for their goof-up, the Pirates arranged the trade for Martinez. Chamberlain hit .283 in 18 games with the Phils, although he was far from a polished big league ballplayer.

The 1991 season demonstrated just how clearly the Phillies had become Lenny Dykstra's team. It also showed that Dykstra, while a hard-driving, aggressive ballplayer, had some trouble conforming to society's norms off the field. During spring training, Dykstra was involved in a probe of illegal gambling in Mississippi. Lenny, it seems, had lost some $78,000 in bets on poker games and golf matches, although the outfielder was not himself a "target" of the probe. Commissioner Fay Vincent placed him on a year's probation.

Dykstra returned to the national headlines in May when he tried to drive himself and Darren Daulton away from John Kruk's bachelor party.

Lenny was drunk, and he crashed his expensive Mercedes into a tree. Both players were badly injured and lucky to be alive. Daulton, whose career had been plagued by knee injuries before this, missed 63 games, while Dykstra was out for 61 games and lost his driver's license.

After Dykstra returned to the lineup in mid–July, he was able to get into 63 games, batting .297, before he crashed into the outfield wall in Cincinnati on August 27. He broke his collarbone, the same one which had been fractured in the auto accident, and his 1991 year was history. It was a year he was happy to forget.

Dykstra's teammates probably felt the same way. Daulton played in only 89 games and batted a sickly .196. Von Hayes suffered a broken wrist and, even more, the indignity of going through the season without a single home run, hitting only .225 with a mere 21 runs batted in. Ken Howell had a sore arm and did not appear in a game.

Manager Nick Leyva was canned by his old friend Lee Thomas after thirteen games, only four of which had been Phillies wins. "I guess there were just times when I wondered if he still had control of the players," Thomas said; "I started to see things I didn't like." Leyva thought it over and then, reflecting on the turnover in managers and farm directors, told a radio interviewer, "Maybe they fired the wrong guy."[9]

The new manager was Jim Fregosi, a star infielder for eighteen years in the big leagues. Fregosi had previously managed seven seasons in the American League, winning a division title with the Angels in 1979. He got the '91 Phillies righted after their abysmal start. They played at a 74–75 pace for him, despite all the crippling injuries, finishing in third place with a 78–84 record. They even won thirteen games in succession, matching the twentieth century club record.

There was some excitement for the Phillies in 1991. Several of the young pitchers made good progress. Mulholland moved into the front rank of National League pitchers with a record of 16–13, and an earned run average of 3.61. Tommy Greene was 13–7 and 3.38, and on May 23 he became the second Phillie pitcher in two years to throw a no-hitter. His gem took place at Montreal's Olympic Stadium when he blanked the Expos, 2–0, walking seven but fanning ten. DeJesus pitched well once again, with a 10–9 mark and an ERA of 3.42, although his 128 walks led the National League.

The major part of the Phillies' pitching excitement came from their new bullpen closer, a longhaired lefthander named Mitch Williams, nicknamed "Wild Thing." One of his former employers described Williams's pitching style as that of "a man with his hair on fire." Williams had been turning managers' hair gray for three years with Texas and two with the

Cubs when the Phillies acquired him in April. Kruk, who loved Mitch, wrote that "left-handed pitchers are wacky and ... you have to be a little nuts to be a closer. So I guess that makes him double bad."[10]

Williams threw very hard, with no pretense at finesse, flinging himself off the mound in an exaggerated follow-through after each pitch. He seldom knew where the ball was going when he let it go, but then neither did the batter, who knew only that it was headed very quickly in his direction. A typical Williams "save" was two walks around a single, followed by two strikeouts and a popup, with the manager ducking back into the runway to light a needed cigarette. In 1991, Williams had a 12–5 record, with 30 saves and a 2.34 ERA. In August alone, he won eight games and saved five.

Dale Murphy supplied some needed punch, with 18 home runs and 81 runs driven in. Ex-Padre John Kruk had a banner year, hitting .294, with 21 roundtrippers and 92 RBIs. Another steal from the Padres, young third baseman David Hollins (picked up in the 1989 minor league draft), spent the first half of 1991 at Scranton-Wilkes Barre but hit .298 in 56 games when the Phillies recalled him.

Finally, a third ex-Padre, infielder Randy Ready, had to exert himself to avoid achieving immortality in a game against his former San Diego teammates on April 28. With none out and two men on, the runners on first and second took off as Tony Gwynn of the Padres hit a hard line drive at second baseman Ready. Randy caught the ball, stepped on second to retire the lead baserunner, and then dodged around the oncoming runner to throw to first sacker Ricky Jordan to complete a triple play.

When reporters pointed out to Ready that all he had to do was tag the runner coming directly at him to become the first National League second baseman in history and only the ninth player ever to record an unassisted triple play, Randy said, truthfully enough, "Well, I don't practice that."

A year and some months later, on September 20, 1992, Phillies' second baseman Mickey Morandini must have thought the situation looked familiar. The Pirates had no outs, men on first and second, and a 3–2 count, when Pittsburgh manager Jim Leyland put his runners in motion. Jeff King hit a low liner toward second, and Morandini made a nice catch of it. The rest was simple. He ran to second to retire lead runner Andy Van Slyke and, having watched Ready mess up the last part of the play, tagged the oncoming Barry Bonds to complete the unassisted triple play which Ready had blown. Morandini said later, "I remember that Spike [Ready] could have had one last year if he hadn't thrown the ball to first."[11]

The city itself underwent a change between the 1991 and 1992 seasons, when W. Wilson Goode turned over the mayoral office to former district attorney Ed Rendell. Goode, the city's first black mayor, had been a disappointment. Rendell was elected in November 1991 after an anticlimactic campaign in which his Republican opponent, former mayor Frank Rizzo, died of a midsummer heart attack. Rendell was a transplanted New Yorker, a Penn grad, and a passionate sports fan. He set out to improve the city's labor situation and to upgrade Philadelphia's municipal credit, and he had a better year in 1992 than the Phillies did.

The Morandini triple play was one of the few highlights of a very disappointing 1992 season, one in which the club fell once again into the Eastern Division cellar with a 70–92 record, despite a number of deals Thomas made during the off-season.

Three trades were consummated in early December 1991, with Von Hayes moving to California for southpaw pitcher Kyle Abbott and outfielder Ruben Amaro (son of the 1960s Phillies shortstop), catcher Darrin Fletcher going to Montreal for setup reliever Barry Jones, and the disappointing Bruce Ruffin switching to Milwaukee for shortstop Dale Sveum. In January, Charlie Hayes went to the Yankees, and just before the season started, inconsistent pitcher Jason Grimsley was sent to Houston for an unheralded righthander named Curt Schilling.

On Opening Day, the Phillies unveiled new uniforms. Discarded were the ones featuring a modernistic "P" which had been worn since 1970, and in their place were suits similar to those of the Whiz Kid era (1950–1969), with the script "Phillies" across the chest. The occasion was spoiled, however, when the second pitch of the season by Chicago's Greg Maddux to leadoff hitter Lenny Dykstra broke the Dude's wrist, and Jim Fregosi could suddenly see what kind of year it was going to be. He knew that he would not have the pitching services of Ken Howell and Jose DeJesus, each of whom broke down in spring training and neither of whom threw another pitch for the Phillies.

Abbott lost and lost and lost, finishing with an unsightly record of 1–14, with a 5.13 earned run average. Barry Jones was terrible coming out of the pen and was let go early in August. Sveum, given the shortstop job, hit .178 in 54 games and was traded to the White Sox on August 10. Dale Murphy, by now a slow and pitiful shadow of the great player he had been, was injured and able to play in only 18 games, batting .161 with two home runs. Chamberlain, too, was a disappointment, batting .258 with only 41 RBIs and suffering a temporary demotion to the minors.

Dykstra came back from the broken wrist in a surprisingly short time, but he suffered two more crippling injuries, was on the disabled list from

June 29 to July 16, and packed his season in when another injury landed him back on the DL on August 16. He hit .301 in the 85 games he was able to play and proved once again that the Phillies went only so far as Lenny Dykstra took them. The team landed in last place on June 24 and never left it, finishing with a mark of 70–92.

Despite the last place finish and the rash of injuries which crippled the team, 1992 was not a total disaster. Darren Daulton, his bad knees finally healthy, astounded the league by copping the RBI crown with 109, the first lefthanded-hitting catcher in major league history to lead in runs batted in. Daulton belted 27 home runs and hit a surprising .270. Kruk led the league in hitting for most of the season, finishing third at .323. Dave Hollins, installed at third base, hit 27 homers and drove in 93 runs, playing with a driven intensity which was sometimes frightening. Curt Schilling pitched well out of the bullpen in sixteen games, so on May 19 Fregosi and pitching coach Johnny Podres gave him a start. Schilling went on to win 14 games.

But Greene missed most of the season with tendinitis in his right shoulder, Dykstra was on and off the disabled list all year, and so many other injuries and players coming and going made it hard to tell the Phillies from their Scranton-Wilkes-Barre farm club. The Phillies' fielding was particularly bad. Fregosi and Thomas felt the team should have been much better than last place, but the numbers were hard to contradict.

Chapter 21

Winning — and Losing — Wild

After the dismal 1992 season, Phillies fans expected general manager Lee Thomas to bid for the big-name players who became free agents at the end of the year, and they were disappointed when the best Thomas could do was three outfielders, Pete Incaviglia, a big, crude slugger who struck out a lot, Jim Eisenreich, a player afflicted with a strange nervous disorder called Tourette's Syndrome, and Milt Thompson, who had been here before.

Another acquisition Thomas made was lefthanded pitcher Danny Jackson, picked up after the expansion draft from the new Florida Marlins. Jackson had been a dominating pitcher in 1988 with Cincinnati, but he had struggled with the Reds, Cubs, and Pirates since then, his arm a question mark, and Pittsburgh left him unprotected in the draft. Finally, Thomas traded journeyman pitcher Mike Hartley to Minnesota for David West, a tall, portly lefthanded pitcher, once heralded as a coming superstar, who had bombed with the Mets and Twins. The fans were not impressed.

"But we knew we weren't one player away," Jim Fregosi said. "Sure, it was a temptation to go out and make a big splash," he said, but he and Thomas knew there were several holes to fill. They set out to fill them the best way they knew how. Thomas felt that his team could now contend in the National League East, where the defending champion Pirates had lost Barry Bonds, Doug Drabek, and Jose Lind to free agency without getting a thing in return.[1]

Fregosi's 1993 Phillies got off to a flying start. Terry Mulholland beat Houston in the opener at the Astrodome, 3–1, to initiate a three-game sweep of the Astros. The Phils lost the home opener to the Cubs, but Curt Schilling's four-hit shutout of Chicago on Easter put them in first place (for good, as it turned out) and set them on a winning tear.

On April 18, at Wrigley Field, they beat the Cubs, 11–10, in eleven innings even though Mitch Williams was unable to hold a four-run lead in the ninth. When John Kruk homered in the fourteenth inning to beat San Diego, 4–3, the next night, after the team had gone seven innings without a hit, the '93 Phillies had a 10–3 record and a growing feeling that they were destiny's darlings.

A week later, the Phils spotted the Giants an 8–0 lead as late as the sixth inning and then came roaring back through the rain to win 10–8 in ten innings. Three days after that, they topped the Padres in San Diego, 5–3, when Thompson reached over the left-center field fence to pull back what should have been Bob Geren's game-winning grand slam.

The next day, in Los Angeles, the Phillies led 7–6 when Williams came in to pitch the ninth. He soon had the bases loaded with no outs, and things looked bleak when Dodger Mike Sharperson hit a line drive up the middle. Dodger manager Tommy Lasorda "started clapping and running out of the dugout to celebrate," as Kruk recalled, when Mickey Morandini speared the ball with a remarkable diving catch. He then crawled over to tag second and double the runner. Thus reprieved, Williams got the final out, and the Phillies had an amazing record of 17 and 5.[2]

"After some of these games," catcher Darren Daulton said later, "I think we have to wake up and read about them the next day to figure out exactly what we did."[3]

The starting pitching was excellent, with Mulholland, Schilling, Jackson, and Tommy Greene shining. Kruk, Hollins, and Daulton drove in runs, and Dykstra seemed to be on base and scoring all the time. Incaviglia and Eisenreich, penciled onto the roster as part-timers, were proving to be much more than that, hitting well and producing runs. Eisenreich was a masterful outfielder, and Inky provided excitement in the field.

David West, the acquisition from the Twins, and 40-year-old Larry Andersen, a former Phillie who had been signed as a free agent, shored up the bullpen as setup men for Williams, and the "Wild Thing" piled up saves, although few of them were without a thrill or two.

A major area of concern was shortstop, where Juan Bell, awarded the position late in '92, was shaky. A rash of errors by Bell, combined with weak hitting, made him a target of the Vet Stadium boo-birds, and the booing shook his confidence further. Mariano Duncan and Kim Batiste were tried at the position, but their range was inadequate for a big league shortstop. On June 1, Bell went to Milwaukee on waivers, and five days later defensive whiz Joe Millette was brought up from the Scranton farm. Millette handled the job in the field, but he could not hit major league pitching at all.

Finally, on July 6, Lee Thomas made the move which he had resisted making, bringing up the club's top shortstop prospect, Kevin Stocker. Soon Thomas wondered what he had worried about. Young Stocker played the field as if he had been in the majors for years, and he hit much better than he had in the minors, ending the season at .324.

The sensational run continued into May. On the 9th, the Phils trailed the Cardinals by three runs in the eighth inning and still won, 6–5, when Duncan hit a grand slam home run off of ace reliever Lee Smith. Daulton's slam beat the Pirates the next night. On June 14, the Phillies held an astonishing lead of 11½ games in the National League East, and the local fans had fallen in love with a most unexpected winner.

These Phillies were scruffy-looking, with the long hair of Kruk, Williams, Incaviglia, and Daulton, and several of them looked a little overweight, but they seemed perfectly in synch with their followers and with one another. When one Phillie failed to drive in a key run, more often than not the next man in the batting order would follow with a two-out hit. If a pitcher put a couple of runners on, Eisenreich would make a tough catch of a foul ball in the right-field corner or Morandini would start a double play. Some of the players were a trifle unconventional for the '90s, but they enjoyed their oddball image. Kruk said, "Honest, we're really not bad people. But you wouldn't want us in your home." Blue-collar Philadelphia took them to its heart. Fregosi was an ideal manager for this collection of nonconformists, because he let them be themselves, asking only that they give him 100 per cent effort on the field. As Dykstra said of Fregosi, "Some managers you just play for. Some you really want to bleepin' win for."[4]

There would be downturns along the way. The first of these came in late June, when Schilling and Greene, almost invincible till then, were pounded in a series in St. Louis. The San Diego Padres came to town and split a four-game series. Two of those games made up a bizarre doubleheader which started at 4:35 p.m. on July 2 and featured six hours of rain delays. The second game started at 1:28 a.m. on July 3 and ended at 4:40 a.m. when Mitch Williams, of all people, singled home the winning run.

On July 7, they played twenty innings against Los Angeles, after Williams failed to hold a two-run lead in the ninth. The Dodgers finally scored in the top of the 20th, but the Phillies came back on a two-run double by Dykstra to win, 7–6. Then the San Francisco Giants came to town and torched the pitching staff, taking three out of four and cutting the division lead to five games at the All-Star break.[5]

The Phillies had three starters on the All-Star team in Baltimore, Daulton and Kruk, both selected by vote of the public, and pitcher Terry Mulholland, picked by N.L. manager Bobby Cox. Third baseman Dave

Hollins also played for the Nationals. The funniest moment in the game came when the menacing-looking, hard-throwing Seattle pitcher Randy Johnson, a 6'10" lefthander, sailed a pitch high over Kruk's head, to the backstop. John gave the pitcher a quizzical look, then bailed out on three ineffectual swings and fled to the safety of the dugout. "I was never so happy to strike out in my life," Kruk said.[6]

After the midseason break, the Phillies saw their lead dwindle to three games over St. Louis before Schilling won a big victory over the Padres. On July 27, the Cardinals came to town trailing by four games. They left three days later seven games behind after a Phillies sweep. Early in August, the Phillies swept three more from Montreal, and on August 12 they led the Cards by eight games and the Expos by thirteen. The next night the Phils came into the bottom of the ninth behind the Mets, 5–4. They got the tying run home, and then little-used infielder Kim Batiste slugged a grand slam home run to win it.

Everyone on the team helped, but the most important contributor was Dykstra, with his base hits, walks, runs scored, high on-base percentage, and attitude. Lenny was without a peer as a leadoff hitter in 1993. Daulton continued to drive in big runs, and Incaviglia maintained an astonishing pace of nearly one run batted in per base hit. Eisenreich and young Kevin Stocker averaged well over .300, and both played excellent defense. Kruk's hitting sloughed off slightly in the second half, but he still came up with his share of timely hits.

Hollins's power was down, after he broke a bone in his hand and went on the disabled list for surgery. Fifteen days later, the intense young third sacker was back on the active list, ready to play. His throwing was affected, and he made a number of bad throws. Still, his speedy return from surgery was awe-inspiring.

The bullpen was a problem area, as middle relievers came and went while Thomas and Fregosi tried to find consistency. They used former Phil Mark Davis from Atlanta, rookie Tim Mauser from Scranton, veteran right-hander Roger Mason from San Diego, Jose DeLeon, ex-White Sox ace Bobby Thigpen, and, in September, another ex-White Sox righthander, Donn Pall. Of these, Mason and Pall were the most effective. As the season went on, the setup men, West and Andersen, showed wear and tear from the heavy work they had been doing all year, and Mitch Williams, the closer, continued to make things all too exciting even as his save total mounted.

When the race entered September, it was no longer the Cardinals but the young Montreal Expos who were the Phillies' closest rivals. Still, a 5–3 win in Cincinnati on the 5th left the Phils 9½ ahead. They won only two games of a seven-game homestand with the Cubs and Houston, although on September 10 they broke the club attendance record set in 1979. Montreal, winning steadily, cut the Phils' lead to five games. In the first Cub game, Terry Mulholland left early with a hip injury, and it became evident that he would be unable to help much during the stretch drive.

The Phillies won two out of three from the Mets at Shea, but the Expos kept pace in their series with St. Louis. The Phillies had a five game lead as they traveled to Montreal for a three-game set starting September 17. The Expos needed a sweep to have a realistic chance in the season's waning days.

In the first game, a frenzied crowd watched as the Expos took an 8–7 win

The popular and fun-loving star of the 1993 champions, John Kruk.

in twelve innings. On Saturday night, before more than fifty thousand fans, the Phillies won, 5–4, behind Tommy Greene's excellent pitching, the hitting of Duncan, Dykstra, and Kruk, and another hair-raising save by Williams. Even though Montreal won the Sunday game with two runs in the ninth, helped by a questionable call by umpire Charlie Williams, the Phils left with a four-game lead and thirteen to play. Jim Fregosi looked back on the games with the Expos and said, "It was a hell of a series, wasn't it?"[7]

On Monday night the 20th, Schilling bested ancient Charlie Hough of the Marlins, 7–1, striking out eleven. On Tuesday, the Phillies again beat Florida, Atlanta pounded the Expos, and the Phillies' lead climbed to 5½ games. The next night Roger Mason got out of a bases-loaded jam in the eleventh inning, blanked the Marlins in the twelfth, and the Phillies won, 2–1, on a hit by Hollins. The magic number for clinching was reduced to six and then to five when the Expos lost the next night.

On September 24, the Atlanta Braves, leading in the west by 2½ games, came to the Vet, with 57,792 on hand. They were blown away, 3–0, by Tommy Greene, who held the hard-hitting visitors to three singles in 8⅓ innings, raising his record to 16–3. Williams fanned the last two Braves in the ninth. The huge crowd pushed the Phillies' home attendance for the year past the three million mark for the first time ever.

The next day, poor pitching and sloppy fielding cost the Phillies a 9–7 loss to Atlanta. When the Expos beat New York, the Phils' lead was reduced to five games. On the 26th, Atlanta once again beat the Phils, but the Mets upended Montreal to cut the clinching number to three. The Phils-Braves game was the final regular season game at Veterans Stadium, and the Phillies were gratified with a new attendance record of 3,137,674.

Still, there was work to be done. On a wet and cold Monday night, before a few thousand less-than-enthusiastic fans at Three Rivers Stadium, Ben Rivera beat the Pirates. Williams picked up save #42 with a scoreless ninth in which he gave up two hits and a walk. When Florida's Pat Rapp beat the Expos, 3–1, the Phillies clinched a tie for the division title.

The next evening, rookie Mike Williams took the ball for the Phillies. Kruk and Dykstra got him a three-run lead, but poor relief work by Bobby Thigpen put the Pirates ahead in the sixth. In the seventh, Stocker singled in a tying run, Dykstra walked to force home a go-ahead run, and Duncan belted the team's eighth grand slam of the season to give the Phillies breathing room. Donn Pall struggled through the final three innings, but when Dave Clark grounded to Kruk with two outs in the ninth and the Phillies holding a 10–7 edge, it was all over. Kruk flipped the ball to Pall covering, and the Phillies had their division winner.

In the champagne-drenched Three Rivers locker room, they shouted and whooped and squirted, and some of them remembered what it was like to finish last the year before. Many paused to give credit to Lee Thomas, who had acquired or drafted 21 of the 25 players on the postseason roster. "He put this squad together," Mitch Williams said. "He deserves this."[8]

As the Phillies waited for the Giants and Braves to settle the N.L. West, they looked back at their accomplishments. They won 97 games and lost 65. Stocker (.324), Eisenreich (.318), Kruk (.316), and Dykstra (.305) batted over .300, and Daulton's 105 RBIs marked his second straight year over the century mark.

Daulton and Incaviglia both hit 24 home runs, and Kruk, Hollins, and Incaviglia all had 85 or more runs batted in. For the first time ever, a team had three men with more than a hundred bases on balls each, in Dykstra, Daulton, and Kruk. And Lenny Dykstra had simply a fantastic year. He led the league in hits, walks, and runs scored, with 19 home runs and 66 RBIs from his leadoff position. The Phillies set a modern National League record as they scored in 174 consecutive games, suffering their first shutout of the season only after the division was won.

The pitching was led by Greene, 16–4 and 3.42, and Schilling, 16–7 and 4.02. Rivera won thirteen games, and Jackson and the injury-plagued Mulholland each won twelve. On top of that, the Wild Thing, Mitch Williams, garnered 43 saves to set a new club record.[9]

On the last day of the season, the Atlanta Braves nosed out the Giants by one game to win the Western Division title. The Braves, under Bobby Cox, had won the playoffs two years in a row against Pittsburgh, only to come up short in the World Series. Atlanta, with the best starting rotation in baseball and sluggers like David Justice, Ron Gant, and Fred McGriff, was a heavy favorite in the National League LCS.

The playoff series began in Philadelphia on October 6, with Curt Schilling on the hill for the Phillies and lefty Steve Avery opening for the Braves. Schilling struck out leadoff hitter Otis Nixon, and then Jeff Blauser and Gant as well, and the crowd of 62,012 cheered wildly. Dykstra led off the first with a double to left-center, moved to third on Duncan's single, and scored on Kruk's infield bouncer. The Phillies led, 1–0.

Schilling fanned McGriff and Justice to start the second, running his strikeout streak to five in a row, before Terry Pendleton grounded out to snap the spell. In the third inning, Incaviglia misplayed two balls hit to left into doubles and Atlanta tied the score. Another Braves run in the fourth was matched by a long Incaviglia home run in the bottom of the inning, and the Phillies took a 3–2 lead on Avery's wild pitch in the sixth. Schilling protected the lead well, getting his ninth and tenth strikeouts of the game in the eighth.

With Schilling's pitch count at 137, Fregosi chose to relieve him for the ninth, bringing in Mitch Williams. The manager made another defensive move which he had been making frequently since Hollins's throwing problems began, putting Kim Batiste at third base. Williams started by walking pinch-hitter Bill Pecota on four pitches, but Mark Lemke hit a double-play ground ball to third. Batiste made the pickup but in his haste fired the ball wide of second and into right field. Pecota hustled to third, and only a quick retrieval in right by Eisenreich kept Lemke at first base.

Rafael Belliard batted for the pitcher and sacrificed pinch-runner Tony Tarasco to second, with Pecota staying at third. When Nixon grounded to Stocker, Pecota scored the tying run and Tarasco took third.

Williams walked Blauser, but he struck out Ron Gant on a 3–2 pitch to end the inning.

Williams gave the big crowd a few more thrills in the top of the tenth. After two outs, Pendleton singled and went to third on Greg Olson's double. With disaster staring him in the face, Williams fanned Tarasco to retire the side. In the bottom of the tenth, Kruk doubled with one out, and Kim Batiste went from goat to hero by pulling a hit into left that easily scored the game-winning run.

Game Two was ugly. Greene started for the Phillies, against Greg Maddux, and Tommy was not sharp. He gave up a two-run, upper-deck home run to McGriff in the first and was knocked out in the third. Poor relief by Thigpen and West resulted in a final score of 14–3, Atlanta. The teams headed south with the series tied.

The *Atlanta Constitution* felt it necessary to warn its readers about the visitors from up north. One headline read: "NL Championship Series Pits America's Team Against Wild-Eyed, Tobacco-spittin', Gut-bustin' Phillies," and the next day it ran an article on Dykstra's tobacco-chewing and spitting habits, writer Doug Cress calling the Phillies "a team that looks like a roving gang of bikers ... in stark contrast to the squeaky-clean Braves."[10]

The Phillies paid no attention. They were more concerned with Terry Mulholland's hip and how he would throw in Game Three. For five innings, he looked like the Terry Mulholland of the early season. In the fourth, back-to-back triples by Duncan and Kruk off Braves lefthander Tom Glavine gave the Phillies a 1-0 lead, which Kruk doubled with a sixth inning home run to left. In the bottom of the sixth, Mulholland paid the price for his lack of innings in September when he ran out of gas. Terry's undoing came with astonishing suddenness, as Blauser singled, Gant walked, McGriff and Pendleton singled, and Justice doubled, accounting for four runs. The Phillies' bullpen faltered, and Atlanta cruised to a 9–4 victory.

Danny Jackson was in excellent form the next day. The lefty gave up a run in the second, but the Phillies came back in the top of the fourth against John Smoltz. Daulton reached base on Lemke's error and, one out later, moved to third on Milt Thompson's double. Stocker's sacrifice fly got the tying run home, and Jackson himself drove home the second run with a single up the middle.

With a 2–1 lead, Jackson kept the Braves at bay inning after inning. When Justice and Damon Berryhill singled with two out in the eighth, Fregosi went to his closer, Mitch Williams. Lemke hit a long fly to left, Thompson made a leaping catch against the wall, and the Phillies still had their lead.

The ninth was another test, courtesy of the Wild Thing. After pinch-hitter Pecota led off with a base hit, Nixon laid down a bunt. Williams, preparing to go to second, tried to barehand the ball and missed it. Runners on first and second with no outs. The next hitter, Blauser, also bunted. Williams had it with plenty of time for a force at third, but this time his throw was bad. Batiste, in again for defense, made an acrobatic catch to keep the ball from sailing down the leftfield line and even kept his foot in contact with the bag to get the out. Gant hit a hard ground ball to Morandini at second. Mickey grabbed it, stepped on the bag for one out and fired to Kruk for the double play that ended the game. The series was tied again at two victories each, thanks to Danny Jackson.

The fifth game in a seven-game series is usually crucial, and Schilling squared off against Avery to determine which team would carry a 3–2 edge back to Philadelphia. The Phillies took an early lead when Duncan singled with one out in the first and scored on Kruk's double. Wes Chamberlain in right field kept the Braves from tying the score in the bottom of the inning. With one out Blauser hit a ball down toward the corner, but Chamberlain cut it off and held the Atlanta shortstop to a single. With two outs, McGriff hit a rocket off the top of the rightfield wall. Chamberlain played the carom perfectly and fired a strike to Stocker. The shortstop's throw home nailed Blauser for the final out.

While Schilling held the Braves scoreless, the Phillies got a couple more runs, including Daulton's ninth-inning home run, to make it 3–0. Schilling walked Blauser to open the ninth, and Gant hit a hard shot to defensive replacement Batiste at third. Kim looked toward second but in pulling the ball out of his glove to throw he dropped it, for a costly error.

Fregosi lifted Schilling in favor of Williams, and things quickly got worse. McGriff singled, scoring Blauser, and Justice's fly ball brought Gant home. Pendleton singled to put runners at the corners, and pinch-hitter Francisco Cabrera bounced a hit up the middle, to score McGriff with the tying run and send the potential winning run to third, with only one out. The Phillies' plight looked grave indeed, and when Lemke slammed a ball down the left field line it looked worse. At the last instant the ball hooked slightly, landing just foul, and the Phils were still alive. Williams then fanned Lemke on a nasty slider, and Pecota, batting for the pitcher, could do no better than an easy fly to Dykstra. The game went on.

Dykstra, who said of himself, "I just like to play in these types of situations," stepped up against flame-throwing Mark Wohlers with one out in the tenth. When he got a 3-and-2 fastball, Dykstra lined it high over the fence in right-center to put the Phillies ahead once again, 4–3.[11]

Now it was the job of 40-year-old Larry Andersen, who usually threw nothing but sliders, to save the game for Williams. Andersen got leadoff hitter Nixon and struck out Jeff Blauser. Finally, Gant took strike three on an unexpected split-finger pitch, and the Phillies had a delicious victory and the lead in the series.

After a travel day, the two teams went at it again on Wednesday night, October 13. A crowd of 62,502 fans turned out at the Vet, and they were primed for victory. Greene started against Greg Maddux, the righthander who won the 1992 Cy Young with the Cubs and would win it again for the Braves in 1993.

After Greene retired the Braves in order in the first, Morandini banged a one-hopper off Maddux's right shin. The Braves' starter insisted he was able to continue, but he seemed not as sharp as usual after that. Greene walked McGriff to open the second. (It was the first of three straight walks he would issue to McGriff, but they kept the Atlanta slugger away from the upper deck.) Justice's line drive, which might have gotten between the outfielders for two or three bases at least, never got past the infield, as second sacker Morandini made a sensational leaping, diving catch. When Pendleton followed with a single, instead of two runs scoring there were just runners on first and second, and they were rubbed out when Morandini turned Berryhill's ground ball into a dandy double play.

Daulton's bases-loaded double down the right field line brought in two runs in the third. In the fifth, Blauser singled home an Atlanta run, but Hollins hit a two-run homer to make the score 4–1, Phillies. A two-run triple by Morandini in the sixth knocked Maddux out of the game. Blauser hit a line-drive two-run homer in the seventh to cut the Phils' lead to 6–3. West pitched a good eighth for the Phillies, and all eyes turned to the bullpen as Mitch Williams strutted in to work the ninth inning. In the Phillies' dugout, Curt Schilling put a towel over his head, hiding his eyes.

With mounted police and motorcycle cops making their appearance, the Wild Thing struck out Berryhill on four pitches. He used six pitches to induce Lemke to hit an easy fly ball to Dykstra in center. He then went to a full count on pinch-hitter Bill Pecota and at 11:17 p.m. blew one by Pecota's late swing for the strikeout that won the National League pennant, the fifth in the club's history. With his one-two-three save, Williams leaped high into the air in triumph before he was swarmed over by his teammates.

There was one more rung on the ladder, the World Series with the American League champion Toronto Blue Jays. But Phillies fans were not worried. They felt that Atlanta was a better ballclub than Toronto, and their

team had polished off the stunned Braves in six games. Fregosi's men prepared to take on the defending world champions in Skydome, the four-
year-old futuristic stadium with the retractable roof, the hotel and Hard
Rock Cafe in back of center field, and an unfailing string of sellouts.

The Blue Jays won the American League playoff series in six games
against the Chicago White Sox. The team, managed by Clarence "Cito"
Gaston, had seen a considerable turnover in its personnel from one year
to the next. To take the places of eight departed regulars (including four
pitchers), general manager Pat Gillick obtained Paul Molitor, Dave Stewart, Tony Fernandez, Rickey Henderson, and rookie pitcher Pat Hentgen.
The heart of Gaston's team remained intact: Roberto Alomar, perhaps the
best second baseman in the majors, center fielder Devon White, right
fielder Joe Carter, first baseman John Olerud, catcher Pat Borders, and
reliever Duane Ward.

The Jays were decided favorites, as the Braves had been in the LCS,
but Pete Incaviglia said, "That's just how we like it." The series opened in
Toronto on October 16, with righthanders Schilling, the MVP-winner in
the National League LCS, and Juan Guzman getting the starting assign-
ments.[12]

A crowd of 52,011 showed up for Game One, and Lenny Dykstra,
tobacco juice and all, started it off by walking on five pitches. He stole second and scored on a single by Kruk. Hollins walked, and Daulton's single
brought Kruk in with the second run. It looked easy, and Guzman looked
hittable, but Schilling was not at his sharpest. Toronto took the lead in the
sixth inning when A.L. batting champion Olerud poled one over the right
field wall to make it 5–4, and Schilling ran out of steam in the seventh.
After two hits with one out, Fregosi brought in David West, who had
retired none of the six batters he'd pitched to in two earlier World Series
games with Minnesota in 1991. In a Phillies uniform West could do no better, although it should be noted that he was pitching with a strained rotator cuff, which the Phillies kept quiet about for tactical reasons. Two
doubles brought in three runs, and West's Series ERA remained at infinity.
The final score was 8–5, Toronto.[13]

If the opening game was a disappointment for Phillies fans, with the
shaky pitching and defense, Game Two looked like a lot of games they had
seen during the summer. Mulholland opened against Dave Stewart, a fierce
competitor and ex-Phillie who had enjoyed his best years in Oakland. In
the third inning, Dykstra and Duncan walked, and Kruk flared a broken-
bat single into center to drive Dykstra in. Hollins then blooped one into
the same area to score Duncan and give Philadelphia a 2–0 lead. After a
groundout, Stewart got ahead of Eisenreich, no balls and two strikes. He

tried to get a high fastball past the Phillies right fielder, but Eisenreich turned on it and drove it over the right-center field fence for a three-run home run.

The Blue Jays reduced the lead to 5–2 in the fourth on Joe Carter's two-run clout. When the Jays scored again in the sixth, Roger Mason came in from the pen and prevented further trouble. In the seventh, Dykstra homered, and the Phillies led, 6–3.

Mason retired the side in the seventh, but Molitor led off the eighth with a double. Mason fanned Carter and then gave way to Williams. Mitch paid no attention to Molitor, who stole third, whence he was able to score on Olerud's fly ball. The Wild Thing walked Alomar, who stole second when Williams again ignored him. Roberto then took off for third base, which was not a smart move with two out, and it looked even worse when Williams whirled and threw to Hollins for the easy putout.

In the ninth, with the Phillies holding a two-run lead, Williams walked the leadoff hitter. Ed Sprague hit a hard grounder to Batiste, in at third base for defense, and Kim, in his anxiety to get a double play started, made a terrible throw to second. Duncan dug it out of the dirt and held on to get the force-out. When the next batter hit a sharp grounder to Stocker, the Phillies turned the double play, ending the game and evening the World Series at one game apiece.

A huge and enthusiastic crowd of 62,689 turned out at the Vet on October 19, for the first World Series game in Philadelphia in ten years. Ready to rumble, ready to roar, instead they sat in the rain and waited. At one point the tarpaulins came off the infield, starter Danny Jackson got all warmed up, the players were introduced, and guest-of-honor Mike Schmidt threw out the first ball. Then it started to pour again, the tarps came back out, the fans scurried back under cover, and the players waited some more.

After a 72-minute delay, the game finally got underway, although it was cold and wet for the rest of the night. When Jackson made his long-delayed appearance, he had little on the ball. He and reliever Ben Rivera were hit hard, and Toronto earned a soggy 10–3 victory.

What the 62,731 fans who showed up on another misty, drizzly night for Game Four saw was the zaniest World Series game ever played. It was the highest-scoring game in Series annals, the longest nine-inning night game in major league history, a game in which thirteen records were set or tied. "You don't expect games like this in a World Series," Joe Carter said. "In spring training, but not a World Series."[14]

Tommy Greene started against Toronto's Todd Stottlemyre, who was carrying on a mini-feud with Ed Rendell, of all people. When the mayor told the press that even he could hit Stottlemyre, the Jays pitcher said he'd like to face Rendell and he would buzz the first three pitches behind Hizzoner's ear.

Greene began badly, giving up three runs in the first inning. In the bottom of the first, Dykstra walked and stole second. After two outs, Stottlemyre walked Hollins, Daulton, and Eisenreich to force in a run. Stottlemyre was looking for Ed Rendell, but instead he found Milt Thompson, who tripled off the center field wall to drive in three and put the Phillies up, 4–3.

In the second, Greene walked Stottlemyre, who had never been to bat in the major leagues before, and then got Henderson and White. When Alomar singled to right-center field, the Toronto pitcher unwisely tried to go to third and was thrown out. After a Dykstra two-run home run, Greene came apart. With one out in the third, he walked Olerud and yielded three successive singles for two runs. Fregosi brought in Mason. After a force-out, Henderson walked to load the bases and Devon White singled to drive in two. The Blue Jays were on top, 7–6, and it was just the third inning.

In the fourth, Dykstra doubled with two outs and scored on Duncan's hit. Tie score. Hollins led off the fifth with a base hit, and Daulton followed with a two-run homer. Eisenreich singled and came all the way around on Thompson's double. After two groundouts, Dykstra slugged another two-run homer to put the Phils up, 12–7. When Duncan followed with a hit, Gaston came out to change pitchers.

The Blue Jay bench was having trouble with the phone to the bullpen, and Gaston was dismayed to see righthander Mark Eichhorn appear on the mound rather than the southpaw he thought he had summoned. He convinced the umpires that he should have Tony Castillo rather than Eichhorn, and Castillo was given time to warm up, as the game clock rolled on.

David West entered in the sixth for the Phillies, and for a while it looked as if he were doomed never to record an out in a World Series game. White doubled. Alomar singled, scoring White. When Carter flied to right, a great cheer went up, as West finally got an out and reduced his earned run average from infinity to 162.00. But that was just one out. Another run scored before West retired the side. Phillies 12–9, after five and a half innings.

The Phillies were not done, as their fans kept up a continuous roar. Hollins led off the sixth against Castillo with a double, and two outs later Thompson singled him home, Milt's fifth RBI of the evening. Andersen set the Jays down in order in the seventh, with two strikeouts. It looked as if Gaston was giving up when he let pitcher Castillo bat for himself. The

Phils nicked the lefthander for another run in the seventh, to make it 14–9, Phillies. The fans whooped and shouted, as an even-up Series seemed ever more likely.

Andersen usually pitched only one inning per game, but he looked so dominant in the seventh that Fregosi sent him out again for the fatal eighth. Larry retired Alomar on a grounder and fooled Carter with a pitch that the Jays' slugger still blooped into right field for a single. Olerud walked, and Molitor blasted a double down the third base line past Hollins, with Carter scoring. Fregosi knew he had gone too far with Andersen, so he brought in Mitch Williams.

Fernandez singled off the Wild Thing, to score Olerud, and Borders walked. Sprague hit for Castillo and was called out on strikes, so with two outs and the bases loaded the Phillies still led, 14–11. All Williams needed was one more out to restore order, although the radar guns were clocking his fastball at 83 m.p.h., far below his norm. That out proved to be several batters away. Henderson singled to left to drive in two runs, and White tripled to score two more. Suddenly the Blue Jays were ahead, 15–14. Sixty-two thousand disbelieving fans sat stunned. The Phillies, out of miracles for this night, went meekly in the eighth and ninth, with four of the six hitters out on strikes. When White caught Hollins's long fly to end the game, it was still 15–14, Toronto.

Despite the tremendous hitting of Dykstra, Duncan, Hollins, Daulton, and Thompson, the Phillies lost the game on bad pitching. "I stunk," said Williams after the game, and no one disagreed with him. One writer said the club "had taken a stake through the heart." The fans were silent as they left the ballpark. Robbie Alomar said later, "In Philadelphia, Phillies fans will remember it for a long, long time. Fifteen, twenty years from now, they'll still be talking about it." Some thought they could do something about it immediately: the Phillies reported to the local police near Williams's South Jersey home the receipt of several death threats against the Wild Thing.[15]

The next evening, Curt Schilling went to the mound knowing there was little or no bullpen behind him after the debacle of the previous night. But he needed no relief at all. With his and his team's backs to the wall, Schilling threw a masterful 2–0 shutout at the hard-hitting Blue Jays and kept the Phillies alive for the trip back to Toronto.

Another crowd of 62,706 was on hand, but these fans, though supportive, seemed quieter and more tentative than the ones who had alternately screamed and groaned through the untidy epic of the night before. But, as Schilling mowed down the Toronto hitters, the crowd came back, their faith restored, their hopes rekindled.

The Phillies scored a run in the first, when pitcher Juan Guzman walked Dykstra. Lenny promptly stole second and went on to third when the catcher's throw went awry. Kruk scored him on a bouncer to second. In the next inning, Daulton doubled against the left-center wall, and, two outs later, Stocker drove him in with a double past first. The Phillies would score no more, but it was enough.

Schilling's moment of truth came in the eighth inning. Borders led off with a single, and a fast rookie named Willie Canate ran for him. Rob Butler batted for Guzman and singled, with Canate going to third. With runners at the corners and no outs, Henderson hit one back to the mound. The ball hit Schilling's glove and popped out, but he quickly found it lying at his feet. He threw it to Daulton, and Canate was hung up off third base for the first out. Schilling fired strike three by Devon White, then went to two-and-two on Alomar. Robbie fouled off four fastballs before Schilling fooled him with a breaking ball that he grounded to Duncan for the third out.

In the ninth, Schilling retired Carter, Olerud, and Molitor in order to nail down his win, the first shutout ever hurled by a Phillies pitcher in a postseason game. With what was at stake, with what had gone before, it would be difficult to find a more perfect definition of a "pressure game" than the one Curt Schilling pitched on October 21, 1993.

The fans cheered and shouted, both for Schilling's great performance and in tribute to the '93 Phillies as they ended their home season. Win or lose, the year would be completed in Canada. But for the baseball fans of Philadelphia, those in Veterans Stadium that Thursday night and those who were home watching on television, it had been a glorious season.

After the travel day, it was Terry Mulholland against Dave Stewart, in a game the Phillies had to win to keep the Series going. There was almost as much pressure on the American League champions, because they did not want a seventh-game situation with shaky rookie Pat Hentgen on the mound.

Game Six did not begin well for the Phillies. Mulholland gave up three first inning runs, and Stewart held the Phils hitless through three. With two away in the fourth, Daulton hit a double down the left field line, and Eisenreich singled up the middle to make the score 3–1. In the bottom of the fourth, the Jays got that run back, and when Molitor homered in the fifth, matters looked dark indeed for the visitors.

Mulholland left after the fifth, to be followed by a very effective Roger Mason. The Phillies were down to single digits in the number of outs they had left, but this was a team which did not give up. Kevin Stocker led off the seventh by walking, and Morandini singled. The unbelievable Lenny

Dykstra stepped to the plate and drilled a home run—his fourth of the World Series—to bring the Phillies to within one. The crowd in Skydome became eerily silent.

Gaston removed Stewart and brought in another ex-Phillie, righthander Danny Cox. Duncan greeted him with a single and, after Kruk fanned, stole second. When Hollins singled, Duncan scored and the game was tied at 5–5. Daulton drew a walk and Eisenreich singled, and the bases were loaded with one out. Al Leiter, a lefthander, came in to pitch. Incaviglia, pinch-hitting for Thompson, swung at Leiter's first offering and lined it to right, deep enough for Hollins to score the go-ahead run. Now it was up to the bullpen.

Mason had pitched two scoreless innings, just about as long a stretch as he ever went, but Fregosi sent him out again in the eighth just to get the righthanded Carter. He did so and, his job well done, Mason left, in favor of David West. When West, obviously laboring, walked Olerud on five pitches, Fregosi had seen enough of the tall southpaw, and he brought in Andersen. Larry struggled mightily, walking one, hitting another, and throwing 27 pitches, but he got through the inning without allowing a run, leaving the bases loaded when he retired Borders. The Phillies took their 6–5 lead into the ninth.

In the top of the inning, Ward retired the Phils in order. In came Williams for the bottom of the ninth, as Schilling, in the dugout, again covered his face with a towel.[16] As he did so often, Mitch walked the first batter, Henderson, on four pitches. White flied to Incaviglia in deep left-center for the first out. On what Williams called "a pretty good pitch," Molitor lined a single to center.

Joe Carter came to the plate and quickly got ahead, 2-and-0. He took a strike on a fastball away, and he looked bad swinging at a slider down and in. The next pitch was a fastball that Williams wanted outside but got inside. Carter swung and got all of it, a line-drive home run that landed in the Blue Jay bullpen beyond the left field fence.

As Carter leaped and danced around the bases, to score behind Henderson and Molitor for an 8–6 victory, a stunned Mitch Williams and his teammates left the field, their season suddenly and shockingly at an end. It was the first time in World Series history that a series has ended with a home run hit by a team that was behind in the game.[17]

The Phillies sat in their clubhouse after the game and talked to the media. They reacted with class and dignity to their loss, and they neither whined nor offered alibis. Williams told reporter after reporter the same thing, "I went out there thinking about getting people out. I didn't get it done." Mason said, "If it's gotta end, that's the way you want it to end.

You don't want it to end because of an umpire's call, or walks. They just beat us."[18]

The Phillies had not been overwhelmed or intimidated by the defending world champions, and they had fought the Blue Jays to the bitter end. They had come back from an awful defeat to win the fifth game, and they had come from behind in the final game, only to lose on bad relief pitching in the ninth. The Phillies simply ran out of innings. Their heads were high in the consciousness of an exciting World Series topping off a superb season.

They flew home to Philadelphia, most of them, and were greeted by a large and adoring crowd at the airport. Mitch Williams flew directly from Toronto to his home in Texas.

Chapter 22

More Losing Seasons

Fans, writers, and eventually even some players, like Len Dykstra and Curt Schilling, suggested after the blown World Series games that it would be best for all concerned if Mitch Williams were to move on. For Lee Thomas, the clinching factor was that fastball clocked at only 83 m.p.h. On December 3, 1993, a deal was struck. The Wild Thing went to the Houston Astros for veteran reliever Doug Jones and pitching hopeful Jeff Juden. Shortly before the '94 season began, Thomas sent Terry Mulholland to the Yankees for three prospects. With both Williams and Mulholland pitching poorly for their new teams, these trades were pluses for the Phillies, but they could not prevent the season from being a bust.[1]

It became apparent, even during spring training, that the magic of 1993 was not to carry over into 1994. John Kruk's pre-season treatment for testicular cancer was only the first of many maladies and injuries which brought down Jim Fregosi's '94 Phillies. The list ranged from reliever Heathcliff Slocumb's chicken pox and Dykstra's appendicitis to shoulder and knee miseries for Tommy Greene and Schilling, two broken bones in the hand for Dave Hollins, and a broken collarbone for Darren Daulton.

The Phillies dropped heavily into fourth place just before the players went out on strike on August 12, effectively terminating the season. Just before the strike began, Steve Carlton, the great "Lefty," was inducted into the Hall of Fame, having received more than 95 percent of the writers' votes. Danny Jackson and Doug Jones had fine pitching years, and Duncan was elected the starting All-Star second baseman, but the rest of the club's work left players, writers, and fans looking toward 1995, hopeful that the endless labor-management strife might finally be resolved.

In the maddening mixture of posturing, threats, scab players, presidential intervention, greed, and general idiocy which constituted baseball's labor "negotiations" in the 1994-95 off-season, Phillies head Bill Giles came off as a moderate. Giles sounded uncomfortable spouting the hard-line positions of the owners as they attempted to rein in their uncontrollable penchant for throwing vast sums of money at ballplayers. In mid–December, Giles made the owners' poor-mouthing look a bit silly when he signed ex-Cardinal infielder Gregg Jefferies to a four-year contract for twenty million dollars.

The only pleasurable moments for Philadelphia's baseball fans during that excruciating off-season were the elections to the Hall of Fame of Mike Schmidt by the writers and Richie Ashburn by the Veterans Committee. The fans were relieved when a Federal judge's ruling on March 31, 1995, brought an end to the strike and a belated start to a new season on April 26, with the schedule shortened by eighteen games.

Astonishingly, Fregosi's Phillies, with a strange-looking starting rotation of Schilling, former relievers David West and Paul Quantrill, and rookies Tyler Green and Michael Mimbs, charged out of the gate as if it were 1993 all over again. Despite disappointing offensive production, the Phillies on June 26 led the N.L. East by five games over Atlanta, and they were 19 games above the .500 level. At that point they hit the wall, and for the next six weeks the club played horribly, dropping far behind the Braves and, briefly, the Expos. In mid–August, with the acquisition of veteran lefthander Sid Fernandez and outfielders Andy Van Slyke and Mark Whiten, the team straightened itself out and managed to get into the race for the wild-card playoff berth eventually won by Colorado. Fregosi suffered season-ending injuries to Dykstra, Schilling, Daulton, West, Tommy Greene, and Tony Longmire, but he kept his players pointed in the right direction. Jim Eisenreich, Mickey Morandini, Jefferies, and Slocumb put together fine seasons for the club, which fell below .500 and finished in a tie with New York for second in its division.

The Phillies experienced a drop in attendance, as did most other clubs in 1995, attributed largely to post-strike bitterness on the part of many fans. Phillies followers showed their true colors, however, on July 30 when a record number of them turned the site of the ceremonies at Cooperstown into a sea of Phillies red for the Hall of Fame inductions of Schmidt and Ashburn.

There was hope — or at least talk — in 1995 that somewhere in the future would be a baseball-only ballpark for the Phillies, with real grass, to replace dismal Veterans Stadium, although the location of and financing for such a project were still unknowns. At the same time, a poll taken for *Philadelphia Magazine* revealed that, though more white respondents named the Phillies as their favorite local team than any other, blacks ranked both the football Eagles and basketball Seventy-sixers ahead of the baseball club, giving Giles and his people something else to chew on.

Nineteen hundred ninety-six was a disaster for the club. Severe injuries plagued Fregosi and his players all season long, and the team landed in last place in its division. Despite losing Jefferies for the first two months with surgery on his left thumb, the Phillies played moderately well at the start of the season and at the end of May stood right at the .500 mark, their 26 wins and losses leaving them tied for third place. June, however, was a crusher; the team won six and lost 21 that month, marked by a six-game road trip to Colorado and St. Louis, all losses, that dropped it into the cellar, never to emerge. Attendance dropped to 1,801,677, the lowest it had been for a full season since 1973, when Danny Ozark managed a third straight last-place finisher.[2]

Rookie pitcher Mike Grace started the season in fine form, and his mark stood at 7–2 when arm trouble brought his season to a close in early June. Dykstra, with a bad back, and Daulton, with knee problems, were limited to forty and five games, respectively. Third baseman Scott Rolen broke his wrist early in September, Mickey Morandini separated his shoulder, and pitcher Sid Fernandez was limited to eleven games with various maladies.

There were a few bright spots. Catcher Benito Santiago, signed as a free agent, slugged thirty home runs and drove in 85, leading the club in both categories, while doing a workmanlike job behind the plate. Ricky Bottalico, installed by Fregosi as his closer, saved 34 games, and he was the only Phil to appear in the All-Star game, played for the fourth time in Philadelphia. Jim Eisenreich hit a solid .361 in part-time duty. Curt Schilling, coming off major shoulder surgery, returned to start 26 games, lead the league in complete games with eight, post a 3.19 earned run average, and pace the club in victories, albeit with just nine. Rolen looked good at third base after he was brought up from Scranton-Wilkes-Barre, although his season-ending wrist injury preserved his rookie status for another year. Recalling better days, pitcher Jim Bunning, who was now a United States Senator from Kentucky, was installed in the Hall of Fame at Cooperstown, capping a remarkable run of Phillies inductions starting with Steve Carlton in 1994.

On May 2, the Phillies picked up from San Francisco a lefthanded hitting first baseman-outfielder named J.R. Phillips. The young man had been considered a hot prospect by the Giants after he led the Pacific Coast League in home runs, but his low batting average had cooled their enthusiasm for him. For the Phillies, J.R. played 37 games, hit .152 with five home runs, and was soon shipped to Scranton and let go at the end of the year. What fascinated Philadelphia fans with J.R. Phillips was his beautiful lefthanded swing which hardly ever hit anything. J.R. had 89 plate appearances for the Phillies, and he struck out 38 times, an astonishing 42.7 percent ratio. He was not around the Vet long, but he left a lasting impression.

In the midst of all this disappointment, there were a number of departures. Outfielder Mark Whiten, counted on to supply major punch, hit only .236 with seven home runs and was released in mid–June. Terry Mulholland, signed as a free agent before the season, was 8–7 for the Phils before being traded on July 31 to Seattle for a shortstop prospect named Desi Relaford. Third baseman Todd Zeile was shipped off with Pete Incaviglia to Baltimore at the end of August. And, on September 30, Lee Thomas fired his old buddy, Jim Fregosi, and named as manager in his place 37-year-old Terry Francona, the son of former Phillies outfielder Tito Francona and himself a veteran of ten injury-filled big league seasons.

Francona received a rude introduction to managing in the major leagues, as the Phillies once again finished last in the East in 1997, with a mark of 68–94. It could have been worse. The club won only 24 games in the first half of the season, losing 61, but showed definite improvement after the All-Star break with a 44–33 log. Attendance dropped off even more, to 1,490,638. Before the season began, the Phils signed slugging free-agent outfielder Danny Tartabull, who had a history of injuries and malingering. As an indicator of what was to come, Tartabull broke his foot in one of his first at-bats, played in only three games, and was 0-for-7 for the year. He was let go at the end of the season. On July 21, with the club firmly in last place, Thomas traded Darren Daulton to the Florida Marlins, whom he led to the world championship before retiring. Nevertheless, there were some outstanding accomplishments and some hope for the future.

Scott Rolen, a 22-year-old from Jasper, Indiana, won Rookie of the Year honors in the National League, with a .283 average, 21 home runs, and 92 runs batted in. The Phillies were fortunate to have gotten Rolen in the free agent draft in 1993. Scott was the leading high school basketball player in Indiana and seemed headed toward Georgia Tech on a hoops scholarship, so no other club wanted to waste a high draft choice on him. The Phillies took a chance in the second round and then learned that Rolen really wanted to play baseball. He moved up quickly through the organization and soon reached the majors. Scott was modest and low-keyed, but he played hard at all times, ran out everything at full speed, and was an outstanding third baseman in the field as well.

Mike Lieberthal, a Californian who had been the club's first round pick in 1990, took a bit longer to establish himself, but by 1997 he was the first-string catcher with promise of being one of the league's best. While his batting average was a modest .246, Lieby slammed twenty home runs, drove in 77, and earned respect for his throwing ability from would-be base stealers.

The other outstanding performance in 1997 was that of Curt Schilling, who enjoyed good health all season long. He won 17, lost 11, and posted a 2.97 ERA. In 254 innings, Curt fanned a league-high 319 batters. He had a 15-strikeout game on July 21 and a 16-strikeout effort on September 1. For good measure, Schilling threw in two scoreless innings in the All-Star game.

The year saw changes in the two top spots in the Phillies' front office. On June 21, Bill Giles stepped down as club president, staying on as chairman of the board, saying that he wanted to devote his time and energy to the stadium issue. His job was taken by David Montgomery, a longtime club executive. After the season, on December 9, Montgomery fired Lee Thomas as general manager, replacing him with Thomas's assistant, Ed Wade. Curt Schilling, who was always good for a quote, commented, "For five years, we haven't gone in the right direction.... My opinion is we had to do something to get better."[3]

To Wade then fell the task of conducting the frustrating and maddening negotiations with the Phillies' top draft choice. The college player of the year in 1997 was a Florida State outfielder named J.D. Drew, who picked a difficult agent named Scott Boras to represent him. Boras and Drew decided that the financial structure for draft picks established by custom up to that time was not rich enough for their taste, and Boras notified the Phillies that they should not draft Drew unless they were prepared to pay him ten million dollars, far above the going rate. Refusing to be intimidated by such tactics, Philadelphia drafted Drew with the second pick in the first round on June 3, and the dealing got underway.

It soon became evident that Drew and his agent were not going to back away from their demand. The Phillies offered Drew more than any other draft choice had ever received, only to have the offer contemptuously rejected. As it became clear that Drew had no intention of signing with the Phillies, Philadelphians decided that the young man and his agent were so greedy and arrogant that they backed the club in its refusal to yield to their demands. Drew went back into the draft in 1998 and was selected by the Cardinals, who gave Drew the money he was demanding.

On December 23, 1997, the club traded veteran second baseman Mickey Morandini to the Cubs in exchange for a young center fielder named Doug Glanville. Glanville, a Penn graduate, hit .300 in 1997, his first full big league season, and was a very good outfielder. When he got to Clearwater, however, he found that Dykstra, who had been on the disabled list for much of the prior four seasons, had missed all of 1997, and

had not been on the active roll since May 19, 1996, was claiming that center field still belonged to him. It made for an ugly situation, with several
days of sparring among Francona, Wade, and Dykstra, before Lenny finally
admitted that his back problems would not permit him to play.

With Glanville in place, and banner years from Rolen and outfielder
Bobby Abreu, obtained from Tampa Bay in a trade for Kevin Stocker, the
Phillies started the year well, going into the All-Star break with a winning
record of 43–42. Even though they could not keep up this pace, finishing with
a mark of 75–87, the Phils improved by seven games over 1997 and moved up
to third place in their division. Rolen hit .290, with 31 home runs, 110 runs
batted in, and a Gold Glove for his third base play, while Abreu, left open to
the expansion draft by Houston, batted .312 with 17 homers and 74 RBIs. First
baseman Rico Brogna drove in 104 runs and played sterling defense. A free-
agent signing brought Mark Lewis, a much-traveled journeyman infielder and
a favorite of Terry Francona; Lewis was installed at second base, where he
gave the Phillies a mediocre performance both at bat and in the field.

1998 was, of course, the year of the big bombers, the year in which
Mark McGwire of the Cardinals slammed 70 home runs while the Cubs'
Sammy Sosa hit 66 and numerous other high totals were recorded. Phillies
pitchers were victimized for their share of these blasts, and few of them
had good records for the season. Curt Schilling was 15–14, with a 3.25
earned run average; his fifteen complete games led the National League,
as did his three hundred strikeouts. Veteran righthander Mark Portugal
won ten and lost five, and a late-season pickup off the waiver wire, Paul
Byrd from the Braves, was 5–2 in eight games at the end of the year. Otherwise, Francona's pitching was not much.

The 1999 Phillies improved a little bit more, finishing with a record of
77–85, two games ahead of their mark for 1998. What was disappointing,
however, was the way they did it. The club started the season well, and at
the All-Star break it was only 7½ games out of first place in the National
League East, six games over the break-even level. Led by Mike Lieberthal,
Curt Schilling, and Bobby Abreu, the Phillies continued to play well, and
after an 11-inning win over the Arizona Diamondbacks on August 6, they
were 13 games over .500 and contending in the race for a wild-card spot in
the expanded playoffs. The next night, Schilling was knocked out by the
Diamondbacks. He went on the disabled list on August 8 with a sore shoulder, and the Phillies started a skid that would see them lose 22 out of 25
games, falling far out of contention. A back injury to Scott Rolen, on top
of earlier injuries to shortstop Desi Relaford and closer Jeff Brantley, aggravated the slide. Once again the best the club could do was third in the N.L.
East, nine games ahead of Montreal and thirteen in front of Florida.

The brightest development of the '99 season was the blossoming of Mike Lieberthal into one of the top catchers in the game. At the age of 27, Mike hit .300, with 31 home runs and 96 runs batted in. A fine thrower and a good handler of pitchers, Lieberthal won his first Gold Glove in 1999. Abreu continued to show that he ranked among the league's top hitters, batting .335 with twenty homers, 93 runs batted in, and a league-leading eleven triples. Glanville hit .325, although his 48 walks were low for a leadoff hitter. Schilling once again led the Phils pitchers, with 15 wins and six losses, although his innings and strikeouts fell off considerably with his shoulder miseries. Byrd compiled a record of 15–11, although most of his wins came in the first half of the season, resulting in his selection to the National League All-Star team. Righthander Chad Ogea, picked up in a trade with Cleveland, was written in as the No. 2 starter, but he was a flop. He won 6, lost 12, had an ERA of 5.63, and was torched for 36 home runs. Moved to the bullpen late in the season, Ogea was let go shortly after its end.

The Phillies had been operating for several years with a payroll around $30 million (imagine what Gerry Nugent would have thought of that!), which was far outstripped by their Eastern Division rivals in Atlanta and New York, as well as by many other clubs. For the year 2000 the mostly-invisible limited partners who made up the club's ownership group allowed Ed Wade to run the payroll up to the $45 million level. Figuring that the team's offense was pretty much a given, with Rolen, Lieberthal, Abreu, Glanville, and Rico Brogna on hand, Wade went out to shore up his pitching staff.

On November 10, 1999, he acquired Andy Ashby, a tall righthander who had won 31 games in the prior two seasons, from San Diego, giving up two former first-round picks, pitchers Carlton Loewer and Adam Eaton, and a useful reliever named Steve Montgomery. Ashby, who had come up through the Phillies organization in 1991, had been left unprotected in the 1992 expansion draft, a serious mistake. Taken by Colorado and later traded to San Diego, Ashby had developed into one of the league's premier pitchers. Three weeks later Wade signed Cleveland's closer, Mike Jackson, for three million dollars, although there were questions about Jackson's physical soundness which caused several teams to shy away from signing him. Jackson, like Ashby, had originally come through the Phillies' system, having been traded away in the Phil Bradley deal of December 1987. The heady feeling generated by these pitching acquisitions was dampened somewhat a few days later when the club was informed that Schilling needed shoulder surgery and would miss the first month of the season.

Nevertheless, hopes were high as Terry Francona entered his fourth year as manager. Ashby would hold the fort as the number one starter until Schilling returned, and Jackson would mop up in the ninth inning of the close ones. Sadly, nothing worked out right. Ashby gave up six runs in six innings in an Opening Day loss, and Jackson hurt his shoulder warming up in the bullpen, sidelining him for the season. The club's offense misfired, and the result was a horrendous April record of 7–17. The Phillies never recovered, never rose from last place, and finished with a record of 65–97, their worst numbers since 1972.

Not long after the season began, Andy Ashby let it be known that he had no intention of signing a contract extension with Philadelphia and that he would become a free agent at the end of the year. With Ashby's pitching mediocre at best, the fans certainly had no objection to Wade getting what he could for him. On July 12, Ashby, sporting a 4–7, 5.38 record in sixteen starts, was shipped to Atlanta for two southpaws, Bruce Chen and Jimmy Osting.

Curt Schilling, after he came back at the end of April, pitched some good games and some not so good, and, as he had done several times in the past, proclaimed his willingness to waive his no-trade clause in order to go to a winning team. This time Wade took him up on it. A couple of weeks after the Ashby deal, Schilling, 6–6 at the time, went to Arizona for three pitchers, Omar Daal, Vicente Padilla, and Nelson Figueroa, and first baseman Travis Lee, once a highly-prized prospect but now more of a suspect.

Curt Schilling was always outspoken, sometimes abrasive and annoying, but one always knew where he stood. In his 8½ seasons with the Phillies, he won 101 games and was always ready to take the ball, even when his physical condition dictated otherwise. In baseball terms, Curt Schilling was "a horse," although someone in the front office said, "If he wasn't our horse, he'd be our horse's rear end."[4]

With the two ace pitchers gone, Wade, Francona, and the Phillies settled down to see what was left. The lineup was unstable at best — Lieberthal and Rolen were both in and out with injuries, Brogna broke his wrist, shortstop Desi Relaford was so erratic that he was traded to San Diego, and Abreu showed a bit of an attitude as his batting average dropped some — and the pitching was very shaky. Young lefthander Randy Wolf, in his first full year in the majors, emerged as the staff leader, with Byrd having an off year, and the acquisition from the Braves, Bruce Chen, looked impressive. Robert Person, acquired as a reliever from Toronto the year before, became a good-looking starting pitcher. Omar Daal, however, lost 19 games (with his Arizona record thrown in), and the bullpen was terrible.

The brightest light in the picture was young Pat Burrell, the number one pick in the 1998 draft coming out of the University of Miami and signed by the Phillies for eight million dollars. Burrell was strong, hard-working, eager to please, and a very talented hitter. He played at Clearwater in the Florida State League in 1998, at Reading in the Eastern League in 1999, and at Scranton in the International League in the first part of the 2000 season. He piled up impressive numbers at each level, and when Rico Brogna broke his wrist Burrell came to the majors. A third baseman in college, he played first and the outfield in the minors, and it was at first base that he broke into the big time. He proved to be adequate at the position, although when Travis Lee was obtained from Arizona Burrell was quite willing to move to left field. What Pat Burrell did do very well was hit. Although he struck out a lot as he adjusted to major league pitching, he still hit for a respectable average of .260 while belting eighteen home runs and driving in 79 runs in 111 games. Phillies fans were looking forward to a long acquaintance with Pat Burrell.

As the team floundered in 2000 and attendance dropped, the fans who came to the games concentrated their frustrations more and more on Terry Francona. His every appearance on the field was met with a chorus of boos. Never a great bench manager or strategist, Francona's relationship with the front office cooled. While Terry Francona was certainly not to blame for all the things which caused 2000 to be a disaster for the Phillies, he realized that managers were usually the first to go from losing ballclubs. It came as no great surprise to him, then, when he was advised on October 1, before the final game of the season, that he and all but one of his coaches were fired. Terry Francona managed that final game, which the Phillies lost, bringing his four year managerial tally to 285–363.[5]

Chapter 23

Glory Nevertheless

On November 1, 2000, the Phillies named as their new manager Larry Bowa, after they had gone through a list of prospective managers that included two of their greatest catchers, Bob Boone and Darren Daulton. The intense Bowa had served for a season and a fraction as manager of the San Diego Padres, back in 1987-88, with a singular lack of success. Since then he had held coaching positions with several teams, with the Phillies until the advent of Francona and with Seattle in 2000. Whether the Phillies would achieve a winning record under Bowa only time and the unfolding of the season would tell, but one thing was clear. Feisty, in-your-face Larry Bowa would bring to the Phillies a leadership style far different from that of Terry Francona.[1]

In any event, whether a managerial change would make much difference was not clear. What promised to be more important was the fact that in the late '90s the Phillies under Bill Giles had somehow become a "small market" team. Major league baseball in the decade of the '90s clearly divided itself between the fiscal haves and have-nots, more commonly known as "big market" and "small market" teams. How Philadelphia, the fifth largest metropolitan area in the country, came to be defined as a "small market" is a puzzle to be worked out by demographers and economists. What it really meant was that the Phillies, no matter what the size of their market, were going to operate on the cheap and therefore become uncompetitive in twenty-first century baseball.

Giles, David Montgomery, and their mostly silent partners clearly had no stomach for the kind of cash outlays which would produce the big payoff of a winner in the new century. The Steinbrenners, Murdochs, Turners, and Buschs were able to pour big bucks into their baseball operations and expected to be rewarded with winners and playoff revenues. The goals of the owners of such teams as the Royals, Pirates, Twins, and the Phillies were more modest: keep expenditures (mostly player salaries) down and hope to be rewarded with a small profit. When big-name free agents came on the market, the Phillies were no longer among the clubs which contended for them.

The remaining factor to be taken into account in Philadelphia was the possibility of a new stadium. It became clear, not long after the Phillies and Eagles moved into it, that Veterans Stadium was a disappointment. The Phillies' lease with the city was considered among the worst in baseball and one of the causes of the club's poor-mouth attitude. Charmless and ugly, the Vet was satisfactory for neither baseball nor football. Its Astroturf became notorious in professional sports circles as the worst around. Sightlines were poor and, on top of its other problems, the Vet started to deteriorate physically, in part because the city was lackadaisical in performing necessary maintenance.

During the mayoral tenure of Ed Rendell, a true sports buff, efforts got under way to locate, finance, and construct two new stadiums, one for the Phillies and one for the Eagles (to match the two being built in Pittsburgh, with state financial assistance that was grudgingly offered to Philadelphia as well). Complicating this effort was the success of downtown ballparks in Baltimore and Cleveland, which led certain groups in Philadelphia to believe these successes could be duplicated here. Rendell pushed for a baseball park at Broad and Spring Garden Streets, but fierce neighborhood opposition stymied that idea.[2]

The result was that John Street, who succeeded Rendell as mayor in 2000, and who was suspected of having little interest in the stadium question in any event, suddenly proposed a site for the ballpark just north of Chinatown, at 12th and Vine, a location which was unappealing to just about everyone else, particularly the residents of Chinatown. After an appropriate amount of flak was directed at Street's proposal, he backtracked and said, all right, we'll put it back in South Philadelphia, next to the Vet, where most observers felt from the beginning that it would wind up. All that needed to be nailed down after that was the financing for two new stadiums.

Anyone who was surprised at the hit-and-miss progress of the new stadium issue clearly had not been a Philadelphian for long. The Phillies owners, who had already enjoyed huge appreciation in the value of their original investments in the team, sat back to see whether the city and state would in fact invest the necessary amounts to fund the new structures and thereby increase substantially again the value of their ownership shares.

So, as Philadelphia continues to be Philadelphia, with its snail-like progress on stadium-building and its rapid turnover of managers, we can look back on what the Phillies have accomplished in the 118 years they have been a feature of summer life in the Quaker City. Glory there has been, but it has been doled out to Philadelphians like a commodity in extremely short supply. One world's championship, five National League pennants, three other years with division crowns, and one strike-ravaged season with a forgettable "first half" championship. Even the Athletics, who were in town only fifty-four years, featured five World Series winners and nine league pennants. Perhaps the most memorable Phillies team of all was the 1964 crew, with its heartbreaking end-of-the-year collapse.

But when they did win, the Phillies made a splash. The 1915 flagwinner, featuring Alexander, Cravath, Rixey and Bancroft, came along just as Connie Mack was destroying the team that gave him his first dynasty. The Whiz Kids in 1950 were the darlings of the town, and the team of Roberts, Ashburn, Ennis, Seminick, et al. is still beloved in the Delaware Valley. The Team That Wouldn't Die won it all in 1980, the only world champion the Phillies have ever produced, and there are thousands of fans who can tell you just where they were when the Tugger fanned Willie Wilson to put it in the win column. The 1983 pennant seemed almost an accident, the result of the Phillies being the team that got hot in September, but it was still much appreciated, with Gary Matthews, John Denny, and Al Holland writing their names in Philadelphia's memory book that year.

And the 1993 team, a surprise aggregation which did a wire-to-wire run against all expectations, came just so close to winning it all. Dykstra, Eisenreich, Kruk, Schilling, Daulton and of course the Wild Thing stirred up old Philadelphia as it had seldom been stirred before. It gave the city a taste of how sweet, how exciting, and how profitable a winner can be, a taste which has been totally lacking since then.

From the first Phillies team, which finished last in an eight-team league in 1883, to the 2000 Phillies squad, which finished last in a six-team division, there was scant progress, and the losing was just as hard on the fandom of Philadelphia.

Even with the scarcity of winners, there have been great players wearing Phillies uniforms over the years. The best of them all — Schmidt, Alexander, Klein, Roberts, Carlton, Ashburn, Bunning, and the great outfield from the 1890s— have been enshrined in baseball's pantheon at Cooperstown. Just below them have been stars like Gavvy Cravath, Johnny Callison, Del Ennis, Cy Williams, Granny Hammer, Chris Short, and Richie Allen. The true believers in town expect Pat Burrell one day to be worthy of the same sort of acclaim.

But as more typical of the Phillies, and perhaps as fitting for a franchise which has lost more games in its history than any other, we should think of some of the lesser lights who have cast their rays upon Philadelphia, in Baker Bowl, Shibe Park, and the Vet. Players like Marv Blaylock, Russ Springer, John Easton, Mitch Chetkovich, Porfirio Altamirano, Pretzels Pezzulo, Gilly Huber, Bill Atwood, Morrie Arnovich, Ted Savage, Bert Haas, and Wally flager. Not Hall of Famers, not even regulars most of the time, they played the game for not much money and not much reward, but there was glory nevertheless in their representation of a great city in the greatest game ever devised.

Notes

Chapter 1

1. Harold Seymour, *Baseball — The Early Years* (New York: Oxford University Press, 1960), 137–38.

2. *Chicago Tribune*, May 1, 1876.

3. *N.Y. Times*, Oct. 19, 1980.

4. *Spalding's Official Base Ball Guide* (1884), 14.

5. *Phila. Inquirer*, July 2, 1883.

6. *Spalding's Official Base Ball Guide* (1884), 54.

7. Under the reserve clause, inserted into the standard contract, a player was "reserved" to his team for the season following that contracted for, in effect keeping a player tied to one team as long as that team chose to hold him.

8. David Q. Voigt, *American Baseball* (University Park, Pa., and London: Pennsylvania State University Press, 1983, 3 vols., vols. 1-2 orig. pub., Norman, Okla.,: University of Oklahoma Press, 1966, 1970), I, 134; on Jersey Bakely, *Phila Inquirer*, April 4, 1897.

9. On Clements, see Robert L. Tiemann and Mark Rucker, eds., *Nineteenth Century Stars* (Kansas City, Mo.: Society for American Baseball Research, 1989), 30.

10. Irwin, who played three seasons for the Phillies and later managed the club in 1894–95, died in 1921 when he jumped from a steamboat cruising between Boston and New York. It was then discovered that for thirty years Irwin had maintained two families, with wives and children, one in Boston and the other in New York; *N.Y. Times*, July 17, 21, 1921.

11. William B. Mead, "The Year of the Hitter," in John Thorn, ed., *The National Pastime* (New York: Warner Books, 1987), 252.

12. Tiemann & Rucker, eds., *op. cit.*, 141. Wood later played for the Philadelphia Brotherhood team in 1890 and for the Athletics in the following year, during which he also managed the Athletics for part of the season.

13. *Phila. Inquirer*, April 13, 16, 17, 18, 23, 24, 30, 1888. Ferguson, who was delirious for most of his three weeks' illness, left a widow to whom he had been married two years; together, they had buried an infant daughter the year before.

255

The *Inquirer*, after reporting the medical attention rendered Ferguson by the eminent Dr. William Pepper and the pitcher's death at 10:30 p.m. on the 29th, said that Ferguson "was a winning player, and one whose services the Philadelphia Club cannot replace."

14. Tiemann & Rucker, eds., *op. cit.*, 42.

15. Bill Hallman spent 1890 in the Players League and 1891 in the American Association, with the Athletics, but in '92 he was back with the Phillies, for whom he covered second base for five more seasons until traded to the St. Louis Browns on May 29, 1897. He returned to the Phillies for three more seasons in 1900-01-02.

16. Voigt, *op. cit.*, I, 103; Tiemann & Rucker, eds., *op. cit.*, 121.

17. The club's owner, George Wagner, was awarded the Washington franchise in the expanded National League.

Chapter 2

1. *Sports Illustrated*, Oct. 18, 1982.

2. "The Old Sport" in the *Phila. Inquirer*, May 26, 1930.

3. Philip J. Lowry, *Green Cathedrals* (Reading, Mass.: Addison-Wesley, 1992), 206; Lawrence J. Ritter, *Lost Ballparks: A Celebration of Baseball's Legendary Fields* (New York: Viking, 1992), 10; *Phila. Inquirer*, April 18, 1897. The distant left field line was brought in, from 500 feet to a more reasonable 335 feet.

4. *Phila. Inquirer*, Oct. 30, 1910 (Boyle interview); Lewis Scheid, "The Tragedy of Ed Delahanty," *Baseball Research Journal*, 1991.

5. *N.Y. Times*, July 10, 1903. The conductor who put him off the train said Delahanty had consumed five drinks of whiskey and was terrifying others on the train with an open razor.

6. The *Inquirer* correspondent covering the game, which the Phils lost 9–8, said it "was not even interesting outside of the batting done by" Delahanty; *Phila. Inquirer*, July 14, 1896. Delahanty had two doubles and a triple the next day.

7. J.M. Murphy, "Napoleon Lajoie: Modern Baseball's First Superstar," *The National Pastime*, spring 1988, 14–15. Geier hit just .232 in 17 games in 1896 and .249 in 349 big league games over five seasons.

8. *Phila. Inquirer*, June 25, 1897.

9. Lajoie and shortstop Monte Cross were said to be in open rebellion against Stallings. "In his declaration of independence... Larry used English that was remarkable for its vigor and for its directness;" *Phila. Inquirer*, June 19, 1898. It did not take long for other players to join in.

10. Frederick G. Lieb & Stan Baumgartner, *The Philadelphia Phillies* (New York: G.P. Putnam's Sons, 1953), 53–54.

11. *Ibid.*, 47.

12. *Ibid.*, 54.

13. Wagner's sale: *Phila. Inquirer*, July 17, 1897; purchase of Shugart and his drinking habits, *Phila. Inquirer*, July 23, 24, 1897. Perhaps the reason Lucid was impressed with Elberfeld was that the first time he pitched against Richmond, Elberfeld touched him for a double and a home run; *Phila. Inquirer*, June 4, 1897.

14. For the electrical spying, see Joe Dittmar, "A Shocking Discovery," *Baseball Research Journal*, 1991.

Chapter 3

1. *Phila. Inquirer*, Dec. 5, 1900.
2. *Ibid.* (column by "The Old Sport," Frank Hough).
3. *Phila. Inquirer*, Dec. 6, 1900.
4. *Phila. Inquirer*, Feb. 20, 1901, for the announcement on Ben Shibe. The paper said that Shibe's presence with the Athletics was a guarantee that the club "will be run on straightforward business principles," with no indication that the writer of these words, Hough, had an ownership interest in the team. The day before, Billy Shettsline of the Phillies expressed indignation at Mack's "inducing the Phillies' players to jump their contracts." *Phila Inquirer*, Feb. 19, 1901. Shettsline declined to comment further when it was pointed out to him that the players being wooed were not under contract but were held solely by the "reserve clause option," which was of questionable legality.
5. Murphy, *loc. cit.*, 20; *Phila. Inquirer*, March 21, 1901.
6. Connie Mack, *My 66 Years in the Big Leagues* (n.p.: Universal House, 1950), 28; *Phila. Evening Telegraph*, March 5, 1901.
7. *Philadelphia Record*, March 23, 1901.
8. Mack, *op cit.,*, 28.
9. Lieb & Baumgartner, *op. cit.*, 65.
10. *Philadelphia Ball Club, Ltd. v. Lajoie*, 202 Pa. 210, 217, 219, 221 (1902).
11. *Public Ledger*, April 22, 24, 1902.
12. *Public Ledger*, May 16, 28, 1902. Lajoie played his first game with Cleveland on June 4. During the 1902 season, when the Cleveland team came to Philadelphia, Lajoie disappeared, apparently going to Atlantic City for a few days. Duggleby rejoined the Phillies on May 5, Fraser on May 16.
13. Bill Brandt article on James Joseph "Jimmy" Hagen in *The Sporting News* (hereinafter cited as TSN), March 7, 1935. When Potter offered young Hagan a job as an office boy in 1903, Hagan asked "whether it was a steady job." Potter said it was, "and I guess he was right." *Ibid.* Many of Hagen's forty-plus years with the Phillies were spent as business manager and traveling secretary.
14. See the *Phila. Inquirer*, Aug. 9, 10, 1903, for graphic descriptions of the disaster. It was discovered that there had been no city inspection of the ballpark since 1895. The first lawsuits were filed on August 10 in Common Pleas Court.
15. Lieb & Baumgartner, *op. cit.*, 70, 78.
16. Dave Anderson, "The Coveleski Brother Act: Harry and Stanley," *The National Pastime*, 2000, 40.
17. Lieb & Baumgartner, *op. cit.*, 83.
18. TSN, March 2, 1933.
19. For Steffens, see *McClure's Magazine*, July 1903.
20. *Public Ledger*, Nov. 27, 1909.

Chapter 4

1. *Phila. Inquirer*, Oct. 28, 29, 1910. Lieb and Baumgartner, *op. cit.*, 89–90, place this trade, which clearly took place in October 1910 and was acquiesced in so reluctantly by Fogel in the following month, in "early 1911," with Fogel

boasting about it as a pennant-winning deal. Lieb even has Jimmy Hagen calling a press conference for Fogel, with the Phillies' president then engaging in repartee with newsman Gordon Mackay, a scene which certainly never took place. This is followed by Rich Westcott and Frank Bilovsky, *The New Phillies Encyclopedia* (Philadelphia: Temple University Press, 1993), 42, 310, 691, as well as by the Macmillan *Baseball Encyclopedia* (9th ed., 1993), 2481, 2515, both of which have the trade occurring in February 1911.

2. *Phila. Inquirer*, Oct. 30, Nov. 1, 3, 1910.

3. The operators of the Syracuse club, who purchased Alexander from Indianapolis without being informed that the young pitcher suffered from double vision, had the last laugh when the impairment cleared up.

4. *Phila. Inquirer*, June 4, 1930.

5. Cravath himself signed his nickname "Gavy," but the sportswriters of the day and thereafter spelled it "Gavvy." At Nicollet Park in Minneapolis, with a right field fence 279 feet from home plate, Cravath had taught himself to hit to right field, a skill which came in very handy at the Phillies' park; Bill Swank, "Before the Babe: Gavy Cravath's Home Run Dominance," *Baseball Research Journal* (2000), 51, 53.

6. *Phila. Inquirer*, Nov. 27, 1912.

7. *Phila. Inquirer*, Nov. 28, 1912. It should be noted, of course, that Fogel's suspicions, however inelegantly presented, may possibly have been correct. There was in these years an undercurrent of gambling influence which would cause Connie Mack to wonder about his team's sweep by the Braves in 1914 and culminate in the 1919 World Series fix.

8. *Weeghman v. Killefer*, 215 F. 168, 169 (W. District, Michigan, 1914). The lower court decision was handed down on April 10, 1914. The Sixth Circuit decision affirming, with an opinion by Judge John W. Warrington, was on June 30, 1914; 215 F. 289.

9. *Phila. Inquirer*, Oct. 15, 1914.

10. *Phila. Inquirer*, Oct. 21, 1914.

11. *Phila. Inquirer*, Oct. 22, 1914. Dooin's contentions were supported by a *Bulletin* writer who said that Dooin "never got the worst of a trade. But the last year or so Dooin couldn't swing any trades and with no money available to buy players— and with nary a peek at the waiver list when it came along— he never had a chance to better the team. He was practically a manager in name only"; *Evening Bulletin*, Oct. 27, 1914.

12. *Phila. Inquirer*, Dec. 13, 1914.

13. *Phila. Inquirer*, Dec. 15, 1914.

14. *Phila. Inquirer*, Jan. 6, 1915.

Chapter 5

1. *Evening Bulletin*, April 9, 1915. "Brains will mix with brawn this year," wrote the *Bulletin* reporter, "and the player who cannot use his head the way it should be used, will be out of a job."

2. *Evening Bulletin*, April 26, 1915.

3. *Phila. Inquirer*, Sept. 1, 1915. "Both men have many good games left in them," the story said. Marquard won two games down the stretch, Cheney none, although both pitched well for Brooklyn in future years.

4. *Phila. Inquirer*, Sept. 19, 1915.
5. *Phila. Inquirer*, Oct. 7, 1915.
6. *Ibid.*
7. *Phila. Inquirer*, Oct. 5, 1915.

Chapter 6

1. *Phila. Inquirer*, Dec. 12, 1917. Alexander, Baker added, "was not a drawing card."
2. *Phila. Inquirer*, July 18, 1918.
3. Jack Coombs left professional baseball for a long and successful college coaching career, at Williams, Princeton, Rice, and Duke, where he put in 24 years. Athletic directors, college presidents, and alumni never bothered a man who had put up with William F. Baker.
4. *Phila. Inquirer*, Aug. 10, 1919.
5. The Phillies' team ERA was 4.17; the earned run average for the whole league was 2.91.
6. *Phila. Inquirer*, June 8, 1920.
7. *Phila. Inquirer*, Sept. 1, 1920; *Evening Bulletin*, Aug. 31, Sept. 4, 1920.
8. *Evening Bulletin*, Sept. 23, 28, 1920. Lieb & Baumgartner, *op. cit.*, 145, and Westcott and Bilovsky, *op. cit.*, 53–54, both have the suspect Phils-Cubs game taking place in late 1919, but they missed by a year. The wires which tipped off William Veeck that one or more of his players had been reached were sent probably by gamblers who, seeing the odds shift strongly in the Phillies' favor, were looking to get money down on the Cubs once Alexander was substituted as the starting pitcher.
9. Rixey won 179 games and lost 148 for the Reds before retiring at the age of 42 after the 1933 season.
10. TSN, Jan. 6, 1921.
11. TSN, March 3, 1921.
12. TSN (Isaminger), April 14, 1921.
13. J.G. Taylor Spink, *Judge Landis and 25 Years of Baseball* (New York: Thomas Y. Crowell, 1947), 130–133.
14. *Phila. Inquirer*, May 15, 1927.

Chapter 7

1. Mead, *loc. cit.*, in Thorn, ed., *op. cit.*, 252.
2. *N.Y. Times*, Oct. 22, 1929.
3. *Phila. Inquirer*, Aug. 19, 1928.
4. *Phila. Record*, Aug. 2, 1929.
5. Westcott and Bilovsky, *op. cit.*, 168.
6. Phillies shortstop Tommy Thevenow's 56 errors were more than anyone else in the league committed.
7. *Phila. Inquirer*, April 19, 1930. The quotes were so far out of character for both Ott and Klein that there must be a strong suspicion that they were dreamed

up by sportswriters in search of a story. It might be noted, when "pop fly home runs" are mentioned, that Mel Ott hit 323 of his career 511 homers at the Polo Grounds, specializing in pulling the ball down the 257-foot right field line, that he hit 40 at Baker Bowl, and that after the Phillies moved in mid–1938 Ott never hit a single home run at Shibe Park, with its sensible dimensions and high right-field fence, in seven-plus seasons.

8. *Phila. Inquirer*, April 20, May 12, 20, 21, 1930. On May 20, Isaminger wrote sadly, "On all sides, here and everywhere, they were heralded as pennant contenders. So far this season, Burt Shotton's men have been sad flops."

9. Dick Bartell, with Norman Macht, *Rowdy Richard* (Berkeley, Cal.: North Atlantic Books, 1987), 85–86.

10. *Ibid.*, 86–88.

11. *Ibid.*, 87.

12. *Ibid.*, 96.

13. *Ibid.*, 96–97.

Chapter 8

1. John A. Lucas, "The Unholy Experiment — Professional Baseball's Struggle Against Pennsylvania Sunday Blue Laws 1926–1934," *Pennsylvania History*, April 1971, 168. The Pennsylvania Supreme Court decision of June 25, 1927, is in *Commonwealth v. American Baseball Club of Philadelphia*, 290 Pa. 136.

2. *Baseball Magazine*, Jan. 1937; Bartell and Macht, *op. cit.*, 109.

3. For a Chicagoan's perspective on this (and other) disastrous deals, see Eddie Gold, "Cubs Trades," *Baseball Research Journal* (1999).

4. Bartell and Macht, *op. cit.*, 111.

5. *Ibid.*, 88.

6. Two of the homers were hit off Pirate starter Jim Weaver, one off Mace Brown, and the game-winner in the 10th inning, just after it started raining, was off Bill Swift; *Phila. Inquirer*, July 11, 1936.

7. *Phila. Record*, June 25, 1938.

8. *Phila. Record*, July 1, 1938.

9. *Phila. Record*, July 2, 1938.

10. Frank Yeutter, "That Hustler and Fine Fellow, 'Doc' Prothro," *Baseball Magazine*, April 1941, 505; Kirby Higbe with Martin Quigley, *The High Hard One* (New York: Viking Press, 1967), 48.

11. Yeutter, *loc. cit.*, 506.

12. TSN, April 4, 1940.

13. Higbe and Quigley, *op. cit.*, 53; *Phila. Inquirer*, April 17–24, 1940.

14. Higbe and Quigley, *op. cit.*, 55; *Phila. Inquirer*, Sept. 27, 1940. Higbe's recollection was off a little here; he says the game was against Brooklyn, and he lost 2–1 on five Phillie errors.

15. Higbe and Quigley, *op. cit.*, 56.

16. TSN, Oct. 17, Nov. 14, 28, 1940.

17. *Phila. Record*, Dec. 2, 1941.

18. *Phila. Record*, Dec. 8, 1941. Lloyd Waner, apparently on the strength of a .316 lifetime batting average, is in the Hall of Fame, though there is still a suspi-

cion that some of the Veterans Committee members who put him in in 1967 thought they were voting for his brother Paul, who had been in the Hall for fifteen years.

Chapter 9

1. *Phila. Record*, Dec. 9, 1941.
2. *Phila. Inquirer*, Feb. 8, 1942. The unpaid bill for the new uniforms was one of the things which Nugent turned over to the league when it took over the club from him the following year.
3. *Phila. Inquirer*, Feb. 15, 1942.
4. *Phila. Inquirer*, April 24, 1942.
5. *Evening Bulletin*, Oct. 21, 1942. Litwhiler's feat has been matched four times since 1942, by outfielders playing in 150 games or more.
6. TSN, Oct. 22, 1942 (Baumgartner on Hughes; one must consider that it became increasingly difficult to find anything positive to write about the Phillies).
7. *Phila. Record*, Nov. 12, 1942.
8. *Phila. Inquirer*, Dec. 3, 1942.
9. *Ibid.*
10. *Phila. Inquirer*, Dec. 13, 1942.
11. *Phila. Inquirer*, Feb. 1, 1943.
12. *Phila. Inquirer*, Feb. 8, 1943.
13. *Phila. Record* and *Evening Bulletin*, both Feb. 10, 1943.
14. Bill Veeck, with Ed Linn, *Veeck — As In Wreck* (New York: G.P. Putnam's Sons, 1962), 171–72. Alfred Wright of *Sports Illustrated*, reviewing Veeck's book in the *New York Times*, said that reading it "is much like sitting with Veeck … through a few long nights in a saloon"; *N.Y. Times* (Book Review), July 29, 1962.
15. *Milwaukee Journal*, Oct. 18, 1942, and phone interview with Rudie Schaffer. For a detailed analysis and complete refutation of the Veeck claim, see David M. Jordan, Larry R. Gerlach, and John P. Rossi, "Bill Veeck and the 1943 Sale of the Phillies: A Baseball Myth Exploded," *The National Pastime* (1998).
16. *Phila. Record*, Feb. 21, 1943.
17. *Phila. Inquirer*, June 2, 1943.
18. *Time*, July 5, 1943.
19. Westcott & Bilovsky, *op. cit.*, 441.
20. *Phila. Inquirer*, Nov. 24, 1943.
21. *Phila. Inquirer*, Nov. 24, Dec. 4, 1943.
22. *Phila. Inquirer*, Dec. 4, 5, 1943. Cox identified his suspect director as L. Wister Randolph, also club vice president, who promptly characterized Cox's testimony as "clap trap" and "balderdash," two terms not often heard in the world of baseball; *ibid.* The whole episode is covered in Spink, *op. cit.*, 283–85.
23. *Phila. Inquirer*, Nov. 24, 1943. Connie Mack, who shared ownership of the Wilmington Blue Rocks franchise in the Interstate League with the new Phillies president, said of the Carpenters, "They are one of the finest families in this country"; *ibid.*
24. *Life*, April 23, 1945.
25. *Phila. Inquirer*, June 30, 1945.

Chapter 10

1. Wright was signed by Rickey as a companion for Robinson, who was clearly marked out as the trailblazer who would integrate Organized Baseball.

2. Danny Peary, ed., *We Played the Game* (New York: Hyperion, 1994), 7.

3. Ennis said Wasdell was his road roommate, "only I didn't get to know him because he never stayed in the room"; *ibid.*, 12.

4. *Phila. Inquirer*, May 10, 1946.

5. Harold Parrott, *The Lords of Baseball* (New York: Praeger Publishers, 1976), 194. Parrott has the series in Ebbets Field mixed up with the subsequent one at Shibe Park.

6. Jackie Robinson, as told to Alfred Duckett, *I Never Had It Made* (New York: G.P. Putnam's Sons, 1972), 71–72.

7. Arnold Rampersad, *Jackie Robinson: A Biography* (New York: Alfred A. Knopf, 1997), 173.

8. Parrott, *op. cit.*, 192. Many years later, in 1998, this conversation of Pennock with Rickey was raised as an objection to erecting a statue of Pennock in his home town of Kennett Square.

9. Pennock died of a massive cerebral hemorrhage suffered as he entered the Waldorf-Astoria Hotel in New York to attend the annual meeting of the National League; *N.Y. Times*, Jan. 31, 1948.

10. Peary, ed., *op. cit.*, 68.

11. *Ibid.*, 69.

12. *Phila. Inquirer*, July 17, 1948.

13. Robin Roberts and C. Paul Rogers III, *The Whiz Kids and the 1950 Pennant* (Philadelphia: Temple U. Press, 1996), 136.

14. On the day he was released, Rowe walked up to Roberts before the game and told the young pitcher he was giving away his curveball. Roberts later wrote, "I always thought it was funny that Schoolie never told me that when we were on the same pitching staff. But after he was released and my performing well could no longer affect his role on the team, he walked out to the outfield in his street clothes to let me know that I was tipping my curve"; *ibid.*, 183.

Chapter 11

1. Roberts and Rogers, *op. cit.*, 219.

2. *Evening Bulletin*, May 12, 1950; Roberts and Rogers, *op. cit.*, 135.

3. *Phila. Inquirer*, Aug. 18, 1950 (Nicholson); *Newsweek*, July 17, 1950 (Konstanty).

4. For Meyer, Roberts and Rogers, *op. cit.*, 290.

5. For Ennis on Seminick, Roberts and Rogers, *op. cit.*, 252. On August 11, New York second baseman Eddie Stanky tried to bother Seminick while Andy was at bat by getting in his line of sight at second and waving his arms up and down, and Sal Maglie hit Seminick on the elbow with a pitch. The next day Seminick went into third so hard that he knocked Giant third sacker Henry Thompson out. Later in the game Stanky was ejected for waving his arms again while Seminick was at bat. Seminick slid hard into Stanky's replacement, Bill Rigney, who jumped

on top of Andy and was pummeled by the Phillies catcher, setting off a donny-brook.

6. *Phila. Inquirer*, Oct. 1, 1950. It would be another fourteen years before the Phillies qualified for *that* ignominy.

7. Lopata added, "We should have sent Milt Stock a World Series share.... Milt probably didn't look back at where the outfielders were playing like he was supposed to"; Roberts and Rogers, *op. cit.*, 316. Milt Stock was the third baseman on the Phillies' 1915 champions.

8. *Phila. Inquirer*, Oct. 2, 1950.

9. (Jenkintown, Pa.) *Times Chronicle*, Sept. 9, 1982; *Newsweek*, Oct. 9, 1950. Yankee outfielder Gene Woodling said, "We swept the Phillies in the World Series, so ... people assume they were overmatched. But that Series was tight"; Peary, ed., *op. cit.*, 140.

10. *Phila. Inquirer*, Oct. 8, 1950.

11. Ennis said his only real regret in baseball "was not winning the Most Valuable Player award in 1950 ... Jim Konstanty did a heck of a job for us in relief, but I felt they shouldn't have taken a pitcher over an everyday player"; Peary, ed., *op. cit.*, 122.

Chapter 12

1. Peary, ed., *op. cit.*, 224.

2. Robin Roberts, "Fifty Years With Whitey," *Elysian Fields Quarterly*, Spring 1999, 30.

3. *Times Chronicle*, Sept. 9, 1982 (Simmons).

4. Frankie Baumholtz, who roomed with him, said Jones "loved to have a good time and he had many of them. Now, this was a guy who could drink. I was amazed by his stamina"; Peary, ed., *op. cit.*, 330.

5. *Ibid.*, 566 (Tim McCarver quoting Simmons).

6. *Evening Bulletin*, July 15, 1954 (Hamey on Moore); *Evening Bulletin*, Mar. 24, 1981 (Ashburn on Jones).

7. Peary, ed., *op. cit.*, 290 (Ennis), 329 (Baumholtz). Smith managed Cincinnati after he left the Phillies, and Reds pitcher Jim Brosnan said, "Mayo Smith was a kind, gentle man and I couldn't figure out how he ever got to be a big league manager. He wasn't the type. He didn't have any idea how to control his ballclub"; *ibid.*, 437. In 1968, Mayo Smith managed the Tigers to a world's championship.

8. Michael Fedo, *One Shining Season* (New York: Pharos Books, 1991), 79.

9. In the minors, Hamner developed a knuckleball and actually made it back to the majors as a pitcher, in a brief 1962 stint with the Kansas City A's.

10. Ed Bouchee said if you hit one off Sanford, "you had better be looking for a lot of chin music the rest of the game"; Peary, ed., *op. cit.*, 363.

11. Bob Uecker and Mickey Herskowitz, *Catcher in the Wry* (New York: Jove Books, 1983, orig. pub. New York: G.P. Putnam's, 1982), 189–190.

12. Hamey, who had ruined clubs in Pittsburgh and Philadelphia, moved on to New York where, in a few years, he actually ran the Yankees into tenth place.

13. Throughout the '57 spring training, it appeared that the first black to play with the Phillies would be a 22-year-old infielder named John Kennedy, formerly

with the Birmingham Black Barons in the Negro American League. Just before the season opened the Phillies made the judgment that Kennedy would not do and traded for Fernandez. Kennedy *did* get into five games with the Phillies, with no hits in two at bats. Because of all the spring publicity, many Phillies fans still recall (erroneously) John Kennedy as the Phillies' first black player. Kennedy went on to four and a fraction minor league seasons but never again played in the major leagues.

Chapter 13

1. *PhillySport*, June 1989; Peary, ed., *op. cit.*, 469 (Bouchee).
2. Post had come to Philadelphia in an even-up swap for pitcher Harvey Haddix in December 1957. He hit 36 home runs in two and a fraction years with the Phillies, after averaging 28.5 homers in his four prior Cincinnati seasons. He led the league in striking out in 1959, as he had done twice with the Reds.
3. TODAY (*Phila. Inquirer*), May 4, 1980 (Dalrymple).
4. *Sports Illustrated*, June 13, 1960.
5. One of the alternatives to Dalrymple was a little catcher named Clarence "Choo Choo" Coleman, who batted .128 in 34 games before going on to become a legend of sorts with the expansion New York Mets.
6. Roberts was cut by the Yankees in spring training but caught on with Baltimore, where he made the pitching adjustments he had refused to make with the Phillies. He went 10–9 and 2.78 with the O's in 1962 and won an additional 42 games over the following four years, to the joy of most Phillies fans.
7. Uecker and Herskowitz, *op. cit.*, 69.
8. Ed Richter, *View From the Dugout* (Philadelphia and New York: Chilton Books, 1964), 8.
9. *Phila. Inquirer*, Nov. 28, 1962.
10. Richter, *op. cit.*, 126–28.

Chapter 14

1. *Sports Illustrated*, April 20, 1964.
2. *Sports Illustrated*, April 13, 1964.
3. *Sports Illustrated*, Sept. 25, 1989.
4. Dick Allen and Tim Whitaker, *Crash: The Life and Times of Dick Allen* (New York: Ticknor & Fields, 1989), 54.
5. No Phillies pitcher had hurled a no-hitter of any kind since Johnny Lush did it in 1906. A subsequent record-keeping decision has senselessly wiped Harvey Haddix's gem, perhaps the best game ever pitched by anybody, from the list of no-hitters.
6. Thomas said later, "There's no doubt in my mind that if I remained healthy, the Phillies would have made it to the World Series"; Peary, ed., *op. cit.*, 602.
7. *Sports Illustrated*, Sept. 25, 1989; *PhillySport*, June 1989. It was, of course, the second time in three games that the Phillies had lost on an ill-advised steal of home. Dumb plays that worked were alien to Gene Mauch's scheme of baseball.

8. *Sports Illustrated*, Oct. 5, 1964.

9. Peary, ed., *op. cit.*, 592; *PhillySport*, June 1989.

10. Roebuck said, "Short could pitch with two days' rest without losing effectiveness. He had one of the strongest arms I ever saw — if he wasn't on the mound, he'd be throwing somewhere else anyway"; Peary, ed., *op. cit.*, 601.

11. *Sports Illustrated*, Oct. 12, 1964; *Evening Bulletin*, Sept. 28, 1964.

12. Allen and Whitaker, *op. cit.*, 55; *PhillySport*, June 1989.

13. A bitterly-disappointed Mauch sat in the Crosley Field clubhouse after the last game and muttered, "If I knew how it was going to come out, I might have done a couple of things different.... When you manage the way I want to manage, you don't miss something by a game or two"; *Phila. Inquirer*, Oct. 5, 1964.

14. Frank Dolson, *The Philadelphia Story* (South Bend, Indiana: Icarus Press, 1981), 88; *Sports Illustrated*, Sept. 25, 1989.

Chapter 15

1. Uecker and Herskowitz, *op. cit.*, 176.

2. *Phila. Inquirer*, July 5, 1965; Allen and Whitaker, *op. cit.*, 6–7.

3. *Phila. Inquirer*, July 4, 1965.

4. *Phila. Inquirer*, July 5, 1965.

5. *Phila. Inquirer*, April 22, 1966. "None of the three Phils [traded away] figured strongly in present plans," added the *Inquirer* article.

6. Uecker and Herskowitz, *op. cit.*, 172. When the light-hitting Uecker was traded to Atlanta on June 6, 1967, Allen said sadly, "He was the best friend I had on this club and now they're sending him away"; *ibid.*, 176. Unfortunately, Uecker was hitting only .171 at the time, and such a figure doesn't lend itself much to job security. Uecker would slip to .146 with the Braves in his last big league season.

7. Allen and Whitaker, *op. cit.*, 64; *Phila. Inquirer*, Aug. 25, 1967. Allen's wife and mother rushed him to the hospital, where his arm was placed in a cast for six weeks.

8. Allen and Whitaker, *op. cit.*, 72.

9. *Phila. Daily News* (special supplement), June 6, 1989.

10. Curt Flood with Richard Carter, *The Way It Is* (New York: Trident Press, 1971), 188.

11. J.W. Callison, with John A. Sletten, *The Johnny Callison Story* (New York: Vantage Press, 1991), 167.

12. At least twenty-five spectators were treated for injuries at the park, with nine of them sent to nearby hospitals; *Phila. Inquirer*, Oct. 2, 1970.

13. *Evening Bulletin*, Oct. 2, 1970.

14. *Phila. Inquirer*, Oct. 2, 1970.

15. Westcott & Bilovsky, *op. cit.*, 526.

Chapter 16

1. *Phila. Inquirer*, July 26, 1989.

2. Dan Prowler in *Phila. Inquirer*, Aug. 20, 1989. The stadiums built in the

late '60s and early '70s were called generically "the cookie-cutter stadiums," for their basic similarity.

3. Their first-round choice, a pitcher named Roy Thomas, never made it to the Phillies. Tony Lucadello's career, scouting methods, and baseball philosophy are detailed in an excellent book by Mark Winegardner, *Prophet of the Sandlots: Journeys With a Major League Scout* (New York: Atlantic Monthly Press, 1990). The scout's fiftieth player to reach the top did so after Lucadello's death, when outfielder Tom Marsh made it with the 1992 Phillies.

4. Lucchesi later managed the Texas Rangers, from 1975 to 1977, in a tenure marked by his being punched by one of his players, outfielder Lenny Randle. For a very harsh assessment of Lucchesi at Texas, based mainly upon interviews with Randle and former Ranger Roy Howell, see Peter Golenbock, *The Forever Boys: The Bittersweet World of Major League Baseball as Seen Through the Eyes of the Men Who Played One More Time* (New York: Birch Lane Press, 1991), 193–95, 217–18.

5. For the devious methods employed by Owens in selecting his manager, see Dolson, *op. cit.*, 182–85.

Chapter 17

1. *Phila. Daily News*, March 21, 1980.

2. Late in 1973, the Kansas City Royals called up Ken Brett's little brother George, who turned out to be an even better hitter than Ken.

3. *Phila. Inquirer*, Sept. 24, 1975.

4. Allen and Whitaker, *op. cit.*, 153–54, 158.

5. Dolson, *op. cit.*, 194.

6. Allen and Whitaker, *op. cit.*, 168.

7. *Phila. Inquirer*, Oct. 10, 1976.

8. *Phila. Inquirer*, Oct. 11, 1976.

9. Johnstone had a tremendous series, batting .778 with 7-for-9 including a double and triple.

10. *Phila. Inquirer*, Oct. 8, 1977. Ozark explained lamely that he'd left Luzinski in because Greg was due up in the bottom of the inning, but this was clearly nonsense.

11. *Phila. Inquirer*, Oct. 7, 1978.

12. *Phila. Inquirer*, Oct. 8, 1978.

13. *Phila. Inquirer*, Sept. 1, 1979.

14. *Phila. Inquirer*, Feb. 18, 2001.

Chapter 18

1. *Phila. Inquirer*, Oct. 19, 1979.

2. *Phila. Daily News*, March 21, 1980.

3. *Sports Illustrated*, July 21, 1980.

4. *Phila. Inquirer*, Feb. 18, 2001.

5. Dolson, *op. cit.*, 267 (Luzinski).

6. *Ibid.*, 268.

7. *Sports Illustrated*, Oct. 6, 1980.

8. Mike Schmidt, with Barbara Walder, *Always On the Offense* (New York: Atheneum, 1982), 178; Dolson, *op. cit.*, 274. On Bowa and his teammates, see quotes from Randy Lerch in Golenbock, *op. cit.*, 116–17.

9. *Sports Illustrated*, Oct. 13, 1980.

10. *Ibid.*

11. *Sports Illustrated*, Oct. 20, 1980.

12. *Ibid.*

13. Manager Bill Virdon told the author that Vern Ruhle himself did not know whether he caught or trapped the ball.

14. Dolson, *op. cit.*, 286.

15. *Phila. Inquirer*, Oct. 13, 1980.

16. *Phila. Inquirer*, Oct. 16, 1980.

17. *Sports Illustrated*, Oct. 27, 1980.

18. Schmidt and Walder, *op. cit.*, 91.

19. Dolson, *op. cit.*, 297.

20. *Ibid.*

21. *Newsweek*, Nov. 3, 1980.

Chapter 19

1. *Newsweek*, Nov. 3, 1980.

2. *Phila. Inquirer*, March 3, 4, 1981.

3. *Phila. Inquirer*, March 7, 1981.

4. *Sports Illustrated*, Feb. 16, 1981; Bill Conlin, in *Phila. Daily News*, June 29, 1989. On March 1, Lerch, a disappointing 4–14 in 1980, was traded to Milwaukee.

5. Kevin Kerrane, *Dollar Sign on the Muscle: The World of Baseball Scouting* (New York: Avon Books, 1985), 255.

6. *Ibid.*, 185.

7. *Phila. Inquirer*, July 19, 1983.

8. Joe Morgan and David Falkner, *Joe Morgan: A Life in Baseball* (New York and London: W.W. Norton, 1993), 263; *Sports Illustrated*, Oct. 17, 1983.

9. *Phila. Daily News*, May 30, 1989. Maddox, during the World Series, told the press that "I wasn't happy being a platoon player. I haven't accepted that role, and I don't want to be that type of player next year. But one thing about our team this year is that a lot of guys— Pete Rose, Gary Matthews, Joe Morgan at times— all had to do things they didn't want to do. But we had to accept some things"; *Phila. Inquirer*, Oct. 12, 1983.

10. *Sports Illustrated*, Oct. 17, 1983

11. *Phila. Inquirer*, Oct. 12, 1983.

12. *Phila. Inquirer*, Oct. 15, 1983; also, *Sports Illustrated*, Oct. 24, 1983.

13. *Phila. Inquirer*, Oct. 15, 1983.

14. *Phila. Inquirer*, Oct. 17, 1983.

15. Morgan and Falkner, *op. cit.*, 269–70; *Phila. Inquirer*, Oct. 17, 1983.

Chapter 20

1. *Phila. Daily News*, May 30, 1989.

2. *Phila. Inquirer*, April 17, 1987.

3. *Phila. Daily News*, May 30, 1989.

4. *Phila. Inquirer*, June 9, 1989. That Woodward was a capable executive was shown when he helped to turn the Seattle Mariners from a doormat to a contender.

5. *Phila. Daily News*, May 30, 1989.

6. *Chicago Tribune*, Oct. 15, 1993 (Royko on Kruk). Royko called Kruk "a throwback to when athletes played as much for the joy of the game as they did for the paycheck." For O'Brien, see John Kruk as told to Paul Hagen, *"I Ain't an Athlete, Lady..." My Well-Rounded Life and Times* (New York: Simon & Schuster, 1994), 73.

7. *Phila. Daily News*, June 19, 1989.

8. *Ibid.* Of McDowell, Kruk said he was "an intelligent man, but in baseball terms, he's a ten-year-old. That's just the way he approaches the game"; Kruk, *op. cit.*, 74.

9. *Phila. Inquirer*, April 24, 25, 1991.

10. Kruk, *op. cit.*, 234. Kruk told Williams "that if I ever faced him I'd stand right on the plate. Because I knew he'd never hit me if I stood there"; *ibid.*, 235.

11. *Phila. Inquirer*, Sept. 21, 1992. Philadelphians, who started to assume these things came up all the time, were startled to learn that Morandini's was the first unassisted triple play by a second baseman.

Chapter 21

1. *Phila. Daily News*, Oct. 5, 1993 (Fregosi).

2. Kruk, *op. cit.*, 211.

3. *Phila. Inquirer*, Oct. 13, 1993.

4. *Chicago Tribune*, Oct. 15, 1993 (Kruk); *Phila. Daily News*, Oct. 5, 1993 (Dykstra).

5. The 20-inning game with the Dodgers was the first in the big leagues for Kevin Stocker, who must have wondered what craziness he had fallen into.

6. Kruk, *op. cit.*, 218.

7. *Phila. Inquirer*, Sept. 20, 1993.

8. *Phila. Daily News*, Sept. 29, 1993.

9. The standard for a "save" had been by this time so liberalized that many observers felt that a save now had little more meaning than the unlamented "game-winning RBI" which was tried for several seasons in the 1980s and then discarded. If a relief pitcher came in to pitch the ninth inning with a three-run lead and managed to retire the opposition without losing all three runs of that lead, he earned a save. Quite a few of Williams's saves were of this kind, and Fregosi seldom brought him in with men on base.

10. *Atlanta Constitution*, Oct. 6, 7, 1993.

11. *Phila. Inquirer*, Oct. 12, 1993.

12. *Phila. Inquirer*, Oct. 15, 1993 (Incaviglia).

13. On West's rotator cuff, Bill Brown, "Worst to First," *The Fan*, December 1993, 26.

14. *Chicago Tribune*, Oct. 22, 1993.

15. *Phila. Inquirer*, Oct. 21, 22, 1993.

16. On the towel business, Kruk said, "here some of our guys were showing up their own teammate.... If you can't watch, go back to the clubhouse"; Kruk, *op. cit.*, 232.

17. The only other time that a World Series has ended with a home run was in 1960, when Bill Mazeroski's blow in the ninth inning ended a tied Pittsburgh-Yankees game at Forbes Field.

18. *Phila. Inquirer*, Oct. 24, 1993.

Chapter 22

1. Williams and Schilling entertained the public for a few days after the trade with an exchange of insults and threats which established that they did not like one another; *Phila. Inquirer*, Dec. 8, 1993. Williams's career as an Astro was disastrously brief. He pitched poorly, and the Houston club released him on May 30, 1994, immediately after its first series in Philadelphia. Jones pitched well for the Phillies for one season, earning 27 saves, before moving on via free agency, while Juden, a large righthander with great potential but a strange personality, won three and lost eight for the Phils over two seasons before being traded to the Giants for Mike Benjamin. Two of the three players obtained for Mulholland, pitcher Bobby Munoz (briefly) and infielder Kevin Jordan, were useful acquisitions.

2. Attendance in 1981 was 1,638,752, but a third of that season was lost to a strike, and the Phillies, having "won" the first half, were really only playing for practice after the strike ended.

3. *Phila. Inquirer*, July 27, 2000.

4. *Ibid.*

5. John Vukovich, the third-base coach, was the one retained, as Hal McRae, Chuck Cottier, Galen Cisco, and Brad Mills were turned loose.

Chapter 23

1. John Kruk, who played for Bowa in San Diego, called him, admiringly, "the little psychopath competitor that he is"; Kruk, *op. cit.*, 112.

2. The Eagles settled early on a site in South Philadelphia, near Veterans Stadium, and then waited in increasing frustration for the settling of the issue of the Phillies' park.

Bibliography

Periodicals

Atlanta *Constitution*
Baseball History
Baseball Hobby News
Baseball Magazine
Baseball Research Journal
Chicago *Tribune*
The Fan
(Jenkintown, Pa.) *Times Chronicle*
LIFE
Newsweek
New York Evening Post
New York Times
Philadelphia *Daily News*
(Philadelphia) *Evening Bulletin*

Philadelphia Inquirer
Philadelphia Magazine
(Philadelphia) *Public Ledger*
Philadelphia Record
Philadelphia Tribune
Phillies Report
PhillySport
Sports Illustrated
The National Pastime
The Sporting News
TIME
Trenton Times
Wilmington *Journal-Every Evening*

Books and Articles

Allen, Dick, and Tim Whitaker, *Crash: The Life and Times of Dick Allen*, Ticknor & Fields, New York, 1989.

Allen, Maury, *You Could Look It Up: The Life of Casey Stengel*, New York, 1979.

Anderson, Dave, "The Coveleski Brother Act: Harry and Stanley," *The National Pastime*, 2000.

Axthelm, Pete, "Those Malevolent Phillies," *Newsweek*, Nov. 3, 1980.

Bartell, Dick, with Norman L. Macht, *Rowdy Richard*, North Atlantic Books, Berkeley, Cal., 1987.

Berkow, Ira, *Red: A Biography of Red Smith*, Times Books, New York, 1986.

Bingham, Walter, "The Dalton Gang Rides Again," *Sports Illustrated*, June 13, 1960.

Bloodgood, Clifford, "The Phillies' School Teacher," *Baseball Magazine*, Sept. 1941.

Brown, Bill, "Worst to First," *The Fan*, December 1993.

Callison, John Wesley, with John Austin Sletten, *The Johnny Callison Story*, Vantage Press, New York, 1991.

Casway, Jerrold, "Locating Philadelphia's Historic Ballfields," *The National Pastime*, 1993.

Curtis, Gerald R., *Factors That Affect the Attendance of a Major League Baseball Club*, unpublished M.B.A. thesis, Wharton School, University of Pennsylvania, 1951.

Dittmar, Joe, "Alexander the Great," *The National Pastime*, 1992.

_____, "A Shocking Discovery," *Baseball Research Journal*, 1991.

Dolson, Frank, *The Philadelphia Story: A City of Winners*, Icarus Press, South Bend, Ind., 1981.

Fedo, Michael, *One Shining Season*, Pharos Books, New York, 1991.

Fimrite, Ron, "The Old and The Relentless Beat the Young and the Restless," *Sports Illustrated*, Oct. 17, 1983.

_____, "Wow, What A Playoff," *Sports Illustrated*, Oct. 20, 1980.

Flood, Curt, with Richard Carter, *The Way It Is*, Trident Press, New York, 1970.

Golenbock, Peter, *The Forever Boys: The Bittersweet World of Major League Baseball as Seen Through the Eyes of Men Who Played One More Time*, Birch Lane Press, New York, 1991.

Higbe, Kirby, with Martin Quigley, *The High Hard One*, Viking, New York, 1967.

Honig, Donald, *Baseball Between the Lines: Baseball in the '40s and '50s As Told by the Men Who Played It*, Coward, McCann & Geoghegan, New York, 1976.

Jordan, David M., Larry R. Gerlach, and John P. Rossi, "Bill Veeck and the 1943 Sale of the Phillies: A Baseball Myth Exploded," *The National Pastime*, 1998.

Kaplan, Jim, and Steve Wulf, "They're Playing the Sweet Swing Music of the 40s," *Sports Illustrated*, July 19, 1982.

Kaplan, Stan, *Who Was On First?*, Dover, NJ, 1988.

Kavanagh, Jack, and Norman Macht, *Uncle Robbie*, Society for American Baseball Research, Cleveland, 1999.

Kerrane, Kevin, *Dollar Sign On The Muscle: The World of Baseball Scouting*, Avon Books, New York, 1985.

Krevisky, Steve, "'XX' and Hoosier Chuck," *The National Pastime*, 1993.

Kruk, John, with Paul Hagen, *"I Ain't an Athlete, Lady..." My Well- Rounded Life and Times*, Simon & Schuster, New York, 1994.

Kuklick, Bruce, *To Every Thing A Season: Shibe Park and Urban Philadelphia 1909–1976*, Princeton University Press, Princeton, NJ, 1991.

Levine, Peter, *A.G. Spalding and the Rise of Baseball: The Promise of American Sport*, New York & Oxford, 1985.

Lewis, Allen, and Larry Shenk, *This Date In Philadelphia Phillies History*, Stein & Day, New York, 1979.

Lieb, Frederick G., and Stan Baumgartner, *The Philadelphia Phillies*, Putnam, New York, 1953.

Lowry, Philip J., *Green Cathedrals*, Addison-Wesley, Reading, Mass., 1992.

McCarver, Tim, and Jim Kaplan, "Lefty Has the Right Approach," *Sports Illustrated*, July 21, 1980.

Montville, Leigh, "Leading Man," *Sports Illustrated*, Oct. 11, 1993.

Morgan, Joe, and David Falkner, *Joe Morgan: A Life in Baseball*, W. W. Norton, New York & London, 1993.

Murphy, J.M., "Napoleon Lajoie: Modern Baseball's First Superstar," *The National Pastime*, 1988.

Neft, David S., Richard M. Cohen, and Jordan A. Deutsch, *The Sports Encyclopedia: Baseball*, Grosset & Dunlap, New York, 1981.

Okkonen, Marc, *Baseball Uniforms of the 20th Century: The Official Major League Baseball Guide*, Sterling Publishing Co., New York, 1991.

_____, *The Federal League of 1914–1915: Baseball's Third Major League*, Society for American Baseball Research, Garrett Park, MD, 1989.

Parrott, Harold, *The Lords of Baseball*, Praeger, New York, 1976.

Peary, Danny, ed., *We Played the Game*, Hyperion, New York, 1994.

Philadelphia Ball Club, Limited v. Lajoie, 202 Pennsylvania Reports 210, 1902.

Pietrusza, David, "Sliding Billy Hamilton," *Baseball Research Journal*, 1991.

Rampersad, Arnold, *Jackie Robinson: A Biography*, Alfred A. Knopf, New York, 1997.

Richter, Ed, *View From the Dugout: A Season With Baseball's Amazing Gene Mauch*, Chilton, Philadelphia and New York, 1964.

Ritter, Lawrence, *Lost Ballparks: A Celebration of Baseball's Legendary Fields*, Viking Studio Books, New York, 1992.

_____. *The Glory of Their Times*, William Morrow, New York, 1966.

Roberts, Robin, with Paul Rogers, "Fifty Years with Whitey," *Elysian Fields Quarterly*, Spring 1999.

_____. *The Whiz Kids and the 1950 Pennant*, Temple University Press, Philadelphia, 1996.

Robinson, George, and Charles Salzberg, *On A Clear Day They Could See Seventh Place: Baseball's Worst Teams*, Dell, New York, 1991.

Robinson, Jackie, as told to Alfred Duckett, *I Never Had It Made*, Putnam, New York, 1972.

Scheid, Lewis, "The Tragedy of Ed Delahanty," *Baseball Research Journal*, 1991.

Schmidt, Mike, with Barbara Walder, *Always On the Offense*, Atheneum, New York, 1982.

Seymour, Harold, *Baseball — The Early Years*, Oxford University Press, New York, 1960.

_____, *Baseball — The Golden Years*, Oxford University Press, New York, 1971.

Smith, Curt, *Voices of the Game*, Diamond Communications, South Bend, Ind., 1987.

Spink, J.G. Taylor, *Judge Landis and 25 Years of Baseball*, Crowell, New York, 1947.

Swank, Bill, "Before the Babe: Gavy Cravath's Home Run Dominance," *Baseball Research Journal*, 2000.

Swindell, Larry, "The All-Time Phillies Dream Team," *Today*, May 4, 1980.

Thom, John, "The 1930 Phillies," *The National Pastime*, 1993.

Thorn, John, ed., *The National Pastime*, Warner Books, New York, 1987.

_____, and Pete Palmer, eds., *Total Baseball*, Warner Books, New York, 1989.

Tiemann, Robert L., and Mark Rucker, eds., *Nineteenth Century Stars*, Society for American Baseball Research, Kansas City, Mo., 1989.

Tomlinson, Gerald, "A Minor League Legend: Buzz Arlett, the 'Mightiest Oak,'" *Baseball Research Journal*, 1988.

Tygiel, Jules, *Baseball's Great Experiment: Jackie Robinson and His Legacy*, Oxford University Press, New York, 1983.

Uecker, Bob, and Mickey Herskowitz, *Catcher in the Wry*, Jove Books, New York, 1983.

Veeck, Bill, with Ed Linn, *Veeck — As In Wreck*, Putnam, New York, 1962.

Voigt, David Quentin, *American Baseball*, 3 vols., Pennsylvania State University Press, University Park, Pa., & London, 1983.

Weeghman v. Killefer, 215 Federal Reporter 168 (1914) and 215 Federal Reporter 289 (1914).

Weigley, Russell F., ed., *Philadelphia: A 300-Year History*, W.W. Norton, New York & London, 1982.

Westcott, Rich, and Frank Bilovsky, *The New Phillies Encyclopedia*, Temple University Press, Philadelphia, 1993.

Winegardner, Mark, *Prophet of the Sandlots: Journeys With a Major League Scout*, Atlantic Monthly Press, New York, 1990.

Wulf, Steve, "Don't Look Back...," *Sports Illustrated*, Sept. 27, 1993.

_____, "In Philadelphia, They're the Wheeze Kids," *Sports Illustrated*, Mar. 14, 1983.

_____, "Out But Not Down," *Sports Illustrated*, Oct. 6, 1980.

_____, "The Orioles All Pitched In," *Sports Illustrated*, Oct. 24, 1983.

_____, "The Year of the Blue Snow," *Sports Illustrated*, Sept. 25, 1989.

Yeutter, Frank, "He Gets His Chance at 60," *Baseball Magazine*, February 1942.

_____, "He's No Ordinary Player," *Baseball Magazine*, May 1942.

_____, "That Hustler and Fine Fellow, 'Doc' Prothro," *Baseball Magazine*, April 1941.

In addition, much use has been made of the annual publications of *The Sporting News*, such as the *Baseball Register*, *Baseball Guide*, *One For the Book*, and *The Dope Book*, and such other annual publications as the *Spalding Base Ball Guide and Official League Book* and *The Little Red Book of Baseball* for various seasons. There have also been the scorecards, programs, media guides and yearbooks issued by the Phillies over the years and the Phillies Phan-o-grams. Basic statistics have, for the most part, come from successive editions of *The Baseball Encyclopedia*, published by Macmillan, and *Total Baseball*, cited above.

Index

Numbers in *italics* refer to photographs.

Aaron, Henry 118, 145
Abbott, Kyle 222
Abrams, Cal 115
Abreu, Bobby 246–48
Adams, Elvin "Buster" 91, 94
Adams, Jack 46, 49
Adcock, Joe 112
Aikens, Willie 189–92
Alexander, Grover Cleveland 39, *40*, 41, 44–45, 48, *49*, 50–57, 59–60, 71–72, 117, 131, 190, 211, 252, 258–59
Alexander, Nathan "Babe" 93
All-Star Game 3–4, 76, 79–80, 94, 100, 126, 141, 169, 216, 226, 241, 243, 245
Allen, Bob 12
Allen, Ethan 1, 78–79
Allen, Johnny 89
Allen, Richie 68, 138–40, 142, 144–45, 147–48, 150–54, *155*, 156–57, 168, 171–73, 252, 265
Alomar, Roberto 234–38
Alou, Felipe 130, 144
Alston, Walter 164
Altamirano, Porfirio 208, 253
Altman, George 141
Altobelli, Joe 204, 206
Amaro, Ruben 129, 132, 135–136, 138, 139, 200
Amaro, Ruben, Jr. 222
American Association 5, 12–14, 16, 22, 24, 256
American Baseball Guild 96
American League 17, 24–26, 28–29, 32–33, 41, 50, 54, 86, 96, 135, 150, 167, 169, 189, 212, 220, 233–34, 238
Andersen, Larry 210, 225, 227, 233, 236–37, 239
Anderson, George "Sparky" 126, 172
Anderson, Harry 125–126, 130
Anderson, Mike 164, 171

Andrews, Ed 10
Arizona Diamondbacks 246, 248–49
Arlett, Russell "Buzz" 74
Arnovich, Morrie 82, 253
Ashburn, Richie 22, 104, *105*, 107, 109–111, 113, 115–23, 126–28, 135, 168, 242, 252
Ashby, Andy 247–48
Astrodome 186, 189, 224
Athletics (original) 5, 7–9, 12–13, 255
Atlanta Braves 167–68, 177, 195, 211, 219, 227–34, 242, 246–48, 265
Atwood, Bill 253
Avery, Steve 230, 232
Axthelm, Pete 193
Ayala, Benny 206

Bahnsen, Stan 185, 217
Bakely, Jersey 8, 255
Baker, Frank 47
Baker, Johnnie "Dusty" 175, 178
Baker, Newton D. 57
Baker, William F. 43–46, 51, 53–62, 64–65, 66, 67, 70, 72–73, 259
Baker Bowl 10, 56–57, 60, 62, 65–72, 74, 77, 79–81, 89, 253, 260
Baldschun, Jack 132, 134, 136, 138–39, 144, 152
Baller, Jay 201
Baltimore Orioles (American League) 204–206, 214–15, 264
Baltimore Orioles (original) 18, 22–23, 27
Bancroft, Dave 46, 48, 52–53, 55, 58, *59*, 60, 252
Bankhead, Dan 100
Barlick, Al 109
Barrett, "Kewpie Dick" 91, 94
Barry, Jack, 50, 52
Bartell, Dick 72–76, 78–79
Bateman, John 159

Bates, Johnny 37
Batiste, Kim 225, 227, 230–32, 235
Bauer, Hank 116
Baumer, Jim 200, 214–15
Baumgartner, Stan *49*, 88–89, 91, 114
Baumholtz, Frank 123, 263
Bayuk Cigar Company 87
Beck, Walter "Boom Boom" 82, 84
Becker, Beals 43, 45, 48
Bedrosian, Steve 211–14, 216–18
Beebe, Fred 37
Behan, Petie 62
Belinsky, Robert "Bo" 151
Bell, Juan 225
Belliard, Rafael 230
Bench, Johnny 173
Bender, Charles "Chief" 40, 47, 55
Benge, Ray 10, 67, 70–71, 74–75
Bengough, Benny 100
Benjamin, Mike 269
Bennett, Dennis 135–36, 138–39, 141, 143–44, 147, 151
Bentley, Jack 65
Bergman, Dave 186, 188, 208
Bernhard, Bill 26–28
Berryhill, Damon 231, 233
Bicknell, Charlie 124
Birmingham Black Barons 264
Blackwell, Ewell 110–13
Blankenship, Rudolph 51
Blanton, Cy 84
Blasingame, Wade 144, 147
Blauser, Jeff 230–33
Blaylock, Marv 253
Bloodworth, Jimmy 112, 117, 119
"Blue Jays" 94–95, 98
"Blue laws" 77, 100
Bochy, Bruce 188
Boddicker, Mike 205
Bolen, Stew 74
Bonds, Barry 221, 224
Boone, Bob 165–67, 169, 171–72, 174, 176–77, 182, 184–85, 188–90, 192, 200, 208, 250
Boozer, John 145
Boras, Scott 245
Borders, Pat 234, 237–39
Borowy, Hank 106–107
Boston Beaneaters 16–18, 21, 23, 30
Boston Bees 80, 83
Boston Braves 46–47, 49–50, 52, 54–55, 57–58, 61, 65, 76, 79, 87, 106, 111–14, 258
Boston Red Sox 50–52, 60–61, 68, 79, 93, 98, 123, 130, 132, 141, 151, 165
Boston Red Stockings 14
Boston Rustlers 41

Bottalico, Ricky 243
Bouchee, Ed 125–26, 128–29, 263
Bowa, Larry 158, 163–64, 166–69, 171, 174–78, 180, 182–86, 188–90, 193, 197, 199–200, 208, 250, 267, 269
Bowman, Bob 125–26
Boyer, Ken 149
Boyle, Jack 17, 19
Bradley, Phil 214–15, 247
Brandt, Jackie 152
Bransfield, William "Kitty" 30, 33–36, 41
Brantley, Jeff 246
Braves Field 50, 52, 113
Brennan, Addison 42, 44
Brennan, William 42
Bresnahan, Roger 42, 47
Brett, George 189–92, 266
Brett, Ken 166, 266
Brewster, Charlie 91
Briggs, John 139
Bristol, Dave 164
Brock, Lou 18
Brogna, Rico 246–49
Brooklyn Dodgers 32, 49–50, 64–65, 71–72, 80–83, 89, 95, 100–102, 109–15, 119, 127, 129, 136, 165, 258, 260
Brooklyn Eckfords 6
Brooklyn Robins 54–55
Brooklyn Superbas 12, 21, 23
Brosnan, Jim 263
Brotherhood of Professional Ballplayers 11–12, 14, 22, 26, 255
Brouthers, Dan 18
Brown, Bobby 116–17
Brown, Francis Shunk 34
Brown, Mace 260
Brown, Ollie 168, 171
Brown, Tommy 115, 119
Brown, Willard 100
Browne, Byron 156
Brusstar, Warren 174, 177–79, 187, 198
Buffinton, Charlie 10–12, 14
Buhl, Bob 152
Bumbry, Al 205
Bunning, Jim 138–41, 143–45, *146*, 147–49, 151–55, 158, 160, 162, 164, 243, 252
Burgess, Forrest "Smoky" 120, 123–24
Burk, Mack 124
Burkett, Jesse 17
Burns, Eddie 49, 51–52
Burrell, Pat 249, 252
Busch, Augustus 143, 250
Busch Stadium 3
Butcher, Max 81
Butler, Rob 238
Buzhardt, John 131–33

Byrd, Paul 246–48
Byrne, Bobby 48
Bystrom, Marty 183–84, 188, 191, 203

Caballero, Ralph "Putsy" 102, 104, 117, 119
Cabell, Enos 187–88
Cabrera, Francisco 232
California Angels 151, 200, 215, 220, 222
Callison, John 128, 130, 132, 134, 136, 138–41, *142*, 144–45, 147–48, 151–54, 157, 252
Camden Yards 3
Camilli, Dolph 78–81
Camnitz, Howie 44
Campanella, Roy 109–10, 114–15, 118
Campbell, Bill (broadcaster) 135, 162
Campbell, William R. "Bill" 208
Canate, Willie 238
Cardenal, Jose 192
Cardenas, Leo 148
Cardwell, Don 129
Carlson, Hal 65
Carlton, Steve 163–69, *170*, 171–72, 174–77, 179–82, 184, 186–87, 190, 192–95, 197–206, 209–12, 241, 243, 252
Carman, Don 212
Carpenter, Robert R.M., Jr. 29, 93, 95, 98, *99*, 101, 104, 106, 118–19, 124, 126–27, 132, 136, 154, 156, 158–60, 164, 199–200, 261
Carpenter, Robert R.M., III "Ruly" 164, 168, 172, 178, 182, 195–97, 199, 200
Carrigan, Bill 50–51
Carsey, Wilfred "Kid" 18
Carter, Gary 185, 209
Carter, Joe 234–39
Carty, Rico 145
Casagrande, Tom 124
Casey, Danny 9–10
Cash, Dave 166–69, 171, 173
Castillo, Tony 236–37
Cater, Danny 139–140, 150
Cedeno, Cesar 186
Cepeda, Orlando 140
Cey, Ron 175, 178
Chalmers, George 39, 41, 44, 48–52
Chamberlain, Wes 219, 222, 232
Champion, Billy 163, 165
Chance, Frank 32, 36
Chandler, Albert B. "Happy" 96, 101
Chapman, Ben 95, 100–102, 104, 106, 122
Chen, Bruce 248
Cheney, Larry 49, 258
Chetkovich, Mitch 87, 253
Chicago Cubs 23, 32–33, 35, 37, 41–42, 47, 49, 54, 56–57, 59–60, 62, 77–79, 82, 88, 91, 94, 98–99, 106–107, 109–10, 113, 120, 124, 127, 129, 131–33, 157, 164, 169, 174, 178, 183–84, 198–200, 202, 208, 213, 218, 221–22, 224–25, 228, 233, 245–46, 259
Chicago White Sox 29, 57, 60, 98, 128, 130, 150, 168, 195, 208, 211, 222, 227, 234
Chicago White Stockings 9–10
ChiFeds 44
Chiozza, Lou 78
Christenson, Larry 168, 170–71, 174–75, 177, 179, 181–82, 186, 188, 191, 196, 198, 202
Christopher, Joe 140
Church, Emory "Bubba" 3, 111–14, 116–17, 119–20
Cicotte, Eddie 57, 60
Cincinnati Red Stockings 8
Cincinnati Reds 3, 21–23, 37, 42, 46, 48, 55, 57, 60, 76, 81, 85, 87, 91, 98, 100, 102–103, 106–107, 109–13, 120, 126, 128, 130, 135, 143–45, 148, 158, 162, 164, 172–73, 175, 178, 197, 201, 211–12, 224, 259, 263–64
Cisco, Galen 148, 269
Clark, Dave 229
Clark, Joseph S., Jr. 103, 118, 120, 139
Clay, Dain 91
Clements, Jack 9, 11–12, 18, 255
Cleveland (AL) 28, 67, 100, 122, 125, 127, 133, 165, 199–200, 202, 211, 247, 257
Cleveland (original) 22
Cline, Ty 145
Cobb, Ty 17
Cohen, Andy 129
Coker, Jim 129
Coleman, Clarence "Choo Choo" 264
Coleman, Jack 7–8
Coleman, Jerry 116–17
Collins, Eddie 47, 58, 82
Collins, Jocko 93, 197
Collins, Phil 71, 74–76
Colorado Rockies 242, 247
Colt Stadium 136
Columbia Park 32
Combs, Pat 218–19
Comiskey Park 195
Concepcion, Dave 162, 173
Concepcion, Onix 191
Conley, Gene 127, 130
Connie Mack Stadium 3–4, 124, 150, 152, 154–55, 158–59
Cook, Dennis 218–19
Cooke, Allan "Dusty" 101, 106
Cooley, Duff 20–21
Coombs, Jack 47, 58, 259
Corey, Fred 7
Corrales, Pat 152, 199, 202–203

Corriden, Frank 32–33
Cosell, Howard 205
Cottier, Chuck 269
Coveleski, Harry 33
Coveleski, Stanley 33
Covington, Wes 132, 134–41, 149
Cowley, Joe 212–14
Cox, Billy 109, 115
Cox, Bobby 226, 230
Cox, Danny 239
Cox, William D. 90–93, 261
Cravath, Clifford "Gavvy" 41, 43–44, *48*,
  49–55, 58, 60, 252, 258
Cristante, Leo 119
Crosley Field 148, 265
Cross, Monte 21, 27–28, 256
Cruz, Jose 188
Culp, Ray 136, 138–39, 147, 149, 152, 154
Curry, Tony 130
Cy Young Award 163, 174, 194, 197, 202,
  208, 211, 213, 233

Daal, Omar 248
Dahlgren, Ellsworth "Babe" *2*(photo), 87,
  91–92
Daily, Ed 9
Dalrymple, Clay 128–30, 132, 135–36, 138–
  39, 143–44, 147, 264
Dalton Gang 131–32, 135
Dark, Alvin 125, 128–29, 140
Dauer, Rich 206
Daulton, Darren 219–20, 223, 225–27,
  229–34, 236–39, 241–44, 250, 252
Davalillo, Vic 175–76
Davis, Curt 78–79
Davis, George "Kiddo" 75
Davis, Mark 201, 227
Davis, Storm 206
Davis, Virgil "Spud" 70–71, 74–77
Davis, Willie 143
Dawson, Andre 185
Day, Charles "Boots" 160
Dean, Wayland 65
Decatur, Art 65
DeJesus, Ivan 199–200, 206
DeJesus, Jose 219–20, 222
Delahanty, Ed 11–12, 14–18, 20–22, 25–27,
  80, 216, 256
De La Hoz, Mike 144
DeLeon, Jose 227
Del Greco, Bobby 130
Demaree, Al 46, 48, *49*, 51, 55
Demeter, Don 132, 134, 136, 138
Dempsey, Rick 205–06
Denkinger, Don 191
Denny, John 201–202, 204–206, 210–11, 252

Dernier, Bob 201, 208
Detroit Tigers 32–33, 50, 91, 122, 127–28,
  138, 208, 212, 263
Detroit Wolverines 9–11
Diaz, Baudilio "Bo" 199–200, 202, 206
Dickson, Murry 123
Dillard, Gordon 215
Dillhoefer, William "Pickles" 54, 56
Dilworth, Richardson 103, 120, 139, 160
DiMaggio, Joe 116
DiMaggio, Vince 87, 95, 98
Dinges, Vance 99
Doby, Larry 100
Dolan, Joe 26
Dolan, Patrick "Cozy" 64
Donahue, Francis "Red" 21, 26–27, 219
Donnelly, Sylvester "Blix" 113
Donovan, Wild Bill 60–61
Dooin, Charles "Red" 27, 32, 35–37, *38*,
  39, 41, 43, 45–46, 48–49, 84, 258
Doolan, Mickey 32, 43–44
D'Ortona, Paul 161
Doyle, Denny 158, 164, 166
Drabek, Doug 224
Drew, J.D. 245
Dreyfuss, Barney 28–29, 43, 72
Drysdale, Don 125
Dubiel, Walt 106
Dudley, Clise 72, 74
Duffy, Hugh 16, 30, 32
Duggleby, Bill 26–29, 31–32, 257
Duncan, Mariano 225–26, 228–32, 234–
  39, 241
Duren, Ryne 136
Durham, Israel W. 34
Durocher, Leo 119, 143
Dwyer, Jim 205
Dyer, Bill 77
Dykstra, Lenny 218–20, 222–23, 225–39,
  241–43, 245–46, 252

Easler, Mike 212–14
Eastern Division 165, 197, 201–202, 209,
  222, 224, 226, 242, 246–47
Easton, John 253
Eastwick, Rawly 179
Eaton, Adam 247
Ebbets Field 1, 71, 100, 110, 114–15, 117, 262
Eichhorn, Mark 236
Eisenreich, Jim 224–27, 229–30, 234–36,
  238–39, 242–43, 252
Elberfeld, Norman "Kid" 21, 256
Elia, Lee 213, 215
Elliott, Hal 71
Elliott, James "Jumbo" 72, 74–76
Ellis, Sammy 144

Ellsworth, Dick 154
Ennis, Del 55, *97*, 99–100, 102, 104,
 106–107, 109–11, 113–20, 122–25, 152, 216,
 252, 262–63
Erskine, Carl 112, 119
Esper, Charles "Duke" 14
Espinosa, Nino 179, 188
Etten, Nick 84, 89
Evers, Johnny 55

Fall River (Mass.) club 19
Farley, Jim 90
Farrar, Sid 8
Farrell, Dick 125–27, 131–32, 154
Federal League 44–47, 54–55
Feeney, Chub 176
Felske, John 209–10, 212–13
Fenway Park 52
Ferguson, Bob 7
Ferguson, Charley 8–11, 255–56
Fernandez, Humberto "Chico" 127–28, 264
Fernandez, Sid 242–43
Fernandez, Tony 234, 237
Ferrick, Tom 117, 131
Figueroa, Nelson 248
Finn, Mickey 75–76
Finneran, Bill 39
Finney, Lou 98
Fitzsimmons, Fred 92, 94–95
Flager, Wally 253
Flanagan, Mike 205
Fletcher, Art 59, 61–62, 64–65
Fletcher, Darrin 219, 222
Flick, Elmer 21–22, 26–28
Flitcraft, Hildreth 87
Flood, Curt 156–57, 162
Florida Marlins 224, 228–29, 244, 246
Fogarty, Jim 8, 10–11, 14
Fogel, Horace 30, 34–37, 42–45, 257–58
Fonseca, Lew 65
Foote, Barry 178
Forbes Field 79, 112
Ford, Curt 215
Ford, Dan 205–206
Ford, Ed "Whitey" 117
Ford, Gerald 169
Forepaugh Park 12
Forsch, Ken 186, 188
Foster, George 173
Foster, George "Rube" 50, 52–53
Fox, Howard 120
Fox, Nelson 11
Foxen, Bill 36
Foxx, Jimmie 3, 95
Franco, Julio 201
Francona, Terry 4, 244, 246, 248–50

Francona, Tito 244
Franklin Field 160
Fraser, Chick 21, 26–30
Freedman, Andrew 22–24
Freeman, John "Buck" 51
Freese, Gene 127–28
Fregosi, Jim 220, 222–24, 226–28, 230–32,
 234, 236–37, 239, 241–44, 268
Frey, Jim 189–91
Friberg, Barney 65, 71, 74
Frick, Ford 88–90
Frisch, Frank 64, 75
Froemming, Bruce 176, 187
Fryman, Woody 155–56, 162–63, 185
Fulton County Stadium 3
Furillo, Carl 109, 115

Gale, Rich 190, 192
Galt, Edith 52
Gamble, Oscar 157, 159
Gant, Ron 230–33
Garber, Gene 167, 169, 171–76
Gardner, Larry 50, 52
Garman, Mike 169
Garvey, Steve 177
Gaston, Clarence "Cito" 234, 236, 239
Geier, Phil 19, 256
Geren, Bob 225
Gerheauser, Al 91
Gibson, Bob 147–148
Gibson, Joel 135
Giles, Warren 196
Giles, William Y. 182, 196, 199–200, 203,
 208–209, 213–15, 241–42, 245, 250
Gillick, Pat 234
Gilmore, James A. 44
Glanville, Doug 245–47
Glavine, Tom 231
Glazner, Charles "Whitey" 62
Gleason, William "Kid" 12, 14, 29, 32
Gold Glove award 169, 209, 211–12, 217,
 246–47
Goliat, Mike 108–109, 111, 113, 117, 119
Gomez, Ruben 126–27
Gonder, Jesse 140
Gonzalez, Tony 130, 132, 134, 136–39,
 141–42, 151, 154–55
Goode, W. Wilson 162, 222
Gorbous, Glen 124
Grace, Mike 243
Grant, Eddie 37
Green, Dallas 130, 167, 179–86, 189, 191–93,
 195, 198–200
Green, Tyler 242
Greene, Tommy 219–20, 223, 225–26,
 228–31, 233, 235–36, 241–42

Greengrass, Jim 124
Griffey, Ken 173
Grimsley, Jason 222
Grissom, Lee 84
Groat, Dick 144, 152–53
Gross, Greg 178, 186–88, 202
Gross, Kevin 202, 210, 212–13, 215
Gullett, Don 172
Gullickson, Bill 198
Gura, Larry 190–91
Guzman, Juan 234, 238
Gwynn, Tony 221

Haas, Bert 103–104, 253
Haddix, Harvey 123, 125, 141, 264
Hagan, Arthur "Cut" 7
Hagan, Jimmy 29, 257–58
Hall, Dick 154
Hall of Fame 10, 15, 30, 56, 59, 103, 126,
    137, 153, 157, 164, 203, 212, 241–43,
    260–61
Hallman, Bill 12, 256
Hamey, H. Roy 123–126, 263
Hamilton, Billy 15–18, 104
Hamilton, Jack 138
Hamner, Garvin 86
Hamner, Granville "Granny" 86, 102, 104,
    106, 109–13, 116–20, 122–23, 125, 127,
    252, 263
Handley, Lee 101
Hanlon, Ned 18, 21, 23
Hansen, Roy "Snipe" 71, 75–76
Haring, Claude 108, 128, 135
Harmon, Terry 168
Harper, George 64–66
Harrell, Ray 82
Harris, Stanley "Bucky" 90–93
Hart, Jim Ray 140
Hartley, Mike 224
Harvey, Doug 187
Hasenmayer, Don 3
Haslin, Mickey 79
Hawks, Nelson "Chicken" 65
Hayes, Charlie 218, 222
Hayes, Von 3, 201–202, 209–10, 212–14,
    218, 220, 222
Head, Ralph 62
Hearn, Jim 112
Hebner, Richie 173–74, 176
Heep, Danny 188
Heintzelman, Ken 104, 107, 109, 112–14,
    117, 119
Hemsley, Rollie 98
Henderson, Rickey 18, 234, 236–39
Hendricksen, Olaf 52
Hendrix, Claude 59–60

Henline, Walter "Butch" 61–62, 65–66
Hentgen, Pat 234, 238
Herbert, Ray 151
Hernandez, Guillermo "Willie" 202, 208
Herr, Tom 215
Herrera, Frank "Pancho" 128–29
Herrmann, Garry 28, 37, 42
Herrnstein, John 139, 152
Herzog, Dorrell "Whitey" 180, 201
Heydler, John 64
Higbe, Kirby 82–83, 260
Hiller, Frank 113
Hisle, Larry 156
Hoak, Don 135–136, 138–139
Hoblitzell, Dick 50–51
Hodges, Gil 109, 113, 115
Hoefling, Gus 212
Hoerner, Joe 156, 158
Hoerst, Frank 84, 88
Holke, Walter 62, 64
Holland, Al 201–202, 204–206, 209–10,
    252
Holley, Ed 75–76
Hollingsworth, Al 81
Hollins, Dave 221, 223, 225, 227, 229–30,
    233–37, 239, 241
Hollmig, Stan 106
Hooper, Harry 50–53
Hooton, Burt 175, 177
Hoover, Buster 8
Hornsby, Rogers 17, 124
Hough, Charlie 228
Hough, Frank 25–26, 257
Houston Astros 186–89, 193, 196–97, 201,
    222, 224, 228, 241, 246, 269
Houston Colt .45s 133, 139, 152
Howe, Art 187
Howell, Ken 215–16, 218, 220, 222
Hubbell, Bill 59, 61
Hubbell, Carl 72, 82
Huber, Gilly 253
Hudson, Charles 202, 204–206, 210, 212
Hughes, Keith 214
Hughes, Roy 98
Hughes, Tommy 83, 88, 97
Hulen, Bill 19
Hume, Tom 211
Humphries, Johnny 98
Huntingdon Street Grounds 9–10, 29–30,
    42–43, 49, 51
Hurst, Don 67–68, 70–71, 74–76, 78
Hutchinson, Fred 143
Hutton, Tommy 174

Incaviglia, Pete 224–27, 229–30, 234, 239,
    244

Indianapolis (NL) club 34
Ingersoll, Charles 34
International League 32
Irvin, Monte 114, 118
Irwin, Arthur 9–10, 18, 255
Irwin, Robert 89

Jack Murphy Stadium 216
Jackson, Alvin 141
Jackson, Danny 224–25, 230–32, 235, 241
Jackson, Grant 127, 156, 158
Jackson, Joe 11, 17, 57, 60
Jackson, Larry 152–153, 155
Jackson, Mike 214, 247–48
James, Bill 47
James, Chris 217
Javery, Alva 87
Jefferies, Gregg 242–43
Jeltz, Steve 214, 219
Jenkins, Ferguson 11, 152, 164
Jennings, Hugh 27
John, Tommy 175–77
Johns Hopkins University 94
Johnson, Alex 81, 139, 144–145, 151–152
Johnson, Ban 24–25, 28
Johnson, Dave 174–75
Johnson, Deron 158, 162
Johnson, Jerry 156
Johnson, John G. 26
Johnson, Ken 119
Johnson, Randy 227
Johnson, Silas "Si" 82, 84, 88
Johnson, Sylvester 79
Johnstone, Jay 166, 168, 173–74, 266
Jones, Barry 222
Jones, Doug 241, 269
Jones, Sheldon 114
Jones, Willie 102, 106–107, 109–13, 115–17, 119, 122–23, 127, 263
Jordan, Kevin 269
Jordan, Niles 119–20
Jordan, Ricky 221
Judd, Oscar 100
Juden, Jeff 241, 269
Jurisich, Al 98
Justice, David 230–33

Kaat, Jim 169, 171–73
Kalas, Harry 162
Kansas City Athletics 132, 263
Kansas City Blues 16
Kansas City Royals 180, 189–93, 219, 250, 266
Kazanski, Ted 124
Keane, Johnny 143
Kelly, Gene 108, 128

Kelly, George 64
Kelly, John B. 90
Kennedy, John 263–64
Killefer, Bill 39, 41, 43–44, 48–49, 51, 55–56, 60, 87
Kiner, Ralph 109, 121
King, Jeff 221
Kison, Bruce 167
Klein, Charles "Chuck" 1, 10, 68, *69*, 70–77, 79–80, 82, 102, 179, 252, 259
Klem, Bill 51, 65
Klippstein, John 136–137, 139
Kluszewski, Ted 3, 112–13
Kluttz, Clyde 98
Knabe, Otto 32, 39, 41, 43–44
Knight, Jack 65
Knowles, Darold 152–154
Konstanty, Jim 106, 109, 111–14, 116–17, 119, 193, 263
Koosman, Jerry 208–210
Koppe, Joe 129
Koufax, Sanford 3, 141
Kruk, John 217–19, 221, 223, 225–27, *228*, 229–32, 234, 238–39, 241, 252, 268–69
Krukow, Mike 199, 201

LaCorte, Frank 186, 188
Lajoie, Napoleon "Larry" 19–22, 25–28, 256–57
Lake, Steve 215
Lakeman, Al 103
LaMaster, Wayne 80–81
Landestoy, Rafael 188
Landis, Kenesaw M. 61, 64, 86, 90, 92–94, 96
Lanier, Max 112
Larson, Dan 199
Lasorda, Tommy 175–76, 204, 225
Leach, Freddy 65, 68
LeBourveau, deWitt "Bevo" 59
Lee, Bill 94
Lee, Cliff 61–62
Lee, Hal 72, 75
Lee, Travis 248–49
Lefebvre, Joe 202, 204–206
Leiter, Al 239
Lemke, Mark 230–33
Leonard, Dennis 189, 191
Leonard, Emil "Dutch" 102, 104, 106
Leonard, Hubert "Dutch" 50, 52
Leonard, Jeff 187
Lepcio, Ted 128
Lerch, Randy 174, 177, 179, 182, 196, 267
Lerian, Walter "Peck" 68, 70
Lewis, Duffy 50–53
Lewis, Mark 246

Leyland, Jim 221
Leyva, Nick 215, 219–20
Lieb, Fred 3, 20–21, 27, 30, 34, 258
Lieberthal, Mike 244, 246–48
Lind, Jose 224
Litwhiler, Danny 1, 2, 84, 88, 91, 261
Lobert, John 37, 39, 41, 43, 45–46, 84–85, 87–88
Lock, Don 153
Locke, Bobby 145
Locke, William H. 43, 72
Loewer, Carlton 247
Lonborg, Jim 165–69, 171–72, 174–75
Longmire, Tony 219, 242
Longstreth, Thacher 120
Lopat, Ed 117
Lopata, Stan 106, 109, 113, 115, 117, 124, 126, 263
Lopes, Dave 176–77
Los Angeles Angels 143
Los Angeles Dodgers 125, 132, 141–43 151, 153, 158, 164–65, 168, 173, 175–77, 185–86, 197, 204, 210, 219, 225–26, 268
Louisville Colonels 21–22
Lowenstein, John 205
Lucadello, Tony 163–64, 266
Lucas, Henry V. 8
Lucchesi, Frank 156, 158, 162, 164, 266
Lucid, Con 21, 256
Luderus, Fred 36, 39, 41, 43, 45, 48, 51–54, 58–59
Lupien, Tony 94
Lush, John 32, 264
Luzinski, Greg 3, 163–64, 166–69, 171–72, 174–77, 180, 182–86, 188, 195, 208, 266
Luzinski, Jean 196
Lyle, Al "Sparky" 183–84, 198
Lynch, Thomas 42–43

Mack, Connie 25–27, 32, 47, 50–51, 55, 81, 84, 108, 199, 252, 258, 261
Maddox, Garry 168, 171, 174, 177–78, 182–91, 203, 205, 211, 267
Maddux, Greg 222, 231, 233
Magee, Sherry 30, 31, 32–34, 36, 39, 41, 43, 45–46, 50
Maglie, Sal 112, 114, 262
Mahaffey, Art 131–32, 134–36, 138–39, 141–43, 145, 149, 152
Malkmus, Bobby 128–129
Mallon, Les 74
Mallon, Mae 73
Manning, Jack 8
Mantle, Mickey 121
Manuel, Jerry 185
Marichal, Juan 140

Marion, Marty 125
Marquard, Rube 49, 258
Marsh, Tom 266
Marshall, Mike 204
Marston, Charlie 19
Martin, Gene 199
Martin, Jerry 174–78
Martinez, Carmelo 219
Martinez, Felix "Tippy" 206
Marty, Joe 82–83
Masley, Robert L. 196
Mason, Roger 227–28, 235–36, 238–39
Mathews, Bobby 5
Mathews, Eddie 144–145
Mathewson, Christy 33
Matthews, Gary 195, 197–98, 200, 202–205, 208, 252, 267
Matuszek, Len 202–203, 205
Mauch, Gene 3–4, 113, 125, 128–33, 134, 135–41, 143–45, 147–55, 159, 264–65
Mauser, Tim 227
May, Merrill "Pinky" 92, 95
Mayer, Erskine 42, 44–45, 48, 49, 50–53, 55, 57
Mayo, Jackie 106, 115
Mays, Willie 118, 121, 126, 140
Mazeroski, Bill 269
Mazza, Dr. Patrick 182, 196
McBride, Arnold "Bake" 173–75, 178, 181, 184–87, 189–91, 200
McCarver, Tim 156, 158–59, 162, 171, 174–75
McClellan, Bill 8
McCormack, Don 185–86
McCormick, Frank 98, 100
McDonnell, Maje 110
McDowell, Roger 218, 268
McFarland, Ed 21
McGee, Willie 218
McGraw, Frank "Tug" 167–68, 171, 174–75, 177–79, 182–86, 188, 190–94, 198, 201, 252
McGraw, John 29, 32–34, 55
McGregor, Scott 205–206
McGrew, Ted 93
McGriff, Fred 230–33
McGwire, Mark 246
McInnis, John "Stuffy" 65–67
McLish, Calvin 135–36, 138–39
McNally, Dave 173
McNichol, James P. 34
McPherson, John 30
McQuillan, George 33–34, 36–37, 48, 49, 55
McRae, Hal 191–92, 269
Meadows, Lee 58–62

Melton, Rube 84, 87–89
Memorial Stadium 205
Menke, Dennis 144
Merkle, Fred 33
Messersmith, Andy 173
Meusel, Emil "Irish" 57–58, 61–62
Mexican League 96–97
Meyer, Jack 131
Meyer, Russ 106–107, 109, 112–13, 117, 119
Miller, Bob 110–11, 113–14, 116–17, 119, 127
Miller, Eddie 103–104, 106, 108
Miller, Russ 67
Millette, Joe 225
Mills, A.G. 5–6
Mills, Brad 269
Milnar, Al 98
Milwaukee Braves 126–27, 129, 132–33, 144–45
Milwaukee Brewers 165–66, 214, 222, 225
Mimbs, Michael 242
Minnesota Twins 139, 165, 211, 224–25, 234, 250
Mitchell, Clarence 65
Mitchell, Fred 29
Mokan, Johnny 62, 65
Molitor, Paul 234–35, 237–39
Money, Don 155, 158, 165–66
Monge, Isidro "Sid" 200–201
Montanez, Guillermo "Willie" 162–63, 166, 168
Montgomery, David 245, 250
Montgomery, Steve 247
Montreal Expos 155–56, 158–60, 171, 173, 183–86, 197–99, 202–203, 215, 220, 222, 227–29, 242, 246
Moore, Earl 36, 39, 41
Moore, Johnny 78–79
Moore, Terry 123
Moran, Pat 39, 45–47, 49–51, 53–57, 68
Morandini, Mickey 221–22, 225–26, 232–33, 238, 242–43, 245, 268
Morehead, Seth 131
Moreland, Keith 181, 184, 188, 190–91, 193, 198–99
Moren, Lew 37
Morgan, Bobby 124
Morgan, Cy 199
Morgan, Joe L. 137, 172, 186, 201–203, 205–206, 208, 267
Morgan, Joseph M. 129–130
Mota, Manny 176
Mott, Elisha "Bitsy" 87
Mulcahy, Hugh 80–83, 97
Mulholland, Terry 218–20, 224–26, 228, 230–31, 234, 238, 241, 244, 269
Mulvey, Joe 11–12

Municipal Stadium 111, 193
Munoz, Bobby 269
Murdoch, Rupert 250
Murphy, Charles 35, 37, 42; estate of 66, 80–81, 89
Murphy, Dale 209, 219, 221–22
Murphy, Morgan 22
Murray, Billy 32–35
Murray, Eddie 204–206
Murtaugh, Danny 84, 92, 98
Musial, Stan 18, 117, 119, 196–97
Myatt, George 156
Myers, Al 11

Nash, Billy 18–19
National Agreement 5, 12, 24
National Association 5, 7–8
National Commission 28
National League 5–7, 11–12, 16, 21–25, 27–28, 32, 42–43, 54, 58–59, 62, 68, 74, 87–90, 94–96, 102, 106–107, 114–15, 121–23, 125, 133, 138, 141–42, 148, 166, 169, 171, 176, 181, 186, 193, 196, 201–202, 204, 208–209, 220–21, 224, 226, 229–30, 233, 242, 244, 246–47
Naylor, Earl 91
Neeman, Cal 129
Negro American League 264
New York Giants 9–10, 22–23, 29, 32–34, 42–43, 45–46, 49, 54–55, 61–62, 64–66, 68, 71–72, 75, 79, 83, 97–98, 102, 110, 112–114, 119
New York Mets 3, 133, 135, 140–41, 148, 151, 167, 170, 183–84, 193, 210, 212–13, 217–18, 224, 227–29, 242, 247, 264
New York State League 39
New York Yankees 60, 68, 89, 98–99, 116–18, 132, 209, 213–14, 222, 241, 263–64, 269
Newcombe, Don 109, 111, 113–15, 119–20
Newsome, Lamar "Skeeter" 98
Nichols, Charles "Kid" 31–32
Nicholson, Bill 100, 109, 111–112
Niehoff, Bert 46, 48, 54–55, 57
Niekro, Joe 186
Nixon, Otis 230, 232–33
Noles, Dickie 184, 186–87, 191, 198–99
Northey, Ron 92, 94, 97, 100, 102
Novikoff, Lou 87
Nugent, Gerald P. 73, 75–77, *78*, 79, 81–83, *84*, 86–91, 247, 261

Oakland Athletics 178, 211, 234
O'Brien, Charlie 217, 268
O'Connell, Jimmy 64
O'Doul, Frank "Lefty" 68, 71–72, 74

Oeschger, Joe *49*
Ogea, Chad 247
Olerud, John 234–39
Olson, Greg 230
Olympic Stadium 220
O'Neill, Steve 122–23
O'Rourke, Patsy 39, 78
Orth, Al 19, 21, 26–27
Osteen, Claude 210, 213
Osting, Jimmy 248
Otis, Amos 189–90, 192
O'Toole, Jim 143
Ott, Mel 68, 72, 75, 259–60
Owens, Jim 131, 135
Owens, Paul 164, 167–69, 173–74, 177–81, 183, 188, 195, 199–203, 205–206, 208–209, 266
Ozark, Danny 164–65, 167–69, 171–72, 174–77, 179, 181, 243, 266

Pacific Coast League 46, 57, 74, 78, 243
Padilla, Vicente 248
Pafko, Andy 119
Palica, Erv 113–14
Pall, Donn 227, 229
Palmer, Jim 205–206
Parrett, Jeff 215–16, 219
Parrish, Lance 212–15
Parrish, Larry 185, 199
Paskert, George "Dode" 37, 39, 41, 46, *48*, 49, 51–52, 54–55, 57
Pasquel brothers 96–97
Passeau, Claude 80–82
Pastore, Jack 200
Paterson (NJ) club 21
Paulette, Gene 59, 61
Pearson, Ike 84, 88, 97
Pecota, Bill 230, 232–33
Peguero, Julio 219
Pellagrini, Eddie 119–20
Pena, Bobby 153
Pendleton, Terry 230–33
Pennock, Herb 93, 95, 98, *99*, 100–103, 118, 262
Pennsylvania National Guard 112
Pennsylvania Railroad 6
Pennsylvania Supreme Court 27–28
Pennsylvania, University of 21
Penson, Paul 124
Pepper, Dr. William 256
Perez, Tony 172, 201, 205, 208
Perkins, Cy 100
Perry, Gaylord 140
Person, Robert 248
Pezzulo, John "Pretzels" 253
Philadelphia Athletics 25–29, 32–33, 36,
40, 47, 51, 55–56, 58, 60, 62, 65, 68, 77, 79–81, 83, 88–89, 93, 95, 108, 116, 123–24, 133, 158, 169, 199, 252, 257
Philadelphia Eagles 158, 160, 242, 251, 269
Philadelphia Keystones 8–9, 20, 255
Philadelphia Magazine 242
Philadelphia Quakers 12
Philadelphia Seventy-sixers 242
Phillips, Adolfo 144, 147, 152
Phillips, J.R. 243
Piatt, Wiley 20–21, 26
Pierce, Ray 65
Pinchot, Gifford 77
Pittinger, Charles "Togie" 30, 32
Pittsburgh Pirates 3, 19, 22–23, 26, 28, 33, 43, 49–50, 57–58, 72–73, 80, 82, 85, 95, 100, 102, 104, 109–10, 112–13, 127 135, 142, 145, 166–67, 170, 173–74, 176, 179, 181, 183, 202–203, 210, 213, 219, 221, 224, 226, 229–30, 250, 263, 269
Plank, Eddie 40, 47
Players League 11–12, 14, 256
Podgajny, Johnny 83, 88
Podres, Johnny 223
Polo Grounds 72, 82, 107, 114, 116, 260
Portugal, Mark 246
Possehl, Lou 119
Post, Wally 130, 264
Potter, James 29, 30, 34, 257
Potter, William P. 27
Powell, Jake 87
Power, Vic 143
Prendergast, Mike 56
Prothro, James T. "Doc" 82–84
Providence Grays 8
Puhl, Terry 187–88
Pujols, Luis 187
Purcell, Blondie 7

Qualters, Tom 124
Quantrill, Paul 242
Quay, Matthew 34
Quinn, John 126–30, 138, 141, 143, 150, 152–54, 157, 163–64
Quisenberry, Dan 190–91

Radatz, Dick 141
Radcliffe, Hugh 124
Rader, Dave 178
Raffensberger, Ken 94, 100, 102–103, 107, 109
Ralston, Robert 26–28
Randle, Lenny 266
Randolph, L. Wister 261
Rapp, Pat 229
Raschi, Vic 116

Rawley, Shane 209–10, 212–13, 215
Reach, Al 6–9, 11–12, 14, 16, 19–20, 25, 28–29
Ready, Randy 217–18, 221
Reagan, Ronald 205
Reardon, Jeff 198
Reardon, Joe 93
Recreation Park 7, 9
Redus, Gary 211–12
Reed, Ron 171, 173–74, 177, 179, 183, 186, 190–91, 198, 201, 204, 208
Reese, Pee Wee 109, 115, 125
Relaford, Desi 244, 246, 248
Rendell, Ed 222, 235–36, 251
Repulski, Eldon "Rip" 124, 126
Reuschel, Paul 169
Reuschel, Rick 169
Reuss, Jerry 204
Reynolds, Allie 116–117
Reynolds, Ken 163
Rhem, Flint 75–76
Richardson, Gordon 141
Richardson, Ken 98
Richmond, John Lee 7
Richter, Francis C. 11
Rickey, Branch 67, 90, 96, 100–101, 129, 165, 262
Rigney, Bill 262
Ring, Jimmy 61–62, 64–65, 67
Ripken, Cal, Jr. 204–205
Rivera, Ben 229–30, 235
Riverfront Stadium 172
Rixey, Eppa Jeptha 42, 44–45, 48–49, 51, 53, 55, 57–58, 60, 252, 259
Rizzo, Frank L. 139, 162–63, 169, 222
Rizzuto, Phil 117
Roberts, Robin 3, 102, 104, 107, 109–20, *121*, 123–27, 129, 132, 168, 211, 252, 262, 264
Robinson, Frank 143
Robinson, Humberto 127
Robinson, Jackie 96, 100–102, 106, 109–110, 115, 120, 127, 262
Robinson, Wilbert 49, 54
Roe, Elwin "Preacher" 109, 119
Roebuck, Ed 139, 144, 149, 265
Roenicke, Gary 205
Rogers, John I. 6–8, 11–12, 14, 16, 20, 23, 25–29
Rogers, Steve 185, 198–99
Rojas, Octavio "Cookie" 135, 138–140, 142, 145, 149, 151, 156
Rolen, Scott 243–44, 246–48
Rose, Pete 162, 172–73, 178–80, 182, 184–85, 187–92, 196–97, 201–203, 205–206, 208, 267

Rowan, Jack 37
Rowe, Lynwood "Schoolboy" 55, 91, 97, 100, 102, 104, 107, 262
Ruch, Lewis C. 72–73
Rucker, Johnny 83
Ruffin, Bruce 212, 219, 222
Ruhle, Vern 187, 267
Ruiz, Chico 143
Rush, Bob 110
Russell, Bill 176, 178
Russell, Jim 115
Russell, John 208
Ruth, George "Babe" 41, 50, 52, 60, 70
Ruthven, Dick 165–67, 169, 177, 179, 184, 186, 188, 190, 194, 198, 202
Ryan, Connie 120
Ryan, Mike 158
Ryan, Nolan 188, 196–97, 211, 213

Saam, Byrum 1, 81–82, 108, 128, 135, 169
Sadecki, Ray 147
Sain, Johnny 111–12
St. Louis Browns (AL) 27, 39, 54, 67, 80, 82, 90, 98, 100, 119, 204, 256
St. Louis Browns (original) 21
St. Louis Cardinals 1–2, 23, 31, 42, 57–58, 67–68, 75, 77–79, 90–91, 97–98, 100, 102, 104, 108, 110–12, 123–25, 127, 141, 143–45, 147–49, 156, 162–63, 166, 171, 173–74, 181, 184, 197, 199, 201–203, 209, 215, 226–28, 242, 245–46
Sambito, Joe 186, 188
Samuel, Bernard 87, 103
Samuel, Juan 201, 208–209, 213–14, 218
San Diego Padres 156, 217, 221, 225–27, 247–48, 250
San Francisco Giants 126, 130, 132, 137, 140, 143, 153, 183, 195, 201, 209, 211, 217–19, 225–26, 229–30, 243, 269
Sand, Henry "Heinie" 62, 64–65, 68
Sandberg, Ryne 11, 199–200, 209
Sanderson, Scott 198
Sanford, Jack 125–126, 263
Santiago, Benito 243
Saucier, Kevin 184
Sauer, Hank 113, 120
Savage, Ted 253
Sawatski, Carl 128
Sawyer, Eddie 106–107, 109–11, 113–14, 116–17, 119, 122–23, 126–29
Sax, Steve 204
Scarce, Guerrant "Mac" 164, 167
Schaffer, Rudie 90
Schanz, Charley 94–95
Schilling, Curt 222–28, 230, 232–34, 237–39, 241–43, 245–48, 252, 269

Schmidt, Michael Jack 122, 163–69, 171–81, 184–93, 195, 197, *198*, 200–210, 212–18, 235, 242, 252
Schofield, Dick 142
Schriver, William "Pop" 11
Schu, Rick 208–209, 214
Schueler, Ron 167
Schulte, Frank "Wildfire" 50
Schultz, Barney 147
Schultz, Howard 101
Scott, Everett 50
Scott, Jack 65–66
Scott, Rodney 185
Seaton, Tom 42, 44–45
Seattle Mariners 214, 244, 250, 268
Seitz, Peter 173
Selee, Frank 18, 21, 23
Selma, Dick 157–58
Seminick, Andy 100, 102, 104, 107, 109, 112, 114, 116–17, 119–20, 124, 252, 262
Semproch, Roman "Ray" 128
Sentelle, Paul 32
Shantz, Bobby 145
Sharperson, Mike 225
Shea Stadium 1, 140–41, 156, 228
Shelby, John 206
Shettsline, Billy 8, 20–22, 28–30, 34, 73, 257
Shibe, Benjamin F. 6, 25–26, 51, 257
Shibe Park 1, 51, 66, 81, 87, 89, 102, 111–13, 119, 122, 158, 253, 260, 262
Shore, Ernie 50–52
Short, Chris 131–32, 134, 136, 138–39, 141, 143–45, 147–48, 151–53, 155–56, 158, 162, 252, 265
Shotton, Burt 67–68, 70, 72–77, 110, 114, 260
Shugart, Frank 21
Sievers, Roy 135–36, 138–39, 141
Simmons, Curt 3, 102, 104, 107, 109–12, 116–20, 122–25, 127, 130, 147
Sims, Frank 128, 135
Sisler, Dick 104, 106, 108–10, 113, 115–17, 119–20, 143–44
Sisler, George 104
Sizemore, Ted 173–74, 176, 178
Skinner, Andy 106
Skinner, Bob 155–156
Skydome 234, 239
Slocumb, Heathcliff 241–42
Smith, Billy 128
Smith, Bobby Gene 128, 130
Smith, Charley 132, 140
Smith, Columbia George 61
Smith, Dave 186–87
Smith, Lee 226

Smith, Lonnie 181, 184, 186–87, 189, 193, 197, 199
Smith, Mayo 122–23, 125, 263
Smoltz, John 231
Snider, Edwin "Duke" 109–10, 115, 121–22
Sosa, Elias 175
Sosa, Sammy 246
Sothern, Denny 70
South End Grounds 41
Southworth, Billy 112
Spahn, Warren 111, 211
Spalding, Albert G. 23
Spalding Guide 7
Sparks, Thomas "Tully" 29–33, 36
Speaker, Tris 18, 50–51
Spindel, Hal 99
Sporting Life 11
The Sporting News 75, 104, 125, 171, 193
Sports Illustrated 131, 144
Sprague, Ed 235, 237
Springer, Russ 253
Stallings, George 20, 58, 256
Stanceau, Charlie 99
Stanky, Eddie 262
Stargell, Willie 212
Stearns, John "Bad Dude" 167
Steevens, Morrie 143
Steinbrenner, George 214, 250
Steinfeldt, Harry 21
Steinhagen, Ruth Ann 107
Stello, Dick 185
Stengel, Charles "Casey" 58, 141, 148
Stephenson, John 141
Stewart, Dave "Smoke" 210–11, 234, 238
Stewart, Sammy 206
Stock, Milt 46, 48, 51–52, 54–55, 60, 115, 263
Stocker, Kevin 226–27, 229–32, 235, 238, 246, 268
Stone, Jeff 208–209, 214
Stone, Ron 159
Stottlemyre, Todd 235–36
Stovey, Harry 5, 7
Street, John 251
Stryker, Lloyd Paul 93
Stuart, Dick 151
Stubbins, Hugh 161
Stuffel, Paul 119
Suhr, Gus 83
Sullivan, Frank 132
Sunday, Billy 12
Surhoff, Rick 210
Sutter, Bruce 201
Sutton, Don 175, 177
Sveum, Dale 222

Swarthmore College 91
Sweetland, Les 66–67, 70–71
Swift, Bill 260

Tabor, Jim 98, 100
Taft family 35, 37, 66
Tampa Bay Devil Rays 246
Tarasco, Tony 230–31
Tartabull, Danny 244
Tate, James H.J. 139, 161
Taylor, Antonio "Tony" 129, 132, 135–36, 138–40, 144, 158–59, 172
Taylor, Bob 140
Taylor, Brewery Jack 19
Tekulve, Kent 210, 212–13
Terry, Adonis 18
Texas Rangers 183, 199, 210, 220, 266
Thevenow, Tommy 72, 259
Thigpen, Bobby 227, 229, 231
Thomas, Frank 141–42, 145, 148, 151–52, 264
Thomas, Lee 215, 217–20, 222–24, 226–27, 229, 241, 244–45
Thomas, Roy A. 21–22, 27–28, 30, 32, 104
Thomas, Roy J. 266
Thomas, Valmy 126–27
Thompson, Fresco 66, 70, 72
Thompson, G.W. 5
Thompson, Henry 100, 262
Thompson, John "Jocko" 119
Thompson, Milt 211, 215, 224–25, 231, 236–37
Thompson, Sam 11, 14, *15*, 16–18
Thomson, Bobby 114, 119
Thon, Dickie 215
Three Rivers Stadium 176, 213, 229
Tierney, James "Cotton" 62
Tincup, Ben *49*
Titus, John 29–30, 39, 41
Todd, Al 78
Tolan, Bobby 171, 173
Toronto Blue Jays 233–40, 248
Torre, Joe 144–45
Tovar, Cesar 165–66
Townsend, Jack 27
Triandos, Gus 138–40
Trillo, Manny 178–79, 181, 184–88, 191–93, 197, 201, 209
Triplett, Coaker 91–92
Troy (NY) Trojans 6–7
Tsitouris, John 143
Turner, George "Tuck" 16
Turner, Ted 177, 196, 250
Twitchell, Wayne 166–67
Tyler, George "Lefty" 47, 59

Uecker, Bob 125, 152–53, 265
Ulrich, Frank "Dutch" 65
Underwood, Tom 168, 171, 173
Union Association 8–9, 20
United States Supreme Court 157
Unser, Del 165–67, 179, 188, 190–91

Valenzuela, Fernando 197, 204
Van Slyke, Andy 221, 242
Veeck, Bill 3, 89–90, 261
Veeck, William L. 59, 259
Verban, Emil 98, 100, 102
Verdel, Al "Stumpy" 87
Veterans Committee 242, 261
Veterans Stadium 1, 3, 160–62, 169, 175, 177, 184, 189, 192, 196, 198, 201, 203–205, 216, 225, 229, 233, 235, 238, 242–43, 251, 253, 269
Vincent, Fay 219
Virdon, Bill 186–88, 267
Virgil, Ozzie 206, 211
Vukovich, George 198, 201
Vukovich, John 162, 165, 179, 215, 269

Waddell, Rube 40, 131
Wade, Ed 245–48
Wagner, John "Honus" 21–22, 36
Wagner brothers 12, 256
Waitkus, Eddie 106–11, 113, 115–17, 119–20
Walk, Bob 181, 184, 189–90, 195
Walker, Curt 61–62
Walker, Harry 102, 104, 106
Wallach, Tim 185
Walling, Denny 186
Walls, Lee 130
Walsh, Jimmy 44
Walters, Ken 128, 130
Walters, William "Bucky" 79–81
Waner, Lloyd 85, 260
Ward, Arch 76
Ward, Chuck 102
Ward, Duane 234, 239
Warneke, Lon 120
Wasdell, Jimmy 87, 91, 94–95, 99, 262
Washington, Claudell 196
Washington Nationals 6, 19, 22, 51
Washington Senators 17, 26–28, 30, 102, 128, 153, 157
Wathan, John 192
Watson, John "Mule" 57
Weaver, Jim 260
Wehmeier, Herman 113, 123
Weinert, Philip "Lefty" 62
Weintraub, Phil 80
Welch, Bob 177, 204
Wendelstedt, Harry 175

West, David 224–25, 227, 231, 233–34, 236, 239, 242
Western Division 175, 186, 229–30
Western League 24
Weyhing, Gus 18
"Wheeze Kids" 201, 203
White, Bill 147–48, 152–53
White, Devon 234, 236–39
White, Frank 190–92
White, Guy "Doc" 27–29
White, Jerry 185
Whiten, Mark 242, 244
Whitman, Dick 109, 117
Whitney, Arthur "Pinky" 1, 67, 70–71, 74–76, 79–80
Whitted, George "Possum" 46, 48, 51, 54–55, 58, 60
"Whiz Kids" 3, 110, 113–14, 116–18, 121, 123, 125–26, 222, 252
WIBG 108
Widmar, Al 135
Wiechec, Frank 112
Wiler, Alfred Day 42–43
Wilhelm, Irvin "Kaiser" 61–62
Willard, Jerry 201
Williams, Charlie 228
Williams, Dick 183–84
Williams, Fred "Cy" 57–58, 61–62, 63, 64–65, 68, 252
Williams, Mike 229
Williams, Mitch 220–21, 225–33, 237, 239–41, 252, 268–69
Williams, Ted 18
Willoughby, Claude 65, 70–72
Wilson, Glenn 208–209, 214
Wilson, Hack 71
Wilson, Jimmy 65, 77–80, 84

Wilson, Willie 192, 252
Wilson, Woodrow 52
Winchell, Walter 101
Wine, Bobby 135–36, 138–40, 203
Wise, Rick 139, 142, 156, 158, 162–64
Wockenfuss, John 208
Wohlers, Mark 232
Wolf, Clarence 34
Wolf, Randy 248
Wolman, Jerry 158
Wolverton, Harry 26–27, 30
Wood, George 10–11, 255
Wood, Smokey Joe 50
Woodling, Gene 117, 263
Woods, Gary 187
Woods, Jim 128–29
Woodward, William "Woody" 214, 268
Worcester Brown Stockings 6–7
WPEN 108
Wright, Harry 8–10, 12, 14, 16, 18
Wright, John 96, 262
Wrightstone, Russ 61–62, 64–66
Wrigley Field 1, 169, 179, 203, 216, 225
Wynn, Jim 139
Wyrostek, Johnny 98, 100, 102, 120

Yankee Stadium 116
Youmans, Floyd 215
Young, Denton "Cy" 41
Young, Dick 119
Young, Mike 214–15
Young, Nicholas 23
Youngs, Russ 64

Zeile, Todd 244
Zernial, Gus 152
Zimmer, Charles "Chief" 29–30